# Broadcast News Writing, Reporting, and Producing

## Third Edition

# Broadcast News Writing, Reporting, and Producing

## Third Edition

**Ted White**
*Southern University*

**Focal Press**
**An imprint of Butterworth-Heinemann**
Boston • Oxford • Auckland • Johannesburg • Melbourne • New Delhi

Focal Press is an imprint of Butterworth–Heinemann.
Copyright © 2002 by Butterworth–Heinemann

 A member of the Reed Elsevier group

Recognizing the importance of preserving what has been written, Butterworth–Heinemann prints its books on acid-free paper whenever possible.

**Library of Congress Cataloging-in-Publication Data**

White, Ted, 1926–
    Broadcast news writing, reporting, and producing/Ted White. — 3rd ed.
        p.   cm.
    Includes index.
    ISBN 0-240-80433-3 (pbk. : alk. paper)
    1. Broadcast journalism.   2. Reporters and reporting.   3. Report writing.   I. Title.
PN4784.B75 W5 2002
070.1'9—dc21
                                                            2001033422

**British Library Cataloguing-in-Publication Data**

A catalogue record for this book is available from the British Library.

The publisher offers special discounts on bulk orders of this book.
*For information, please contact:*

Manager of Special Sales
Butterworth–Heinemann
225 Wildwood Avenue
Woburn, MA 01801-2041
Tel: 781-904-2500
Fax: 781-904-2620

For information on all Butterworth–Heinemann publications available, contact our World Wide Web home page at: www.bh.com

10 9 8 7 6 5 4 3 2 1

Printed in the United States of America

To my wonderful grandchildren:

*Brian, Dennis, Eric, Leslie, and Dayna*

*And to the late* CBS News *correspondent, Doug Edwards, a friend and colleague who was loved by all who had the good fortune to work with him.*

The late *CBS News* correspondent
Doug Edwards

# Contents

# Foreword

Broadcast news seems so simple that most viewers and listeners figure there's nothing to it. For several years now, I have done four "Osgood File" broadcasts on the CBS Radio Network each morning. Each broadcast has two and a half minutes of editorial content, $4 \times 2.5 = 10$. Therefore, my friends figure, I work only 10 minutes a day—nice work if you can get it. As with most things that seem simple, however, there's a whole lot more to radio and television news reporting than meets the eye or ear. It's been said that, as with sausage and cheese, it's better if the public doesn't ever find out exactly how our product is made or how early one has to get up every morning to make it. (In my case, 2:30 A.M. is the answer to the last part, by the way. Do you still want to be a news writer or reporter?)

At the heart of radio and television news broadcasting are the reporting and writing. You can have the greatest studio in the world, the most state-of-the-art equipment, the hottest signal, the catchiest news theme music, and the niftiest news set anybody ever designed, but if your reporting and writing aren't good, nothing is going to happen. You have to find out what's going on, talk with the principals and witnesses, gather your information, assemble your facts into a coherent story, and then tell it. The writing part is easy. As *CBS News* correspondent Terry Smith's father used to say: "All a writer has to do is open a vein and bleed all over the page." Nothing to it. Terry's father was the legendary sportswriter Red Smith. What he said may be true, but it isn't helpful advice about how to become a writer or reporter, whether for print or broadcast. Easier on your health, and easier on the carpet, is Ted White's approach.

Ted and I worked together at *CBS News* in New York. Our colleagues were wonderful people like Walter Cronkite, Douglas Edwards, Eric Sevareid, Lowell Thomas, Hughes Rudd, Dallas Townsend, and Richard C. Hottelet. We had great editors like Hal Terkel and Marian Glick who had learned from the masters, Edward R. Murrow himself and Murrow's own radio editor and writer, Ed Bliss. Our bosses were Joe Dembo and Emerson Stone, and their bosses were people like Richard Salant and Fred W. Friendly. That was the news broadcasting school Ted White and I went to. There was never a better one.

So, when Mr. White tells students about radio and television news, he knows whereof he speaks. And when he writes in this book about the nuts and bolts of how to gather news and organize it so that it makes sense, he knows whereof he writes. You may decide, after reading this book, that broadcast news writing and reporting are not for you. This would be a sensible decision nobody could argue with. But if you do pursue this dodge anyway, you won't find anybody better to show you the ropes than Ted White.

*Charles Osgood*

# Preface

*Broadcast News Writing, Reporting, and Producing* examines the skills, techniques, and challenges of working in broadcast news. Along with complete coverage of the fundamentals, the text presents up-to-date examples and issues through actual scripts and interviews with the people who bring us the news.

As you read the book, you may notice the extensive coverage of reporting. Eight of the book's 23 chapters focus on everything from basic skills and specialty reporting to research techniques and ethics, including a detailed discussion of the ethical issues involved in the O.J. Simpson murder case and the controversy over Connie Chung's interview with Mrs. Kathleen Gingrich, mother of former Speaker of the House Newt Gingrich.

I believe this is the most complete assemblage of reporting techniques and scripts by outstanding correspondents available in a broadcast news text. Journalists such as Betsy Aaron, Bob Dotson, the late Charles Kuralt, Charles Osgood, Susan Stamberg, and Richard Threlkeld not only provided scripts for the book but also discussed how they write and report. The work of such distinguished reporters as the late Edward R. Murrow and the late Pauline Frederick is also examined and analyzed closely. I also spoke with numerous producers about their philosophies and techniques and what it takes to get newscasts on the air every day and night.

Supplementing this is the emphasis throughout on real-life situations. The problems that reporters, writers, assignment editors, and producers face every day are discussed in detail. You'll find entire chapters devoted to interviewing, covering breaking stories, delivering the news, and finding a job.

Whenever possible, I've relied on the voices of the experts—through interviews and transcripts of actual broadcasts—to teach future professionals how it's done.

Instructors may want to assign the writing, review, and discussion exercises at the end of each chapter. These exercises ask students to apply what they've read, not just to summarize it. In conjunction with outside assignments, these exercises can provide enough material for an entire course. (You'll find answers to the exercises in the Instructor's Manual, along with sample syllabi and my suggestions for organizing the course, whether it be a reporting, writing, or all-in-one course. The Instructor's Manual is available at www.focalpress.com.)

This book would have been impossible to write without the assistance of a great number of people. Much of this help came from colleagues in the broadcast news industry with whom I worked over the years. Significant contributions also came from journalism professors, research assistants, editors, and a variety of administrative assistants and public relations personnel throughout the country. I will try to thank by name all who have helped produce this book, but there have been so many of you that I am likely to miss a few. Please forgive me if one of them is you.

At the top of the "thank you" list is Ben Silver. Our relationship goes back more than 20 years to when we both worked for *CBS News*. Ben, now professor emeritus of the Walter Cronkite School of Journalism at Arizona State University, was a gold mine of information. I thank him for locating some of the scripts and gathering much of the quoted material in the book, particularly that dealing with the technological advances in the broadcast industry and the vigorous news operations going on in Phoenix, where he lives.

Charlie Osgood, too, has been a friend and colleague over the years, and the foreword he wrote for the book is greatly appreciated. So are the scripts that he has permitted me to reproduce. It was nice to see Charlie take over *Sunday Morning* from the very talented late Charles Kuralt. Kuralt graciously allowed me to use two of his famous "On the Road" scripts when I assembled the previous editions of this book. I also appreciate the help I received from Karen Beckers, who was Kuralt's wonderful secretary. Many thanks also to Lori Knight, Audrey Forman, and Jennifer Halloran, who have worked over the years for Charlie Osgood.

The list of other correspondents who assisted me is extensive. Betsy Aaron and Richard Threlkeld allowed me to share their scripts and insights with you. I thank them also for providing photos from their private collections.

My appreciation to Roger Welsch for sending me one of his "Postcard from Nebraska" stories. Thanks also to Bob Faw and David Culhane for all their help over the years.

*60 Minutes* correspondent Ed Bradley gave me new insight into, among other things, the hopes and problems of African Americans in broadcast journalism. I thank *Dateline NBC* correspondent Robert McKeown (formerly of *CBS News*) for sharing with us, as so many others did, what it was like to report during the Gulf War.

The *ABC News* team also provided me with many pages of copy. Special thanks to all who took time to speak with me, including former *Nightline* correspondent Jeff Greenfield and news correspondents Morton Dean and Barry Serafin. News commentator Paul Harvey contributed a sample of his unique writing style; thanks also to his secretary, June Westgard.

Friend and former colleague Rob Sunde, a veteran of CBS and ABC, provided useful information for young people trying to get started in broadcast news. Former *ABC News* Vice President Walter Porges and Arnot Walker were also a great help.

NBC News correspondent Bob Dotson was more than generous, giving me not only a sample of his splendid writing but very detailed notes on how he thinks and works when he's putting a story together. NBC's Roger O'Neil is not only an excellent journalist, but also refreshingly frank in describing the short-comings of many of those working in broadcast news. Thanks to Chris Vanocur of KTVX-TV in Salt Lake City for sharing his Olympic scandal exposé with us.

I appreciate the assistance received from Don Browne, former executive vice president of *NBC News,* from Katherine McQuay, manager of news information at NBC, and from producer Kathryn Keeney.

The news staff at CNN was very cooperative. Former anchor Bernard Shaw, in particular, gave his views on a variety of subjects, including the Gulf War and the problems associated with reporting live and covering politics. Thanks also to Howard Kirsch of *The Washington Post* and Keith Woods of the Poynter Institute.

CNN investigative reporter Jim Polk provided a lot of good advice about a beat he has covered for several decades. Reid Collins, another former CBS col-league, gave samples of his excellent writing, as did former CNN medical cor-respondent Dan Rutz. Thanks also to friend and former CNN colleague Don Shoultz, an editor-producer for *Headline News*; and to my former CNN boss, Ed Turner.

Many thanks also to the people at NPR, where, as Susan Stamberg reminds us, women journalists have made tremendous progress. I thank Susan and Cokie Roberts for their scripts and input on a variety of subjects and issues in broad-cast news. I also appreciate the time that Nina Totenberg spent with me dis-cussing her involvement in the leak of sexual harassment charges made by Anita Hill against Judge Clarence Thomas.

Some network producers were very helpful, among them Paul Friedman, former executive producer of ABC's *World News Tonight*; Steve Friedman, exec-utive producer of NBC's *Nightly News*; Linda Mason, former executive producer of *Sunday Morning*; Joel Bernstein, a producer for CBS's *Evening News*; and Phil Scheffler, a senior producer for *60 Minutes.*

I received a great deal of assistance from colleagues at radio and TV sta-tions throughout the country. Much of that help was provided by stations in Baton Rouge. Special thanks to friend and colleague John Spain, former station manager of WBRZ-TV, who has provided extraordinary information about a variety of aspects of broadcast news for two of my earlier books.

Management and staff at WAFB-TV, the other major station in Baton Rouge, were equally cooperative. My thanks to Station Manager Ron Winders and WAFB-TV anchor-reporter Paul Gates, who provided excellent examples of his work.

Thanks also to former *60 Minutes* producer Chris Szechenyi and Mark Lagerkvist of News 12 Long Island for providing details on how they write and produce their excellent investigative reports.

My appreciation to Will Wright, news director of WWORTV in New York, for recalling how he rose from desk assistant at CBS to become one of only a handful of African-American news directors at major TV stations. Wright and African-American journalist Sheila Stainback provided valuable information and advice for minorities who hope to succeed in broadcast news.

Others at local stations who provided information and scripts include: Jack Atherton, WTVJ-Miami; Jerry Bell, news director of KOA-TV, Denver; News Director Chris Berry and reporter Kris Kridel of WBBM Radio, Chicago; Tom Bier, news director of WISC-TV, Madison; Jerry Brown, weathercaster for KUTV, Salt Lake City; Christine Devine, anchor for KTTV-TV, Los Angeles; Ed Godfrey, news director of WAVE-TV, Louisville; News Director Jim Boyer and anchor Bill Elder of WWL-TV in New Orleans; Edwin Pferffer and Gordon Peterson of WDVM-TV in Washington; anchor Jerry Turner of WJZ-TV in Baltimore; and John Bobel, president of Talentbank.

Many thanks to the crowd at KPNX-TV, Phoenix: Executive Producer Julie Frisoni; Producer Marey Morse-Lay; and anchors Kent Dana and Lin Sue Cooney.

My appreciation also to those at KTSP-TV in Phoenix including investigative reporter Steve Kraft. Thanks also to News Director Dennis O'Neil, and Producer Lisa Hudson and Kathy Matz of KTVK-TV, Phoenix.

I received a lot of help from Marty Haag, former vice president of News and current consultant for the A. H. Belo Corporation, which owns several stations, including KHOU-TV in Houston and WFAA-TV in Dallas. Penny Scott and reporter Don Wall of WFAA-TV were a great help, as was Kerry Oslund, executive producer of news at KCAL-TV, Los Angeles, and Bill Bauman, news director at KCRA-TV, Sacramento.

Special thanks and a hug for friend and colleague Nan Siemer, who provided students with information on how to survive in our business. My appreciation also to WTOP anchor John Lynker for providing a photo of himself in action; a nice reminder of the days some 20 years ago when I edited John's scripts at WINS, the first all-news station in New York.

Thanks also to the many journalism professors who shared information with me, including several at the University of Missouri: Karen Frankola, Rod Gelatt, John Ullmann, and Vernon Stone, former research director for the Radio and Television News Director's Association (RTNDA).

I thank Ed Bliss, Professor Emeritus at American University and another transplanted *CBS News* writer and editor. He's the author of *Now the News*, a great book on the history of broadcast news.

Other professors who made contributions to the book include: David Dick, a former *CBS News* correspondent; Robert Mulholland, chair of Broadcast News at the Medill School of Journalism at Northwestern University and former president of the NBC network; Susan Morris at the University of Pittsburgh; Lou Prato, who heads Northwestern's program in Washington, D.C.; Travis Linn of the University of Nevada at Reno, a former *CBS News* bureau chief in Dallas;

Bill Small, a former senior vice president of *CBS News*; Paul Thaler, author of *The Watchful Eye*; and Stephen Doig of Arizona State University.

My appreciation to other professors who reviewed the manuscript in its early stages: Professor Emeritus Ben Silver, Arizona State University; Elmer Lower, former *ABC News* president; Marsha Della-Giustina, Emerson College; James L. Hoyt, University of Wisconsin at Madison; Kate Andrews, Syracuse University; Mark Harmon, Texas Tech University; Andrew Stern, University of California at Berkeley. Thanks also to Professor Robert Lissit of Syracuse University for his support and feedback.

Special thanks also to my good friend and former student, Lennie Tierney, who has learned so much about TV news photography that he can teach his old mentor a few tricks. Thanks also to all the other students, too many to name, who have made me proud by becoming successful in news.

Lots of people shot photos for us, and many others dug pictures and scripts out of files and archives. These people include Kathy Ozatko of Madison, Wisconsin, Kenneth Keller of Southern Illinois University, and Marty Silverstein of CBS. The shooters included James Terry and Christopher Rogers of Baton Rouge and Mike Coscia of WFAA-TV, Dallas.

Special thanks to Carol Lichtenberg, curator at the Historical Photograph Collection at Washington State University, for finding photos of Edward R. Murrow. Thanks to Catherine Heinz, director of the Broadcast Pioneers Library, for telling me where to look for things I needed.

Help also came from Richard Lobo, president and general manager of WTVJ-TV in Miami, and from Carmen Perez, PR director for that station. I also thank Lori Konopka and Su-Lin Cheng of CNN and Abenaa Abboa-Offei and Leslie Halpern at ABC Radio for supplying pictures.

My appreciation also to Mata Goodwyn and Margery Sly, archivists at Smith College, for locating a script written by the late Pauline Frederick.

I am indebted to voice coaches Carol Dearing, Mary Berger, and Jeff Puffer for providing excellent information on voice control and other aspects of anchoring and reporting for radio and TV.

During three years of writing and research, I attended many conferences and meetings of broadcast groups (particularly those held by the Radio and Television News Director's Association) and reviewed many journals and magazines such as *The Communicator* and *Broadcasting and Cable TV* so that I could include the comments and observations of many whom I was unable to interview.

Here's a list of those I have quoted, in one way or another, throughout the book: investigative reporters David Anderson, Jack Anderson, and Peter Benjaminson; *ABC News* correspondents Sam Donaldson and Judy Muller; *NBC News* commentator John Chancellor; Bob Engleman of Scripps-Howard; former *CBS News* Vice President Peter Herford; *CBS News* anchor Dan Rather and correspondent Leslie Stahl; *Wall Street Journal* reporter Robert Goldberg; Craig Le May, editor of the *Freedom Forum Journal*; Robert Logan, director of the

Science Journalism Center at the University of Missouri; CNN environmental reporter Deborah Potter; Bill Kovach, chairman, and Tom Rosensteil, vice chairman, of the Committee of Concerned Journalists; Jeffrey Marks, president of RTNDA; Walter R. Mears, vice president and Washington bureau chief of the Associated Press; Professor William Metz, University of Nevada; attorney and former reporter Bruce Sanford; Penny Parrish, news director of KMSP in Minneapolis; Doug Ramsey of the Foundation for America Communications; network news veterans Liz Trotta and Ed Fouhy; and the staff at Brill's *Content* magazine.

I also received help from Tom Goodman, director of media relations for CBS, and PR associate Eldra Gillman; Lynn Ross of AARP in Washington; Charlie Folds, PR director for WSVN-TV, Miami; Dr. Terry Kennedy, Southern University; the Gallup and Roper research and polling organizations; and Marvin Kalb, former network news correspondent and director of Harvard's Shorenstein Center on the Press, Politics, and Public Policy.

A number of people were helpful in the report on the Oklahoma City bombing, including Bill Perry, who was working for the Oklahoma PBS network when the blast occurred; his colleague, reporter Charles Newcomb; Joyce Reed, the news director of KWTV; News Director Jim Palmer and reporter Billy Rodely of WKY radio; Susan Kelley, news director of KOCO; Melissa Klinzing, news director at KFOR-TV; and KTOK-TV News Director Jerry Bohnen. We also received lots of help in our coverage of school violence from the Freedom Forum and, in particular, Robert H. Giles, a senior vice president of the Forum, and Bob Haiman, a Freedom Forum fellow. Assistance also was provided by KUSA-TV's Ginger Delgado.

I also thank Brill's *Content* contributing editor Jon Katz; Poynter Institute's director of the Ethics Program, Bob Steele; sociologist Stephen Gorelick of the City University of New York; Nell Hancock, an assistant professor at the Columbia University Graduate School of Journalism; James Garbino of Cornell University; Richard Wald, senior vice president of *ABC News*; James Glassman, a fellow of the American Enterprise Institute; Sig Bedingfield, vice president of CNN; and the *American Journalism Review* writer Sherry Richiardi. Also contributing thoughts to our news coverage of violence were Chris Cramer, president of CNN's international division, psychiatrist Frank Ochberg, Roger Simpson of the University of Washington at Seattle, and Michael Sorkin of the *St. Louis Post Dispatch*.

Helping us to try to sort through the events of the Waco, Texas, conflict were Anson Shupe and Jeffrey K. Hadden, authors of *Armageddon in Waco*, James T. Richardson, an expert in new religions, Shelly Katz, a Time Life photographer, attorney Dick de Guerin, and James Wood, editor of the *Journal of Church and State*.

Sharing information with us on a variety of subjects were Michelle Kosinski of WSOC-TV in Charlotte; Peter Landis, director at NY1; Barbara Cochran, president of RTNDA; Chuck Peters of the Gazette Company of Cedar Rapids; Rick

Ragola, president of WFLA-TV; *Tampa Tribune* reporter Lisa Greene; Greta Van Susteren, legal correspondent for CNN; James Rosen, a Washington correspondent for *Fox News*; Steve Sweitzer, news operations manager at WISG-TV in Indianapolis; Jim Disch, director of news and programming for CLTV in suburban Chicago; Jack La Duke of WCAX-TV in Burlington, Vermont; CBS spokesman Kevin Tedesco; *New York Times* media critic Caryn James; *New Yorker* writer Jeffrey Toobin; attorney Raoul Felder; the *New York Times*' Jim Rutenberg; John Moody, vice president of Fox TV Channel; Steve Capus of MSNBC; reporter Edna Buchanan of the *New York Times*; Jan Schaffer of the Pew Center for Civic Journalism; and Tom Bier, news director of WISC in Madison.

Thanks also to colleagues Frank Coakley, Dr. Howard Jacobson, Dr. William Turpin, Professors George Crutchfield and Bill Giles, and attorney Dan Schaneville for their friendship and support over the years.

Finally, thanks to Marie Lee, Tammy Harvey, Maura Kelly, Terri Jadick, and Kevin Sullivan at Focal Press.

# Acknowledgments

Aaron, Betsy, "Marines in Lebanon," September 14, 1993. Transcript from *ABC News*, reprinted by permission. Copyright 1983.

Atherton, Jack, "The Price of Fame" transcript, December 5, 1989, and "Ford Follow" transcript, July 16, 1991. Excerpts courtesy of National Broadcasting Company, Inc. All Rights Reserved.

Carter, Hodding, quotation about journalists today, from a speech on government and journalism by Hodding Carter, Assistant Secretary of State for Public Affairs/Department Spokesman.

Devine, Christine, "Deadly Fires" newscast, KTTV-TV, Los Angeles. Script excerpts courtesy of Fox Television Stations, Inc. © 1992 Fox Television Stations, Inc.

Dotson, Bob, "Cave Rescue." Excerpts courtesy of National Broadcasting Company, Inc. All Rights Reserved.

Ellerbee, Linda, *NBC News Overnight*. Excerpts courtesy of National Broadcasting Company. All Rights Reserved.

Frederick, Pauline, report from United Nations, December 5, 1963 story. Excerpts courtesy of National Broadcasting Company, Inc. All Rights Reserved.

Gates, Paul, lead story on weather. Used with permission of WAFB-TV, Baton Rouge.

Harvey, Paul, "Rebirth of a Nation." Used with permission of Paul Harvey News.

Kirk, Bruce, marked script. Used by permission of Bruce Kirk, KPNX-TV Broadcasting, Phoenix, Arizona.

Kridel, Kris, David Chreck murder story. Used with permission of Kris Kridel, WBBM-AM, Newsradio 78, Chicago.

Kuralt, Charles, "On the Road in Montana," 1975, and "On the Road in Vermont," 1976. Used with permission of *CBS News*.

Lagerkvist, Mark, Series on HMOs, 1995. Used with permission of News 12 Long Island.

Murrow, Edward R., "Orchestrated Hell," "Permit Me to Tell You," and "The Fault, Dear Brutus," from Ann M. Sperber, *Murrow: His Life and Times*, New York: Bantam Books, 1986. Originally published by Frendlich Books.

Olmstead, Jill, excerpts from "How to Find a Job in Radio/TV." Used with permission of Jill Olmstead, The American University.

Osgood, Charles, "Obituary for Dr. Seuss" and "Newsbreak." Used with permission of *CBS News*.

Parker, Nancy, story on prison visit. Used with permission of WAFB-TV, Baton Rouge.

Roberts, Cokie, feature story on Congressman Morris Udall. © Copyright National Public Radio, 1992. Excerpts from National Public Radio's *Morning Edition* news were originally broadcast on National Public Radio on April 19, 1991, and are reproduced with permission from National Public Radio. Any unauthorized duplication is prohibited.

Rutz, Dan, chronic fatigue syndrome story. © 1992 by Cable News Network, Inc. All rights reserved.

Sevareid, Eric, *CBS Evening News* excerpts. Used with permission of *CBS News*.

Stamberg, Susan, interview with Alfred Eisenstadt. © Copyright National Public Radio © 1992. Excerpts from National Public Radio's *Morning Edition* news were originally broadcast on March 13, 1991, and are reproduced with permission from National Public Radio. Any unauthorized duplication is prohibited.

Threlkeld, Richard, "Obituary for Dr. Seuss." Used with permission of *CBS News*.

Wall, Don, environmental report on possible dangers of electromagnetic field, WFAA-TV, Dallas. Used with permission.

Welsch, Roger, "A Postcard from Nebraska," from *Sunday Morning*. Used with permission of *CBS News*.

WISC-TV, Madison, Wisconsin, "Butter River Fire story," used with permission of Tom Bier, News Director.

# Introduction

This book was in the final stages of production when, on September 11, 2001, terrorists hijacked four airliners and flew two of them into the World Trade Center towers, one into the Pentagon, and one into a field in Pennsylvania. We "stopped the presses" to attempt as best we could to include as much as possible about the media coverage of the terrorist attacks within our time constraints. In the following paragraphs, I have attempted to show what was being said and reported by major national news organizations and some of the local radio and TV stations in New York City at the time the terrorism began and for the next few hours after the disaster. I have included some broadcast segments with dramatic eyewitness reports from civilians and journalists who were at the scene in an effort not only to convey the horror of the events, but also to show how the news media functioned during the worst terrorist attack in the nation's history. Because of the time constraints for publication, extensive coverage could not be included here. However, more comprehensive information can be found on the companion website for this book, attached to www.focalpress.com.

Most Americans can recall what they were doing when President Kennedy was assassinated, and it appears that the same will be true about the day terrorist attacks killed thousands of Americans following the coordinated hijacking of four airliners. Like millions of Americans, the author was on his way to work, listening to National Public Radio, when news of the disaster first broke. NPR's Carl Kassell had this to say:

> Details are sketchy but it appears a plane has crashed into the upper floors of the World Trade Center in New York City. CNN is quoting witnesses as saying it was a two-engine plane that flew right into the trade center. Witnesses report hearing a huge explosion, and heavy smoke can be seen billowing from the building at the moment. Otherwise, witnesses said they saw a small commuter plane smash into the building, so it appears a plane has crashed into the upper floors of the World Trade Center in New York.

Kassell read some other news stories and a few minutes later recapped his earlier information and added that there was a new report saying that an explosion had rocked the second trade center building.

The World Trade Center south tower (L) bursts into flames after being struck by hijacked United Airlines Flight 175 as the north tower burns following an earlier attack by a hijacked airliner in New York City, September 11, 2001. (Courtesy Reuters/Sean Adair.)

Meanwhile, at 8:52 AM on CBS's *The Early Show*, Bryant Gumbel was saying, "We understand that there has been a plane crash on the southern tip of Manhattan. You're looking at the World Trade Center. We understand that a plane has crashed into the building. We don't know anything more than that. We have no idea how many were on board or what is the extent of the injuries." Gumbel then spoke to an eyewitness, identified only as Stuart, who was working at a restaurant near the trade center. He told Gumbel, "I literally saw what—it seemed to be a small plane bounce off the building, and then I just saw a huge ball of fire on top and then a lot of smoke was coming out." As Gumbel spoke to the man the audience was looking at a picture of smoke coming out of the trade center building. Stuart continued: "I heard a sort of crashing sound. I looked up quick enough to actually see something go into the building. But everything happened so fast, I wasn't quite sure what I was looking at."

Another eyewitness, Wendell Klein, a doorman at the Marriott World Trade Center, told Gumbel he was standing right in front of the hotel across from the trade center when he heard an explosion. Then, he said, "All of a sudden, stuff just started falling, like bricks and paper and everything, and so I ran inside to get away form the falling debris and glass and so forth, and cars were crashing into each other." Klein said that when the falling material "kind of stopped" he heard a man screaming. "When I looked over there was this guy on fire so I like ran over and I tried to put the fire out on him. And he was like screaming and I just told him to roll, roll, and he said he can't. And then another guy came over with his bag and kind of put the flames out on him."

Gumbel then spoke to another witness, Theresa Renault, who told him that about 10 minutes earlier there appeared to be an explosion at about the 80th floor of the trade center building. Looking out her apartment window, Renault said, "Major flames are coming out of the fire and it looks like the building is still on fire inside." At that point, Renault saw the second plane hit the other tower. She told Gumbel, "Oh there's another one. Another plane just hit right— oh my God, another plane has just hit. It hit another building, flew right into the middle of it. My god it's right in the middle of the building." She added, "It definitely looked like it was definitely on purpose." When Gumbel asked Renault why she said *definitely on purpose,* she responded, "Because it flew straight into it." Renault said that both buildings were completely on fire.

Almost in disbelief, Gumbel announced that they were rewinding the video-tape to see if a second plane had hit. Seconds later, Gumbel told his audience, "Yeah, we see it right now. We see a plane right now coming in and impacting on what would appear to be the north side of the tower." Next, Gumbel was connected with a man who was on the 24th floor of a building with a view of the trade center who also saw the planes hit the buildings. Frederick Snyder said his 51-story building shook when a plume of flame shot out of the trade center. He then saw the plane that had crashed into the building fall down. "There was a tremendous amount of smoke and then it started to rain huge pieces of paper, and the paper continued to come down." Snyder added, "I was sitting at my desk when a second jet, a fairly large plane, flew in over the south end of Man-hattan and deliberately flew directly into the trade center." Gumbel asked Snyder why he said the plane flew deliberately into the building. He responded, "Because there was no doubt in my mind that both planes were using the trade center as a target. They weren't in trouble, they weren't in distress. They weren't falling from the sky. They aimed for it. And they did a very good job."

While Gumbel was on the air, another commercial airliner had plowed into the Pentagon in Washington, D.C., but that would not be confirmed for more than an hour. At 9:43 AM, Gumbel reported and showed pictures of smoke coming out of the Pentagon.

> Oh my goodness, we're looking at a live picture from Washington and there is smoke pouring out of the Pentagon. It would appear that there has been another major explosion. You are looking at a scene of an apparent blast aftermath . . . We don't know whether this is the result of a bomb or whether it is yet another aircraft, but there is smoke pouring out of the Pentagon.

A short time later, Gumbel informed the audience that all airports and all tunnels and bridges leading into New York City had been closed. Shortly after this report, President Bush spoke to the nation from Florida, where he was pro-moting his education program.

*CBS News* correspondent Bill Plante reported from Washington that the entire White House staff was evacuated. He said the Secret Service had moved everybody away from the White House grounds and "kept telling us that we have to remain a block away."

While Gumbel was carrying much of the burden of covering the story in New York for CBS, Dan Rather was making his way to the studios. Gumbel turned the mike over to Rather after reporting that there had been a second explosion on Trade Tower 2. After taking over, Rather said that there were unofficial reports that a portion of one of the trade towers had collapsed.

Rather was able to reach correspondent Harold Dow, who was near the trade towers. He reported that there had been another explosion and that literally the top of the building came down, sending smoke and debris everywhere. Dow added, "I had to do all I could to run to get away from the debris. Me and a number of other people are trapped in a subway here, in a shoe store, actually trying to get away from most of the debris." He continued, "It is a surreal and devastating scene over here, something like I've never seen before."

Rather then reached another correspondent at the scene, Mika Brzezinski. Here is part of his report:

> I was standing with *CBS News* correspondent Byron Pitts when the collapse occurred. And literally plumes of smoke and gases as the collapse happened began to roll our way, and that is when the crowd went wild. People just began to run. Our live truck shut down, crews were running, reporters were running, and the cops were literally just waving their arms saying "go, go, go."

Following this report, correspondent Jim Stewart told Rather and the nation that police in Washington had closed down the Capitol, the House and Senate, and the Justice Department. One building that had not been closed down, Stewart said, was the FBI. He said the FBI had established an emergency command post in the center of its building.

At NBC, *Today Show* hosts Katie Couric and Matt Lauer were interviewing an author when the attacks occurred. Lauer interrupted to say, "We're going to go live now and show you a picture of the World Trade Center, where I understand a plane has crashed into the center here in New York City." Like the other networks, NBC also was able to get eyewitnesses on the air quickly as they showed live pictures of the trade center buildings on fire. Eyewitness Jennifer Oberstein said, "I have to tell you it's quite terrifying. I'm in shock right now. I came out of the subway and was heading to work when I heard a big boom, looked up and there was a big ball of fire . . . I've never seen any fire like this in the air, and the pieces of building were flying down . . . It looks like the top, maybe 20 floors . . . It's horrible. I can't even describe it."

Moments later, at 9:00 AM, Lauer said, "We're back with dramatic pictures of an accident that has happened just a short time ago. You're looking at the World Trade Center in lower Manhattan, where just a few minutes ago, we're told, a plane crashed into the upper floors of one of the trade towers. You can see fire and flames, or smoke billowing from that tower." The anchors continued to interview eyewitnesses. Dan Dietrich said he saw one plane crash into the middle of the top floors of one of the towers, and 10 minutes later he saw another plane crash into the other tower. "There was a huge fireball and a gaping hole in the side of the tower," he said, adding, "As we were looking into it, another plane came in low, I believe from the other side, and hit the middle of the other tower. I saw both planes, two separate planes, crash into each tower."

MSNBC reporter Ashleigh Banfield told a dramatic story of being engulfed in a cloud of debris so thick that she had to kick in two glass doors to an apartment building just to keep from suffocating.

Will Wright, the news director for Fox station WWORTV, which is on the New Jersey side of the Hudson River, said he was about to leave for the station when he received a phone call from one of his producers saying a plane had just crashed into the World Trade Center. The producer told Wright that she had already reached the station and was dispatching crews to the scene. Wright said some of his crews were able to hire pleasure boats to take them across the river because the tunnels and the George Washington Bridge had been closed. He said other crews walked across bridges to get to the scene.

Meanwhile, at 8:51 AM, after the first plane hit, ABC's *Good Morning America* went from a Charles Gibson interview with the Duchess of York to a picture of the World Trade Center. Gibson and Diane Sawyer were on the air when the second plane hit. ABC quickly began a special report that included a live shot of the second plane hitting the trade center. Correspondent Dan Dahler called in from the roof of his apartment building four blocks away from the trade center on his cell phone—the first network correspondent to do that. By 10 AM, Peter Jennings took over. An ABC spokesman said Jennings walked right into the building and sat down in the anchor chair. The network's three-day coverage of the disaster was the longest continuing coverage of any story in the history of ABC.

Shortly after the crash, local stations in New York began calling up reinforcements from co-owned stations outside the city. WNBC-TV, for example, called in reporters and crews from sister stations in Philadelphia, Providence, and the Hartford-New Haven markets. NY1 cable station pulled in reporters from a similar Time-Warner cable operation in Tampa. Because CNN lost its microwave facility on the trade center, it was forced to set up a temporary receiver on the roof of its New York headquarters. An official noted that the network had never had to do that before, but as he put it, "Desperate times call for desperate measures."

Radio coverage of the disaster also helped millions in New York City and the neighboring area to know what was going on, because all but one local TV station, WCBS-TV, were knocked off the air when their transmitters were destroyed at the trade center.

At the all-news radio station, WINS, executive sales account executive Joan Fleisher went to the roof of her apartment building at 8:50 AM and described what was going on at the trade center. News Director Ben Mevorach was walking across one of the bridges to Manhattan and reported live on his cell phone as the second trade tower collapsed. He said 15 of his reporters finally got to the trade center, city hall, and area hospitals.

ABC News Radio aired its first special report at 8:52 AM and provided its stations with 91 hours of anchored coverage through the first weekend. CNN Radio delivered 96 newscasts per day.

*Broadcasting and Cable* magazine, in an issue devoted to the disaster, noted that much of the live coverage and dramatic pictures came from traffic reporting helicopters ringing Manhattan. Those choppers delivered live pictures of the second passenger jet plowing into Tower 2. The magazine also noted that as the twin towers stood for their final hour, TV crews had time to capture images of frightened evacuees pouring through the streets, trapped office workers   clinging to the outside of the buildings, and—most chillingly—terrified jumpers choosing to plunge to their deaths rather than face the 2,000-degree flames consuming the upper floors.

*Broadcasting and Cable,* the industry's major trade magazine, said of the news coverage: "Considering the wall-to-wall coverage, radio and television reporting was remarkably informative, maybe even calming." But it pointed out some mistakes, too. It noted that ABC, MSNBC, and FOX all reported a car bomb explosion outside the State Department, and that when police detained 10 people at New York airports two nights after the disaster, stations widely and erroneously reported that some were armed with knives. The day after the tragedy, many networks also reported that the official death toll from the Pentagon fire would be around 800, but Pentagon officials said that the final number would be hundreds fewer than that figure.

In a special report on the media coverage in *The Communicator*, the magazine published by the Radio and Television News Directors' Association, Gil Geisler wrote that when life in the United States was at its worst, broadcast journalism was at its best. She said the story was chaotic, but the storytellers were calm. She said television made every citizen an eyewitness.

Geisler, who is with the Poynter Institute in St. Petersburg, Florida, wrote that you could see "the conscious decision of TV directors to stay with the pictures during the coverage. This was not a day to see the faces of anchors; their voices sufficed." Geisler added, "Viewers needed to see the towers, the Pentagon. The sheer magnitude of the damage needed to be on screen for all to see."

Geisler also pointed out that at a time of budget strain, layoffs, and cutbacks, "Networks took the high road and dropped commercials, foregoing millions of dollars in revenue, and poured untold dollars into overtime, satellite bills and the care and feeding of crews."

*Newsweek* magazine's special report on the disaster noted that television doesn't always get tragedy right, but, "The media's work on the terrorist attacks did something that seemed nearly impossible considering the disastrous coverage of election night 2000." The magazine said the media exercised commendable caution and rightfully kept the grisliest images from the public. But it noted one unfortunate exception, what it called the "seemingly endless" video of someone plunging from the trade center. CBS, FOX, and CNN showed the footage repeatedly, though NBC wisely aired it only once.

At this writing, it is still too soon to analyze completely the broadcast media's performance during this crisis, particularly in respect to the non-breaking news aspects of the coverage. There is strong evidence that the late night talk shows, as is their penchant, engaged in irresponsible and speculative discussions about the disaster.

# A Changing Industry

Most of the original edition of this book was written during the conflict in the Persian Gulf and its aftermath. The timing offered a variety of opportunities to observe the broadcast media as they moved into a new role: the live reporting of a war on television. For the first time, the American people, along with most of the world, thanks to CNN, watched a war much as they would a Super Bowl. The instant coverage of rockets falling on Israel and Saudi Arabia brought the war into living rooms as never before. This coverage of the war showed us how dramatically the technology of electronic journalism had matured, and we would see the impact of these technical advances again in the coverage of the terrorist attacks on the United States.

Long before the Gulf War, many TV stations had expanded their newscasts from 30 minutes to an hour or more of news in the late evening. So it was not unusual, especially in the larger markets, to see local reporters competing with network journalists during the Gulf War, a trend that would continue in the coverage of subsequent world events, such as the terrorist attacks in the United States and the O.J. Simpson murder trial. The significance of this trend for journalism students is that, as more local TV stations begin to rely on their staffs to cover events outside their listening area, more jobs will become available for people breaking into the field.

One of the most significant developments in broadcasting in the past five years was the growing influence of Rupert Murdoch's FOX network and that of General Electric's MSNBC. Another positive factor is the growing profitability of local TV news. Most TV stations are profitable. But the explosion in cable and satellite dish programming has taken a heavy toll on traditional broadcasters. The saturation of information from these sources and from the Internet has cut deeply into audiences for traditional broadcast stations and networks.

For now, at least, the local TV news job market is healthy. But also remember that competition for jobs in broadcast news is keen, and that is not likely to change. The field is crowded because the profession is a dynamic one. It's often exciting, colorful, mostly rewarding and often glamorous, attracting many people who want to be a part of the action. But do not be overly alarmed—there always will be room for achievers. If you are determined to be among those broadcast journalism students who "make it," you will need plenty of determination, motivation, and hustle.

You do not have to be a born genius to become a good broadcast journalist. It never hurts, of course, but it's certainly not a requirement. As in all professional fields, you must be intelligent. However, there are other characteristics and skills that you must have or develop as well. These include: (1) an insatiable curiosity about the world around you; (2) a desire to change those things and circumstances that you perceive to be unfair, improper, or unlawful; and (3) persistence and aggressiveness in discovering the truth.

## Is Journalism for You?

The late Frank Graham, a sports columnist, once observed that journalism will kill you, but it will keep you alive in the meantime. An exaggeration, perhaps, but the lifestyle does not encourage a healthy or emotionally stable way of life. As one broadcast reporter puts it, "You have to be a little crazy to want to spend your life working lousy hours, eating bad food, probably drinking too much and fighting with your wife or girlfriend because you had to miss dinner for the 99th time or had to break a date."

The late veteran broadcaster and commentator John Chancellor noted that journalism is difficult work. "It's often frustrating, frequently exhausting, not the way to get rich." He said, "Every slip is out there in print or public view, to draw scorn, wrath or lawsuits." In *The News Business* (which Chancellor co-authored with Pulitzer Prize-winner Walter R. Mears of The Associated Press), the authors also wrote that journalism is "exciting, fascinating, constantly challenging and changing work."

## What Role to Play?

Do you hope to be in front of the cameras or behind them? Most journalism students want to be on camera as TV anchors. The odds are not quite as bad as for college quarterbacks making it to the NFL, but the competition is still formidable. Fortunately, there are more TV stations—and an even greater number of radio stations—than there are pro football teams.

If you are determined to be an anchor, keep in mind that it takes more than a college degree or an internship. Most anchors must first put in their time as reporters. In time, and with appropriate skills, a reporter may be given a shot at anchoring on weekends or holidays when the "stars" have a day off. If you are intent on being an anchor, then work hard at developing your reporting skills. If your goal is to be a broadcast reporter, sharpen your writing skills because they are the essence of good reporting.

Many of you will say, "I don't want to write or report, I want to be a producer." But TV news producers also pay their dues. They frequently start out as writers and associate producers, sometimes as researchers and even as desk assistants. Like the other people in broadcast news, producers get their jobs because they demonstrate many different skills. News judgment (i.e., the ability to sort out what should and should not go into a newscast, and what should be highlighted and what downplayed) is one of the most crucial skills. If the producer's news judgment is not sound, the program will not be successful.

Whatever role you hope to play, this book will help you achieve your goals. It concentrates on three areas—writing, reporting, and producing—which are the cornerstones of broadcast journalism. If you are successful in finding a place in the broadcast news industry, you will probably find yourself using these skills daily. Before you start on developing them, however, let's examine some other fundamentals that will help prepare you for a career in broadcast journalism.

# Your College Education

There is a continuing debate among news executives over the value of a journalism degree. Many professional journalists argue that a liberal arts education is more important than a program in journalism. "Give me young people with a well-rounded liberal arts education," say many news executives, "and I'll teach them how to be journalists."

It is a strong argument, which is why a great many college broadcast journalism programs require students to take most of their credits in liberal arts. While you may want to focus solely on your journalism courses, keep in mind that all the history, economics, political science, and language courses you are required to take will inform you as a journalist and will enrich your life as well.

An increasing number of job ads placed by news directors seek journalists who have some strong interest or background in such areas as health, business, or law. Almost any concentration in a secondary area, including political science or sociology, may improve your chances of finding a position in broadcast news.

Another advantage for those entering the broadcast news market is a second language. Spanish is particularly useful for journalists working in markets in the Southeast, Southwest, and West and also in major northern cities, such as New York and Chicago, which have large Spanish-speaking populations.

# Internships

Never pass up a chance to work as an intern for a radio or TV station while you are in school. Such work can be a tremendous advantage because it gives you an opportunity to observe firsthand what you are learning in your classes. Interns are often asked to write and work at the assignment desk or to help the producer. Yes, there will probably be a lot of coffee runs, and you will take many calls from complaining listeners, but anything you do that gets you inside a radio or TV station is well worth it even if you do not get paid. However, interns sometimes do receive minimum wage, if not more.

One of the greatest advantages of an internship is that you meet the people who do the hiring. Many students, after graduation, remain with the stations where they worked as interns. Many become reporters, producers, and assignment editors. Even if there is no job waiting for you at the station after your internship, you have something substantial to put on your resume. If you performed well, you have some good references too.

An internship also allows you to see what broadcast news is really like. You may discover that it is not what you want to pursue as a career. Some students discover during an internship that it's not for them. If you are not "pushy" by nature and are not comfortable with pressures and deadlines, it is better to discover that as quickly as possible.

# Your First Job

Like entry-level positions in many fields, your first job will not pay much. One disadvantage of working in broadcast news is that a lot of other people want to do it. News directors know that, and pay accordingly. They also know that if you "have what it takes" you will not be staying with the station for long. There is not much union representation except in larger markets, and you are unlikely to begin in one of those. However, for most people who end up in broadcast news, money is secondary. There is always the hope of ending up in New York, Chicago, or Los Angeles, where salaries are substantial, but you cannot depend on that happening. So, most people work in broadcasting for the very reasons that they got involved in the first place: it's fun, exciting, and yes, sometimes glamorous. There also is the satisfaction of knowing that you are doing your part to keep people informed, sometimes making things better in your community, and correcting injustices.

This introduction has given you an overview of the important requirements and rewards of a career in broadcast journalism. The remaining chapters focus on the process of developing the writing, reporting, and producing skills and techniques necessary to succeed in broadcast journalism.

At the end of each chapter, there are exercises to help determine how well you are absorbing all this new information. If you find that you are having trouble, go back and review the material. Much of the information you need to complete the assignments successfully is detailed in the chapter itself, but at times you will also have to use other resources. Locating outside information is the first step in a research process that will become a part of your everyday life if you become a broadcast journalist.

# 1 Broadcast News Writing Mechanics

Before you can get a driver's license, you have to learn how to drive a car. Before you write broadcast news, you must learn good grammar and know how to use a computer. You also must understand what news is and how writing broadcast news copy differs from other types of writing. As noted in the Introduction, you must quickly learn about accuracy and responsibility. You also need to learn the vocabulary of broadcast journalism, terms such as *wrap*, *voiceover*, *standup*, and *cutaway*.

Before you have finished working with this book, you will have learned about all these things and many more. This chapter starts with the mechanics of broadcast news writing, the small but essential details of preparing a script correctly. Learning these mechanics is like learning how to use the controls on a dashboard.

## Some Basics

Computers have replaced typewriters in newsrooms and classrooms, so margins and spacing are now set electronically, not manually as used to be the case with typewriters. Radio news is written on a full page, and television newswriters work with what is called the *split page*, which is discussed later in this chapter.

Set the margins on your computer so that there are approximately 10 spaces, or one inch, on each side, depending on the computer program that you are using. Type the copy double- or triple-spaced depending on the wishes of your instructor.

## Correcting Copy

In the days of the typewriter, corrections were made carefully with a pen or pencil between the lines. Today corrections are done electronically, but when the finished copy comes off the printer, some errors may still need correcting before airtime. The words being changed must be completely crossed out, and the words being substituted must be written clearly just above the crossed-out words. If the required corrections are too elaborate and the script becomes difficult to read, you should retype it.

Standard newspaper copyediting symbols are not permissible in broadcast copy. Here are two examples of corrected copy. The first is edited for print, the second for broadcast:

```
The mayor says he's binging the two sides in the newspaper

strike to the bargaining table today and is hopeful that an

agreement can be reachd before the end of the week. The

strike is now in its 3rd week. The major issue are job

security and the newspaper's demand that the union accept

a 20% reduction in wages.
```

```
                        bringing
The mayor says he's binging the two sides in the newspa-
          strike                    table            hopeful
per strike to the bargaining talbe today and is hupeful that
                             reached
an agreement can be reachd before the end of the week. The
                        third week.                   issues
strike is now in its 3rd weeek. The major issiue are job
                                  demand
security and the newspaper's demnand that the union accept
      percent
a 20% reduction in wages.
```

Poorly corrected copy increases the possibility that an anchor will make a mistake. As might be expected, anchors are particularly sensitive about stumbling over a word or sentence, and, if the mishap is the writer's fault, you can be certain that the newscaster will let someone know about it as soon as the newscast is over or, more likely, during a commercial break.

# Slugs

Every page of the news script must be identified. These identifications are called *slugs*, and they are placed in the upper left-hand corner of the page. The slug includes a one- or two-word description of the story, such as Fire, Newspaper Strike, or Missing Boy. The slug also includes the date, the time of the newscast, and the writer's initials. Here's an example:

Fire

2/10/01

9 a.m.

TW

Slugs are important because they allow the writer, producers, anchors, director, and a variety of other people involved in putting a newscast together to quickly locate a particular story in the script. This capability can be vital when, for example, the position of the story in the script must be changed or the story must be dropped just as the newscast begins or when it is already on the air.

# The Split Page

Preparing a TV script is somewhat more complicated than preparing a radio script. A TV script is divided into two vertical sections and is known as the *split page*. All technical instructions and identification of video and graphics fall in the left portion of the split page, and the script to be read by the anchor or reporter appears in the right column, along with sound bite outcues and times. Several examples of split pages, and how they are used, are included throughout this book.

As you examine those scripts, you will notice that each station has its own way of using the split page. Experienced broadcast journalists adjust easily to the slight variations as they move from station to station.

# Avoiding Abbreviations

All words in broadcast news copy, with a few exceptions, must be spelled out. Abbreviations are not permitted because they would force anchors to interpret their meaning, inviting confusion and mistakes.

|               *Wrong*               |               *Right*               |
| ----------------------------------- | ----------------------------------- |
| Lt. General                         | Lieutenant General                  |
| Ass't. Sec. of State                | Assistant Secretary of State        |
| Union Pres. Felix Jones             | Union President Felix Jones         |
| John St. and Norfolk Ave.           | John Street and Norfolk Avenue      |

It is permissible to use abbreviations when the names of organizations are better known by their initials than by their full names (e.g., FBI, NBC, and CIA); however, to make it easier for anchors to read, writers place hyphens between the letters.

F-B-I

N–B–C

C-I-A

# Avoiding Split Words and Sentences

If there is not enough room on a line of copy to complete a word, the entire word must be carried over to the next line. Words should not be hyphenated because splitting words at the end of a line could confuse the anchor. The same is true with sentences that cannot fit on one page. Part of a sentence should not be carried over from one page to another.

Forcing anchors to jump from the bottom of one page to the top of the next when they are in the middle of a sentence invites trouble. It cannot be stressed too often that writers must avoid anything that increases the chance that the anchors will stumble over copy.

If a sentence cannot be completed on a page, it should begin on the top of the next page. Type the word MORE at the bottom of the page so the anchors know that the story continues on the next page. Otherwise, they may pause unnecessarily, believing that a new story starts on the following page. Some newsrooms prefer to use an arrow at the end of the page to indicate that more copy is coming.

# Punctuation

The opening of this chapter stressed the importance of using correct grammar in broadcast copy, but you should be aware that certain exceptions are made to standard grammatical rules. For example, use commas to indicate a pause, not simply for grammatical reasons. Some writers use a dash instead of a comma to indicate a pause, but dashes should be used sparingly, usually to indicate longer pauses. Unless you are writing for yourself (when you can do whatever is comfortable for you), you should not use an ellipsis (. . .) to indicate a pause

**Figure 1.1**  ABC News World Headquarters, 1998. (©2000 ABC, Inc.)

or as a signal that you have eliminated part of a quotation because those dots could confuse anchors. And you should never use a semicolon.

Capitalize certain words, like *Not* and other words you think the anchors should emphasize. This technique is especially helpful when the anchors might not have an opportunity to go over the copy before they read it on the air. Keep such emphasis to a minimum, however, because the anchor is usually the best judge of which words to stress.

# Names and Titles

Titles are always used before a person's name in broadcast copy, never after it. For example, Secretary of Defense John Smith should be used rather than, as newspapers write, John Smith, Secretary of Defense. Using the title first alerts the listener to the name that will follow and reflects conversational style.

It is acceptable to break up the name and the title. For example:

> The secretary of the Navy said today that joint maneuvers would begin in the Atlantic next week. John Smith told reporters that Canadian and British vessels would join part of the Atlantic fleet in the maneuvers.

If you use names in your copy, make sure you double-check their spelling and pronunciation. If you are reporting an accident or a fire in which injuries or deaths occurred, ask the police officer or fire chief to confirm any names you're unsure about. Wire services are a good source for checking names and pronunciations. (More information on that topic is discussed in Chapter 8, "Delivering the News.")

Names are not always essential to a story. Scripts written at a small-town radio or TV station should certainly include the names of those who were killed or injured in a fire at the local paper plant. But the names of three people from another state who were injured on the freeway would be of little interest to the local audience. It would be sufficient to say the following:

> Three Florida residents suffered minor injuries after their car spun out of control on the freeway and hit a guardrail.

If those three people live in a small town in the station's listening area, however, then the names and addresses should be mentioned. The story might read as follows:

> Three Centerville people are recovering from minor injuries suffered this afternoon when their car went out of control on the freeway and hit the guardrail. Police identified the injured as Pam and John Rose of the 300 block of Blackwell Avenue and Peter Noyes, who lives at 177 Sunshine Road.

Some news directors prefer to omit the house numbers, limiting the address to the street. In many cases, the determining factor is the size of the community. A radio station in a community of 5,000 will give more details about the injured than a station in a city of 100,000. A newscast in a larger city might merely identify the neighborhoods in which the injured people lived.

But in that community of 5,000, the second paragraph of the story might give more details:

> The injured were on their way home from a P-T-A meeting. The Roses both teach at Johnson High School. They were giving Noyes a ride home when the accident took place.

The added details are of interest because in a small community the chances are that many of those listening to the newscast know the three people. If they do not, they may still be interested for other reasons: most of the audience will be familiar with Johnson High School, they may be members of the PTA, and some may have attended the PTA meeting.

## Middle Initials

Do not use middle initials unless they are part of the name a person is known by or they are needed in a story to identify people with similar names. For example, some politicians and celebrities, like the following, always use their middle initials, so you would be correct to use them in the story:

The late Edward R. Murrow

George C. Scott

The late President John F. Kennedy

The same goes for middle names. They should never be used unless the individual does so. It would sound strange to hear the name of the late Dr. Martin Luther King Jr. mentioned without the Luther.

### Foreign Names

It was sometimes amusing, but more often embarrassing, to hear radio and TV anchors trying to pronounce all the foreign names during the Gulf War. Everyone quickly learned the name and pronunciation of the president of Iraq, Saddam Hussein. The king of Jordan was easy: King Hussein. But anchors used a variety of pronunciations for the president of Syria, Hafeez Assad, and the emir of Kuwait, whose full name is Sheik Jabiral-Ahmadal-Sabah. The emir was usually referred to simply as Sheik al-Sabah, and the Saudi Arabian monarch was usually called just King Fahd. Palestine Liberation Organization (PLO) leader Yasir Arafat was almost always initially referred to by both names.

Pronunciation is discussed further in Chapter 8, "Delivering the News," but for now remember that foreign names are used in broadcast copy only if they are essential. The names of foreign heads of state, ambassadors, and foreign ministers who are often in the news must be mentioned, but secondary foreign officials can usually be identified by title alone.

When a foreign name is used, it must be used according to custom. In some foreign countries, such as China, the surname is the first and most important name, not the last. For example, the late Chinese leader Mao Tse-tung is referred to as Chairman Mao.

# Ages

A person's age should be used in a news story only if it is significant for some reason. Most of the time, it is irrelevant. There certainly would be no need to give the ages of Pam and John Rose or Peter Noyes, who were involved in the earlier accident example; however, if the Roses' five-year-old daughter had been involved in the accident, her age would be worth mentioning because she is so young. And if Noyes' 87-year-old mother was in the back seat, her age should also be given.

Sometimes it is also acceptable to give ages in crime stories. If two teenage boys were involved in a hit-and-run accident, their ages should be reported. If an 80-year-old man tried to hold up a bank, his age is the most interesting part of the story because it's unusual to hear of a senior citizen committing a crime.

If a 78-year-old woman's vehicle crossed a divider and collided head-on with another car, give her age because it could have been a factor in the accident. Perhaps not, but until police determine the cause of the accident, the woman's age should be included. It also should be noted if, for example, police said that one of the tires on the woman's car had blown out and possibly caused the accident.

Other reasons for giving ages include exceptional accomplishments or unlikely occurrences. For example:

A 16-year-old graduates at the top of her law school class.

A 60-year-old Hollywood actor marries a 22-year-old woman.

A 44-year-old woman gives birth to quadruplets.

## Marital Status

It is not necessary to specify whether someone is married, divorced, or single unless the information is directly related to the story in some way. There would be no reason to say whether someone who was arrested for driving while intoxicated is single or married. But when a candidate is running for mayor, most people want to know whether he or she is single or married. It may influence how some people vote.

During the Gulf War, many servicewomen were on duty in the desert. A soldier usually was identified as a married woman when the reporter discovered that her husband was also in the service, or, perhaps, was home looking after the children. For the most part, however, reporters were more concerned with servicewomen's role in the Gulf War, not their marital status, and that was appropriate.

## Race

As with marital status, race should be noted only if it is relevant to the story. For example, you would mention race or ethnicity if a city elected its first Hispanic member of the city council or if an African American student graduated at the top of the class in a predominantly white college. But a person's race should be mentioned in a crime story *only* if it is necessary for identification purposes while police are still looking for a suspect. If a person has already been arrested for a crime, there is no reason to indicate the person's racial or ethnic background. Race and diversity are discussed further later in the book.

## Numbers

The fundamental rule to remember about the use of numbers in broadcast copy is that they should be rounded off and spelled out when any chance for confusion exists. For example, a budget figure of $60,342,960,000 should be rounded off to "more than 60 billion dollars." Such a figure is spelled out because it would

**Figure 1.2**   An anchor reviews copy.

be virtually impossible for a newscaster to deal with all those numbers in the middle of the copy.

The convention is to spell out single-digit numbers, and eleven, and to use figures for 10 and for 12 through 999. For larger figures, use words or word-figure combinations. Here are some examples:

There are only eleven days left until Christmas.

There were 45 students in the class.

There were three people at the table.

There were 600 prisoners of war.

There were 75-thousand people in the stadium and another 15-thousand were turned away.

Single-digit numbers with million, billion, and so on are expressed in words, such as:

It will take another three million dollars to complete work on the project.

Some figures reaching the news desk are expressed in decimals:

The stock market was up 6.88 points.

Unemployment was down .01 percent for the month.

The Navy asked for an additional 5.5 billion dollars.

Some newscasters will say the stock market was up "six point 88," but most prefer to eliminate the decimal and round off the figure to "almost seven points." As for the other examples: recast them for broadcast copy to read, "Unemployment was down one tenth of one percent for the month," and "The Navy asked for an additional five and one-half billion dollars."

## Timing Stories

It is essential to know how to time copy. If you are writing for yourself, use a stopwatch as you read each page of copy aloud, and then write the time on the page. Be sure to read the copy aloud because the timing would be different if you read it silently.

If you are writing the copy for someone else, it is more difficult to estimate time because everyone reads copy at a different pace. On average, newscasters read at a speed of about 15 or 16 standard lines of copy per minute.

For television, because of the split page and the use of bold type for the teleprompter, most newscasters take about one second to read each line of copy. Most computer programs have the ability to time each story. As you become familiar with the equipment you use to write scripts, you'll learn how best to time the material. You must know this information so that you can estimate how many lines of copy you need to write for a given story. You may often be told by a producer: "Give me about 20 seconds."

## Review Questions

1.  Why can't you use standard newspaper copyediting techniques when you are correcting mistakes in broadcast copy?
2.  What is a slug, and where does it go on your copy?
3.  Most abbreviations are not permitted in broadcast copy. Give examples of some exceptions.
4.  What should you do if you cannot complete a sentence on one page?
5.  Do titles go before or after a name in broadcast copy?
6.  Explain when you should and should not give the street address of someone involved in a car accident.
7.  Should you ever give a person's middle name or initial in broadcast copy? Explain.
8.  When is it proper to give a person's age in broadcast copy?
9.  When should you mention a person's racial or ethnic background?
10. How would you express the following sentence in broadcast copy?

    The Centerville School Board approved a budget of 1.5 million dollars.

11. How would you express the figure in the following sentence?

    There were 49,883 people at the game.

# Exercises

1. Photocopy the following broadcast copy or retype it exactly as it appears and then, with a pen or pencil, correct the errors.

   The President called on Iraqis to overthrow the regime of President Haddam Hussein. He suggested this solution would be the best way to bring Iraq buck into the community of peace-luving nations.

   Pete Williams, Assistant Secretary of Defense, praised the press for its coverage of the Gulf War and defended the military's use of the pool system in reporting the War. Williams said the press accurately reported the war. He denied complaints that the press was unable to report the war accurately because of interference by the military.

2. Rewrite the following to reflect good broadcast style:

   Ted Kennedy, the Democratic senator from Massachusetts, said he would vote against the Supreme Court nomination.

   Colin Powell, the Secretary of State, was critical of China's refusal to allow the American spy plane to be flown home.

3. Read through your local newspaper until you find three stories that use numbers that would have to be changed for broadcast. Type the material so that it reflects proper broadcast style.

4. Using the same newspaper, find three examples of names and titles that would have to be rewritten for broadcast. Type the material in broadcast style.

5. Rewrite a one-page story from a newspaper and, after you have corrected the copy, time it and note the time on the page.

# **2** Broadcast News Writing Style

Chapter 1 helped acquaint you with some of the rather tedious but necessary basics of broadcast news writing. The next step is to learn broadcast news writing style. Broadcast style is different from other styles of writing, principally because broadcast copy is written for the ear, not the eye, unlike most other writing. Much of the news "writing" heard on radio and television is actually "rewriting." Although broadcast news reporters write original copy when they are covering a story, a considerable portion of the news on radio and television is gathered from the Associated Press (AP) news wire and rewritten in broadcast style or taken off the broadcast wire and read on the air without a rewrite. This chapter focuses on rewriting copy obtained from the wire.

## Rewriting Wire Copy

One semester, a student stopped me at the end of a class and said: "Professor White, I need some help. I have an internship and an opportunity to write some broadcast copy. Can you give me some tips?"

I was puzzled and amused. He was carrying a copy of my textbook under his arm. "It's all in the book," I told him. "Everything I've learned about writing is there. I have no secret, no 'quick fix.' It's all important."

He looked at me, nodding his head in agreement. "I know," he said, "I've read it all, but isn't there something special, something particularly important that I should remember when the editor gives me some wire copy and says, 'rewrite this'?"

I was still amused by his question and his apparent panic at the idea of having to write a story from wire copy in an actual broadcast newsroom, rather than in the classroom. Then suddenly I remembered being in a similar situation before this young man was even born. There was, indeed, one essential point to learn about rewriting wire copy.

"Look," I said, "there actually is one thing that you can do when you are given that wire copy, that you must learn above all else. Get rid of it as fast as possible. Read it, digest it, and then discard it. After that," I said, "write what you remember and don't look at the wire copy again until it's time to check your facts."

You may find it difficult to surrender the wire copy and rely only on your memory, but that is the only way to be certain that you rewrite what is basically newspaper-style wire copy into conversational broadcast copy. The AP does offer a broadcast wire written in a conversational style, but we are not concerned with that wire. This book prepares you to do what the broadcast news service writer does with the service's newspaper wire copy.

Getting accustomed to reading and absorbing material and then expressing it in your own words takes practice. Once you have conquered the temptation to refer to the original wire copy or newspaper copy as you write, you will discover that your broadcast copy will be easy and natural for you, or anyone else, to read on the air.

Of course, when I wrote that example, most newsrooms were still using actual wire copy. Today, most newsrooms receive the wire copy through the computer, and if that young man were to take a similar test today, he might be writing on the computer from wire copy received on the computer, but the principal is still the same.

# Conversational Style

Writing in conversational style means writing for the ear. Newspapers, obviously, are written for the eye, which means that if readers do not understand something, they can return to the paragraph or sentence and read it a second time. In broadcast news, however, the audience has no such luxury; they hear the copy just once. So, broadcast copy must be written clearly and simply. Thoughts must be expressed quickly with brief, crisp, declarative sentences. They must be aimed at ordinary people, which means the words must be understood immediately, without second thought. If the audience does not understand the copy, nothing else matters.

# Contractions

Broadcast newswriters must write the way most people speak. When we have a discussion with another person, we automatically do several things of which we usually are not aware. For example, we almost always use contractions. We are more likely to say "I'm going to work now, Frank," than "I am going to work now, Frank." And we might add, "Let's get together for lunch again soon," instead of "Let us get together again soon." In other words, if we contract our words in conversation, we should do the same in broadcast copy. Here are some other examples:

**Figure 2.1**   Newsroom at WAFB-TV, Baton Rouge. (Photo by
Christopher J. Rogers)

Good morning, I'm Jack Jones with the late news.

Here's a rundown of the top stories we're covering.

We've just received word that teachers are walking out of classrooms at Willow
   Street High School. . . .

If you're driving to work, expect serious delays on the freeway because of an
   accident at the James Street exit. . . .

There's no word from the mayor yet on rumors he'll resign. . . .

In the above copy, most pronoun-verb combinations have been contracted;
however, sometimes—for emphasis—it is better not to contract words. For
example:

The mayor says he will seek reelection.

Because the word *will* is key to this particular sentence, it would be better to
avoid the contraction *he'll*. The newscaster would want to emphasize the word
*will*.

## Reading Your Copy Aloud

Reading copy aloud helps you determine when words should be contracted,
which words should be emphasized, how clear the sentences are, and how well
the copy flows from sentence to sentence. Writers should not be embarrassed
about reading copy aloud in the newsroom. The ear, not the eye, is the best
judge of well-written broadcast copy. It is almost impossible to catch some

poorly written phrases or sentences without testing them on the ear. In particular, you may not realize how complicated a sentence is until you read it aloud.

# Avoiding Information Overload

Often, copy that is difficult to understand contains too much information in any one sentence, a situation known as information overload. Some of the nation's finest newspapers are guilty of overloading sentences, but, as mentioned earlier, readers can always reread complicated passages. Here's an example of some copy from a major city newspaper and how it could be simplified for broadcast:

> President Saddam Hussein of Iraq, besieged by tenacious domestic rebellions that continued to threaten his control of key cities, Saturday promised broad political reforms that he said would transform his totalitarian regime into a multiparty democracy.

Quite a mouthful. It is not well written, even for a newspaper, but in its present form, this passage would sound outrageous if read on the air. The first phrase to go should be "besieged by tenacious domestic rebellions," which is obviously not "conversational" copy. The next passage to be revised would be "transform his totalitarian regime into a multiparty democracy."

The example sentence would be greatly improved if it were broken into two sentences. What is the most important detail? It is Hussein's promise to make reforms. So, the story could start out like this:

> Iraqi President Saddam Hussein promises sweeping political reforms that he claims would lead to a multiparty democracy.

Then the second sentence could deal with the other major thought—the rebels:

> Saddam made the promise Saturday as rebels continued to threaten his control of key cities.

Notice that the word *tenacious* was dropped. Tenacious is not a bad word, but it works better in print than on the air. It is an "elitist" word, and not everyone in the audience will know its meaning. Remember that unless the words are understood, nothing else matters. In a report heard on National Public Radio, two elitist words were used within 20 seconds of each other: *ubiquitous* and *eclectic*. Such words have no place in broadcast copy. The reporter who used them had a good story to tell, but many listeners in his audience missed the meaning of the story because they did not understand the words.

Here's another newspaper lead that needs revising for broadcast:

> The Energy Department proposes to spend $2.4 billion next year and up to 3.7 billion in each of the following four years to bring the nation's nuclear

weapon production plants into compliance with environmental and safety laws, according to Energy Secretary James D. Watkins.

If you read that sentence to some friends, and then ask them to tell you what it says, you would probably find that unless they have unusual abilities of concentration and recall, they would be unable to repeat all the details. That lengthy, involved sentence could be turned into the following good broadcast copy:

> The Energy Department wants to spend almost two and one-half billion dollars next year to improve the nation's nuclear production plants. The funds would be used to bring the plants into compliance with environmental and safety laws. Energy Secretary James Watkins says the government is willing to spend almost 15 billion dollars over the next four years to continue the cleanup and safety checks at the nuclear weapon production plants.

If you read the new sentences to your friends, they would probably remember more about the story than they did when you read them the newspaper version. Let's examine how the newspaper copy was rewritten.

First, it was broken into three parts to reduce the number of details in one sentence. Listeners understand information better if they hear it in small doses. The newspaper version mentions two large figures, $2.4 billion and $3.7 billion. In the broadcast version, the first figure was explained in the first sentence, and the second figure was mentioned in the third sentence.

The first figure, $2.4 billion, was rounded off to "almost two and one-half billion dollars." It is best to round off figures and to eliminate use of the decimal in broadcast copy because the result is easier for most people to understand. The second figure, "up to $3.7 billion in each of the following four years," was totaled and rounded off. The result, "the government is willing to spend almost 15 billion dollars over the next four years," is easier for listeners to grasp because they don't need to do the math in their heads. Notice, too, that dollars is spelled out in broadcast copy.

No attempt was made in the first sentence to discuss exactly how the Energy Department plans to spend the money. It was enough to tell the audience that the department wants to spend this money to improve the plants. Now that the audience has digested that information, it is told how the money is going to be used: "to bring the plants into compliance with environmental and safety laws." And then, in the third sentence, the audience learns that the energy secretary wants even more money in the coming years to complete the job. Just in case the audience was not paying complete attention, how the money is to be used was mentioned again in the closing words "to continue the cleanup and safety checks" at the plants.

Last, the middle initial D was dropped from Secretary Watkins' name because he does not use the initial consistently.

# Avoiding Relative Clauses

Other sentences that produce information overload are those that contain relative clauses. Relative clauses are introduced by the relative pronouns *who*, *which*, *that*, *what*, *whoever*, *whichever*, and *whatever* and add information to simple sentences. Newspapers often use relative clauses to stress one point about a person or thing over another in a particular sentence. Because relative pronouns refer to nouns that precede them, TV and radio audiences may have trouble identifying the noun and pronoun as the same person or thing. Take this example of a newspaper story:

> The comments from the State Department spokesman came in response to a report in the English-language *Tehran Times*, which quoted a source as saying Iran would work toward restoring diplomatic relations with the United States if Washington gave assurances it would release frozen Iranian assets.

Whereas newspaper readers would immediately know that *which* refers to *Tehran Times* because the words are next to each other, a broadcast audience might have to stop and think about what *which* refers to. When this copy was rewritten for broadcast, the relative pronoun *which* was removed and the sentence was cut in two. The noun *newspaper* was used again instead of the pronoun:

> The State Department spokesman made the comments after a report appeared in the English-language newspaper The Tehran Times. The newspaper quoted a source as saying Iran would work toward restoring diplomatic relations with the United States if Washington promised to release frozen Iranian assets.

Another change in the rewrite included recasting the passive construction in the first sentence to make it active.

*Which*, when used as part of a clause that adds descriptive detail about a noun, also presents unnecessary problems for broadcast writers. Take this print copy:

> Two people were killed today when a small plane, which was on a flight from Key West to Miami, crashed into the ocean off the coast of Key Largo.

All these details will be simpler for your audience to digest if you give the number of dead and where the crash took place in the first sentence and explain the departure and destination of the plane in the second sentence. Here's a broadcast version:

> Two people died today when a small plane crashed into the ocean off the coast of Key Largo. The plane was on a flight from Key West to Miami.

Relative clauses introduced by *that* contain information important to the meaning of a sentence, not just additional details. For example:

> The truck that jackknifed on the freeway today was carrying flammable liquid.

The *that* clause identifies which particular truck was carrying flammable liquid.

In some sentences, *that* can be omitted because the sentence sounds more natural and is clear without it. For example:

The governor says that he'll leave the capital by plane this evening.

Dropping *that* makes the sentence more conversational:

The governor says he'll leave the capital by plane this evening.

## Eliminating Long Words

Short words are usually easier to understand than long ones and, crucially for broadcast news, where time is precious, they take less time to deliver. For example:

Police *abandoned* the search.

is more difficult to say than

Police *gave up* the search.

Here are examples of long words and some shorter ones that could replace them in broadcast copy:

| AVOID | USE |
|---|---|
| extraordinary | unusual |
| acknowledge | admit |
| initiate | start, begin |
| transform | change |

Certain words should be avoided because they are difficult to pronounce on the air. Here are some examples:

| AVOID | USE |
|---|---|
| burst into | broke into |
| coaxing | tempting |
| recrimination | countercharge |
| autonomy | independence |
| deteriorate | grow worse |
| allegations | charges |
| intermediaries | go-betweens; negotiators |

If you are unsure about other words you find yourself using, remember that reading them aloud is the best way to decide whether they are appropriate broadcast words. If a word is difficult to say or sounds strange or confusing to the ear, don't use it.

# Conjunctions

Coupling pins such as *but* and *and* are often helpful in connecting sentences or parts of sentences. Using conjunctions to link ideas to one another often can help broadcast copy sound more conversational; however, do not overuse conjunctions. Remember also that some conjunctions that work in print, such as the *however* in the previous sentence, do not always work as well in broadcast copy. Use *but* instead of *however* in broadcast copy.

# Prepositions

Prepositions can also help make copy more conversational, particularly when used to eliminate the possessive, which tends to make listeners work harder to follow the meaning. Here are some examples; the first uses the possessive:

> The Senate Armed Services Committee's spokesman announced a series of new hearings on budget cuts.

Here is a preposition used in the same sentence:

> A spokesman *for* the Senate Armed Services Committee announced a series of new hearings on budget cuts.

See how much easier it is to read the version with the preposition. It is more natural. The preposition is more likely to be used than the possessive in conversation.

# Pronouns

We use a lot of pronouns during conversation, and they serve a useful purpose in broadcast copy. They eliminate the need to repeat a person's name. Some difficulty arises, however, when pronouns are used too far from the person's name or more than one name is mentioned in the sentence or paragraph. Examine this troublesome use of a pronoun:

> The Boy Scout of the Year award was given to Frank Jones by Mayor Harris. Immediately after the presentation, he slipped and fell on the stage.

Who slipped and fell on the stage, the mayor or the Boy Scout? The pronoun *he* does not work here because two males are mentioned in the sentence. The person who fell should be identified by name.

# Modifying Phrases

Some writers, in their eagerness to tell the story, often get the details right but put the words in the wrong order, thus changing the meaning of the sentence. Look at the following example:

> Russian officials said political prisoners arrested by the KGB during former
> communist regimes have been released at a news conference today.

Because of the placement of the modifying phrase *at a news conference*, this sentence implies that the prisoners were released at the time of the news conference. What the writer meant to say is:

> Russian officials said at a news conference today that political prisoners
> arrested by the KGB have been released.

When you use modifying phrases, be sure to place them as close as possible to the word(s) they describe or identify. Here's another example:

> The two cars collided in heavy rain on Interstate 95 during the rush hour.

It's true that the "heavy rain" did fall on the highway, but it also fell elsewhere. Recast to be less ambiguous, the sentence would read this way:

> The two cars collided on Interstate 95 in heavy rain during the rush hour.

# Avoiding Clichés

In preparation for writing this book, I watched television news in several major cities. The reporting was often good, but the writing was just as often horrible. When you watch and listen to news for hours at a time, you realize how badly broadcast copy can be written, not only on local stations but on the networks as well.

Newspaper writers often turn out a lot of long, cumbersome copy that sometimes takes several readings to digest. But, to these newspaper writers' credit, their writing is rarely as cliché-filled as the copy produced by broadcast writers and reporters.

Broadcast news managers often argue that their writers do not have as much time as newspaper writers to produce copy, which is often true. They also point out that some of the cliché-filled copy I complain about is not very different from the way people talk. "We're writing conversational copy, aren't we?" asked one news director. "So what's wrong with a few clichés? We use them all the time in conversation."

Some people might find that argument persuasive, but writing in a conversational style does not mean adopting all the bad habits of conversation. Many people hold conversations without using clichés.

The American College Dictionary defines a cliché as "a trite, stereotyped expression." In his book *Newswriting*, William Metz says a cliché is "a phrase that has been used so often that it has no zip, has outlived its usefulness. A cliché is a worn-out phrase." He adds: "These barren, impotent word combinations are used by careless and lazy writers."

We all use clichés from time to time, but you should avoid using clichés in broadcast copy as much as possible, even though some clichés are heard every night on news programs. For example, killers are often "cold-blooded"; "slaughter" is always "bloody"; and events "come on the heels of" other events. Broadcasts during political campaigns in particular inundate listeners with clichés, such as "hats in the political ring," "campaign trails," "political hay," and "political footballs."

Here are some more clichés that should be (if you will excuse the cliché) "deep sixed":

Airliners that become "ill-fated planes" after they crash

Politicians and others who "take to the airwaves"

Lobby groups and others who are "up in arms"

People who end up "in the driver's seat"

Facts that are "difficult to swallow"

Plans brought to a "screeching halt"

Comments or actions that add "fuel to the storm" (a mixed metaphor)

Troublesome situations that are a "can of worms" or a "Pandora's box"

And why are so many things "put on the back burner"? What is wrong with "delaying action" or referring to something as having "a low priority"? Say simply that people are "delaying" or "avoiding" something, rather than "dragging their feet." Police should be "searching for" or "looking for" or even "hunting for" a missing person, not "combing the woods" for him or her.

Broadcast writers who use "cooling their heels," "tight-lipped," and "Mother Nature" should be "tarred and feathered." Although some newsmakers insist on referring to something as being "miraculous," do not use the word to describe some spectacular escape from death or injury unless you are quoting the newsmaker. Use instead "unbelievable," "amazing," or "incredible."

"Rampage" is another "worn-out" word that will never go away. Instead of using the cliché to tell a prison riot story, describe what's actually going on inside the prison. For example:

> Prisoners at Center City jail this afternoon took five guards hostage, burned cellblocks, and demanded that Governor Wilson come to the jail to hear their demands.

A tabloid TV station in Miami, in its story about the arrest of a suspect in the Florida State University serial killings, reported the following:

> People are breathing easier tonight because a suspected serial killer is
> behind bars.

As it turned out, the suspect was then released for lack of evidence, so we can assume that the *breathing* in the community became heavier again.

A network sportscaster reporting about a series of injuries in the NBA wrote this sentence:

Officials are scratching their heads for an explanation.

All of the above are examples of "lazy" writing. Whenever you are tempted to use a cliché, make the extra effort to think of a fresh way to express your point.

## Writing What You Mean

During the Gulf War, the English language also came under attack. It was not an Iraqi boat that was sunk in the gulf, it was a ship. A *boat* is something you paddle or sail. If you are referring to anything larger, use the word *ship*.

In writing broadcast copy, be precise. Use the right word. If you do not, your credibility, a key factor in building a career, comes into question.

Here are a few words and phrases commonly used incorrectly on the air:

The consensus of opinion is that the war will be over within a few months. [*Of opinion* is redundant; consensus means "general agreement."]

There was bad weather over the gulf due to a fast-moving storm front. [*Due to* means "owing to"; use *because of*.]

The fighting is different than last week's. [*Different* here takes the preposition *from*; however, it is correct to say: The fighting is different than he expected.]

The number of people injured was over a dozen. [*Over* implies a spatial relationship; use *more than*.]

The house is further down the road. [*Further* means "in addition to"; use *farther* to refer to distance.]

Since you are going downtown, please get me a newspaper. [*Since* refers to a relationship of time; use *because* to indicate a causal connection.]

These phrases are just a few examples of improper word usage. A good background in English grammar is important. Most college journalism programs insist that you take one to two years of English, but it is not always easy to find classes that emphasize grammar. Ask your adviser to recommend a professor who teaches courses on grammar.

## Good Grammar and Some Exceptions

The same rules of grammar apply to both print and broadcast copy—most of the time. Writers do take a few liberties in broadcast copy because of its conversational nature. You'll recall that commas can be omitted from broadcast copy unless they indicate a pause and that subordinate clauses should be avoided in broadcast writing. Another exception: Verbs can sometimes be dropped from sentences, as is often done in conversation.

For example, if you are talking to your letter carrier and say: "Looks like snow today, Helen," no one is going to object because you did not say: "It appears as if we are going to get snow today, Helen." Therefore, it would be natural for a newscaster to say, particularly in headlines: "Three injuries tonight on the turnpike, that story when we return." Few people will take offense because the newscaster did not say "There were three injuries tonight on the turnpike." (Verbs are discussed further in Chapter 3, "More Style Rules.")

# Summary

This chapter suggests that you use conversational style in writing broadcast copy. The material in the chapter is meant to help you learn to write as you speak. Most of us use brief sentences, with few subordinate clauses, and choose easy-to-understand words in everyday conversation. Communicating information to a radio or TV audience is best done in everyday language, simply and with sincerity.

Keep in mind that reading your copy aloud is the best way to test how well you are using conversational style. Your ears, not your eyes, will tell you if your copy is good.

# Review Questions

1. Where would you use contractions in the following sentences?

   The governor says he will leave on vacation tomorrow.
   There will be a dozen people at the reception.
   The workers say they will walk off the job at noon.
   Here is the latest word from the Weather Bureau.
   Now let us take a look at what happened in baseball tonight.

2. Would you use a contraction in the following sentence? Explain.

   The president says he will sign the bill.

3. What's wrong with the following sentence, and how could it be improved for broadcast?

   Two years after the crash of a helicopter into the Washington channel, the D.C. Fire Department has not provided scuba equipment and training for its fireboat personnel, despite an order from Congress to do so accompanied by an appropriation to pay for it.

4. Here is another complex sentence. How could you improve it for broadcast?

   Higher rates for electricity could be one result of the miners' strike against the Pittston Coal Company, which has forced some utilities to curtail sales of power to neighboring companies and to buy more expensive types of fuel, according to an industry spokesman.

5. Here is a list of words that are not particularly good for broadcast. Think of an appropriate substitute for each.

| | |
|---|---|
| emblazoned | facilitate |
| ascent | perquisites |
| capitulation | stupefied |
| exodus | disperse |

6. Keeping in mind the suggestions for using prepositions and conjunctions, how could the following sentence be improved for broadcast?

The circus's chief lion trainer did not take part in the show because he was sick; however, the apprentice trainer took over, and his performance was loudly applauded.

7. There's a pronoun problem in the following sentence. Identify it, and explain how the sentence should read.

The governor accused his opponent, Frank Smith, of mudslinging. After the exchange, he predicted he would win the election.

8. What words and phrases might you use to replace the clichés in the following sentences?

The prisoners rampaged for more than an hour.
The White House announcement came on the heels of China's tough words about Taiwan.
The Republican candidate said he had no doubt that the tax issue would become a political football.
The gun lobby was up in arms because of congressional approval of the Brady bill.

# Exercises

1. Correct any misused words and phrases in the following sentences:

The consensus of opinion was that the Republicans would gain control of the House.
Due to the bad weather, we decided not to go boating.
There were over a thousand people in the ballroom.
The car rides like an expensive one should.

2. Rewrite the following wire-service sentence for broadcast.

Thunderstorms that raged through the South, and bad weather elsewhere, have been blamed for at least 23 deaths and the presumed drowning of a North Carolina man swept away by a swollen creek the night before he was to be married.

3. Take a story from the wire or a newspaper. Read it carefully, and then put it aside. Now rewrite the story in broadcast style without looking at the copy again. When you have finished, look at your copy and make a note of anything important that you forgot or any information that you wrote incorrectly.

4.  Watch a program of any kind on television, and then write a story about it, describing it as you would to a friend.

5.  Read over your story from exercise 3 or 4, and make any changes you think will improve the copy. Then read the copy aloud, and note any changes you would make that you did not notice when you read the copy to yourself.

6.  Find a newspaper story that has at least one subordinate clause in the lead, and rewrite it in broadcast style.

7.  Look through your newspaper for words that you think are too long or might be difficult for a broadcast audience to understand. Look them up in a dictionary or thesaurus to find synonyms that would be more appropriate for broadcast copy.

# 3 More Style Rules

Like Chapter 2, this chapter focuses on broadcast writing style rules. Much of this chapter is devoted to the use of verbs, adjectives, and other parts of speech. It also examines the various ways broadcast writers express time, quote people, and attribute information.

## Verbs

### Present Tense

Broadcast news must always present an image of immediacy. Without deceiving an audience by treating an old story as if it were fresh, the broadcast newswriter's job is to tell the news as though it is in progress or has just recently happened. If a story is still developing or has just cleared the wire, a newswriter should make it sound as new and exciting as possible because most of the audience will be hearing the story for the first time. Use of present-tense verbs, particularly present-progressive verbs, which suggest ongoing action, adds to that immediacy. For example, in covering a meeting at the White House that is still in progress, a writer would best say:

The president is meeting with his cabinet this morning to discuss the budget.

Only if the meeting had ended by the time of the newscast would the writer use the past tense:

The president met today with his cabinet to discuss the budget.

When writers use the past tense, they tell the audience that the event has already taken place, while some aspect of it may actually still be in progress. Look at the following examples to see how the use of present-tense verbs focuses on the continuing action:

*Poor*: Members of Congress ended their session today and headed for home.

*Good*: Members of Congress are on their way home today after ending their session.

*Poor*: A hurricane warning was issued tonight for Florida and Georgia.

*Good*: A hurricane warning is in effect tonight for Florida and Georgia.

## Present Perfect Tense

Another verb tense that gives a sense of immediacy is the present perfect, which suggests that an action started in the past and is continuing into the present. For example:

The president has left Camp David for Andrews Air Force Base.

The present perfect tense is useful when the status of the story is not certain. In this case, it may be known that the president left Camp David, but it may not be clear when he is going to arrive at Andrews Air Force Base.

## Mixing Tenses

Because a news story may mention events that happened at different times or report a statement that still holds true but was made earlier, it is acceptable to mix tenses in broadcast copy. For example, a story may begin with the present tense and then change to the past tense in later sentences so that the story makes sense. Here's an example of changing tenses:

Mayor Jones says he hopes to keep property taxes at their present level. He made the comment during a speech earlier today before a meeting of the Chamber of Commerce. The mayor told the group he expects that an improving economy and a reduction in city expenses will eliminate the need for higher property taxes.

The first sentence uses the present-tense verb *says*, but the rest of the paragraph uses past-tense verbs because it would sound strange to continue the present tense once it is established that the mayor made the comments earlier in the day. But suppose the mayor has not yet delivered the speech. The story might be handled this way:

Mayor Jones says he hopes to keep property taxes at their present level. Jones will say this tonight in a speech to the Chamber of Commerce. The mayor says he believes that an improving economy and a reduction in city expenses will eliminate the need for higher property taxes.

In this case, the present tense is used to describe opinions the mayor holds now, and the future tense is used to describe when he will express those opinions. The fourth and fifth sentences might continue with the future tense:

The mayor will also tell his audience that he expects to attract new business to the city. He'll say he has a promise from Governor Williams for extra state funds to take care of the city's needy.

## *Active Verbs*

Good broadcast copy also makes use of active verbs, not passive ones. Active verbs speed up copy and give it more punch because they focus on the action rather than the receiver of the action.

*Poor*: Three buildings were destroyed by the fire.

*Good*: The fire destroyed three buildings.

*Poor*: The Dow Jones was pushed up 50 points today after buyers took over on Wall Street.

*Good*: Buyers took over today on Wall Street, sending the Dow Jones up 50 points.

## Says *Is a Good Verb*

Don't be afraid to use *says*. Many writers think they have to find different ways to avoid using a form of *say* because they think it is a boring verb. As a result, they use forms of *exclaim*, *declare*, *assert*, *announce*, and other words that they believe mean the same thing as *say*. The problem is that these other words are not synonyms for *say*; each has a different connotation.

## *Strong Verbs*

Although these verbs should not be used in place of *say*, sometimes they do accurately describe the situation. For example:

The United Nations Security Council declared today . . .

The White House announced that Peter Grant would become the new Secretary of the Interior.

"We'll walk this picket line 'till hell freezes over!" exclaimed union leader Frank Chilton.

As for *assert*, it is difficult to think of an occasion when it would be appropriate to use that word in broadcast copy.

In writing broadcast copy, look for strong verbs that vividly describe the action:

*smother*, rather than *put down*, an uprising

*echo*, rather than *repeat*, an opinion

*clash*, rather than *disagree*, over strategy

*lash out at*, rather than *attack*, opponents

*muster*, rather than *collect*, enough votes

When choosing verbs, think about the image you want to create. For example, a tornado *roars*, but it also can *sweep through* a neighborhood. A hurricane can *destroy* a beachfront, but *demolish* gives a stronger picture. A high-school student might be *expelled*, but a deposed leader would be *exiled*. Battalions can *move through* the desert, but if they are doing it quickly, as they were in the Gulf War, they might be said to *race* through.

# Limiting Use of Adverbs and Adjectives

Like good verbs, adjectives and adverbs sometimes add color to broadcast copy, but they should generally be avoided. Many adjectives add unnecessary detail, and rather than enliven the copy, they weigh it down. Here's an example of a sentence with too many adjectives and adverbs:

> The *diesel-powered* train was quickly moving around the *very sharp* curve when suddenly there was a *loud, screeching* noise and the cars near the *very* front of the train *rapidly* started to leave the track.

The sentence would be more effective without most of these adjectives and adverbs because they add little meaning. It is not important to know that the train is *diesel powered*, because most are. *Quickly moving* could be replaced by the strong verb *racing*, and the adverb *very* could be omitted because intensifiers are "filler" words that rarely add meaning. *Rapidly* could be eliminated because it is a given that the cars would leave the tracks quickly if the train was *racing* around the curve. Finally, *started to leave* could be replaced by the more vivid *jumped*. The cleaned-up sentence would read:

> The train was racing around the sharp curve when suddenly there was a screeching noise as the cars near the front of the train jumped the track.

*Screeching* was left in the sentence because it is a strong, colorful adjective that describes the noise. *Loud*, however, was eliminated because a screeching noise is, by definition, loud.

# Attribution

One of the basic requirements of good news writing and reporting, whether for newspapers or broadcasts, is proper attribution. The chapters on reporting deal with the various types and methods of attributing information. Right now, let's examine the proper style of attribution used in broadcast scripts, which differs from the style used in newspapers and newspaper wire copy.

For the most part, newspapers use attribution at the end of a sentence, what is called *dangling attribution*. For example:

> Hundreds of people have been killed in Russian army attacks in Chechnya, according to The Associated Press.

Attribution in broadcast copy, if used in the lead sentence, is always at the top of the sentence. For example:

> The Associated Press reports hundreds of people have been killed in Russian army attacks in Chechnya.

The attribution can also be *delayed*; that is, it can be mentioned in the second sentence. For example:

> Hundreds of people reportedly have been killed in Yugoslav army attacks on Croatia. The report comes from The Associated Press.

# Using Quotes

Most of the time, quotes are paraphrased in broadcast copy. Newspapers have the luxury of providing long, detailed quotes of politicians, government officials, and other newsmakers. But broadcasting time restrictions require a distillation of such information. Because of the importance of some statements, direct quotes can occasionally be used. But even then, the writer must keep them to a minimum.

Here is a sample of a quote that appeared in a newspaper:

> "This is an example of the worst brutality I have ever come across," was the way the judge described the beating of a man arrested by police.

The broadcast version would read:

> The judge said the beating of a man arrested by police was—in his words— "the worst brutality I have ever come across."

The quote also could have been paraphrased:

> The judge described the beating of the arrested man as the worst brutality he had ever come across.

If a quote is too important to paraphrase, the actual words must be used. Most writers and broadcasters avoid using the terms *quote* and *unquote* at the beginning and end of a direct quote, but you occasionally hear them on the air. There are better ways of handling a direct quote. Here's one way:

> The President said the Republican-sponsored welfare reform bill would—and this is a direct quote—"take food out of the mouths of poor children."

Some newscasters use a direct quote after saying "and these are the president's exact words." Other anchors simply pause a second before a direct quote and change the inflection of their voices, but not all newscasters do this effectively. If you are writing the script, be explicit and use an introductory phrase to indicate you are quoting someone directly.

# Expressing Time

Because broadcast news usually reports or describes events that are currently happening, it is not always necessary to use the word *today* in broadcast copy. If events are not current, point that out quickly.

If a story says that 18 people have been injured in a train crash in Center City, listeners are going to assume that the accident occurred today unless the broadcaster explains that it happened last night or at some other time. Repeating the word *today* throughout a newscast, then, would become tiresome.

Those writing or reporting for an evening or late-night newscast should be specific. If the story is about something that is going on while the newscast is on the air or took place a short time earlier, the copy should stress the word *tonight* or use a phrase such as *at this very moment*, *a short time ago*, *within the past hour*, or *earlier this evening* to alert the audience that this news is fresh.

A story should never lead with the word *yesterday*. If a story happened the day before, something new must be found to freshen the story and eliminate *yesterday* from the lead. (Chapter 4, "Writing Broadcast Copy," presents details on the subject of updating leads.)

# Looking Ahead

Some newscasts alert the audience to events that are expected to happen in the future. The information should be as specific as possible. An example is as follows:

> The president is expected to leave the White House in the next 15 minutes or so for Andrews Air Force Base, where he'll board Air Force One for the trip to London.

Another example:

> At any moment now, members of the United Nations Security Council will be considering new proposals on the crisis in the Middle East. We were told a few minutes ago that members were already beginning to arrive at the Security Council chamber.

This sort of specific time reference adds immediacy and drama. It's much better than saying:

> The United Nations Security Council meets today to consider new proposals on the crisis in the Middle East.

One final note: Whenever you use a specific time reference, such as *tonight* or *a few minutes ago*, place the reference as close as possible to the verb whose action it describes.

**Figure 3.1**
*60 Minutes* correspondent
Ed Bradley. (CBS Photo
Archive)

# Transitions

Transitions are phrases and words that signal relationships between sentences. Some broadcast writers use transitions to carry listeners from one story to another, but in a newscast, transitions should be used with care and in moderation. If a transition is natural, it can be effective, but most transitions tend to sound contrived.

Here's an example of good use of a transition:

> Centerville Mayor Frank Jones is flying to New York City at this hour to take part in talks with other mayors on how to deal with Washington's cut in funds for American cities.

> Also traveling today is Centerville Police Chief Robert Potter. He's on his way to Chicago to meet with officials in that city to discuss the fight on drugs.

The transition *also traveling today* works here because it links stories about similar events of equal importance. But here's a bad example:

> Centerville Mayor Frank Jones is flying to New York City at this hour to take part in talks with other mayors on how to deal with Washington's cut in funds for American cities.

> Also traveling tonight, Hurricane Dorothy. It's headed our way at about 10 miles an hour and could slam into the mainland in the morning.

In this example, the transition is forced. Unlike the natural connection of two city officials who are traveling on government business, there is nothing logical about connecting the movement of the mayor and that of a hurricane.

That example was not made up. The names have been changed, but the transition tying together the movement of an official and a hurricane was actually broadcast.

Here is another example of an effective transition:

> The Justice Department wants to know if there are patterns of police brutality anywhere in the country. The Department has ordered a review of all police brutality complaints filed with its civil rights division during the last six years. The order comes amid an outcry over the police beating of motorist Rodney King in Los Angeles—an attack videotaped by a witness and aired across the country.

> Los Angeles isn't the only place where authorities are investigating allegations of police brutality. In Georgia, witnesses say more than a dozen police officers pounced on a suspected prowler they caught after a chase from Atlanta to Stockbridge. The Atlanta and Clayton County police departments are conducting internal investigations. (*AP Radio*)

The transitional sentence *Los Angeles isn't the only place where authorities are investigating allegations of police brutality* is quite logical.

The prize for bad transitions must go to this report from a Miami station:

> The pope wasn't the only one celebrating a birthday today. Five years ago today, Mount St. Helens volcano erupted.

# People, *Not* Persons

One final style note regards the use of the term *people* as opposed to *persons*. When more than one person is involved in a story, it is more conversational to refer to these individuals as *people*, even though some style books continue to insist that a small group should be referred to as *persons*. For example, in conversation we are more likely to say that "five *people*" are going to join us for dinner than we are to say that "five *persons*" will be joining us.

# Summary

Verbs play a vital role in broadcast news writing. One of the most important messages of this chapter is to use present-tense verbs in broadcast copy as much as possible. People turn to radio and television because they want to know what is happening *now*. When you write broadcast copy, try to make the news sound fresh without being dishonest or misleading.

Using the *right* verb is also crucial. Remember that you don't always need to look for ways to replace *says*. It's a good verb. Look for strong verbs that vividly describe the action, but make sure they don't send the wrong message.

This chapter also discusses attributing information in broadcast copy. If you *need* to include an attribution, always place it at the beginning of your sentence.

# Review Questions

1. How could the verb tenses in these sentences be improved for broadcast?

   The President said he would veto the tax bill unless Congress made some major changes. He spoke to reporters at the White House a short time ago.

   Rescuers went through the wreckage of the burned-out building looking for more bodies. They said they expect to work all day and night looking for more victims of the fire.

   The hurricane slammed into Hollywood, Florida, a few minutes ago, and our reporter had this report from the beach area.

2. What's wrong with the verbs in these sentences?

   There was applause when the birthday cake was brought out by the chef.
   The gunman was grabbed by the sheriff as he tried to run from the bank.

3. How could the verbs in these sentences be improved for broadcast?

   The teacher declared that the student outing was postponed because of rain.
   The Mayor asserted that she would seek another term.
   The President exclaimed that he would go to Camp David for the weekend.

4. What's wrong with the attributions in the following sentences?

   The nation's economy is going to continue to be strong, according to a leading economist.

   Hundreds of people were injured in rioting in Cincinnati following the police shooting of an unarmed African-American man, according to the police.

5. What's wrong with the transition used to link the following sentences?

   Forest fires swept through several states on the West Coast today, destroying hundreds of thousands of acres of trees. Also under fire is our town's police chief, who is accused of failing to control some of his officers.

# Exercises

1.  Using stronger verbs, rewrite the following copy.

    An earthquake has hit San Francisco. Police say several people may have been killed. There is no report on injuries, but rescue workers looked through several wrecked buildings for possible victims. Hundreds of frightened residents left their homes. It was the strongest quake to hit the city in several years.

    Power lines were down in some areas. Police say they fell when cracks developed in the pavement.

    Utility company officials are in the area to examine damage. They said some power lines were broken during the quake and present a danger.

2.  The following remarks were made by President Bush. Write a story showing how you would use them in broadcast copy.

    President Bush said the energy situation had reached the crisis stage. He added that "there are no quick fixes for the problem."

    The President's remarks came at a news conference a day after he outlined his energy plan.

3.  Find two related stories on the wires or in the newspaper. Rewrite them in broadcast style, and use a transition to tie them together.
4.  Using wire copy or newspaper stories, find three sentences that use the passive voice, and rewrite the sentences in broadcast style.
5.  Find as many verbs as you can on the front page of your local newspaper that you think could be stronger or more colorful. Replace them.

# 4 Writing Broadcast Copy

The hardest part of writing broadcast copy is getting started. Sometimes you will have difficulty moving your fingers. Your brain will seem dead. You may feel hypnotized by the glow from your computer screen. Break the spell! Type the first thing that comes into your mind. Don't worry whether it is good, just write. Get started. It will get easier.

You may find that the first sentence you write works as an opening for your story, or you may need to write a few sentences before you come up with one that you like. This chapter focuses on writing an effective opening sentence, or lead, for a news story.

## Leads

The *lead* is the most important part of a news story because it sets the tone for all that follows. The lead must grab or "hook" the audience's attention in as few words as possible. The hook can be an exciting or dramatic sentence, a clever phrase, an intriguing fact, or a provocative quote.

### The "Five W's and H Rule"

Unless the story is a feature, the lead must include an element of news. It must begin to address the traditional journalistic concept of discovering information. To guarantee that all of the important news elements are reported in a story, journalists have devised a rule that requires newswriters to answer six basic questions: *who, what, where, when, why,* and *how.* This rule is referred to as the *"five W's and H rule."*

At one time, most newspaper editors expected every lead to answer all of these questions. But few newspaper editors still require this, and broadcasters never follow the rule; however, at least one or more of the questions must be answered in the lead of the story for it to be news. By the end of the story, most—if not all—of the questions should be answered.

An opening sentence that contains no news is referred to as a *non-news lead*, and such leads are unacceptable in a news story. Here's an example:

> The Chairman of the Joint Chiefs of Staff has met with reporters.

This lead could become news by answering some of the journalistic questions. *Why* did the chairman meet with reporters? *What* did he tell them? For example:

> The Chairman of the Joint Chiefs of Staff, Colin Powell, told reporters this morning that the United States would probably continue to keep troops in Iraq for several months.

This revised lead does not deal with all five W's and the H, but it is a start. The *who* is the Chairman of the Joint Chiefs of Staff. The *what* is the issue of maintaining troops in Iraq. The *where* is Iraq. The *when* is for several months. Still unanswered are the *why* and the *how*. These questions would be answered in the balance of the story—if the answers are available.

This revised lead is an example of a *hard lead*. Such leads address the most important aspect of a story immediately. You can lead off your story in a variety of ways, and all of them are examined in the following sections. The decision about which kind of lead to use depends on several factors, the most important of which is the nature of the story. Is it a feature or breaking news? Is the story sad or upbeat? Is it about people or an event? Is the story about politics, a war, a medical development, or the kidnapping of a child? Is the story brand new or continuing? The lead is like the foundation of a house. How the foundation is built determines how the rest of the house will look. The lead sentence determines how the rest of the story should be constructed.

## Hard and Soft Leads

In choosing a lead, decide first whether it will be hard or soft. As you saw in the previous example, a hard lead tells the audience the vital details of the story immediately. Hard leads are usually used for breaking news:

At least 30 people were injured in the collapse of the building.

More than a dozen people were arrested in the drug bust.

The government announced today that 150 thousand more Americans were employed in November.

A soft lead takes a more subtle approach; it alerts the audience to the news that is to follow. This approach is sometimes called "warming up" the audience. The following soft leads could be used for the previous stories:

A building collapses in Center City. At least 30 people have been injured.

A major drug bust in New York City. More than a dozen people are under arrest.

An improvement in the unemployment figures. The government announced that 150 thousand more Americans were employed in November.

**Figure 4.1**   An anchor and producers go over a script at WTVJ-TV, Miami. (Courtesy of WTVJ-TV, Miami)

The soft leads may not sound as exciting or dramatic as the hard leads, but they do invite the audience to keep listening. Notice that two of the example soft leads are not full sentences but phrases that serve the same purpose as headlines in a print story. Soft leads can be helpful to listeners carrying out other tasks or fighting traffic on the way to the office, by giving them time to shift their attention to the news.

Many editors discourage soft leads because they tend to slow down a newscast, particularly if used too often. But used in moderation, soft leads add variety to broadcast copy. Experienced editors tend to be flexible in dealing with a writer's style, including the kinds of leads writers choose. Good editors recognize that there is not just one way to write a story. They might say: "Well, it's not the way I would have written it, but it's not bad."

## The "Right" Emotion

One challenge in writing a lead is deciding on the appropriate emotion, or tone, to express in the story. The tone depends largely on the kind of story you are going to tell. For example, if the story is about something amusing, you would establish a lighthearted tone in the lead. Let's look at an example:

> A Center City schoolteacher got enough kisses today to last—well, maybe not a lifetime, but a few weeks, anyway. Marilyn Rutland kissed 110 men at the

annual fund-raiser for the local zoo. At ten bucks a kiss, Rutland raised
eleven hundred dollars for the zoo, and when she turned the money over to
zoo officials, she joked that all the animals were not behind bars.

Even stories about accidents can sometimes be treated lightly:

"I'll never drink hot coffee in the car again." That's what John Semien said
when he left the Center City hospital. This morning, Semien's car struck a fire
hydrant, bounced off a tree, and smashed into the window of a flower shop.

Semien said he had bought a container of coffee at a McDonald's drive-
through, and as he tried to add sugar and cream he lost control of the car
when the hot coffee fell between his legs.

Stories about tragedies, as you would expect, require a more serious, straightforward approach:

It's now believed that the death toll in the earthquake in Mexico has reached
more than 50.

or

At least three people are reported dead in the collision this morning of a half-
dozen cars on the freeway.

For these leads, the writers chose to give just the facts, a decision that creates a
quiet tone that underscores the loss of life described in the stories.

Although every story requires the writer to choose a certain tone, features
and nonbreaking news stories allow more flexibility than does breaking news.
Some writers are effective at evoking joy, pathos, and other emotions from an
audience through the tone they create. Look, for example, at these leads written
by former CNN anchor Reid Collins. His story about the invasion of Kuwait
began: "A rich little country died at dawn today." On the rioting at the Viennese
Opera Ball, Collins wrote: "A night at the opera in Vienna was a Marxist nightmare—part Karl, part Groucho." And his lead on a story about Mikhail
Gorbachev's busy day was: "Like a juggler with too many plates in the air,
Mikhail Gorbachev was stage right, stage left, and stage center today. So far, no
breakage."

Notice that Collins creates an air of sadness in his Kuwait lead, whereas he
suggests the chaos and confusion of the riot in his lead about the Vienna opera.
Similarly, his image of Gorbachev as a juggler effectively elicits a picture of
Gorbachev frantically rushing around trying to hold his country together. These
leads tell the audience not only what the stories are about, but also how the
writer wants the audience to feel about them.

## The Quote Lead

Sometimes a *quote*, like the "hot coffee" example used earlier, can provide an
excellent hook for a story:

"Life is short and life is sweet. So take time to enjoy what you have." Marine Captain Russell Sanborn says that's one of the lessons he learned as a prisoner of war in Iraq. He and some other former P-O-W's told their stories today at news conferences in the Washington area. (*AP Broadcast Wire*)

Here is another example:

"The first thing I'm going to do is quit my job and take a trip around the world." That's what lottery winner Bill Turpin said when he redeemed his ten million dollar winning lottery ticket.

Quote leads should be used sparingly, however. Unless the quote is comparatively short, the listener may miss its connection with the rest of the story.

## The Shotgun Lead

The *shotgun*, or *umbrella*, lead can be effective for combining two or more related stories:

Forest fires continue to roar out of control in California, Oregon, and Washington State. The drought that has plagued the three states is now in its second month. Fires have scorched more than a million acres of timberland in California and another half million acres in Oregon and Washington.

The advantage of the shotgun lead is that it allows the writer to eliminate the boring alternative of reporting the fires in three separate, back-to-back stories. Here is another example:

Congress today is looking at administration proposals that would increase the number of crimes punishable by the death penalty and make it easier for police to collect evidence.

The writer would then devote a few sentences to each of the White House recommendations.

## The Suspense Lead

The object of the *suspense lead* is to delay telling the key information until the end of the story.

National Public Radio's Susan Stamberg used an effective suspense lead in her story about a famous photographer:

STAMBERG:    Edith Shane had run over to Times Square from her job at Doctors Hospital. She wanted to be part of the celebration. Off duty, she wasn't supposed to be in her uniform, but she was. The sailor, Bill Schwhitzgood—all these names popped up years later, by the way, and the two never did meet formally—the sailor grabbed the

**Figure 4.2**
V-J Day Times Square,
New York City, August 14,
1945, by Alfred Eisenstaedt.
(Alfred Eisenstaedt/Life
Magazine © Time Inc.)

nurse in glee just as he had grabbed all those other women, but this was different. The nurse is caught gracefully in the sailor's arms. Her body twists a bit in his embrace. They look as if they could be dancing. It's the Eisenstaedt moment.

EISENSTAEDT: If this nurse in white would have been in a dark uniform, wouldn't have been a nurse, wouldn't have been a picture or vice versa. If the, if the nurse was in white and he would be in white, wouldn't be a picture either. It was just a coincidence that he was in navy blue and she was in white and she was thin. If she would have been fat, it wouldn't have been a good picture either.

STAMBERG: The late Alfred Eisenstaedt was one of the original staff photographers for Life magazine, not a person to snap five rolls of film to get the single perfect shot. He has been seen standing absolutely motionless for an hour or more, waiting for a sailboat to move to exactly the right spot before he released the shutter. That August day in 1945, the day of the Eisenstaedt moment, he took more pictures than usual and knew he had something.

EISENSTAEDT:   I know this was the best picture I took on that day. I knew that.

STAMBERG:   What Alfred Eisenstaedt didn't know then is that of all the thousands of images in his long career, this one of the sailor and the nurse would be the one he's known for.

EISENSTAEDT:   When I someday go to heaven and I'm not living anymore, maybe probably everybody will say, "Oh, this is the photographer who took that picture," and everybody remembers that picture.

STAMBERG:   Photographer Alfred Eisenstaedt just celebrated his 92nd birthday. He lives in New York, still goes into the Life magazine offices every day, and still takes photographs, Eisenstaedt moments. U.S. troops continue coming back from the Persian Gulf, and it is possible one of the homecoming photographs will capture the end of Operation Desert Storm, but in this age of the moving image, it's unlikely that the picture will mean to future generations what VJ Day Times Square has come to mean in the past nearly half century. In Washington, I'm Susan Stamberg.

Stamberg does not tell her audience until the final paragraph that Eisenstaedt has just celebrated his 92nd birthday and that this is why she is talking about him and his work on this particular day. She decides to grab her audience with a story about a sailor and a nurse. The listeners have no idea why she is telling them the story, but it is bound to get the audience's attention. And the picture Stamberg paints is a colorful one:

> . . . the sailor grabbed the nurse in glee just as he had grabbed all those other women, but this was different. The nurse is caught gracefully in the sailor's arms. Her body twists a bit in his embrace. They look as if they could be dancing. It's the Eisenstaedt moment.

The last sentence of Stamberg's opening introduces Eisenstaedt for the first time, but listeners still do not know who Eisenstaedt is unless they guess he is the famous photographer. Then, Stamberg intrigues listeners some more by letting Eisenstaedt speak for himself. At that point, the audience realizes that the story is about Eisenstaedt the photographer and about a famous picture he took more than 45 years earlier.

Stamberg doesn't fill up her script with a lot of details about the career of the famous photographer. She decides to remind listeners of the man by telling about his most famous picture, one that captured a moment in history at the end of World War II.

### The Delayed Lead

Instead of saving the most important information until the end of the story, as in the case of the suspense lead, the *delayed lead* just withholds the most important details for a few sentences.

> The scene in the locker room of the Center City Rockets was quieter than usual last night although the team won by three goals. There also was a lot less swearing than usual and no nudity. Also new in the locker room last night was Heather Tierney.

> The sports reporter for the Center City Times is the first woman to be allowed in the team's locker room. Club officials broke the female ban after Tierney threatened to go to court to win the right to enter the locker room after games.

If the delayed lead had not been used, the story probably would have started out this way:

> For the first time, last night a woman reporter was allowed in the locker room of the Center City Rockets.

The delayed lead gives writers another option for adding variety to a script, but, like some other leads mentioned earlier, it should not be overused.

### Negative Leads

*Negative leads*, which include the word *not*, should be avoided. A positive lead can easily achieve the same result. There is always the chance someone in the audience might miss the word *not* and reach the wrong conclusion about what is happening. Here are some examples:

*Avoid*: Striking newspaper workers say they will not return to work.

*Use*: Striking newspaper workers say they will continue their walkout.

*Avoid*: The mayor says he will not raise the city sales tax.

*Use*: The mayor says he will keep the city sales tax at its present rate.

## Updating and Reworking the Lead

One of the most effective methods to attract and hold listeners is to convince them that the news is fresh. Some days the news is plentiful, but on slow days newswriters need certain skills to make the news sound exciting and timely. One skill is to *update* leads, which means finding something new to say in stories used in an earlier newscast. Another skill is the ability to *rework* the original lead to include new developments. For example, take a story about the arrest of a dozen men on narcotics charges. Police say the men were found in a cocaine "factory" where they were "cutting" more than one hundred million dollars' worth of cocaine.

Here's the first version of the lead:

> Police have arrested a dozen men during a raid on a cocaine factory in Center City. They say the men were cutting more than 100 million dollars' worth of cocaine.

An hour later, the lead might say:

> A dozen men are under arrest after police raided a building in Center City. Police say the men were cutting more than 100 million dollars in cocaine.

Still later, the lead might read:

> Police are guarding an estimated 100 million dollars in cocaine that they scooped up in a raid on a Center City building. A dozen men are behind bars in connection with the raid. Police say the men were cutting the cocaine when the raid took place.

Another possible updated lead might say:

> A dozen men are being held for arraignment on narcotics charges following a raid on a Center City building. Police say they found about 100 million dollars' worth of cocaine in the building. Police say the men were in the process of cutting the cocaine when the officers broke into the building.

As new developments occur in the story, there will be added opportunities to rework the lead. Within a few hours, detectives may reveal details about how they found out about the cocaine factory. They also may give more details about the raid. For example:

> Center City police now say that their raid on a cocaine factory that resulted in the arrest of a dozen men came after two months of surveillance by detectives.

A skilled writer can tell the story many times without making it sound stale.

## Constructing the Rest of the Story

Once you have the lead of a story, its foundation, you are ready to construct the rest of the story by building on the lead. The audience has been prepared for what is to come. Now you must provide the details in a clear and logical manner.

In broadcast news, you can use more than just words to accomplish your goal. You can employ sound on radio and use both sound and pictures to help tell the story on television. Those techniques are examined later. For now, let's just deal with words, returning to the story about General Colin Powell mentioned earlier in the chapter. We'll start with a hard lead:

> The Chairman of the Joint Chiefs of Staff, General Colin Powell, says U.S. troops will stay in Iraq for several months.

The listeners now know part of the story. It's not much, but it is sufficient to grab their interest. A general whom they have come to know over the months is telling them something important: that their sons, daughters, husbands, wives, and other relatives and friends—at least some of them—are not coming home right away. The audience will want to hear the general's explanation.

> General Powell says American forces will stay in Iraq to enforce provisions of a pending U.N. cease-fire agreement. He says the troops would also prevent Iraq from using chemicals and air strikes to defeat rebels trying to overthrow President Saddam Hussein.

Now the audience knows why troops will remain in Iraq. What it does not know yet is how the troops are going to prevent Iraq from using chemical weapons and air attacks against the rebels. The next sentence addresses the question:

> General Powell did not explain how U.S. forces would prevent Iraq from using chemicals and air attacks against the rebels.

Once the general made reference to the chemicals and air attacks, the statement had to be explained to the audience even if the general did not elaborate. Otherwise, the audience might have been asking the question and accusing the newscaster of withholding the information. What's next? Because the third sentence mentions the rebels, that aspect of the story could be expanded:

> General Powell also said he was surprised by the strength of the revolt against the Saddam regime. He further denied that the U.S. forces are trying to play a role in influencing the outcome of the rebellion.

The general had much more to say to reporters, and newspapers carried the story in greater detail. But the broadcast newswriter, who had eight other stories to cover in a three-minute newscast, told the Powell story in just 20 seconds. The essential details were given; nothing vital was left out. This is key to broadcast newswriting: Condense the important material and eliminate the unimportant without distorting the story or facts.

# Summary

Writing broadcast copy is like building a house. This chapter focuses on the foundation—the lead. You now know many different ways to open your story. Some leads may be more appropriate than others, depending on the nature of the story, but remember that there is always more than one way to lead your story.

In the first four chapters, the emphasis has been on the basics of broadcast news writing. Now that you know how to construct a news story and include all the important details in your story in a logical manner, you are ready to learn about what many believe is the most important aspect of news writing: color, the subject of Chapter 5.

# Review Questions

1. Many writers have problems writing the first sentence of a story. How can they overcome this block?
2. What is the most important part of a news story? Why?
3. Although the five W's and H rule is basically a print journalism concept, it does have application for broadcast journalism. What are the five W's and H, and what is the major difference in the way they apply to print and broadcast journalism?
4. What is the difference between hard and soft leads?
5. How does emotion play a role in determining the lead sentence and how the rest of the story is written?
6. Do quote leads work for broadcast? Explain.
7. What is a shotgun lead?
8. What is a delayed lead?
9. How do you update a lead?

# Exercises

1. Using the following information, write both hard and soft leads:

   A tanker registered to the Zabo Oil Company of Panama has run aground. This happened off the coast of Charleston, South Carolina. One half million gallons of oil already have spilled into the Atlantic. It is believed that another half million gallons are still on the ship.

2. Write a quote lead based on the following information:

   A man on welfare, Bill Nelson, found a purse on the street. When he opened it there was $5,000 inside. Nelson counted it a dozen times. After two hours, he went to the police station and turned over the money to the officer at the desk. When questioned about his honesty, Nelson said, "I may be poor but I am honest."

3. Using the information from exercise 2, write a delayed lead.
4. Write a shotgun lead using the following information:

   Forest fires in Oregon have burned more than 10,000 acres of timberland and the flames are threatening thousands of additional acres. In California, firefighters are battling flames that already have destroyed 15,000 acres of woodland.

5. Use your imagination to figure out ways to update these leads:

> The president is scheduled to leave this afternoon for a vacation in Florida, where he will work on a new budget.
>
> Hurricane Sally is off the coast of Jacksonville, Florida, and could hit the mainland within the next three hours.
>
> Striking autoworkers are meeting at this hour to decide whether or not to accept the auto industry's latest contract offer.
>
> The countdown has begun at Cape Canaveral for the launching of the space shuttle Atlantis.

6. Using any of the types of leads discussed in this chapter, write a story from the following information:

> Lori and Kevin were married today. It was exactly 30 years ago to the day that they met. When they were teenagers the two had dated for about a year after meeting on a blind date in 1963. "I remember the date, of course, because it was my birthday," said Lori Scott. Lori and Kevin Rowce broke up following a fight. They both married and had children and had not seen each other for 29 years. Kevin contacted Lori when he heard from a friend that her husband had died. Kevin had been divorced a number of years ago. They decided to marry after dating for the past year. They were married on New York's Staten Island ferry. "That's what we did on our first date," Kevin said.

# 5 Color: The Key to Good Writing

The last few chapters stressed that broadcast news writing should be conversational—written the way we would speak with a friend at a restaurant or on a street corner. What makes such conversations memorable? An element known as *color*. Who are the people who most hold our attention in social conversations? Interesting people, of course; people who can tell a yarn with a flair; people who make us laugh; people who sometimes shock us and on occasion make us cry. They may be people who fascinate us because of the way they use the language or the way they dress or because they just act differently. The people we like to meet are colorful people. They may not know it; that's just the way they are. Their style comes naturally. Color in broadcast copy should be just as natural.

## Color Should Be Natural

Color should not be forced or achieved with clichés or hype. Strong verbs, and adjectives used in moderation, add color, but they must be selected carefully. Poorly chosen verbs and adjectives can destroy copy. "Colorful" words do not always produce colorful copy.

The people involved in a story, and what they have to say, are likely to add color. Broadcast writing should honestly reflect the feelings and emotions of those people. Sound bites and pictures of the newsmakers themselves often provide the humor, pathos, and other emotions that make the story a success. But using the voices and pictures of colorful people to provide the color for the story is almost a given. The real challenge is bringing color to the script through words, much as a good painter adds the proper strokes to a canvas to bring it to life.

Color is provided by observing and paying close attention to details and using those details in your copy. Listen to and watch carefully people engaged in conversation. Does John use his hands like an orchestra leader to make his point?

Does Mary whisper and look away in embarrassment when she tells her story, as though she's afraid someone will hear her? Is there a hole in the sole of Frank's shoe? Does Ann look directly into Pat's eyes as she speaks? Do Paul's hands shake? These are the things that good writers look and listen for if they hope to let the audience know and understand Paul and Ann and John and Mary.

Ernest Hemingway's name often comes up during a discussion of good news writing. Hemingway was one of America's best storytellers, and as one of his biographers noted, Hemingway's work as a journalist taught him "certain lessons in verbal economy" that he carried over to his novels. Hemingway's short, crisp, uncluttered, journalist-like sentences—skills he learned as a newspaperman for the *Kansas City Star*—marked his career as a novelist.

Here's a sample of Hemingway's writing from *The Old Man and the Sea:*

> He was an old man who fished alone in a skiff in the Gulf Stream and he had gone eighty-four days now without taking a fish. In the first forty days a boy had been with him. But after forty days without a fish the boy's parents had told him that the old man was now definitely and finally salao, which is the worst form of unlucky, and the boy had gone at their orders in another boat which caught three good fish the first week.

Consider what Hemingway tells us in only three sentences. We know that the fisherman is old and that he fishes in the Gulf Stream and that he certainly is very unlucky. We also know that he had a young companion in his boat until the boy's parents also reached the conclusion that the old man was unlucky. The old man is now fishing alone.

Hemingway tells us more about the character of the boy in the next sentence:

> It made the boy sad to see the old man come in each day with his skiff empty and he always went down to help him carry either the coiled lines or the gaff and harpoon and the sail that was furled around the mast.

And we quickly learn about the condition of the boat:

> The sail was patched with flour sacks and, furled, it looked like the flag of permanent defeat.

Hemingway's description of the old man is next:

> The old man was thin and gaunt with deep wrinkles in the back of his neck. The brown blotches of the benevolent skin cancer the sun brings from its reflection on the tropic sea were on his cheeks. The blotches ran well down the sides of his face and his hands had the deep-creased scars from handling heavy fish on the cords. But none of these scars were fresh. They were as old as erosions in a fishless desert.

In only two paragraphs we already have a clear picture of this fisherman and his young friend. We can see them together by the sea, the young boy sad with worry about the old man and the fisherman weary and broken by age and bad luck.

Consider Hemingway's detail—the kind of detail mentioned earlier that is so important in the development of colorful copy:

The old man was thin and gaunt with deep wrinkles in the back of his neck.

The brown blotches of the benevolent skin cancer . . .

The blotches ran well down the sides of his face.

. . . his hands had the deep-creased scars . . .

But none of these scars were fresh. They were as old as erosions in a fishless desert.

We know more about this old man in just two paragraphs than most writers could tell us in two pages.

## Emulate the Best

A good way to learn how to use color in a story is to look to the masters of the craft. Read E. B. White, James Thurber, and other good essayists and read the scripts in this book by such distinguished broadcast journalists as the late Charles Kuralt, Charles Osgood, Cokie Roberts, and Susan Stamberg. Examine the writing of the late Pauline Frederick of NBC News and the late Edward R. Murrow of CBS News—the most distinguished of all broadcast journalists. One of the best ways to practice good techniques is to adopt the styles of successful writers.

The late *CBS News* correspondent Charles Kuralt, a master of colorful writing, suggested that you also look in style manuals and usage guides— "browse through Fowler or Eric Partridge or Bergen Evans from time to time." He wondered how many people keep Otto Jesperson's seven-volume *Modern English Grammar* on a shelf in the bathroom.

*CBS News* correspondent Charles Osgood, also known for his colorful writing, is "fascinated by the writings of people like John McPhee and Loren Eiseley, both wonderful craftsmen and artisans in their use of the language, who like to deal with subjects that have to do with science." He also says: "You can get a lot out of reading novels simply because we refer to every news story that we do as a story."

Osgood notes that all stories, whether they are novels or news, have to be constructed "according to some kind of logical plan with a beginning, a middle, and an end." He comments that if there has to be development and character and other elements in a novel, writers "should at least pay some homage to it in doing a news story."

Interestingly, both Osgood and Kuralt spoke of rhythm and music when they talked about writing. Osgood says language starts with the ear: "A child learns the language by hearing people speak it. He hears words. He learns to say words long before he learns to read them. There's music in language." Osgood says that, like music, language has rhythm: "There's a shape, form and character to it. It's language, it's music, it's a noise."

Kuralt said: "I know that I hear the rhythms of writers I have read and admired in my head. Sometimes," he added, "I can even remember which writer's rhythm I am feeling. I think good writers hear the music of good writing they've read. The great writers compose new music for the rest of us to hear when we sit down to type."

Kuralt also said that good writing "takes patience." He thinks "it's worth sitting there until you remember the right word," recalling that Mark Twain once said that "the difference between the right word and the nearly right word is the difference between lightning and a lightning bug."

# Kuralt on the Road

Many of Charles Kuralt's colleagues would say that his name should be added to the list of great writers. Kuralt was by everyone's definition a "writer's writer." Many successful network correspondents acknowledge that they have learned from him.

Kuralt's "On the Road" TV series brought joy to millions. In 1975, he did a special series called "On the Road to '76" to mark the upcoming 200th anniversary of the nation's independence. Kuralt did a historical story from each of the 50 states, and one of his stops was Little Bighorn, Montana.

On the Road to '76
MONTANA
Kuralt-Bleckman-Colby-Quinlan
September 4, 1975
Kuralt on camera SOF

This is about a place where the wind blows, the grass grows, and a river flows below a hill. There is nothing here but the wind and the grass and the river. But of all places in America, this is the saddest place I know.

SOF pull back from sparkle on river

The Indians called the river the Greasy Grass. The white men called it the Little Bighorn.

Saddle gap in mountains, pull back to wide grassy plains

From that gap in the mountains to the east, Brevet Major General George A. Custer's proud 7th Cavalry came riding early in the morning of

| | June 25th, 1876, toward the Little Bighorn. |
|---|---|
| Looking down at river | Custer sent one battalion, under Major Marcus Reno, across the river to attack what he thought might be a small village of hostile Sioux. His own battalion galloped behind the ridges to ride down on the village from the rear. |
| grassy valley | |
| pan down from hill | When at last Custer brought his 231 troops to the top of a hill and looked down toward the river, what he saw was an encampment of 15-thousand Indians stretching for two and a half miles—the largest assembly of Indians the plains had ever known—and a thousand mounted warriors coming straight for him. |
| . . . to broad plain below (right after slate in roll 2) | |
| zoom back from river | |
| view of hills . . . | Reno's men, meantime, had been turned, routed, chased across the river, joined by the rest of the regiment, surrounded, and now were dying, defending a nameless brown hill. |
| . . . pull back to Meador's grave on hill | In a low protected swale in the middle of their narrowing circle, the one surviving doctor improvised a field hospital and did what he could for the wounded. The grass covers the place now, and grows in the shallow rifle trenches above which were dug that day by knives and tin cups and fingernails. |
| pan from grass . . . | |
| . . . to post with cross on it | |
| shallow rifle trench . . . | |
| . . . and peer over side | |
| Kuralt on camera | Two friends in H Company, Private Charles Windolph and Private Julian Jones, fought up here, side by side, all that day, and that night stayed awake, talking, both of them scared. Charles Windolph said, "The next morning, when the firing commenced, I said to Julian, 'We better get our coats off.' He didn't move. I looked at him. He was shot through the heart." |
| camera tilts down to gravestone | |
| view from hilltop | Charles Windolph won the Congressional Medal of Honor up here, |

survived, lived to be 98—he didn't die until 1950—and never a day passed in all those years that he didn't think of Julian Jones.

wide shot showing
white hills in distance

And Custer's men, four miles away? There are stones in the grass that tell the story of Custer's men.

one you can read

The stones all say the same thing. "U.S. Soldier, 7th Cavalry, fell here, June 25th, 1876."

montage of grass and
stones, first one or two,
then—

The warriors of Sitting Bull and under the great Chief Gall struck Custer first and divided his troops.

Another bunch of stones,
larger group
Then a big group

Two Moon and the Northern Cheyenne struck him next. And when he tried to gain a hilltop with the last remnants of his command, Crazy Horse rode over that hill with hundreds of warriors, and right through his battalion. The Indians who were there later agreed on two things—that Custer and his men fought with exceeding bravery, and that after half an hour, not one of them was left alive.

Zoom through grass . . .

. . . to stone that has
Custer's name on it.

WS battlefield, stones in
distance

The Army came back that winter. Of course, the Army came back—and broke the Sioux and the Cheyenne, and forced them back to the starvation of the reservations, and in time murdered more old warriors and women and children on the Pine Ridge Reservation than Custer lost in battle here.

More grass and stones

Kuralt on camera

That is why this is the saddest place. For Custer and the 7th Cavalry, courage only led to defeat. For Crazy Horse and the Sioux, victory only led to Wounded Knee.

Saddest shot of battlefield,
maybe backlit stone with
grass

Come here sometime, and you will see. There is melancholy in the wind, and sorrow in the grass. And the river weeps.

Maybe one last zoom to river.          Charles Kuralt, CBS News, on
                                       the road to '76 in Montana.

Kuralt once commented that the Little Bighorn story was a challenge: "There was really nobody to interview there. There's nothing there but grass, water, and gravestones, but I wanted to do a story anyway. We were not in a hurry to do this one; we had a whole day to walk around the battlefield and think. We didn't shoot anything."

Kuralt said he had been reading about the battle and had several books about the Little Bighorn battlefield. After the daylong tour of the battlefield, he said, "I went back to the bus and wrote the story, and afterwards we went out and shot it." The late *CBS News* correspondent admitted, "We broke my rule and reversed the order, but I was writing to pictures I knew we were going to shoot." Kuralt said it was one of the few times that he worked "almost like a movie script writer."

Kuralt said that when the story went on the air, "it was beautiful . . . all mood, all writing, and some beautiful photography." He added: "You can fill the story with words and not do any interviews at all if you have a good story to tell and a skillful photographer at work."

**Figure 5.1**
The late *CBS News* correspondent
Charles Kuralt and crew work on
one of his "On the Road" reports.
(Courtesy of CBS News)

Kuralt stressed how important it is to write to the picture. "Write something that will add to the experience of the viewer in seeing the picture," he said, "but when you can, have the courage to remain silent and let the picture tell the story. Give people time to feel something."

There is another Kuralt script in Chapter 14, "Putting the Television Story Together," in which Kuralt discussed the importance of pictures.

# "A Postcard from Nebraska"

Colorful writing and good pictures make good TV news. *CBS News* special correspondent Roger Welsch's success in marrying the two elements has made him a frequent contributor to the *Sunday Morning* program. Here is the script of one Welsch story, with Kuralt's introduction:

| | |
|---|---|
| Kuralt O/C | To prepare us for Thanksgiving, the great harvest festival we celebrate this Thursday, Roger Welsch has sent us another postcard from Nebraska. This one is reverent. Between the lines you can hear Roger giving thanks. |
| V/C<br>Video of corn fields | (Welsch)<br>It won't be long before these fields are empty. The corn picked, the squash tucked away in the cellar. Well, we managed to get some sweet corn into the freezer. It'll be a long time before we taste the sweetness of corn dripping with butter right off the cob. As for the |
| Video of melons and Placke's Market | melons, there's no saving them. They're here . . . and then they're gone. But it wasn't long ago back in Dannebrog, when Dan or Eric, maybe it was Harriet, said, "Hey, Roger, Placke's has sweet corn and melons for sale, let's go." It doesn't take me long to respond to an invitation like that. It's a special time of the year. An ephemeral moment that has to be grasped right now before it's gone and the fields are empty and cold. |

| | |
|---|---|
| Video of people at Placke's | (SOT Unidentified Person)<br>"That ought to do it." |
| Video of highway and produce places | V/O<br>Highway 281 near Saint Libory is peppered with produce stands. Some little more than rustic sheds, some fairly fancy markets where local farmers sell their squash, tomatoes, peppers, onions, and sweet corn. This is my idea of a supermarket. |
| Video of people at market | There's no question that the merchandise here is fresh. It was picked this morning from fields within walking |
| Video of produce picking | distance of where we're standing right now. |
| SOT | (SOT Unidentified person)<br>"Those have got a high sound to them. You've got to have a low sound." |
| V/O<br>Market footage | V/O<br>Personal service? Well, the family that's selling me my groceries this morning picked it and planted it, watered it, and weeded it. In every sense of the word this watermelon is the Plackes' watermelon, until I pay for it. Then in every sense, it's mine. |
| Video of watermelons and watermelon eating | (SOT Unidentified person)<br>"You guys going to eat that?" |
| V/O | V/O<br>And taste? Nothing beats the taste of melon straight out of the field. |
| SOT | (SOT Unidentified person)<br>"That's good, waited all summer for that." |
| V/O<br>Video of Welsch at market | V/O<br>Spaghetti squash? |

| | |
|---|---|
| SOT | (SOT Unidentified person) "Yes, they're very good." |
| V/O Video of market | V/O Well, I'm going to try some of those. |
| SOT | (SOT Unidentified person) "OK." |
| V/O | Sure, part of the attraction of buying produce like this is the price. It's not expensive and the Plackes usually consider 13 ears of corn a dozen and round off the total of your bill from $9.37 to $9 even. I don't know what I'm going to do with these red peppers, but they're too pretty to pass up. |
| SOT | (SOT Salesperson) "OK . . . a dollar, 78, 40." |
| V/O Video of people picking produce | V/O But, do you know what I think makes this food taste especially good? Handing over my money to the very folks who grew the sweet corn and who picked the watermelon and know the peppers by name. Sure the food is cheaper. But frankly I'd pay more knowing that the money goes to the farmers. And, of course, it's better tasting, but I attribute part of that to the fact that the folks who sell it to me want it to taste better. |
| Welsch O/C at market | O/C They have to look me in the eye when they sell it to me and when I come back the next week and next year. I've been buying produce at the Placke stand now for 15 years. One of the Plackes' nephews was a classmate of mine at the |

| | |
|---|---|
| | University of Nebraska 10 or 20 years ago or so. Thanks a lot, Marilyn. I appreciate it. |
| SOT | (SOT Unidentified person) "Yeah." |
| V/O<br>Video at market | V/O<br>These folks are not just businessmen, they're friends and neighbors. There are a lot of reasons to complain about the weather out here on the plains. Sometimes it seems as if complaining is our favorite of all season sports. But when the heat of summer is gone and before the winter's blizzards sweep across these fields . . . at that short and lovely moment when the sweet coolness of autumn is evident, it's then that the Saint Libory produce stands remind us how good things out here can be. How rich and how full and how tasty. |

Welsch's story relies heavily on words as well as pictures. Welsch had only a few short sound bites to punctuate the narration, which meant the narration had to be longer, particularly because the stories on "Sunday Morning" usually run at least twice as long as the two-minute stories on most other news programs.

The story succeeds only because the script is so well written. Normally, without interviews it is difficult to sustain so much copy. But the combination of excellent pictures and colorful words allowed this story to run as long as it did. In the hands of a less talented writer, the story most certainly would have been shorter.

# Crisp and Clear

Welsch's writing style is crisp and clear. He picks short sentences and phrases and makes each word work for him. His sentences are conversational and often incomplete.

> It won't be long before these fields are empty. The corn picked, the squash
> tucked away in the cellar.

The squash could have been *stored* in the cellar, but *tucked away* is so much
more colorful.

The first section of this chapter discussed the importance of using your
senses in writing broadcast copy. Welsch uses his senses well:

> It'll be a long time before we taste the sweetness of corn dripping with butter
> right off the cob.

Welsch also involves the audience. He brings the viewers into the story with lines
such as:

> I don't know what I'm going to do with these red peppers, but they're too
> pretty to pass up.

Most of us have said the same thing at one time or another as we shopped and
spotted food that we just could not resist buying. We identify with Welsch's feelings, and that makes his writing effective.

He involves the audience again later in the script:

> But, do you know what I think makes this food taste especially good?
>
> Handing over my money to the very folks who grew the sweet corn and who
> picked the watermelon and know the peppers by name.

Welsch speaks with us, not to us. It's conversation, not narration. His script effectively mixes strong and tender thoughts:

> But when the heat of summer is gone and before the winter's blizzards
> sweep across these fields . . . at that short and lovely moment when the sweet
> coolness of autumn is evident, it's then that the Saint Libory produce stands
> remind us of how good things out here can be.

And then he reinforces the thought with the final line of the script:

> How rich and how full and how tasty.

If you spot some similarity between the writing styles of Roger Welsch and
Charles Kuralt, you may see why so many Welsch stories wound up on "Sunday
Morning."

## Use Your Senses

The novelist William Burroughs once observed that if a writer "can't see it, hear
it, feel it, and smell it he can't write it." You will not be able to use all of your
senses every time you sit down at a computer. But on most occasions, you should
be able to draw on the two senses most useful to a journalist—seeing and
hearing.

Here's an excellent example of how a writer used those senses, a script written by *NBC News* correspondent Bob Dotson about a cave rescue in Carlsbad, New Mexico. The actual script is produced in its entirety because it shows an unusual technique employed by Dotson. In the left-hand column, among the video notes, Dotson tells in great detail what he is seeing and hearing.

| SLUG | SHOW | WRITER | DATE | TIMING | LC |
|---|---|---|---|---|---|
| Cave Rescue = | = NN/DD = | dotson | Thu May 16 10:48 1991 | HOLD | 2:11 260 |

"NN CAVE" 4/4/91
W/BOB DOTSON
CARLSBAD, NEW MEXICO
SPOT RUNS: 2:31
SUPERS: BOB DOTSON
CARLSBAD, NEW MEXICO
[LEAD INFORMATION]

Imagine slithering through a block of swiss cheese a mile and a half long. Climbing up a thousand-foot maze dragging a broken leg. That's what it was like for Emily Mobley. She clawed her way beneath the earth for 4 days, after an 80-pound boulder slipped and crushed her in a cave. It took 60 people to rescue her. Emily's ordeal ended at 3:15 EDT this morning.

ANCIENT INVASIONS OF ICE HAVE CREATED AN ENORMOUS UNDERGROUND CATHEDRAL. ONE LONE CLIMBER—HIGH ABOVE— CLINGS TO ITS SPIRE. THE LIGHT FROM HIS HELMET LAMP DABS THE CAVERN WITH COLOR.

NAT SOT: (RESCUER)
"IS THE WHOLE TEAM READY?"

OTHER RESCUERS APPEAR IN
THE BEAM OF LIGHT. THERE
IS A SQUEAKING OF PULLIES
AND ROPES. RESCUER IS
RAPPELLING DOWN.

                        V/O
Shadows chase shadows. Now
and then a whisper of sliding rope.

ONE RESCUER SLITHERS IN
AND OUT, MOMENTARILY
LOSES CONTROL. TUMBLES,
BUT RIGHTS HIMSELF.

                      NATSOT: (RESCUER)
                    "OKAY, EASY, EASY!"

A THIN LINE OF RESCUERS,
CARRYING EMILY, HUFF
THEIR WAY THROUGH A
TIGHT OPENING, THEN PICK
CAUTIOUSLY ALONG LOOSE
GRAVEL.

                        V/O
The anxious, uneven breathing
of 60 people lugging one of their
own.

MOBLEY IS LASHED TO A
MAKESHIFT STRETCHER.
ONLY THE RESCUERS'
WITS AND A LENGTH OF
ROPE KEEP HER FROM
PLUNGING INTO ETERNAL
FREEFALL.

                      NATSOT: (RESCUER)
             "I GOT IT!"

                        V/O
Emily Mobley was at the bottom of the
deepest cave this country has ever seen.
In a cavern so big there are explorers at
the opposite end that don't even know
the 4-day rescue took place.

A RESCUER SQUINTS ACROSS
THE BLANK STONE, TRYING
TO SEE THE CRACKS HE
HAD MEMORIZED THE
NIGHT BEFORE, THEN
COMMENCES AGAIN THE
STEADY ROUTINE OF THE
CLIMB.

NATSOT: (RESCUER)
"MUCH BETTER! MUCH
BETTER!"
V/O
The darkness would have been total
without her friends.

NATSOT: (RESCUER)
"LOOKING GOOD! "MOVE A
LITTLE FASTER." "KEEP HER
COMING!"

RESCUERS MUST BE MORE
THAN BRAVE. THEY MUST BE
METICULOUS AND ABOVE ALL
ORDERLY. EACH STEP MUST
BE THE SAME. EXACTLY THE
SAME. AGAIN AND AGAIN.

V/O
They tugged her to the top an inch at a
time. One-and-a-half miles.

NATSOT: (RESCUER)
"KEEP ON MOVING."

EMILY IS BREATHING OUT
THE PAIN.

(MOBLEY)
"YEAH, I'M FINE. JUST KEEP
MOVING ME."

THE RESCUERS LIE ON THEIR
BACKS AND PASS THE
STRETCHER OVER THEIR
HEADS.

V/O

In places they cushioned her weight with their own bodies. And always kept a light for her to see above.

NATSOT: (RESCUER)
"REAL SLOW AND EASY GUYS."

EMILY'S SMILE SHOWS
THROUGH THE DUST AND
GRIME ON HER FACE

V/O

Emily showed her appreciation with a grin . . . lit from inside.

SOT: (MOBLEY)
"UM, IF I HAVE TO BREAK MY LEG, I CAN'T THINK OF BETTER PEOPLE I'D RATHER BE AROUND."

SHE IS HOOKED TO
ROPES THAT WILL LIFT
HER INTO DARKNESS.
SHE SPINS UP AND AWAY

NATSOT: (RESCUER)
"ON THREE . . . ONE, TWO . . ."
NATSOT:
[THE CLANKING AND HUFFING BELOW CONTINUES UNDER DOTSON's STANDUP]

CUT TO DOTSON ON CAMERA
WITH RESCUE TEAM NEAR
MOUTH OF CAVE. SUPER: BOB
DOTSON, CARLSBAD, NEW
MEXICO

[Standup] The ordeal below did not build character, but it revealed it. What matters down there are energy, muscle, and will. Qualities her friends had in abundance. Otherwise she would not have survived.

TEAM STRUGGLES FOR
FOOTING AT THE BOTTOM OF
A TALL STACK OF LOOSE
ROCKS.

NATSOT: (RESCUER)
"OKAY, WE CAN CARRY HER ON
OUT."

EMILY'S WORDS ARE
BRAVER THAN SHE
LOOKS.

SOT: (MOBLEY)
"AS LONG AS I DON'T STEP ON MY
LEG, I'M FINE."

THEY FACE THIS LAST
CHALLENGE WITH HOPE AND
A CERTAIN HORROR. RISK IS
AS MUCH A CLIMBER'S TOOL
AS A ROPE.

V/O
They are all expert climbers. So is
Emily. She was mapping this new cave
when a loose rock started this test of
friendship.

NATSOT: (RESCUER)
"ALL RIGHT. . . ."

EACH CLIMBER STEADIES
THE NEXT. HAND HOLDING
HAND, THEY LIFT EMILY OUT
OF THE DARKNESS.

V/O
Pals came from all around the country.
A cry of need seems to carry further in
darkness. Or perhaps we listen closer.

THEY SCRABBLE UP, HUNGRY
NOW TO REACH THE TOP.

NATSOT: (RESCUER)
"HOLD ON!"

THE COMMONPLACE
HORIZONTAL WORLD OF
MORTGAGES, GIRLFRIENDS,
AND FAMILY SEEM FAR
AWAY. THEY HAVE FORGED
AN INTENSE RELATIONSHIP

WITH EACH OTHER AND THE
ROCK.

NATSOT: (EMILY)
"AM I EXCITED! YOU BET I AM!"

AT LAST! THEY ARE OUT.
UNDER A FULL MOON, HUGS,
HANDSHAKES, CONQUEST!

V/O

Finally, the light above did not need
batteries.

NATSOT: (RESCUER)
"CHEERS FOR EVERYBODY!"
NATSOT: (CROWD WHISTLES
AND APPLAUSE)

Emily's friends felt as old as thick mud.
Nearly 100 hours in that pewter world.

RESCUER ON CAMERA
TURNS AND SPEAKS FOR
ALL WHO LABORED SO
LONG.

SOT: (RESCUER)

"WE'RE REAL PLEASED TO GET
HER OUT ALIVE. AND GET HER
OUT IN ONE PIECE. IT WAS REAL
SPECIAL TO ALL OF US."

EMILY'S FRIENDS GENTLY
SLIDE HER INTO A WAITING
AMBULANCE. SHE GIVES
THEM A THUMBS UP THROUGH
THE WINDOW AS IT DRIVES
OFF INTO THE NIGHT.

Deep within themselves they had
discovered the people they wanted to be.
Bob Dotson, NBC News, Carlsbad, New
Mexico.

If you go back to the Welsch script, you will note that limited information is
included in the video column. The Dotson notes, in contrast, are so literary, and

include such detail, that they could have easily provided a second script for the story.

Dotson's broadcast script is lean by comparison with the notes. You may find yourself wondering why Dotson did not employ more of the well-written notes in the actual script. One important reason is time. The story that was broadcast ran 2 minutes and 11 seconds. Dotson did not really have the option of adding more narration because of the time constraints placed on him by his producers. And second, although Dotson is a splendid writer, he is primarily a "picture person." He selects his pictures first and then writes his script to the pictures. Some reporters believe that the script should be written first and then the pictures selected to support the words. That long-standing debate is discussed later in detail, in the reporting section. For now, let's examine Dotson's style.

Dotson gives his script a lean, almost poetic quality. He captures emotion and color by selecting his words carefully:

Shadows chase shadows. Now and then a whisper of a sliding rope . . .

The anxious, uneven breathing of 60 people lugging one of their own . . .

The darkness would have been total without her friends. . . .

In places they cushioned her weight with their own bodies . . .

Emily showed her appreciation with a grin . . . lit from inside . . .

Pals came from all around the country. A cry of need seems to carry further in darkness. Or perhaps we listen closer.

Dotson's words—like Emily's rescuers—are strong, caring, and proficient. Both got the job done.

Now examine the words that did not get into the script. They tell us that their author, although a "picture person," has mastered the skill and art of good writing:

Ancient invasions of ice have created an enormous underground cathedral. One lone climber—high above—clings to its spire. The light from his helmet lamp dabs the cavern with color. . . .

Only the rescuers' wits and a length of rope keep her from plunging into eternal freefall.

A rescuer squints across the blank stone, trying to see the cracks he had memorized the night before, then commences again the steady routine of the climb. . . .

They face this last challenge with hope and a certain horror. Risk is as much a climber's tool as a rope.

Remember that these words are not written for a broadcast audience but for Dotson's and the editor's reference. He and his co-workers are the only people who will read the video notes. (We examine Dotson's work in more detail in Chapter 14, "Putting the Television Story Together.")

**Figure 5.2** *NBC News* correspondent Bob Dotson. (Courtesy of NBC News)

## Color Comes in Many Shades

You have read some examples of outstanding, colorful writing by top broadcast journalists. All of the scripts display an element of entertainment, humor, and enlightenment. They may have brought a smile to your face and, perhaps, even a tear or two. But color comes in many shades; it is not just humorous or entertaining.

Color can be expressed in writing about dramatic or frightening situations:

> The man held his gun to the side of the woman's head and you could see that both of them were scared. Her eyes were bulging. So were the veins on her neck as she looked down at the grey steel barrel moving down to the side of her neck. The gunman's hand shook nervously and menacingly.

Color can appear in the middle of a report on a congressional debate:

> The senator's face was beginning to turn red. His fists were tight and you could see he was about to give in to the anger that was swelling within him. I don't think I have ever seen the senator from Oregon as angry as he was at that moment.

Color can be used to describe an FCC hearing:

> Neither side was happy about the decision. The networks warned they could go broke and the Hollywood producers said the decision could mean the public would see fewer creative programs. Someone said it was a battle between the rich and the wealthy.

In discussing color in broadcast copy, *NBC News* correspondent Roger O'Neil says, "If I am successful it's because I take a great deal of pride in telling a story rather than giving people facts and figures, most of which no one remembers anyhow. It seems to me," he continues, "the great failing of local reporters that I watch across the country is that they are not good storytellers."

For a story to be successful, O'Neil says, an audience "must be provoked" by the story or "moved by it, or be happy or sad about it." He adds that he is talking about a human interest story, not a news story from the White House.

## Colorful Obituaries

Just about any event or situation that is worth news coverage has potential for colorful writing—writing that influences and affects an audience in a dozen different ways. This is true even of obituaries. Former *CBS News* correspondent Richard Threlkeld wrote many obituaries over the years. Here is an example that displays his special talents.

| V/O | Threlkeld |
|---|---|
| Montage of Dr. Seuss characters | Dr. Seuss wasn't a real doctor, but he was at least as instrumental in the upbringing of a couple of generations of kids as Dr. Spock. |
| Clips from various Seuss videos | And not just American kids. Everywhere, in 18 languages, they know about ziffs and zuffs and nerkles and nerds. |
| Seuss video clips and kids reading books | They called his books "children's books," but the children knew better. "Children like my books," said Dr. Seuss, "because I treat them as equals." |
| SOT of kids reading books and commenting on them. Video of Cat in Hat | (SOT . . . kids) |
| | V/O |
| | And the books are about grownup things, after all. About taking responsibility. |
| PIX of Cat in Hat book | "I know it is wet and the sun is not sunny, but we can have lots of good fun that is funny." |
| PIX of Horton Hatches the Egg | About loyalty. "I meant what I said and I said what I meant. An elephant's faithful, one hundred percent." |
| Seuss movie | About prejudice. |

| SOT | (SOT) |
| --- | --- |
| | "Ronald, remember when you are out walking, you walk past a sneetch of that type without talking." |
| V/O | V/O |
| Seuss video | So, Dr. Seuss wasn't all stuff and nonsense, even though creatures in his world were pretty weird and called each other funny names. When you grew up, you were always amazed at how many people in the real world reminded you of somebody you met in Dr. Seuss. Somebody asked him once, who was his favorite? |
| SOT T. S. Geisel | (SOT) |
| | "I think the Grinch, maybe." |
| SOT Grinch video | "I'll be coming back someday." |
| V/O Grinch movie | V/O |
| | The Grinch has been coming back to our living rooms every holiday season for 25 years now, trying and failing to steal Christmas. |
| SOT END of Grinch Xmas movie, sad kids in window and cat walks by | (SOT) |
| | Dr. Seuss never had any children of his own. But he is survived by millions of children, past and present, all over the world. Richard Threlkeld, CBS News, New York. |

Threlkeld says that he tries, in his obituaries, to capture the "essence" of the particular person. He says that because of time limits in broadcasting, "You aren't able to include all the nuances as you would in a newspaper obit. But," he adds, "the advantage in broadcasting is that the nuances, quite often, come in the pictures and sound."

For the Dr. Seuss (T. S. Geisel) obit, Threlkeld said, "I got every piece of information in print that I could find and culled through it looking for particular things that would lead me to the essence of the person and his work." Threlkeld said that he was fortunate to have the Dr. Seuss TV special that is broadcast every Christmas, and he bought all the Dr. Seuss books available.

Threlkeld said that he had the advantage of living through two generations of Dr. Seuss—as a child himself and as a parent reading the stories to his children. "As I looked at all the visual material," he said, "I thought of the things that affected me when I was a kid. I realize now, of course, that Dr. Seuss was not only entertaining but also teaching children things. I asked myself what he was trying to teach and, in the case of Horton the Elephant—'an elephant's faithful one hundred percent'—he was teaching loyalty to children." Threlkeld said that in the Dr. Seuss books he was able to find three or four examples to demonstrate "these principles of good, decent living that [Dr. Seuss] was trying to teach."

Threlkeld said that it was not easy finding sound bites because Geisel was something of a recluse. But he was able to find one bite that worked. As for the readings from Dr. Seuss' books, Threlkeld said he decided he was the right one to read them because he had "read them out loud" to his children. "I tried to let the viewer look at the life's work of this man," he said, "that's what you do in an obituary."

Dr. Seuss was special—and an inspiration—to another *CBS News* correspondent, Charles Osgood, who likes to use rhyme in many of the stories he writes for the "Osgood File" on CBS Radio. The title of Osgood's first book is *Nothing Could Be Finer Than a Crisis That Is Finer in the Morning*, and he dedicated the book to Dr. Seuss, who, he said, "gave me a new way to look at the *neuss*." Dr. Seuss sent Osgood a note in reply saying, "Nothing could be finer than to be an Osgood inspiriner."

In his script about Dr. Seuss' death, Osgood used his marvelous flair for rhyme to express some "personal thoughts about inspiration . . . and immortality."

And now the news . . . what can I say? My inspiriner passed away?
That he just died and went to heaven . . . at the age of 87?
I do not like that . . . Sad I am.
For in his books . . . Green Eggs and Ham . . .
The Cat, the Grinch, and Lorax too . . .
There's something that keeps coming through.
It's there, if anybody looks
In 47 of his books.
The ones that kids enjoy so much . . .
His play with words, his special touch.
And yet in just that way he told
Of war and peace . . . and growing old . . .
From the sublime to the absurd . . .
He always picked the perfect word.
And if no perfect words were known . . .
He made up new ones of his own.
You read his stuff . . . I'm sure you did
And as you read it to your kid
You smiled because you really knew

**Figure 5.3**
Former *CBS News* correspondent
Richard Threlkeld prepares to do a
report. (Courtesy of CBS News)

That it was also meant . . . for you.
Your kids will read those books again
As grown-up women . . . grown-up men.
And their kids also will enjoy . . .
Reading to THEIR girl and boy.
Although it's true the MAN is gone . . .
His genius will go on and on.
A spark that was much more than clever
Dr. Seuss will live forever.
So tell the kids they shouldn't cry.
Inspiriners never die.

Osgood says that one of the nice things about radio is "you don't have the problem of fighting pictures, because there you're creating a picture from the very beginning." He adds, "I think radio is a superior visual medium because the picture is not literal."

The *CBS News* correspondent recalls that when the late Rod Serling made the move from radio to television he wrote a line for a drama that said, " 'Once there was a castle on a hill' and he was asked 'What kind of a castle do you want? Do you want ramparts? Is this a medieval castle? What kind of castle is it?'

Serling answered, 'I don't know. Let each person build his own castle.' "

Osgood says, "That's what you do in radio. The listener fills in. But you have to help him, you have to give him enough information so that he can build his castle. You give him materials to build with."

## Frederick, Ellerbee, and Aaron

No discussion of good writing would be complete without examining the writing of one of the nation's best journalists, the late Pauline Frederick, who was United Nations correspondent for *NBC News* for many years. The following is the script of a broadcast from December 5, 1963, two weeks after the assassination of President Kennedy.

FREDERICK:  This is Pauline Frederick, NBC News, New York, with United Nations. The rifle shots that were heard around the world, reverberated through the halls of the United Nations.

Then came a time to weep, a time to mourn, and a time to be silent. Slowly the tempo of living resumed—the carrying out of assigned duties—the pleading for and against causes—the passing and defeating of resolutions. Even though it could be assumed that all was the same, it was not. An accustomed underpinning was gone, a certainty that permitted assault on the accepted, a questioning of the unquestioned. There is a new subdued quality about business here.

One important Western Delegate says that Africans who were once talking freely about drastic measures have lost their fire. They seem frightened, not because they fear the tangible but because suddenly where there was the known there is the unknown. As when a father drops the hand of his child in the dark. This feeling has been particularly evident in the Security Council.

The Africans had demanded an urgent meeting of the Council to take new steps to force South Africa to free all of its people or be read out of the community of nations. The Council was called for Monday morning, November 25. Instead, this became a time to be silent.

When the Council did convene a week ago, President Sir Patrick Dean gave voice to the sudden realization of members of a change that affected them all, afflicted them with a sense of uncertainty because there was change. Sir Patrick said: "Inevitably, and rightly, the United States assumes a large share of our total responsibility under the Charter of the United Nations for the continuing peace of the world. President Kennedy was second to none in his recognition of that fact and in the steadfast support he gave, in word and deed, to the purposes of the United States and to the authority of the Council."

After all the urgency for Council action, only two visiting African foreign ministers were ready to speak. After their words, the Council adjourned until Friday.

The debate since then has repeated most of the words that have been said many times on the subject—there have even been suggestions that South Africa should be deprived of its privileges in the General Assembly. But they were spoken with less zeal than has marked the African demands heretofore. And when Norway's Sievert Nielsen proposed a compromise to bridge the demands of the Africans for sanctions and the more moderate views of the western industrial powers, he succeeded in gaining African support.

The resolution would deny materials for arms-making to South Africa, and the Secretary-General is asked to set up a group of experts to work with South Africa in peacefully according human rights to all of its people.

**Figure 5.4** The late NBC correspondent Pauline Frederick files her report from the United Nations. (Sophia Smith Collection, Smith College)

> Not that the Africans have given up thoughts of extreme pressure against South Africa eventually, if necessary.
>
> But the moment appears to be a time to heal.
>
> This is Pauline Frederick, NBC News, United Nations.

Frederick began her career with ABC, where she became the first woman correspondent with the networks. She went on to spend 22 years with NBC. She retired at 65. She continued to work for National Public Radio and was the first woman to moderate a presidential debate. She died in 1990.

Another respected woman journalist is Linda Ellerbee, who also spent many years with NBC before moving to ABC. Here is one of her stories, written for "NBC News Overnight":

> Doing something just because you really want to do it can make trouble. Especially if you're about the only one who does it. Consider the case of Roy Warren and Elizabeth Sargeant of Massachusetts.

> They got married on June 12. Mr. Warren has six brothers. Miss Sargeant has none. For that reason, Roy Warren took her surname and became Roy Sargeant. The priest, said Mr. Sargeant, freaked out. The Department of Motor Vehicles told the ex-Marine it was illegal to change his name on his license. It wasn't. The Social Security office considered the name change for three days.

> Mr. Sargeant is still carrying his marriage certificate to prove he is not Mr. Warren. Perhaps we ought to be more easy about something that is really a simple thing, but we're not.

> On the other hand, we may take pride in being somewhat more advanced in our notion of equality than the Irish government. The European Economic Community, or Common Market, pointed out to the Irish government that it had not yet implemented the agreed sex-equality legislation. The Dublin government immediately advertised for an equal-pay enforcement officer to correct the situation. The advertisement offered different salary scales for men and women. And so it goes.

Another woman who managed to break through the "women need not apply" attitude at the networks in the 1940s and 1950s was Betsy Aaron. She had too much talent to be ignored. She worked for both CBS and ABC. Here's one of her reports from Lebanon:

Marines in Lebanon
9/14/83
Aaron/Irving

| | |
|---|---|
| NATL SOT: POEM | What Lebanon Means To Me: I lay on the ground with my face in the dirt and wonder what I'm doing here. The bullets go by, the mortars explode, the rockets scream in my ear. |
| V/O | Corporal Thom Stephenson. Hometown Cherry Hill, New Jersey. In Beirut since May . . . and now much older than his 23 years. |
| NATL SOT: STEPHENSON | How has this changed you? I think about what's going on in the world now. |
| V/O | The Americans occupy three positions protecting Beirut's airport. Alpha . . . hugging the runway . . . the company with four men killed in action. Bravo . . . overlooking the airport. The company taking the most shelling. And Charley . . . way out at the end of the runway. The company closest to the Lebanese Army troops. The company hit with the heaviest artillery. |
| SOT: POEM | I wait for a minute and I run for my hole and dive for the comfort inside. Sand in my tee shirt, sand in my socks, and the temperature's at least 105. |
| V/O | He's not kidding. It's just plain hot here . . . all the time. Hot and dirty. |
| SOT: SGT FOSTER HILL | Most everybody is used to the luxuries of home and it's hard when it's taken away from you. |
| V/O | Just over a week ago it rained shrapnel all over Charley Company . . . for most of a day and a night. There's only one way to handle shrapnel. |

| | |
|---|---|
| SOT: SGT HILL | We got an old saying here in the first platoon. If you want to hide behind the wall you must dig behind the wall. |
| V/O | So that's what they do . . . |
| SOT: LT ARTHUR HARRIS | The deeper the better. And we're trying to make it a little more comfortable in our bunkers because it looks like we'll be there for a while. |
| V/O | And when they're not digging, they're filling sandbags . . . more bags than they'd ever dreamed they'd fill. Walls of sandbags lining bunkers dug deeper since the Marines began taking casualties. |
| NATL SOUND SEQUENCE WITH GUNFIRE = OBSERVERS IN BUNKERS ON BINOCULARS AT MAP . . . ON PHONE V/O | It's a front row orchestra seat to a show where the plot unfolds daily. |
| CONTINUE NAT SOT: V/O | The Marines call them men. They are very young men. |
| SOT: POEM | As I sit here melting, sweating away, I'll remember her voice on the phone . . . She said keep your head low, don't be a hero, we all want you home in one piece. |
| NAT SOT: PROMOTION CEREMONY V/O | A month ago all 165 men in Charley Company would have turned out for this promotion ceremony. But it's dusk now, and the fighting in the mountains is picking up. It always does . . . in the evening. |
| CONTINUE CEREMONY V/O | There is a tradition in a Corps long on tradition. For officers above the rank of those promoted to pin the stripes on . . . so they'll stick. |
| CONTINUE SLAPPING SEQUENCE V/O | And at sunset . . . |
| ATL SOT: | Lowering of the colors. |

| | |
|---|---|
| V/O | So far just another day in Lebanon . . . a place where Marines are glad to get eggs and pancakes for dinner . . . when it's the first hot meal they've had in 9 days. |
| NAT SOT: W/ SOT HILL | Oh goody—give me the one with the big bug. |
| V/O | Meals and mail—pretty big items in a Marine's day. Time to try and forget the fighting. But then there is news of shelling at company headquarters. There are casualties . . . but no details. |
| SOT: SGT HILL | We haven't done anything to hurt anybody. We just trying to keep the peace and somebody just wants to hurt us and provoke us into violence against whoever is doing this to us. EDIT What's going through your mind? Just praying we get through the night. |
| V/O | Charley Company is now operating under Condition One. No lights . . . everyone under cover. The men in headquarters sit in the dark and talk. |
| SOT: TAPE 5 5:00 | I wanted to see what it would be like in a hostile environment. This was the most hostile you can get. |
| SOT: TAPE 5 4:30 | There was so much incoming and they dropped boom, boom, boom. All you could see of the three of us was the tops of our boots. I just dove for my life. |
| V/O | And finally with the Druze and the Lebanese Army still going at each other . . . Charley Company goes to sleep. |
| NATL SOT GUNFIRE IN DARK V/O NAT SCENES OF UP AND AT 'EM. END SEQUENCE WITH NAIL SOT: V/O | Reveille is 4:30 a.m. An ungodly hour to get up save for one thing: It is clear . . . and cool.<br><br><br>First shot of the morning. The monotony of the routine can get to you . . . a little breakfast . . . a little work . . . write a letter . . . chase your dog . . . |

NATL SOT:
SOT: POEM

blow off steam.
There is no more jogging . . .
no more basketball.
listening post . . . gunfire.

    I can't help but wonder why these people fight. I guess diplomacy isn't their style. Bombs and grenades, death and destruction. We'll keep our heads low for awhile.

STANDUP

    Despite the casualties . . . despite the sitting duck conditions, despite the debate in Washington . . . the Marines who are here say they should be here. And they're convinced that, no matter how bad things get here, they'd be worse without the Marines. Now the Marines are supposed to say that. But they say it as if they really believe it. ". . . we have a job to do."

NATL SOT: PVT MICHAEL MCCARTY
V/O

    And yet both enlisted men and officers freely talk about the problems of this peacekeeping mission, especially the problem of staying on the defense when you're being attacked.

CAPT CHRIS COWDREY
CHARLEY COMPANY
COMMANDER

    We are not out here banging away at the drum and trying to start something up, or trying to take lives unnecessarily. We are here really taking more licks than we really deserve, or are justified in receiving.

SOT: MCCARTY

    If they would let us get out and fight and move around or if they would take us out of here. The choice doesn't really matter. But it's just a fact sitting here in this particular area it's like we're trapped down.

SOT TO STEPHENSON

    Should you and the Marines be in Lebanon? I don't know . . . that's a tough one I think about all the time.

V/O

    Betsy Aaron for Nightline with Charley Company in Beirut.

**Figure 5.5** Former *CBS News* correspondent Betsy Aaron reporting from Lebanon while she was still with ABC.

Aaron said the package was designed to accomplish several goals: to show the American people what it was like in Lebanon for Marines and to reveal that the Marines didn't understand why they were there and what they were supposed to accomplish. "They had a little boy attitude," she said, "they thought that they were there to do some good." Aaron said that some of the Marines in her story were later seriously wounded in the bomb attack on the barracks that killed 220 Marines.

"We were the first reporting team to spend the night with the Marines," she said, "and we wanted to know how they felt because we were convinced it was an ill-fated mission. You could look at the mountains and the sea that surrounded them," Aaron said, "and you knew they were sitting ducks. That was important for Americans to see, to let them know what we had stepped into."

Aaron said that wasn't the first war she covered. She reported on the Six Day War in the Middle East and the war on Cyprus between the Greeks and Turks, which she said was the worst "slaughter" she had ever covered.

# Murrow and His "Boys"

You have read scripts written by some of America's top broadcast journalists—communicators effectively using language in a colorful, eloquent, and sometimes classic manner. The best of these men and women point to one individual who set the standard on a rooftop in London more than 50 years ago.

Shortly before World War II, the head of CBS, William S. Paley, decided that he wanted the nation's top broadcast news operation. Edward R. Murrow would get it for him.

Murrow was already on the payroll, working in London for CBS, when he was told by his New York office to start hiring the best reporters he could find to work in the key capitals of Europe. He did, and "Murrow's Boys," as they came to be known, *did* give Paley the best broadcast news team in the nation. It also established a dynasty that would allow CBS to dominate broadcast news for more than 40 years.

Among the "boys" were Bill Downs, Charles Collingwood, Richard C. Hottelet, Alexander Kendrick, Larry Le Sueur, David Schoenbrun, Eric Sevareid, William L. Shirer, and Howard K. Smith. The team was to broadcasting what the Babe Ruth Yankees were to baseball. CBS would continue its successful recruiting, adding to its roster the talented Winston Burdett, Walter Cronkite, Douglas Edwards, Robert Pierpoint, Harry Reasoner, Daniel Schorr, and Robert Trout.

# "This Is London"

In the 1940s, Murrow quickly established a reputation as the most notable broadcast journalist covering the war in Europe. His nightly reports from London rooftops—with sounds of bombs and anti-aircraft and sirens in the background—became a ritual for millions of Americans.

Murrow's skill with words set him apart from other broadcast journalists. Here are some excerpts from some of Murrow's reports:

> There are no words to describe the thing that is happening. [But he found them.] A row of automobiles, with stretchers racked on the roofs like skis, standing outside of bombed buildings. A man pinned under wreckage where a broken gas main sears his arms and face . . . the courage of the people; the flash and roar of guns rolling down streets . . . the stench of air-raid shelters in the poor districts. The fires up the river had turned the moon blood red . . . Huge pear-shaped bursts of flame would rise up into the smoke and disappear. The world was upside down.

This rooftop report was delivered as anti-aircraft fire lighted the sky:

Out of one window there waves something that looks like a white bedsheet, a . . . curtain swinging free in this night breeze. It looks as if it were being shaken by a ghost . . . The searchlights straightaway, miles in front of me, are still scratching that sky. There's a three-quarter moon riding high. There was one burst of shellfire almost straight in the Little Dipper.

One of the best examples of Murrow's writing is a report he made after flying on a combat mission to Berlin aboard a British bomber called "D for Dog." Here are excerpts from Murrow's script that display his extraordinary use of words to capture the mood and drama of everything that passed before him:

We went out and stood around a big, black, four-motored Lancaster, D for Dog. A small station wagon delivered a thermos bottle of coffee, chewing gum, an orange, and a bit of chocolate for each man. Up in that part of England the air hums and throbs with the sound of aircraft motors all day. But for half an hour before takeoff, the skies are dead, silent, and expectant. A lone hawk hovered over the airfield, absolutely still as he faced into the wind. Jack, the tail gunner, said, "It would be nice if we could fly like that . . ."

The take-off was smooth as silk. The wheels came up, and D-Dog started the long climb. As we came up through the clouds, I looked right and left and counted fourteen black Lancasters climbing for the place where men must burn oxygen to live. The sun was going down, and its red glow made rivers and lakes of fire on the tops of the clouds. Down to the southward, the clouds piled up to form castles, battlements, and whole cities, all tinged with red.

We were approaching the enemy coast. The flak looked like a cigarette lighter in a dark room—one that won't light. Sparks but no flame. The sparks crackling just above the level of the cloud tops.

The blue-green jet of the exhausts licked back along the leading edge, and there were other aircraft all around us. The whole great armada was hurtling towards Berlin.

We were still over the clouds. But suddenly those dirty gray clouds turned white. We were over the outer searchlight defenses. The clouds below us were white, and we were black. D-Dog seemed like a black bug on a white sheet.

The same moment the sky ahead was lit up by bright yellow flares. Off to starboard, another kite [plane] went down in flames. The flares

**Figure 5.6**
The late *CBS News* correspondent
Edward R. Murrow risked his life to go
on a bombing raid over Germany during
World War II. (Historical Photograph
Collections, Washington State University
Libraries)

were sprouting all over the sky—reds and greens and yellows—and
we were flying straight for the center of the fireworks.

Suddenly a tremendous big blob of yellow light appeared dead ahead,
another to the right and another to the left. We were flying straight
for them.

And then with no warning at all, D-Dog was filled with an unhealthy
white light. I was standing just behind Jock and could see all the
seams on the wings. His quiet Boots voice beat into my ears. "Steady,
lads, we've been coned." His slender body lifted half out of his seat
as he jammed the control column forward and to the left. We were
going down.

Jock was wearing woolen gloves with the fingers cut off. I could see
his fingernails turn white as he gripped the wheel. And then I was
on my knees, flat on the deck, for he had whipped the Dog back into
a climbing turn. . . .

The small incendiaries were going down like a fistful of white rice
thrown on a piece of black velvet. . . .

> The cookies—the four-thousand-pound high explosives—were bursting below like great sunflowers gone mad. . . .
>
> I looked down, and the white fires had turned red. They were beginning to merge and spread, just like butter does on a hot plate. . . .
>
> We flew level then. I looked on the port beam at the target area. There was a sullen, obscene glare. The fires seemed to have found each other—and we were heading home . . .

Two other journalists, on other Lancasters in that raid over Berlin, did not return home. Murrow had the incredible ability—and it was the reason he was so effective—to use words to transport the listener onto a plane or a London rooftop or into an air-raid shelter.

Listen also for the rhythm of Murrow's words in the "D for Dog" report:

. . . the skies are dead, silent, and expectant. A lone hawk hovered over the airfield, absolutely still as he faced into the wind. . . .

The sun was going down, and its red glow made rivers and lakes of fire on the tops of the clouds.

. . . clouds piled up to form castles, battlements, and whole cities, all tinged with red. . . .

The flak looked like a cigarette lighter in a dark room—one that won't light. Sparks but no flame. The sparks crackling just above the level of the cloud tops.

The blue-green jet of the exhausts licked back along the leading edge . . .

It was no wonder that Murrow won great respect from his audiences and peers. Traveling on a near-death ride through hell, Murrow captured and held pictures of everything that was going on, including details like Jock's "woolen gloves with the fingers cut off." Then, like a composer, he put a score to the word pictures he brought back to the studio: he added the dozens of different sounds and sights that were exploding around him, the "fistful of white rice thrown on a piece of black velvet" and the fires that were "beginning to merge and spread like butter does on a hot plate." The broadcast became known as "Orchestrated Hell."

## "Permit Me to Tell You"

One of Murrow's most moving reports from Europe came from his visit to the infamous Buchenwald concentration camp after the fighting was over.

> Permit me to tell you what you would have seen, and heard, had you been with me on Thursday. It will not be pleasant listening. If

you are at lunch, or if you have no appetite to hear what Germans have done, now is a good time to switch off the radio, for I propose to tell you of Buchenwald. It is on a small hill about four miles outside Weimar, and it was one of the largest concentration camps in Germany, and it was built to last.

There surged around me an evil-smelling horde. Men and boys reached out to touch me, and they were in rags and the remnants of uniform. Death had already marked many of them, but they were smiling with their eyes. I looked out over that mass of men to the green fields beyond where well-fed Germans were ploughing.

A German, Fritz Kersheimer, came up and said, "May I show you around the camp? I've been here ten years." I asked to see one of the barracks. . . . I was told that this building had once stabled eighty horses. There were twelve hundred men in it, five to a bunk. The stink was beyond all description.

When I reached the center of the barracks, a man came up and said, "Remember me? I'm Peter Zenkl, one-time mayor of Prague." I remember him, but did not recognize him. He asked about Benes and Jan Masaryk. I asked how many men had died in that building during the last month. They called the doctor; we inspected his records. There were only names in the little black book, nothing more—nothing of who these men were, what they had done, or hoped. Behind the names of those who had died there was a cross. I counted them. They totalled 242. Two hundred and forty two out of twelve hundred in one month. . . .

As we walked out in the courtyard, a man fell dead. Two others— they must have been over sixty—were crawling toward the latrine. I saw it but will not describe it.

In another part of the camp they showed me the children, hundreds of them. Some were only six. One rolled up his sleeve, showed me his number. It was tattooed on his arm. D-6030, it was. The others showed me their numbers; they will carry them till they die.

An elderly man standing beside me said, "The children, enemies of the state." I could see their ribs through their thin shirts. The old man said, "I am professor Charles Richer of the Sorbonne." The children clung to my hands and stared. We crossed to the courtyard. Men kept coming up to speak to me and to touch me, professors from Poland, doctors from Vienna, men from all Europe. Men from the countries that made America.

We went to the hospital; it was full. The doctor told me that two hundred had died the day before. I asked the cause of death; he shrugged and said, "Tuberculosis, starvation, fatigue, and there are many who have no desire to live. It is very difficult. . . ."

We went again into the courtyard, and as we walked we talked. The two doctors, the Frenchman and the Czech, agreed that about six thousand had died during March. Kersheimer, the German, added that back in the winter of 1939, when the Poles began to arrive without winter clothing, they died at the rate of approximately nine hundred a day. Five different men asserted that Buchenwald was the best concentration camp in Germany. They had had some experience of the others.

There were two rows of bodies stacked up like cordwood. They were thin and very white. Some of the bodies were terribly bruised, though there seemed to be little flesh to bruise. Some had been shot through the head, but they bled but little. All except two were naked. I tried to count them as best I could and arrived at the conclusion that all that was mortal of more than five hundred men and boys lay there in two neat piles.

I pray you to believe what I have said about Buchenwald. I have reported what I saw and heard, but only part of it. For most of it I have no words. Dead men are plentiful in war, but the living dead, more than twenty thousand of them in one camp. And the country round about was pleasing to the eye, and the Germans were well fed and well dressed. American trucks were rolling toward the rear filled with prisoners. Soon they would be eating American rations, as much for a meal as the men at Buchenwald received in four days.

If I've offended you by this rather mild account of Buchenwald, I'm not in the least sorry.

Murrow's success during World War II was just the start of his career. His prestige and popularity as a broadcaster grew dramatically after the war. He was by far the most well-known broadcast journalist in the early years of television. With the best producer in the business, Fred Friendly, at his side, Murrow's TV programs were among the most popular in the 1950s.

## "The Fault, Dear Brutus"

One of Murrow's programs was "See It Now," a weekly 30-minute examination of often-controversial subjects. The most memorable episode was the one in which Murrow took on Senator Joseph McCarthy, who had established a national reputation with his anti-communist witch-hunt. McCarthy had charged that the State Department and Pentagon were riddled with communists. Murrow challenged McCarthy's tactics. At the end of the program, Murrow concluded with a biting attack on the senator:

> This is no time for men who oppose Senator McCarthy's methods to keep silent, or for those who approve. We can deny our heritage and our history, but we cannot escape responsibility for the result. As a nation we have come into our full inheritance at a tender age. We proclaim ourselves, as indeed we are, the defenders of freedom—what's left of it—but we cannot defend freedom abroad by deserting it at home. The actions of the junior senator from Wisconsin have caused alarm and dismay amongst our allies abroad and given considerable comfort to our enemies. And whose fault is that? Not really his; he didn't create this situation of fear, he merely exploited it and rather successfully.

> No one familiar with the history of this country can deny that congressional committees are useful. It is necessary to investigate before legislating. But the line between investigation and persecution is a very fine one, and the junior senator from Wisconsin has stepped over it repeatedly. His primary achievement has been in confusing the public mind as between the internal and external threat of Communism. We must not confuse dissent with disloyalty. We must remember always that accusation is not proof and that conviction depends upon evidence and due process of law. We will not walk in fear, one of another. We will not be driven by fear into an age of unreason if we dig deep in our history and our doctrine and remember that we are not descended from fearful men, not from men who feared to write, to speak, to associate, and to defend causes which were for the moment unpopular.

> Cassius was right. "The fault, dear Brutus, is not in our stars but in ourselves."

Because of Murrow's great popularity with the American people, his criticism of McCarthy is considered by many to be an important factor in the eventual downfall of the senator.

Murrow's influence on broadcast journalism was overwhelming. Eric Sevareid, one of the first "boys" to be hired by Murrow, was impressed by his boss from the beginning, and the admiration never ended: "He could absorb and reflect the thought and emotions of day laborers, airplane pilots, or cabinet

**Figure 5.7**
The late *CBS News* correspondent
Edward R. Murrow on the set of an
early TV show, *See It Now*. (Historical
Photograph Collections, Washington
State University Libraries)

ministers and report with exact truth what they were. . . . One can read his broadcasts now, years later, in the printed form for which they were never intended and find London all around—its sights and sounds, its very smells and feeling through the changing hours, all brought back."

Murrow, who died in 1965, would have liked that tribute. He probably would have replied that Sevareid was no "slouch" either.

## Eric Sevareid: Writing with Class

Many adjectives have been used over the years to describe the splendid writing of the late Eric Sevareid during his almost 40 years with *CBS News*. His writings have been described as "majestic," "magnificent," and "elegant." His colleague Walter Cronkite spoke of Sevareid's "beautifully chosen words of wisdom," which made him "one of the finest essayists of the century."

There is no doubt that Sevareid's reports and commentaries stood a notch above most of the writing heard on the air. What he had to say was always important. Sometimes he expressed his strong feelings about the responsibilities of journalists, as he did in a commentary on the *CBS Evening News* on the night of his retirement. Here is part of that commentary:

Mine has been here an unelected, unlicensed, uncodified office and function. The rules are self-imposed. These were a few: Not to underestimate the intelligence of the audience and not to overestimate its information. To elucidate, when one can, more than to advocate. To remember always that the public is only people, and people only persons, no two alike. To retain the courage of one's doubts as well as one's convictions, in this world of dangerously passionate certainties. To comfort oneself, in times of error, with the knowledge that the saving grace of the press—print or broadcast—is its self-correcting nature. And to remember that ignorant or biased reporting has its counterpart in ignorant and biased reading and listening. We do not speak into an intellectual or emotional void.

In another commentary, speaking specifically of electronic journalism, Severeid wrote:

It is a marvelous and frightening instrument, broadcasting, as part of this marvelous and frightening century. But ordinary men must use it as ordinary men have made this century what it is. Bad men can use it to their advantage, but in free societies, only for a time—and a shorter time, I think, than in previous eras. The camera's unblinking eye sees through character faster than the printed word.

And on the subject of democracy, Severeid wrote:

Democracy is not a free ride. It demands more of each of us than any other arrangement. There can be no rights and privileges without responsibilities. My forebears here were at ease with the word "duty." They knew that self-denial was not just a puritanical test of character, but a social necessity, so that others, too, might have elbow room in which to live. They believed, as I do, that civilized life cannot hold together without these old and now sometimes derided values. The reason is simple: only people with a sense of personal responsibility can help others or, for that matter, be helped. There can be no final solutions. From solutions arise new problems, of lessened severity, we are entitled to hope. Time is life. If one uses it to ameliorate the problems, he has lived successfully.

No other people have that chance more than do Americans. The world still looks to this country as the critical experiment in the relations of man to man. This is a fabulous assignment history has given us. From what I have read of the past, and from what I remember of my own generation's beginnings, I believe we are not failing in this assignment, and will not.

At Sevareid's retirement, NBC's John Chancellor said, "With his colleague Edward R. Murrow, he [Sevareid] brought a level of excellence and distinction to broadcast journalism it had not enjoyed before."

The late Charles Kuralt said that Sevareid "was one of the better writers who ever worked around here, one I always admired and whose work I used to read." Kuralt added: "When I got to know him I discovered that he was never entirely comfortable with the lights and the cameras and the makeup and all of the things you have to put up with in television. He said working in television is 'like being nibbled to death by ducks.'"

Kuralt also said that once when Sevareid was "feeling particularly grumpy about television [Kuralt] heard him murmur, 'One good word is worth a thousand pictures.'"

## Good Things from Local Stations

All of the scripts that you have read so far have been by network journalists. Usually, they have more time to tell their stories than do their counterparts at local radio and TV stations. As a beginning journalist, you can also benefit from examining the work of fine local broadcast writers, who are working within the time constraints you will probably face in the early part of your career.

Well-written scripts do not have to be long. The challenge will be to tell your stories quickly without sacrificing quality. Here are examples of good writing from local journalists:

SLUG: GRANDMA 2
DATE: Wed Oct 30, 1991
REPORTER: NP
NEWSCAST: 5P
ON CAMERA

PARENTS OFTEN FIND THEMSELVES
SHOULDERING THE BURDENS OF
THEIR CHILDREN LONG AFTER
THOSE CHILDREN BECOME ADULTS
... AND WHEN PARENTS BECOME
GRANDPARENTS ... THE EMOTIONAL
LOAD CAN BE EVEN HEAVIER ... IN
OUR SERIES GRANDMA'S HANDS ...
WAFB'S NANCY PARKER REPORTS
ON A GRANDMOTHER WHO'S
TAKEN HER GRANDSON INTO HER
HOME ...

|  | WHILE <u>HIS</u> PARENTS ARE BEHIND BARS. (SOT PKG) |
|---|---|
| Opening shot of Paul and grandmother walking into prison | |
| V/O | (V/O) It's visiting day at Saint Gabriel Prison. Judy Hill and her 9-year-old grandson Paul come here a couple times a month. |
| Nat sound up | (SOT) Door slams shut as Paul and his grandmother sign prison visitors' book. |
| Dissolve to Paul's mother entering the room and nat sound of Dotty Hill saying "Paul" and hugging him | (V/O) This is where Paul's mother, Dotty Hill, is serving time. (nat sound) |
| | (V/O) The reunions are always sweet for Dotty and her son. For three years now Paul has been in his grandmother's care. His mother watches him grow, visit by visit. |
| SOT Dotty | (SOT) "Let me see how big you've gotten . . ." |
| Mug shot of mother full screen | (V/O) Dotty Hill and her son were separated in May of 1989 when she was brought to Saint Gabriel on a drug distribution conviction, facing an eight-year sentence. |
| SOT Fade to Dotty bite, music up softly (love theme from "Dying Young") | (SOT) "I was arrested and they brought me to jail and I took it hard. The first thing  that came to mind was where I was going to put my son. I'm |

going to be in prison the rest of my life."

Full Screen
Font: 530 INMATES
397 HAVE CHILDREN
12% OF CHILDREN IN
FOSTER CARE 88%
WITH FRIENDS AND
FAMILY

(V/O)
But she's not alone. St. Gabriel officials say of the 530 inmates at the prison, 397 have children. Twelve percent of these are in foster care, 88 percent are with friends and family.

Fade music out
SOT
Dissolve to grandmother
bite

(SOT)
"I pray a lot. I tell her to pray a lot, that she's gonna get out. I want him to be with his mother. He needs to be with her."

Fade to Dotty bite

"She is the mother to him instead of me. Even when I was out she was a mother to him. I loved him and gave him material things. I didn't give him the mother's love, but she did."

Fade to Parker asking
question and Paul
responding

Parker: "What's the worst part about not having your mom around?"
Paul: "I missed her."

O/C standup

(O/C)
Paul's grandmother not only has to raise him but she has to deal with his emotions as well. Not only is his mother in prison here at Saint Gabriel but his father is also behind bars.

SOT
Fade to bite of
grandmother
Music up
Nat sound of woman
guard slamming jail door.
Dissolve and freeze
and then slo mo of Paul
and mother hugging
and saying goodbye.

(SOT)
"I try to explain to him that they did something wrong and when you do something wrong you have to pay for it. But as long as she needs me, I'll be there. Even when she gets out, I'll be there for both of them."

V/O                                    (V/O)
                                       Nancy Parker, Channel 9 News, Baton
                                       Rouge.

The 50th anniversary of Pearl Harbor was a special occasion, so Executive Producer Rod Haberer of station KPNK-TV in Phoenix was given more airtime than
usual for this story, which he wrote and produced for anchor Kent Dana. (Note
that Haberer's script format is somewhat different from the earlier one by
Parker. He identifies, by number, the tapes he is using and at what time on the
tape the sound bites are located. As is the case in many newsrooms, Haberer
also uses the symbol VG (video graphic) instead of Font.

PEARL HARBOR
ANCHOR LEAD-IN:
50 YEARS AGO TONIGHT . . . MUCH OF THE WORLD WAS AT WAR. BUT
AMERICA WAS SITTING THIS ONE OUT. THAT IS, UNTIL THE FOLLOWING
MORNING. AMERICA'S ILLUSION OF PEACE WAS SHATTERED ALONG
WITH THE HULL OF THE BATTLESHIP ARIZONA. MORE THAN A
THOUSAND MEN WERE KILLED WHEN A JAPANESE BOMB EXPLODED
ABOARD THE SHIP . . . DURING THE AIR RAID ON PEARL HARBOR. KENT
DANA REPORTS.
(SOT FULL RP)
(ALL GRAPHICS PRE-PRODUCED)
END TAPE 5:42 OUT: CALLED A MAN (FADES TO BLACK)

TOMORROW MORNING, AT 7-55 A-M . . . PRESIDENT BUSH WILL BE
ABOARD THE USS ARIZONA MEMORIAL . . . TO LAY A WREATH OVER
THE SHIPWRECK THAT STILL HOLDS AN ESTIMATED 900 MEN
ENTOMBED SINCE DECEMBER 7TH, 1941.

TAPE 29A 20:07                         (NAT SOT EXPLOSIONS)
VG: LORRAINE MARKS                     IN: On that day, 1177 men were
USS ARIZONA                            killed, the largest single naval
HISTORIAN                              disaster in United States history.

                                       LORRAINE MARKS LIVES IN
                                       PHOENIX, AND IS THE OFFICIAL
                                       HISTORIAN FOR THE USS ARIZONA
                                       REUNION ASSOCIATION. HER
                                       HUSBAND, WHO DIED FIVE YEARS
                                       AGO, SERVED ON THE ARIZONA. A
                                       SURVIVOR, ED MARKS WAS ASHORE
                                       WHEN THE ARIZONA WAS
                                       ATTACKED.

TAPE 29A 3:50                                    (SOT FULL)
MARKS                           IN: In 1985 he went back to the last
                                reunion that he could attend. And a
                                television reporter asked him why, after
                                all these years do you attend these
                                reunions? And for the first time, I saw
                                him cry . . . because he said we can't
                                forget those guys.

TAPE 29B 3:07                                    (SOT FULL)
MARKS                           IN: I know my husband suffered all
                                those years, he wouldn't talk about it.
                                There's a lot of women I know who say
                                their husbands just won't talk about it.

TAPE 28A 5:40                                    (SOT FULL)
STRATTON                        IN: Kind of a tough day.

STILL STRATTON                  DONALD STRATTON, WHO NOW
TAPE 28b 26:30                  LIVES IN YUMA WAS ABOARD THE
                                ARIZONA ON DECEMBER 7th, 1941,
                                AT HIS BATTLESTATIONS ON THE
                                ANTI-AIRCRAFT DIRECTOR ABOVE
                                THE BRIDGE.

TAPE 25A 3:50                                    (SOT FULL)
STRATTON                        IN: General quarters sounded and
VG: DONALD STRATTON             everyone was on their battlestations
USS ARIZONA BB39                as far as I knew.

TAPE 28A 4:44                                    (SOT FULL)
STRATTON                        IN: When the bomb hit, it shook that 33-
                                ton ship like you'd shake a piece of
                                paper.

TAPE 28A 5:26                                    (SOT FULL)
STRATTON                        IN: The people in the number one and
                                number two turrets and those manning
                                stations to bring ammo from up below
                                and all that, that was in the forward
                                part, never had a chance.

TAPE 29B 1:00                                    (SOT FULL)
MARKS                           IN: The Japanese planes came,

battlestations sounded, the band threw down all their instruments and went to their battlestations.

TAPE 29B 1:30                   (SOT FULL)
MARKS                           IN: And their battlestations were in the bowels of the ship, passing ammunition, and everyone in the band that day was killed.

STILL USS VESTAL                WHEN THE ARIZONA EXPLODED,
TAPE 26 16:12 & 17:00           THE U-S-S VESTAL WAS STILL TIED UP ALONGSIDE, AND THE VESTAL WAS THE ONLY WAY OFF THE ARIZONA FOR STRATTON AND OTHERS STILL STRANDED.

TAPE 28A 7:53                   (SOT FULL)
STRATTON                        IN: I would say 50 to 60 manned that station, but there was only six of us went across this . . . as you know, the Vestal was tied up alongside.

TAPE 29A 16:12                  (SOT FULL)
MARKS POINTING TO               IN: This is the Vestal tied up alongside
PAINTING                        . . . the repair ship . . . and this is the ship that threw a line over the aft section of the mainmast where Don Stratton was.

TAPE 28A 8:10                   (SOT FULL)
STRATTON                        IN: We pulled over the heavier messenger line, and tied if off to the Arizona, and we crawled across to the Vestal.

TAPE 28A 8:54                   (SOT FULL)
STRATTON                        IN: I was burned over 60 percent of my body.

                                STRATTON SURVIVED . . . BUT SO MANY OTHER YOUNG MEN DIDN'T. LIKE JAMES RANDOLF VAN HORNE.

TAPE 29C 4:50                   (SOT FULL)
MARKS                           IN: He was a sophomore in Tucson High

School and he heard Admiral Kidd, rear
Admiral Kidd, talk about the navy.

TAPE 29C 5:18                          (SOT FULL)
MARKS                          IN: He quit school, and he joined the
                               navy, both he and the admiral died just
                               a few months later.

TAPE #1 17:43                          (SOT FULL)
VG: PAUL STILLWELL             IN: I talked to the son of the Arizona
AUTHOR/BATTLESHIP              admiral who was on board, and in
                               1942 his mother got a package from
                               Hawaii that had in it her husband's
                               naval academy ring, and that had been
                               found fused to the conning tower right
                               in front of the bridge, and apparently
                               that was all that was left of Admiral
                               Kidd.

STILL ROBERTS                  ANOTHER 17-YEAR-OLD KILLED
TAPE 29D 47:30                 THAT DAY . . . WAS WALTER SCOTT
                               ROBERTS.

TAPE 29B 14:03                         (SOT FULL)
MARKS                          IN: The navy department deeply regrets
                               to inform you that your son, Walter
                               Scott Roberts, Junior Radioman First
                               Class US Navy, is missing following
                               performance of his duty and in the
                               service of his country.

STILL BRITTON                  AND 17-YEAR-OLD CHARLES
                               EDWARD BRITTON OFTEN WROTE
                               HOME . . . ON JULY 19TH, 1941, THIS
                               NOTE TO HIS MOTHER.

TAPE 290 14:08                         (SOT FULL)
MARKS                          IN: I was not able to send you the five
                               dollars I got off you . . . a 17-year-old
                               boy borrowing money from his mom.

                               PHOTOGRAPHS OF HER SON AND HIS
                               LETTERS HOME ARE ALL THAT
                               CHARLES EDWARD BRITTON'S
                               MOTHER HAD TO REMEMBER HER
                               BOY. BUT SHE WOULD BE PROUD,

AND MOST LIKELY MOVED TO
TEARS, TO HEAR THE WORDS
LORRAINE MARKS HAS WRITTEN
INTO THE HISTORY BOOKS OF THE
USS ARIZONA.

TAPE 290 12:48                          (SOT FULL)
MARKS                         IN: Where his remains are now are
                              uncertain, but the soul of this 17-year-
                              old departed that day, December 7th,
                              1941, from the starboard side of the
                              quarterdeck of the burning and sinking
                              battleship USS Arizona BB39. His name
                              is engraved in stone along with 1176 of
                              his shipmates on the wall of the USS
                              Arizona memorial that spans the sunken
                              hull in Pearl Harbor, Hawaii. His service
                              to his country and ultimate sacrifice
                              earned him the right at the tender age
                              of 17 to be called a man.

Haberer was asked how he felt about doing all the work on the Pearl Harbor
story, while Dana simply anchored the story. His reply: "It's the way TV has
evolved recently. It's much more anchor driven than it used to be. People like
the anchors and they want to see and hear more of them. It's our job to make
the anchors look as knowledgeable and as strong as we can make them look."
He said he accepts that the anchors are going to get credit for the work he does;
"it's just part of the job." (More on this topic is discussed in Chapter 18, "Ethics.")

The following story was written by Kris Kridel of radio station WBBM in
Chicago.

David Chereck Murder/Kris Kridel
[neighborhood traffic sounds]
In the three weeks since the murder of their son, Alan and
Esther Chereck's brick home in Skokie has been filled with people:
investigators and reporters, family friends, and . . . most important
to David's mother . . . his friends.
AUDIO:    His friends came. They just kept coming and they keep
          coming and, uh, and it just shows how much he was
          loved.
KRIDEL:   Esther Chereck says David's friends sit in his room and
          talk about him.
AUDIO:    More kids than I realized really knew and cared about
          David. The cards that we've gotten tell us memories of

KRIDEL: David and they fill in those blank spots that you don't share with your teenager.

KRIDEL: The Cherecks have learned, for instance, how David once helped a grammar school classmate.

AUDIO: One year she wouldn't have made her math class, if he hadn't helped her through it, she wouldn't have passed. He never boasted. We never knew these things about him.

KRIDEL: On the piano and in the nearby etagere in the Cherecks' living room are David's academic awards, his artwork, and pictures of him at all ages.

AUDIO: In fact, I put more of them up. Having him around, especially when I was sitting shiva, was a comfort. As you see, he has a bright smile and, uh, he's there with me. I don't think he'll ever leave us.

KRIDEL: It is a great comfort to the Cherecks that David's classmates at Niles West High School are organizing an art scholarship fund in his honor.

AUDIO: We just love them for what they want to do for David.

KRIDEL: David's parents are appealing to people who may have any information about his murder to step forward and help.

Kris Kridel, WBBM Newsradio 78

[neighborhood traffic sounds fade]

**Figure 5.8** Kris Kridel of radio station WBBM in Chicago. (Courtesy of WBBM-Chicago)

# Summary

No one expects you to turn out copy of the quality shown in this chapter right away. Working color into your stories effectively will not come easily or quickly. At the outset, the real challenge will be to write respectable broadcast news copy with speed. You will not have days (unless you are working on a documentary or special report) to write your story. Often you will be dealing in minutes and, at best, an hour or so if you are working on a TV script. But there will be enough time for you to write clearly and accurately while you are developing the skill of writing colorfully.

Don't wait until you are covering a story to develop your observation skills. Start to watch people and take notes about their appearance, how they talk and look, and anything unusual or different about them. Observe people the next time you go to the cafeteria or a ball game. Also start to develop your other senses. If you are in a crowded, smoke-filled room, think about how you feel. There are special smells just about everywhere: in a gym, in the corridors of a high school and a hospital, in a church. How many times have you entered someone's home and said: "Something really smells good. What's cooking?" Let all your senses work for you full-time, and put what they tell you into your copy.

# Review Questions

1. List the various ways you can bring color to your copy.
2. Why do so many broadcast news professionals recommend that aspiring journalists read the works of Ernest Hemingway?
3. Give the names of other well-known nonbroadcast writers who might help develop your writing style.
4. Why is the writing of Charles Kuralt so admired? Give some examples of sentences or phrases in his "On the Road" script that you particularly like, and tell why you like them.
5. What is it about the stories of *CBS News* special correspondent Roger Welsch that makes them so successful? Give some examples.
6. Give some examples of color in the writing of NBC's Bob Dotson. How would you describe Dotson's style?
7. Is color restricted to feature stories? Discuss.
8. Why is Edward R. Murrow's writing so well respected? Give some examples of the style that made him famous.

# Exercises

1. Examine one of the biographies of Edward R. Murrow, and summarize some of the statements made about his writing.

2. Listen to NPR's *All Things Considered*, and make notes on stories that you think are colorfully written.

3. Watch a network newscast and the local newscast that precedes or follows it. Keep notes on the stories that you believe are well written, and why.

4. *Sunday Morning* on CBS is considered by many to be the best news program on the air. Watch it, and report on the stories that you like most. Explain why.

5. Describe, in as much detail as possible, your closest friend. Include the individual's physical appearance and any habits or mannerisms he or she might have. Tell what you like and/or dislike about the person and why you consider him or her to be your closest friend.

# 6 Writing for the Radio Newscast

It is difficult to generalize about radio news operations and news programs because they seem to be constantly changing. One statement that can be made, however, is that newscasts on radio are getting shorter and less frequent.

However, many radio stations (mostly in large- and medium-sized markets) still take pride in their news operations and maintain writing and reporting staffs of a dozen or more. Some of these stations, particularly those that provide "all news," may have staffs twice that size. In small markets, radio news is often the product of a one-person news staff. Many people who begin their careers in radio will probably work in that environment, which has some advantages. It's an opportunity to develop the skills that you learned in school: writing, reporting, interviewing, working with sound, and editing. It also offers time to develop that most important of broadcasting skills—news judgment. But working alone also has some disadvantages. No one will be there to help correct and guide you when you need it most.

This chapter discusses the factors you should consider when preparing for and writing radio newscasts. Getting to know the audience is the first consideration.

## Your Audience

One of the continuing debates in both print and broadcast news is whether the news should provide the kind of information that people need to know or the information they want to know. Most journalists agree that the answer lies somewhere in the middle. People must be informed, but it also makes sense to tailor the news for the audience. A station programming easy-listening music probably would not want to provide the same kind of news as a rock station. The rock station would have a relatively young audience, and the soft-music station would have an older audience. If you were the news director at the rock station, you would be looking for stories that might appeal more to young people. The writing style also would be lighter and less formal than it would be, for example, for the audience of a classical-music station.

The story selection also would be different for news delivered in urban and rural areas. Stories about the weather would be important in farm country, whereas stories about traffic congestion would be important in the city.

Although you need to consider all these factors, your main concern in covering the news is the news itself. A story of overwhelming importance, whether it is local, national, or foreign, always takes precedence over the rest of the news.

# Organizing Material

Before radio newswriters decide which story should lead a newscast and which stories should follow, they must know what news they have to work with. A good way to start is to call the police and fire departments to see if anything is going on, then read the newspapers carefully. Newsrooms keep a file marked "futures" that alerts the staff to special events scheduled in the listening area that day and during the upcoming month or later. Check this file next. In a small community there may not be much going on, and, if that community is served by an equally small station, any material in the futures file was probably put there by the newsperson who will be covering the event.

Also check the news wires immediately. Of particular importance are the stories that the wires periodically move about events in the local area. After you have read the copy and decided which stories you want to use, you are ready to sort out the material.

Most newspeople list on a pad all the stories they have to work with and try to figure out a tentative order in which the stories will appear in the script. Other writers print out the stories on the computer they wish to use and arrange the stories in the order they wish to use them, so that the most important stories are at the top and the less important ones at the bottom. There is no right or wrong way to organize copy, so look for the method that is the most comfortable for you.

Writers using computers organize their copy in a variety of ways. Some move the stories they wish to consider for their newscast into a separate computer file. Later, when they are ready to rewrite the stories, they split the screen so that they can look at the wire copy on one side and use the other half, the blank side, to rewrite the copy in broadcast style.

Once that story is written it is saved, and the writer moves on to the next one, and so forth. When all the stories are written, the writer prints them out and puts them in the order in which they will be read on the air.

Many newscasters read the copy right from the computer screen, particularly when urgent material moves on the wire.

**Figure 6.1**   Anchor John Lynker of WTOP-Radio,
Washington, reads a newscast. (Courtesy of WTOP-Radio)

## Writing from the Back

One thing that just about all newswriters agree on is that the first stories they
write are those that will not change. Working in this way is called *writing from
the back* because the stories that are not likely to change are usually those that
are read in the latter part of the newscast.

"Breaking" stories, as their name suggests, will probably change considerably before airtime, so they should be written last.

## The Lead Story

The method for selecting the first story in the newscast—the lead story—may
sound simple: just pick the most important story. But how do you decide which
story is most important? Should a local, national, or international story be the
lead? Does the time of day affect the decision? Will any of the stories affect the
local audience in some way? The answers to these questions can help you determine which story should lead the newscast.

Most of a station's listeners will be more interested in what is happening in
their community than in the rest of the world. There are exceptions, of course,
as during the NATO air attacks on Yugoslavia when most Americans turned on
their radio and TV sets to get the latest on the war. The same was true during
the sensational O. J. Simpson murder trial.

But first, let's examine how we decide what's news to a local audience. News
in a town of 5,000 is not necessarily news in a city of 50,000. And what is considered news in that medium-sized city may not be too important in a city of a

million or more. Here are some story choices on a particular day at a radio station in the hypothetical town of Centerville, population 10,000.

1. The president says he is encouraged by the progress being made in the basketball strike negotiations.
2. The Labor Department says unemployment rose another one-half of one percent.
3. The governor says he will make major cuts in services and state workers' jobs rather than raise taxes.
4. The wife of Centerville's mayor gives birth to triplets.

The story of most interest in Centerville, and the story that most listeners would be talking about that day, is the birth of triplets to the mayor's wife. But 100 miles north, in the state capital, the birth would be less important, and the governor's comments on cuts in jobs and services would be the top story. The network newscast would lead with the jump in unemployment because that story holds the most interest for a national audience.

Suppose we add another story to the list: a three-car accident on the freeway near the state capital. While the story may not sound too important, suppose the accident was at 8 A.M., and those three wrecked cars had created a gigantic traffic jam. It most certainly would be the lead story on the 8 A.M. news for stations in the capital because that is "drive time," the highest-rated listening period for radio. The people listening to their radios on the way to work are more concerned about when they will get to the office than they are about the governor's comments on taxes and jobs. How about the audience in Centerville? Because the accident took place over 100 miles away, the Centerville listeners would have no interest in it. The network radio audience would not even know about the accident because it would not be important enough to make the wires.

Keep in mind that when you start to prepare your newscast, you should not be overly concerned about which story will lead it. The chances are that what appeared to be the most important story an hour earlier may be overshadowed by a new story that broke before airtime. That is the nature of the news business. On some very busy news days—unlikely in Centerville—a story that was considered the lead at one point may not even get into the newscast. That's why each story should be on a separate sheet of paper to allow for a quick reshuffling of the script.

# The Rest of the Newscast

You can use the formula you established for choosing the lead story to pick the rest of the stories in the newscast. Once you have selected the lead, determine which of the remaining stories would hold the most interest for your audience, then the next most interest, and so on. The stories would then be broadcast in that order.

There are important exceptions to this formula, however. Sometimes, it makes sense to place stories back-to-back because they have something in common. During NATO action in Yugoslavia, for example, it was not unusual for newscasts to carry a report of the air raids and then follow it up with a story from the White House or the State Department concerning some diplomatic aspect of the military action. Those two stories were often followed by a third that might have been a reaction-type story from Congress on the bombing or a poll of American opinion.

Another example would be the linking of weather-related stories. If part of the nation is suffering a drought and another section is in the middle of serious flooding, it would be logical to report those two stories together in the newscast. Without such logical connections, the rule is to report the news in its order of importance.

# Localizing the News

When writing for a local station, always look for some local angle in national and international stories. If a British airliner crashes in Europe, the first thing to check is whether any Americans were on board and, if so, whether any were from the local listening area.

During the Gulf War, local radio and TV newscasters were always interested in getting interviews with service personnel who were from their area. When casualties occurred, it was the responsibility of news organizations to find out if any local men and women were killed or injured.

If a person wins a million-dollar lottery it's a good story, but if the person happens to be from the listening area, it's a "great" story.

# Story Length

The length of a story is determined by the length of the newscast, the importance of the story, and the availability of news at that particular hour. If there is not much news to report, the stories may have to be longer than they would be normally. If there is a lot of news, most stories should be short to allow sufficient time for the major stories.

Before you start to write, you must determine how much time you actually have for news in a newscast. In Chapter 1, you learned that most newscasters read approximately 15 or 16 lines of copy per minute. So, for a three-minute newscast, you would need approximately 45 to 48 lines of copy.

But is the newscast really three minutes long? Probably not. Let's say there are two commercials, each running 30 seconds, in the newscast, which leaves two minutes of news. If there is a 10-second weather report, five seconds for stocks, and another five seconds to sign off, the two minutes have been reduced another 20 seconds. What is left is one minute and 40 seconds. If that time is converted to lines, you have about 25 lines in which to cover all the news. That is why you must learn to condense your stories. You may have as little as three lines to tell some of those stories.

# Actualities

The voices of the newsmakers are called *actualities* or *sound bites*. They are the heart of radio news.

In Chapter 5, you learned that color is often provided by the voices of the people in the story. A good writer can tell the story without the actual voice, but he or she faces a greater challenge. Even the best newswriters would tell you that if given a choice, they would rather have the actual sound bite provide the color than their paraphrase of what was in the sound bite. Regardless of the writer and newscaster's talents, it's not possible to capture all of the nuances in a sound bite with a paraphrase and the newscaster's voice. How can anyone better express the remarks of New York City cab drivers than they themselves? And how would the newscaster make up for the missing sounds of the city in the background—the natural sound—without the tape? Good tape is essential.

# Wraparounds

The combination of sound and words is known as a *wraparound*. This technique, as the name suggests, uses the voice of the newscaster or reporter at the beginning and end of a story or report and the voice of the newsmaker in the middle. You might want to think of a wraparound in terms of a sandwich. There can be more than one thing between the two slices of bread. Wraparounds often have more than one sound bite in the middle. The anchor or reporter may wrap several different pieces of sound with script. Here's an example:

A Conrail freight train today left the tracks near Centerville, causing some major problems for passenger trains that also use the tracks. Railroad officials say the locomotive and eight of the train's 14 cars were derailed. They blamed a broken rail.

Remarkably, there were only two injuries—to the engineer and his assistant—and they were not serious. Engineer Brian Potter spoke to us at the hospital.

(sound bite)

15 sec.

Out-cue: ". . . I was plenty scared."

Conrail engineer Brian Potter. He's in good condition at Centerville General Hospital.

The train was on its way to Southern California with a load of steel and lumber when the accident took place shortly before midnight. Freezing temperatures—dipping into the teens—will make the job of cleaning up a very unpleasant one and will hamper efforts to get service back to normal. But Conrail spokesman Mark Florman is optimistic.

(sound bite)

20 sec.

Out-cue: ". . . we will know more in a few hours."

Conrail spokesman Mark Florman.

He also said that Conrail passenger trains will be detoured, causing some delays probably for 48 hours.

# Lead-Ins

Every sound bite, wraparound, and report from the scene included in a news script must be introduced by a line or phrase known as a *lead-in*.

Here is one possible lead-in the anchor could have used to introduce the train wreck wraparound if it were done by a reporter at the scene:

A train wreck in Centerville during the night.

Reporter Carolyn Matherne has the details.

(Take wraparound)

Runs 1:10

Out-cue ". . . Carolyn Matherne reporting for KTHU Radio."

The most important thing to avoid when writing a lead-in is redundancy. One of the worst style errors is a lead-in that says exactly the same thing as the first line of the wraparound or sound bite. The way to avoid this problem is for the writer or anchor in the newsroom and the reporter at the scene to discuss in advance what each is going to say.

# Teases

The short sentences used in a script to hold the audience's attention just before a commercial break are called *teases*. The idea of a tease is to give the audience some reason to keep listening, rather than turning the dial. This is best accomplished by giving just a hint of what is to come after the commercial. The cleverer the tease, the greater the chance the audience will put up with the commercial.

If the train wreck wraparound were to follow a commercial, this is the way it might be teased:

> Freezing temperatures add to the problems of a Centerville train wreck. That story after this.
>
> (Commercial)

If the news is long enough, or being written for an all-news station, it's effective to tease two or more stories before going to a commercial. Such a tease gives the writer more opportunities to hook listeners. If they are not interested in the first story that is teased, they might go for the second or third one.

# Headlines

*Headlines* are another form of tease. Headlines come at the top of a newscast and should reflect the most interesting and exciting stories to be covered in the upcoming newscast. Often, a headline for an offbeat story is an effective tease. Here is a sample:

> A tornado rips through a small Kansas town, killing six people.
>
> The cost of living climbs for the third straight month.
>
> Governor Jones says he will veto legislation that would restore the death penalty.
>
> And a pet cheetah scares a lot of people when he decides to take a walk down Main Street.
>
> Those stories and more on the six o'clock news.
>
> Good evening, I'm Bill Giles.

Some radio newscasts start with only one headline:

> Six people die in a tornado in Kansas.
>
> Good evening, I'm Bill Giles with the six o'clock news. The tornado ripped through Centerville, Kansas . . .

**Figure 6.2**   Jim Hickey of ABC Radio News in the control room.
(© 2000 ABC, Inc.)

Many stations, particularly those that have shortened their newscasts, have eliminated headlines completely on the grounds that they are redundant and take
up too much time. On many other radio stations, the only news is the headlines.

## Pad Copy

Copy written for protection against mistakes in timing and unexpected changes
in the newscast that could affect the timing is called *pad copy*. Most of the time,
such copy will not get on the air, so the stories that are selected as pad copy
should be relatively unimportant.

Because most radio newscasts are relatively short, pad copy normally consists of only a few short pieces totaling perhaps between 30 seconds and a
minute. More pad copy might be written for longer newscasts.

Note that the chief reason for pad material is to avoid one of the scariest
situations in broadcast news: running out of something to say before the
program is scheduled to end.

# Back Timing

Getting off the air on time takes some planning. If a newscast runs over, or is short, it sometimes can create problems for the programs that follow the news. This is particularly true if network programming comes after the newscast.

One way to guarantee that this situation does not happen is called *back timing*. The final segments in the newscast are timed and then deducted from the length of the newscast. Let's look at an example. Suppose the last two items in a newscast are the stocks and weather. Both are timed. It will take 10 seconds to read the stocks and another 20 seconds for the weather. The standard close for the newscast takes another five seconds to read. The newscaster will need 35 seconds, then, to read the last three items. So, 35 seconds are deducted from the total time of the newscast. The newscaster now knows that he or she must begin reading those three final items at exactly 2:25 into a three-minute newscast. The three final items should be placed in a separate pile within easy reach on the studio table. The time 2:25 should be written boldly on the top page of this back-timed copy. When the clock reaches the 2:25 mark in the newscast, the reader simply picks up the three pages and begins reading them, regardless of where he or she is in the newscast. Some stories may have to be dropped, and often they are, but that is the only way to guarantee that the newscaster gets off the air on time. In newsrooms that are computerized, the timing and backtiming are done by the computer itself.

# Summary

Working in a radio operation in a small market has always been a good way to break into broadcast news, although many people seem to find the glamour and the pay of TV more appealing. In radio, you do get a wonderful opportunity to learn how to do everything; you would be the writer, reporter, announcer, and technician. In these days of automation, you might be the only "live" person in the building.

As the only member of the news staff, you would quickly learn how to organize your time and effort because you would have little or no help. Your news judgment would be tested every day. You would get an excellent opportunity to hone your writing and reporting skills. You would also be preparing yourself for the next job in a bigger market.

Even if your main interest is television, the things that you learned in this chapter are important because radio news provides an important foundation for work in television news. The principles of radio news writing also apply to television news, which is discussed in the next chapter. You will be required to make some adjustment because of pictures, but if you have absorbed the material in this chapter, you are well prepared to move along.

# Review Questions

1.  Why is it important when you are writing broadcast news to know about your audience?
2.  You are the only newsperson working at your radio station. When you arrive for work, you have two hours before you read your first newscast. Explain how you would get prepared.
3.  Explain the meaning of the term *writing from the back*.
4.  If you were writing news in Centerville, Kansas, a market of 10,000, which story would you pick for the lead of your newscast? (a) United States forces drop emergency relief supplies to flood refugees in Mozambique; (b) Ten thousand autoworkers go on strike in Detroit; or (c) Centerville welcomes home ten of its service men and women who served in the NATO air attacks on Yugoslavia. Explain your choice.
5.  If you were writing for a radio station in Ann Arbor, Michigan, which of the stories in Exercise 4 would you lead with? Why?
6.  After you have selected the lead of your newscast, how would you determine the order of the rest of the stories?
7.  What does localizing news mean? Give examples of how you could localize a story about a fire at a rock concert that caused some deaths and injuries and a story about the National Basketball Association draft.
8.  If you were writing a two-minute newscast for radio, approximately how many lines of copy would you need?
9.  If you have three commercials in the two-minute newscast, one of them 30 seconds and the other two 10 seconds each, how many lines of copy would you need to write?

# Exercises

1.  Using the stories reported on the front page of a newspaper, prepare headlines for a radio newscast.
2.  Using those same headlines, write teases for two of the stories that will appear later in your radio newscast.
3.  Read the front page of the newspaper, and decide which of the stories you would lead with in a newscast.
4.  What other stories on the front page, and in the rest of the newspaper, would you use in your newscast, and in which order?
5.  Go to a local radio station that has a news operation, and watch how they put a newscast together. Prepare a report on what you saw.

# 7 Writing for the Television Newscast

The major difference between radio and TV news is, of course, pictures. When you write for television, pictures are always crucial to a story. In radio, you must create pictures in your mind—as did Edward R. Murrow and other great broadcasters who used the medium effectively—and then find the words to paint those pictures for your audience. In television, you can show the actual pictures.

## Combining Words and Pictures

The battle over which are more important in television news—the words or the pictures—is endless. There is no doubt that words are vital and that some broadcast writers use them more effectively than others. The late Charles Kuralt is an example of a writer whose words rival the pictures for prominence in a story. But even Kuralt would be hard pressed to tell his stories without pictures. His talent was in his ability to strengthen the pictures with words. *Great* pictures and *great* words make great television news.

The beauty of good pictures is that they do not need a lot of words—just some good ones. The challenge for TV writers is to avoid clashes with the video. Do not tell viewers what they are seeing. Instead, support the video by saying what the video does not or cannot reveal. Fill in the blanks, but do not overpower the video. Give your viewers time to savor the pictures.

Such advice assumes that you have good pictures to work with. If you don't, then the words do become crucial because they are needed to prop up the video. But because TV news is not about using poor video, stories with bad pictures are likely to be dropped for more appealing ones unless the messages they convey are too vital to be eliminated completely.

If the pictures are poor, however, you can be sure you'll be asked to tell the story quickly. A common criticism of television news is that it relies on the pictures too much, but right or wrong the formula is not likely to change: poor pictures, short stories; good pictures, long stories.

# Sound Bites

As in radio, sound bites, the words of newsmakers, are key to telling a good TV news story. An advantage for TV writers is that TV sound bites feature the faces of the newsmakers as well as their voices. Good TV newswriters weave their copy between and around the sound bites, much in the way that radio writers create wraparounds. This combination, called a *package*, is the best way to tell a news story on television. The chapters on reporting will deal extensively with building packages.

# The Television Newswriter

In television, as in radio, a writer's duties depend on the size of the newsroom. In a small market—and even in some medium-sized markets—no one is assigned solely to writing. The anchors, reporters, producers, and perhaps an intern from a local college write the news. Television newsrooms in big markets and at the networks usually have several writers and, perhaps, associate producers who also write. Those who write television news have three basic writing tasks: read stories, voiceovers, and lead-ins.

# Read Stories

*Read*, or *tell*, stories are read by the anchors without the use of pictures except for those that usually appear next to the anchor's head. Visually, read stories are the least interesting in TV news. They are virtually the same as radio copy. They are, however, a necessary part of the TV newscast because they give the anchors exposure to the audiences. Anchors are paid well, and the audience expects to see their faces on camera at least part of the time.

Sometimes, read stories are used because no video is available. Read copy might even lead the newscast if it is about a breaking story that is just developing. We all are familiar with the phrase *film at eleven*, which usually indicates that it's too early for video, but it will come later.

Read stories are most often those that are not important enough to require video or whose video would be dull. At the same time, read stories play a major role in the TV newscast—they break up the other types of material. Too much of anything tends to be boring, so the read stories provide a change of pace.

Finally, read stories are easiest to work with in a newscast because they are flexible. They are the putty that fills in the holes of the newscast. Read stories often play the same role as radio pad copy; they provide an opportunity to make adjustments that guarantee that the newscast gets off the air on time. If the TV newscast is long, the read stories are the likely stories to be dropped. If the newscast is short, more read stories are likely to be used.

# Voiceovers

The second type of assignment given to TV newswriters is the voiceover (V/O), copy that the anchor reads while video or other graphics are shown. The video can either be silent or have a soundtrack that is kept low for natural effect, a technique referred to as *sound under* or *natural sound*.

Remember: The copy must complement the video. It should not duplicate what is obvious to viewers. Avoid phrases such as "what you are seeing here" unless the video is difficult to understand. For example, if you are showing video of a train derailment, rather than tell your viewers "What you are seeing is the derailment of a Conrail freight train that left its tracks last night," you would say "A Conrail freight train left its tracks last night," and let the pictures show the derailed train.

To write voiceover copy intelligently, you need to look at the video and take notes. When viewing the video, use a stopwatch to time each scene. The cameraperson sometimes shoots a series of short shots that may require little editing, but individual shots are often too long to use without editing. Let's consider the train wreck story discussed in the last chapter.

The cameraperson shot a long, continuous *pan* of the wrecked cars that lasts about 30 seconds. There's another shot of a derrick hovering over the scene for 20 seconds and a third 20-second shot of railroad workers huddled around a hastily made trashcan fire to ward off the frigid weather. Finally, there's an additional 30 seconds of video that shows some of the train's wrecked cargo—an assortment of steel rods and girders and lumber. The total running time of the video is one minute and 40 seconds. The producer asks the writer for a 20-

**Figure 7.1**
Anchors Bruce Kirk and Lin Sue Shepherd of KPNX-TV in Phoenix read scripts before going on the air. (Courtesy of KPNX-TV, Phoenix)

second voiceover. The writer, then, must lift an assortment of brief shots from the video that can be strung together in some logical order that will make sense when the narration is added. (In a small newsroom, reporters often write the script and edit the videotape. In a large operation, a tape editor follows the writer's or reporter's instructions.)

Now that the writer has notes on the length of each scene, she must decide how to *edit*, or *cut*, the video. (*Cut* is a film term that has carried over to video. All editing is done electronically; the videotape is not physically cut.) The writer decides to use part of the long pan of the wreck scene first. The cameraperson held steady on the scene at the end of the pan, knowing that the writer might wish to use part of it. It is poor technique to cut into a pan, but it is acceptable to use part of it as long as it comes to a stop before the next shot. The writer uses eight seconds of the pan. Then the writer selects five seconds of the wreckage video that shows the steel girders and the lumber spread over the tracks and terrain. Four seconds of the derrick at work follow, and the voiceover closes with three seconds of the railroad workers around the trashcan fire.

The writer gives her instructions to the tape editor, and then returns to her desk to type out the script from her notes and wire copy. In preparing the script, the writer uses a format different from that used in radio.

### The Split Page

In Chapter 1, you learned that TV scripts differ from radio scripts because they contain both the newscaster's words and an explanation of how the video is to be used. The format for a TV script is known as the *split page*. In Chapter 5, you saw examples of many such scripts.

The split page is divided vertically so that about 60 percent of the page is in the right column and about 40 percent is in the left. Those writing TV news do so on computers. Although their product is often sent electronically to the teleprompters, scripts also are normally printed out from the computers, as a backup, in case the computers malfunction. Most TV newsrooms are still using scripts printed by the computers.

The right side of the split page is reserved for the copy that will be read by the anchors, the running times (which also appear on the left), and the outcues (final words) of any videotape that has sound. The anchors—and this is important to remember—will be able to see only the right side of the script on their teleprompters. It is also important that you write only in the column on the right side. If you write outside the column, the words will not appear on the teleprompter screens.

### Video Instructions

The left side of the script is set aside for the slug and for video and audio instructions and tape times for the director. Because of the limited space on the left side of the script, abbreviations are used for the various technical instructions. Here are some common ones:

1. O/C, "on camera," tells the director that at this point in the script the anchor will be on camera.
2. V/O, "voiceover," means the anchor is reading copy while the audience is seeing something else, such as silent videotape or graphics.
3. SIL indicates "silent" videotape and is used in combination with the V/O symbol.
4. SOT lets the director know that there is "sound on tape." It could be a sound bite with a newsmaker or a report from the field that was taped earlier.
5. ENG, "electronic news gathering," tells the director that the video is on a videocassette.
6. FONT, an abbreviation for the manufacturer Videfont, indicates that names, titles, and other information are superimposed over videotape or graphics to identify newsmakers, locations, and various other pictures appearing on TV screens. Many stations use the term *super* or the abbreviation VG (video graphic) instead of FONT.
7. SL, ESS, or ADDA indicate that pictures or graphics of some sort will be shown next to the anchor. SL stands for "slide"; ESS refers to Electronic Still Storage, an electronic graphics and video computer system; ADDA is the name of a computer system that also provides electronic storage. If the word *box* appears next to any of these abbreviations, the graphic will be enclosed in a box next to the anchor, rather than fill the entire screen. Other technical abbreviations are used by writers to help the director. You will learn them once you start working with video on a regular basis.

Here is the split-page script used for the train wreck story discussed earlier:

TRAIN WRECK 3/15 6pm tw
O/C Smith Box ADDA

SMITH
A Conrail freight train today left the tracks near Centerville, Kansas, causing some major problems for passenger service trains that also use the tracks.

V/O SIL (TRT: 40 sec.)

V/O
Railroad officials say the locomotive and eight of the train's 14 cars were derailed. They blamed a broken rail. Remarkably, there were only two injuries—to the engineer and his assistant—and they were not serious.
The train was on its way to southern California with a load of steel and lumber when the accident took place shortly before midnight.

The wreckage was scattered over a
wide area. Within hours a derrick was
sent to the scene to help clean up the
mess. Officials say the job will take
days.

Freezing temperatures—dipping into
the teens—will make the cleanup
difficult and unpleasant.

Smith O/C Tag                                      O/C
Railroad officials say that while the
wreckage is being removed and repairs
made to the tracks, Conrail passenger
trains will be detoured. This probably
will cause delays for at least 48 hours.

If you examine this script, you will see that the slug *TRAIN WRECK* is in the
upper left-hand corner along with the date, the time of the newscast, and the
writer's initials.

On the next line in the right column is *SMITH*, the name of the anchor.
Because most newscasts have two or more anchors, the name of the anchor
reading the copy must always be displayed at the top of the right-hand column.

On the next line at the left is *O/C Smith*, which lets the director know which
anchor is on camera. Underneath that are the words *Box ADDA*, which tell the
director that a picture will be displayed in a box next to the anchor's head. In
this case, it could be a generic train wreck graphic that TV newsrooms keep on
hand along with scores of other such graphics. (It also could be a freeze frame
of part of the video that would be shown with the voiceover. But if that were the
case, the writer would have to indicate it by typing *SIL/FF* ["silent/freeze frame"]
next to *Box ADDA*.)

The anchor's script continues on the right side. Below the first sentence, you
see the V/O symbol, which means that at this point in the script the video will
be shown. The anchor continues reading, but the audience no longer sees his
face.

The V/O symbol is also displayed in the left-hand column with the abbreviation for silent videotape, *SIL*, for the benefit of the director. In parentheses is
the total running time of the videotape (TRT: 40 seconds), which tells the director that there are actually 40 seconds of wreckage footage on the videocassette.
Because the V/O copy should take only about 30 seconds to read, the director
has a 10-second cushion to avoid going to black, which is something of a nightmare for directors and their bosses. To avoid that problem, tape editors always
"pad the tape"—cut more tape than the writer requests.

When the anchor has finished reading the V/O copy, he returns on camera
(which is why we show *O/C* in both columns) to read a final sentence about

delays in rail service brought on by the wreck. That final sentence is called a *tag*, and the writer of this script has added the word *tag* after O/C in the left column just to remind the busy director that this is the end of the story.

## *Sound on Tape*

Those writing news for TV must also learn to write voiceover scripts that include sound on tape (SOT). Because the voices and pictures of newsmakers are a vital part of TV news, a great deal of the sound on tape is provided in the middle of reporter packages and is of no real concern to the newswriter. But sound is often worked into the anchor's script without the help of the reporter, and that is the newswriter's function.

Let's go back to the train wreck story and suppose that there is some sound on tape of one of the workers trying to keep warm around the trashcan fire. The writer decides to add that sound on tape to the script at the end of the voiceover before the anchor comes back on camera. A sound bite used at the end of a voiceover is abbreviated VO-SOT or V-SOT. The script would look like this:

```
SOT :15                              TRACK UP
FONT: Mark Florman              OUTCUE ". . . get any railroad worker
                               warmer."
                               Time :15


O/C Smith                               O/C
                               Railroad officials say that while the
                               wreckage is being removed and repairs
                               made to the tracks, Conrail passenger
                               trains will be detoured. This probably
                               will cause delays for at least 48 hours.
```

The sound-on-tape symbol and the time appear in the left-hand column to indicate that sound on tape will be used at this point in the script. The director now knows that when the anchor reads the last words of the voiceover, ". . . difficult and unpleasant," it is time to bring in the sound on tape.

The terms *Track Up* and *Time:15* also appear in the right-hand column along with the outcue, the final words of the sound bite. This lets the anchor know that a 15-second sound bite comes up before he returns on camera to read the last sentence in the story. The abbreviation *FONT* in the left column means that the name and identification of the railroad worker is to be superimposed over the lower portion of the screen while the railroad worker is speaking. The director will signal the font operator to punch up the information approximately three seconds into the sound bite.

After the sound bite instructions, the symbol O/C is written on both sides of the script to indicate that the anchor returns on camera to wrap up or "tag" the story, or to begin a new story.

# Lead-Ins

The third common scripting chore for the TV newswriter is preparing *lead-in* lines for sound bites and reporter packages. Writing television lead-ins is similar to writing lead-ins for radio wraparounds but is slightly more complicated. As with radio lead-ins, the information in the first line of the report or sound bite cannot be repeated in the lead-in.

Unlike radio lead-ins, those for television require some additional instructions for the director because while the anchor is leading into the report or sound bite on camera, some visual is usually shown in a box next to the anchor.

TRAIN WRECK 3/15 6pm
tw O/C Smith

                                                  SMITH
                                    A Conrail train has derailed in Kansas
                                    and we have a report from the scene
                                    from our reporter Frank Coakley.

SOT :55                                          TRACK UP
FONT: Frank Coakley               Outcue: ". . . Frank Coakley reporting."
                                  Time :55

The writer used a soft lead-in because she knew that Coakley would provide the hard-news lead. He started his report this way:

> The engine and eight cars of the Conrail train left the tracks around midnight near the town of Centerville. Fortunately only two people were injured slightly.

This lead-in is effective because it allows the reporter's opening words to build on it as he tells the rest of the story.

# Headlines and Teases

Depending on the size of the news operation, headlines and teases usually are turned out by the writer, the editor, or a producer.

As always, the major difference between headlines for television and those for radio is that headlines and teases on television are normally supported with pictures. Some network newsrooms forgo the traditional headline approach, preferring to have the anchors talk briefly about the top story before going to a reporter for details. But local news almost always leads the newscast with head-lines, which are most effective when used with flashes of video. Here's a sample of how one local newsroom scripts headlines:

| | |
|---|---|
| HOWARD (DEE) | (HOWARD)<br>Coming up on Action News at Six . . . |
| V/O #5 (liquor store) | Police search for two men who killed a liquor store owner during a holdup. |
| RUNS :04<br>WIPE TO v/O #3<br>(Mayor shaking hands) | (DEE)<br>Mayor Thompson honors a citizen who rescued a child from a burning building. |
| RUNS :04<br>WIPE TO V/O #2<br>(Unemployment office) | (HOWARD)<br>And unemployment in Center City reaches a new high. |
| RUNS :03<br>O/C Howard (Gail) | Good evening, I'm Howard Pass. |
| | (DEE)<br>And I'm Dee Danaher. Those are some of the stories we're covering on tonight's Action News. |

In the left column, *HOWARD* indicates that one anchor reads the opening line of the newscast and the first headline, while *(DEE)*—note the parentheses—indicates that the other anchor is also on camera. Both anchors quickly disappear from the screen, but Howard is heard reading the first headline over video showing the scene of the liquor store holdup. The video runs about four seconds. After the first headline, the video wipes to a shot of Mayor Thompson shaking hands with a hero while Dee reads that headline. The second voiceover also runs four seconds. The video wipes a third time to a three-second shot of workers standing on line at an unemployment office. Howard reads that headline, as indicated, over the video. Then both anchors return on camera as Howard says "good evening" and identifies himself. Dee does the same and reminds the audience that the stories just teased would be covered in the upcoming newscast.

The numbers next to the voiceover symbols indicate which playback machines are used in the control room, information that is vital to the director. If the director or his or her assistant calls for the wrong machine, the wrong video would appear, and the newscast would get off to a confusing start. Some stations give numbers to the tapes instead of the machines. In that case, the tape numbers would be placed on the scripts so that the director could call for the proper one.

Later in the newscast—before the commercials—teases are used in an effort to hold the audience. The same voiceover technique used in headlines is used for teases. Many producers also include fonts over the video to give it extra punch. For example, these words might appear at the bottom of the appropriate video:

Police hunt killer . . .

Hero honored . . .

Unemployment climbs . . .

The point of such teases is to hook viewers, to keep their interest in the news during the commercial. Teasing three stories increases the chance that your audience will be interested in at least one of the upcoming stories.

# A Team Effort

As you can see, writing television news is more complicated than writing radio news. Although one individual writes the television story and may even edit the videotape used in the story, the final product involves other people in the newsroom.

In radio, writers usually pick the stories they wish to tell their audience. In television, those who write the stories are told what to write and how long the stories should be. In radio, one person may do it all—record interviews on the phone, cover a news conference, and include in the newscast some of the tape he or she has edited. There are no one-person newsrooms in television, although at small stations you may be expected to play more than one role.

As in radio, television affords opportunities to learn how to do several different jobs. Writers often go on to other positions as reporters, anchors, and producers. Some move over to the assignment desk, where the people "find the news," a subject discussed in Chapter 9.

# Summary

This chapter introduces a variety of terms used in television news, such as *split page*, *voiceover*, *package*, and *font*, and describes a television writer's most common writing assignments.

In carrying out these assignments, you need to learn to work with both words and pictures; broadcast news professionals have strong views on which is more important—the words or the pictures. The truth, of course, is that *both* words and pictures are critical to a successful TV news script. Television is a visual medium, and the pictures must be effective, but if the words that go with those pictures are unclear, confusing, or contradictory, the story will fail because no true communication will take place.

Choose your pictures carefully, and do the same with your words.

# Review Questions

1. What is the major difference between writing for radio and writing for television?
2. How will poor pictures affect TV news stories?
3. How important are sound bites to a TV news script? Why?
4. What is a read story?
5. Why are read stories important to a TV newscast? List the different ways they are used.
6. What is a voiceover? Describe what the audience sees and hears during a voiceover.
7. Describe some of the things to remember when writing for pictures in a voiceover script.
8. Is it better to have too few or too many words in a voiceover? Explain.
9. Explain the steps that a writer takes in selecting videotape to be used in a voiceover.
10. Explain the term *split page*, indicating the dimensions and how the page is used.
11. Why must you be careful in observing the margins on the split page?
12. Explain the purpose of fonts and give some examples.
13. Explain the following abbreviations: SL and ADDA.
14. What does *SL Box* in a script mean?
15. What does *TRT* mean, and why is that term important for a director?
16. What is an outcue, and why is it important to the director and anchor?
17. What is the most important thing to remember when writing a lead-in to a sound bite or a correspondent's report?

# Exercises

1. Take a story from the wire or a newspaper and rewrite it on a split page as a read story. It should be 20 seconds long.
2. Using the same piece of copy, prepare a V-SOT. Suppose that you have a sound bite from someone who is involved in the story. Using the split page, indicate the proper symbols and time for a 10-second sound bite. You have 30 seconds for the entire story.
3. Suppose that you have a reporter covering a story about a tornado hitting Centerville, Kansas. Three people have been killed, and more than a dozen have been injured. Write a lead-in for a live report, indicating also what the reporter's first sentence will say.
4. Using wire copy or the front page of a newspaper, script three headlines for a TV newscast.
5. Using the same copy, script two teases that will come before your first commercial break.
6. Go to a local TV station and observe who is doing the writing. Talk to either a writer or a producer on how the writing is assigned, and report on what you discover.

# 8 Delivering the News

Many of you have hopes of anchoring news. How long it takes you to end up at the anchor desk depends mainly on two factors. The first one is talent—your ability to deliver the news. The second consideration is the size of the market in which you begin your career.

If you have talent and start working in a relatively small market, you may reach the anchor desk quickly. You will still, however, have to prove you are ready for that job by impressing the news director with your reporting ability. Also, remember that not all reporters become anchors; some good reporters do not have the special talent required to anchor news. Similarly, some anchors make awful reporters. This chapter discusses the qualities you need to anchor or report in front of a camera or microphone.

## Credibility

Ask news directors what they look for in reporters and anchors and most will tell you *credibility*. They want people who are believable, people who come across as knowledgeable about and comfortable with what they are doing.

Jeff Puffer, a voice coach for one of the nation's major broadcast consulting firms, Frank Magid Associates, says he knows many "reliable anchor-reporters with good potential who just don't seem comfortable in the anchor chair. In person they're spontaneous and charming. But on the air they're wooden, with unnatural speech rhythms and awkward inflection."

Puffer says that when he's instructing anchors and reporters, he expects them "to show two qualities in their reading: intelligence and genuine sensitivity." He says he looks for "emotion that is appropriate for the story, the person, and the occasion. I want them to demonstrate that they know what they're reading and that they're thoughtfully weighing the facts as they speak." Puffer says: "I always want them to say it with feeling, not artificially, but with sensitivity and maturity."

It is not always easy for anchor-reporters to accomplish these goals, and those who coach people in delivery techniques use a variety of methods. Puffer says he doesn't concentrate on speech pathology material such as breathing, diction, and resonance. "We're involved in matters relating to interpretation, making the voice sound spontaneous and conversational, like an ad-lib."

Puffer admits that his methodology could be called "unconventional or unorthodox," but, he says, "given what we have been finding in neuroscience research, we know that the whole of human intelligence is not just the left side of the brain, the intellectual side. It's also intuition, artistry, abstractions, pattern recognition, and the like."

# One-Way Communication

Puffer says the difficulty in broadcast training is the "noninteractive environment." He points out that there is "no give and take, it's largely one way. The result of that strained environment is that the communicators do not automatically use all their self-expression when looking into a camera or speaking on mike as they would in a face-to-face dialogue." Puffer adds: "What we try to do is restore that quality and feeling in the delivery. We try to trigger that part of the brain that is responsible for artistry, abstraction, etc."

Puffer also notes that he's not trying to make a person's voice sound like someone else's. "We all have developed and cultivated a wealth of knowledge regarding what is appropriate interpersonal communication over the years," he says. "We all know the tools; we know how loud to speak; how to emphasize and articulate our words; how to use our face and eyes with accompanying gestures; no one has to tell us how to do these things. The idea," Puffer adds, "is to tap into those resources and help bring them into the environment that is not interactive, like the broadcast studio."

# Getting Help with Your Delivery

If you are having problems with your voice, diction, and delivery, it's a good idea to deal with the problems while you are in college. Speech and debating courses sometimes help, but if you have serious problems, you may need a voice coach. Voice coach Carol Dearing advises students who are intent on being in front of a microphone or camera to "do all they can to prepare themselves before they leave college." She says that without professional help, some students "fall into habit patterns that will work against them."

## *Dialects*

Traditionally, station managers and news directors look for people who speak "standard American speech" when they hire on-air personnel. That's another way of saying they like Midwestern voices, which are considered "neutral."

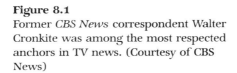

**Figure 8.1**
Former *CBS News* correspondent Walter Cronkite was among the most respected anchors in TV news. (Courtesy of CBS News)

Don't count yourself out if you were not born and reared in South Dakota. Some dialects can be eliminated with good coaching. If they cannot be corrected, it's still possible to work in an area where your dialect is the primary one. "If you have a Southern dialect you can work in the South," says coach Dearing, "but you are not likely to get on the air in Chicago." She said that same rule applies to people who were born and reared in Chicago. "If they have a strong big-city dialect they are not likely to make it in Dallas."

Mary Berger, a speech pathologist at Columbia College in Chicago who works with young people, says it's important to let students know, if they have a dialect that reflects a minority racial or ethnic background, that there is "nothing wrong with them. Many have been told that they are stupid because of the way they speak. Once you tell them that you do not intend to change the dialect but develop a new 'style' for use in the work place, they relax." Berger explains her methods in her book *Speak Standard, TOO*.

Like Jeff Puffer, Berger says many of her colleagues may consider her approach to speech problems "unorthodox." She recalls that she was asked by Columbia College to design a course after the college got feedback from graduates indicating that they were having trouble finding work because of voice problems.

"What we find in our classes," she notes, "are a lot of students with high-pitched, nasal-sounding, unpleasant voices not acceptable for air. We don't try to correct those problems in the traditional way, working on pitch and inflection, etc. What we do is give them an 'indirect hint' that says, 'Your voice is different but you can change it without too much help from us.'"

Berger says the first thing she has the students do is record their voices and then listen to them. "They detect immediately the high pitches and other things that they would like to change. Then we say, 'OK, now pretend that you are someone else, like newscaster Bill Curtis or a general giving orders to troops.' Amazingly, their voices suddenly get deeper."

Berger stresses that there are times when students obviously cannot change their readings. "When their voices are straining, for example, when they try to change their pitch, we direct them to people who deal with such problems."

Voice coach Carol Dearing says that pitch is one of the most troubling problems for young people. "Young ladies," she says, "usually have too high a pitch. When they read their copy, it sounds as if they are much younger and less credible than they really are." But Dearing warns young women that trying to change the pitch of their voice dramatically without professional help can be dangerous.

Dearing says another common problem is articulation. She says many people going into broadcasting have a minor lisp. But Dearing says this problem is easily correctable and should not prevent anyone from moving forward as a reporter or an anchor.

### *Listening to Yourself*

In the chapters on style, you learned that it is always a good idea to read your copy aloud because your ear catches mistakes and detects poorly constructed copy that your eye misses. Similarly, reading aloud alerts you to any problems you have with pronunciation, articulation, and awkward speech patterns.

## Getting Pronunciation Help

Newscasters should avoid using words that are difficult to pronounce. The mind understands the meaning of many words, but sometimes it has trouble relaying the pronunciation to the tongue, which causes newscasters to stumble over their copy. Tricky words and phrases invite trouble.

Sometimes writers and anchors have no choice, however. Proper names, for example, cannot be changed. Spelling them correctly does not guarantee that they will be pronounced correctly. The writer of a newscast must identify the correct pronunciation of any difficult names in a script. Reporters should ask the people whom they are interviewing for the proper pronunciation of their names. Names of towns also should be checked if there is any doubt. For example:

Biloxi in Mississippi is pronounced Bi-lok'-si.

Acadian in Louisiana is pronounced E-kay'-di-en.

Kankakee in Illinois is pronounced Kang'-ka-ke.

Cairo in Illinois is pronounced Ka'-ro.

If a job takes you to a new part of the country, it is a good idea to seek out someone who has lived in the area for some time. Colleagues who have been working at the station will be able to help, and someone at the local library or historical society will probably be happy to answer questions about the pronunciation of nearby towns or local family names.

The wire services send out pronunciation guides to their customers (see Figure 8.2). These are particularly useful when covering national and international stories. If your news operation is computerized, these guides should be stored for future use.

In cities large enough to have a wire service bureau, the staff will help its clients find the proper pronunciation of a name or place in the city or state. The

---

**NEWS**
*Hanan Ashrawi:* hah'-nahn ash-row'-ee
*Hafez Assad:* hah'-fez ah'-sahd
*Azerbaijan:* ah-zur-by-jahn'
*Bosnia-Herzegovina:* bahz'-nee-ah hurts-uh-goh-vee'-na
*Ciudad Juarez:* see-yoo-dahd' wah'-rehz
*Alberto Fujimori:* foo-jee-moh'-ree
*Moammar Gadhafi:* moo'-ah-mahr gah-dah'-fee
*Yegor Gaidar:* yay'-gohr gy'-dahr
*Hans-Dietrick Genscher:* hahnz'-dee'-trihk gen'-shur
*Guantanamo Bay:* gwan-tah'-nah-rnoh
*Inuit:* en-yoo-ft'
*Ahja Izetbegovic:* ah-lee'-yuh ee-zet-beh'-goh-vitch
*Kabul:* kah'-bool
*Francois Mitterrand:* frahn-swah' mee-teh-rahn'
*Hosni Mubarak:* hahs'-nee tnoo-bah'-rahk
*Jorge Muniz:* hohr'-hay rnoo'-nyees
*Nagorno-Karabakh:* nuh-gohr'-noh kah-ruh-bahk'
*Najibullak:* nah-jee-boo'-lah
*Nunavut:* noon'-uh-vuht
*Turgut Ozal:* toor-guht' uh-zahl'
*Sarajevo:* sehr-uh-yay'-voh
*Tanjug:* tahn'-yoog

**SPORTS**
*Danielle Ammaccapane:* ahm-uh-kuh-pahn'-ee
*Bill Koch:* kohk
*Mario Lemieux:* leh-myoo'
*Liselotte Neumann:* lee'-suh-lot noy'-muhn
*Bob Plager:* play'-gur
*Brian Sutter:* sut'-ur

**Figure 8.2**   An AP pronunciation guide.

wires also have a phonetics desk that helps with hard-to-pronounce names in national and international news stories.

In Chapter 1, you learned that it is not always necessary to use the names of foreign dignitaries. If you do use them, it is a good idea to refer to the dignitaries by their titles during the rest of the story, particularly if the names are unusually difficult to pronounce.

When using difficult names, write them phonetically in the copy to help the person who will be reading the script. (See Figure 8.3 for an example of how to spell phonetically.) The phonetic spelling can be given after the word or written above the word. Writers working on a newscast should ask the anchors which style they prefer. Here are examples of the two methods:

Cayuga (Ka-yoo'-ga) Indians still live on the land.

(Ka-yoo'-ga)
Cayuga Indians still live on the land.

Dictionaries, which give the proper pronunciation of words as well as their meanings, are invaluable tools. Several dictionaries of pronunciation are also available for purchase, and most newsrooms keep copies on hand. If you are unsure about the pronunciation of a word, look it up.

# Pacing

What else can you do to improve your delivery? *CBS News* correspondent Charles Osgood says pacing is important. Osgood advises using a pause to get attention when you want something you just said "to sink in. . . . A pause can be very telling, provided you know something." He says the "most remarkable pacer in our business is ABC newscaster Paul Harvey. You can drive a truck between 'Paul Harvey' and 'good day.' He's doing that for a reason."

Osgood recalls times when he's been traveling with a news crew and everyone is talking among themselves until Harvey begins broadcasting. "When Paul Harvey comes on the radio," Osgood says, "everybody stops [talking] and listens to Paul Harvey. You cannot not listen to that man."

Osgood says: "You can hate him. You can think he's terrible. You can disagree with him completely as far as his politics are concerned. But you can't not listen to him, because he has got you. He has found out how to say, 'Hey, shut up. I'm talking now.'"

Here are excerpts from a "Paul Harvey News" broadcast "One Vote," which aired on April 4, 1996:

One voter in each precinct in the United States will determine the next President of the United States.

One vote. That's a big weapon you have there, Mister.

-A-
AY for long A (as in mate)
A for short A (as in cat)
AI for nasal A (as in air)
AH for soft A (as in father)
AW for broad A (as in talk)

-E-
EE for long F (as in meat)
EH for short F (as in get)
UH for hollow F, or schwa (as in the)
AY for French long E with acute accent (as in Pathe)
IH for middle E (as in pretty)
EW for EW dipthong (as in few)

-I-
IGH for long I (as in time)
EE for French long I (as in machine)
IH for short I (as in pity)

-O-
OH for long O (as in note or though)
AH for short O (as in hot)
AW for broad O (as in fought)
OO for long double O (as in fool or through)
OW for OW diphthong (as in how)

-U-
EW for long U (as in mule)
OO for long U (as in rule)
U for middle U (as in put)
UH for short U (as in shut)

**Consonants**
K for hard C (as in cat)
S for soft C (as in cease)
SH for soft CH (as in machine)
CR for hard CR or TCH (as in catch)
Z for hard S (as in disease)
S for soft S (as in sun)
G for hard G (as in gang)
J for soft G (as in general)
ZH for soft J (as in French version of Joliet)

**Figure 8.3**   A phonetic pronunciation guide from UPI.

**Figure 8.4**
News Commentator
Paul Harvey. (Courtesy
of Paul Harvey News)

In 1948, just one additional vote in each precinct would have elected Dewey. In 1960 one vote in each precinct in Illinois would have elected Nixon. One Vote.

One morning in 1844, a grain miller from DeKalb County, Indiana, was walking toward his mill. It was election day but he had work to do and did not intend to vote. Before he reached the mill, however, he was stopped by friends who persuaded him to go to the polls. As it happened, the candidate for whom he voted won a seat in the state legislature . . . by a margin of one vote.

Now . . . When the Indiana Legislature convened, the man elected from DeKalb cast the deciding vote that sent Edward Allen Hennegan to the United States Senate. Then, in the Senate, when the question of statehood for Texas came up, there was a tie vote. But who do you suppose was presiding as President pro tempore? Hennegan. He cast the deciding vote from the chair.

So Texas was admitted to the Union because a miller in DeKalb County, Indiana, went ten minutes out of his way to cast . . . one vote.

More?

Thomas Jefferson was elected President by one vote in the Electoral College. So was John Quincy Adams. Rutherford B. Hayes was elected President by one vote. One vote gave statehood to California, Idaho, Oregon, Texas, and Washington. The Draft Act of World War Two passed the House by one vote.

Almost two hundred million Americans are eligible to vote this year. Fewer than half will.

Plato said it: "The penalty good men pay for indifference to public affairs is to be ruled by evil men."

So your one vote is important. Historically you use it . . . or you will lose it.

Tell the world if you don't want to vote, but don't pretend it makes no difference. Tell the world you no longer want to think and act for yourself, but don't figure you can relax and let George do it. Because sometimes George sells his vote for a bottle of cheap booze to the very men who stand for everything you are against.

If you're not sure for whom you should vote, turn to a newspaper you can trust. Because everything we've won in 10 wars at the point of a gun can be taken away a vote at a time.

Edmund Burke said it another way: "All that is necessary for the forces of evil to win in the world is for enough good men to *do nothing*."

Osgood says that when he writes for himself he uses a lot of ellipses (series of three dots). "I want to remind myself that that is supposed to be a pause. I will also capitalize certain words . . . because I want to hit that particular word for it to work."

The *CBS News* correspondent also says it's important to remember when you are on the air that "you're talking to somebody, which means that you have to be conscious at all times that there's somebody there." Osgood notes that you can't assume people are listening; you "have to get their attention, you don't automatically have it."

# Marking Copy

Most newscasters mark copy to help them remember when to pause or to emphasize certain words. They mark the copy as they read it aloud, which also helps them control their breathing. Long sentences require extra breath, so newscasters must either pause more often or rewrite the sentence. Otherwise, they sound as though they are running out of breath. Often, inexperienced newscasters try to speed up their delivery when they realize that they might have trouble getting through a complicated sentence, but that's a poor solution. If you find yourself leaning toward this solution, rewrite your copy until you can read it at a normal pace.

Here is an example of copy marked by a newscaster.

| | |
|---|---|
| | B) THE SALT RIVER PROJECT'S WEST VALLEY SERVICE CENTER HAS BEEN CLOSED AFTER TESTS SHOW THE PRESENCE OF LEGIONNAIRES' DISEASE |
| TAKE 1/2¼ VO :00 | S-R-P CLOSED THE CENTER AT TOTH AVENUE AND VAN BUREN. . . AS A SAFETY PRECAUTION. |
| VG: 79TH AVE & VAN BUREN SRP CENTER CLOSED | THAT'S AFTER THE PRESENCE OF A WATER-CARRIED BACTERIA THAT CAUSES LEGIONNAIRES' WAS FOUND. |
| | THE COMPANY DID NOT WANT TO ENDANGER ITS 200 EMPLOYEES AT THE CENTER . . . SALT RIVER SAYS IT EXPECTS TO REMOVE THE BACTERIA AND RE-OPEN THE |
| END TAPE :20 | BUILDING TUESDAY. |
| | LEGIONNAIRES' IS A RARE DISEASE NORMALLY FOUND IN HUMID CLIMATES . . . BUT THERE WERE 17 CASES REPORTED IN ARIZONA. |

Bruce Kirk, an anchor at KPNX-TV in Phoenix, who marked the example script, uses slash marks to indicate pauses and underlines words that he wishes to emphasize. Some anchors use a double underline for words that require extraordinary emphasis. Other anchors use all caps for words they wish to stress. Some anchors use ellipses to indicate pauses, and others use dashes. Some anchors like their scripts typed in all caps, whereas others prefer upper- and lowercase (which, according to studies, is easier to read).

Christine Devine, an anchor for KTTV in Los Angeles, who marked this next example, says she doesn't always have time to mark her script, but when she does "it results in a better show." Devine uses a bracket to let herself know she's starting to read a new paragraph and a new thought, and she uses brackets after a sound bite so she doesn't lose her place. She uses an ellipsis to signify the end of a phrase, but not the end of a thought.

Devine underlines key words for emphasis, which seems to be standard practice among anchors. She also routinely underlines "not." In addition, Devine says she underlines for contrast when, for example, contrasting Republicans and Democrats.

| ANCHOR | (CO) |
|---|---|
| I-DEADLY FIRES | TWO PEOPLE ARE DEAD TONIGHT AFTER SEPARATE FIRES IN TWO SOUTHLAND CITIES. |
| | A BLAZE SWEPT THROUGH A HOME IN ORANGE EARLY THIS MORNING . . . FATALLY INJURING AN ELDERLY WOMAN AND LEAVING HER HUSBAND CRITICALLY INJURED. |
| | OFFICIALS SAY THE FIRE WAS SPARKED BY A NATURAL GAS EXPLOSION IN THE COUPLE'S KITCHEN. |

# Characteristics of Successful Anchors

Jim Boyer, the news director of WWL-TV in New Orleans says that "people watch people. They don't watch helicopters or satellites and they prefer to watch people they like and are comfortable with." Boyer says one of his anchors, Bill Elder, has anchored on WWL for 20 years. Boyer says viewers are comfortable with him. He's like an old friend telling them what's going on and it's very easy for them to watch. Elder says it's also important for anchors to be involved in the production of the show. He says he writes at least a third of the news, even on days when he's working on special projects.

Edwin Pfeiffer, General Manager of WDVM-TV in Washington, says his top anchor, Gordon Peterson, is respected for both his reliability and his credibility. But he adds, he's also liked because people appreciate his wry sense of humor as a reflection of a person who isn't all that serious about himself. Jerry Turner, an anchor with WJZ-TV in Baltimore, says it's important to "keep up with things. I make it a point," he says, "to keep up with all the rock bands and things like that which appeal to younger people."

John Bobel, the President of TALENTBANK, stresses that it is important for anchors to understand that there is more to the job than looking and sounding good on the air. They also should be involved in the community through personal appearances or charity work. Bobel says it's important for anchors to be working journalists. They should be able to handle a school board meeting or a foreign story with equal ease.

Most news directors use the same language when they speak about successful anchors, and words like *credibility*, *honesty*, and *genuine* keep cropping up, along with concern and caring about what's going on in the community. Another common denominator is that successful, top-rated anchors are all genial people who are well liked by their co-workers and their viewers.

# Ratings Wars

Of course, what keeps anchors in their jobs, particularly for long periods, are ratings and the numbers. These factors are especially important for the celebrity-type anchors who come into our homes every morning to provide entertainment in addition to news. Almost every local TV station has programs now that copy the network shows like *Good Morning America* and *Today*. The local shows often complement the network productions.

Nowhere on television is the battle for ratings and survival as keen as it is in the morning, with CBS, ABC, and NBC trying to come up with fresh approaches to news and entertainment. On the plus side, this mixture is more palatable than the stuff that often tries to pass as news in the late evening hours—a subject that we have discussed in great detail, particularly in Chapter 22, "Tabloid Journalism."

Those who produce the morning shows rely more on personalities than anything else, although some of the anchors have strong news backgrounds. Morning anchors have changed frequently, and the ratings have flip-flopped over the years, but *Today* has been dominant most of the time, with *Good*

*Morning America* in the second slot. CBS has had trouble finding the right formula and the right anchors for *The Early Show*.

Despite spending a reported $30 million on a new studio, *The Early Show* had little success in finding viewers in 2000. CBS is reportedly paying almost $5 million a year to Bryant Gumbel to try to rescue its morning prime viewing time from the doldrums it has suffered for so long. But according to Brill's *Content* magazine, Gumbel, who is one of the most successful African American news and sports personalities on TV, faces a difficult task. Since *The Early Show* was relaunched with Gumbel and coanchor Jane Clayson in fall 1999, the program has scored lower ratings than it did before when it featured lesser-known hosts. According to the April–May Nielsen ratings of 2001, the CBS program scored a 2.0, while *Good Morning America* pulled a 3.3 and *Today* averaged a 5.2.

Gumbel's career certainly has been distinguished. He started out writing freelance articles for *Black Sports* magazine in 1971 and quickly became a staff writer. The next year he moved into TV as a weekend sportscaster at KNBC-TV in Los Angeles, and in 1976 he became the station's sports director, a position he held until 1980. He was a frequent sports reporter during that time for NBC and *Today*.

A year later, Gumbel became a co-anchor with Jane Pauley on *Today*. While he was with *Today* for 15 years, he worked with executive producer Steve Friedman and formed the strong alliance and friendship that still exists today. Gumbel left NBC for CBS in 1997. It still remains to be seen how this talented and controversial personality will do over the long haul in his new role with *The Early Show*.

# Cosmetics

It has always been true that anchor people, in addition to having good voices, also must be attractive on camera. Fortunately, the problem of "looks" is not quite as bad as it once was when it was virtually impossible to get on camera unless you were beautiful or handsome. News managers still want people with pleasing faces, regardless of race or gender, but we do see anchors wearing glasses, and wrinkles are not outlawed, as they once were. But those who select their on-camera talent often want to change their looks and delivery, even though they liked them well enough to hire them.

Among the absurdities that anchors must sometimes put up with from their bosses is this particularly amusing one related by *ABC News* correspondent Judy Muller when she was still at CBS. According to Judy, her boss called her into his office to complain about the way she was saying the traditional cutaway phrase before a commercial break—"Now this." At the time, Muller didn't think the criticism was very funny. She said it is memorable to her because it "took aim at possibly the only thing I was secure about at the time: my on-air delivery."

Muller was puzzled because she asked herself: How many ways can you say "Now this?" But she said she dutifully practiced different inflections: with

**Figure 8.5** Hillary Clinton joins *The Early Show*'s Bryant Gumbel at a town meeting hosted by WTVH-TV in Syracuse, New York. (CBS Photo Archive)

authority, drawn out in a provocative manner, queried in an inquisitive manner, "every way until I had it just right, which is basically the way I was saying it before, but with a touch of suspense."

This encounter with a boss over such a petty issue is described by Muller as a lesson in understanding that, just when you think you've got a thing wired, something comes along to short-circuit that notion, to pull you up short and remind you that now, of all things, you "must deal with *this*. It may be something petty, or improbable, or unpredictable, but you cannot proceed without dealing with it."

Muller obviously did not forget the lesson. Many years later when she wrote her memoirs she called the book: *Now This* (Putnam Publishing Group, 2000). In her book, Muller also recalls an incident when she moved into TV reporting for the first time and was given some advice on how to improve her appearance.

A consultant hired by ABC News to help new correspondents took Muller into a screening room where they looked at some of the correspondent's stories. After viewing a few of them, the consultant told Muller that she obviously did not need any help with her writing or delivery. Muller then asked about her looks. "Well," the consultant replied, "I really only have one word for you." Muller asked: "And what would that word be?" The consultant leaned close to Muller and whispered in her ear: "*Scarves*. I think they will help soften your angular face." Muller said that during her radio career she didn't have to worry about her angular face. She said that she never realized that she *had* an angular face.

Muller said she began to understand that the "face" thing is important to the people who hired you, like the day she arrived at the Los Angeles Bureau with a new, very short haircut, and the person on the newsdesk said with a shocked expression: "Did you talk to *New York* before doing that?" Muller replied: "No, I didn't know I had to." As for the consultant, Muller said despite the advice she never managed to get into scarves, much less figure out how to tie them.

Muller says despite all the attention given to cosmetics by TV producers and managers, she still believes that, scarves or no scarves: "A reporter's best accessory is the string of words that, like so many pearls, can make for a beautiful story."

Muller added that good camera presence has always been an asset for television reporters, but more and more, at least at the magazine shows, correspondents are increasingly valued more for that attribute than their writing skills.

In her memoir *Reporting Live* (Simon & Schuster, 1999), Lesley Stahl, a long-time *60 Minutes* correspondent, recalls that when she was hired for the job by Executive Producer Don Hewitt, he told Stahl that there was just one thing that he wanted her to change. Sensitive to what he was about to tell Stahl, he prepared her: "I have to do something that I'm afraid is going to make you angry," he went on. "You're going to be really upset with me. I hate to say this." Stahl replied: "What already?" Hewitt blurted out: "I hate your hair, you have to change it, it's too stiff."

Stahl writes that if she had been younger, "I would have chafed at the insult—how dare he." But she wasn't offended. She told Hewitt that because she couldn't be futzing with her hair in the middle of covering the White House, with everything that was going on, she teased her hair and sprayed it and forgot about it. But she told Hewitt: "If you want me to change it, no problem, I'll change it." Stahl said that she spent as much time as she could spare on her appearance. She got her hair done twice a week and bought enough makeup "to open my own boutique."

Stahl recalled another occasion when she and a group of correspondents were meeting with the President of CBS News, Eric Ober, and he complained that there seemed to be a reluctance at the network to discuss cosmetics. He noted that one of CBS' finest correspondents, Bob Simon, needed voice lessons. Stahl said eyes met in horror, and she yelled out: "Guess it's time for my facelift!" "No!" said Ober. "Older is more authoritative. People want their news from older-looking people." "Thanks," replied Stahl.

Stahl also admitted that there were many times when she was anxiety-ridden on the air when she was co-anchor of *CBS Morning News*. "I never froze," she said, "but I tightened up when the camera light went on. I did this strange thing," she continued, "that showed some teeth that was supposedly my smile, but I couldn't look into that camera and be me." She added: "That's the most important thing for anybody on television. The audience can sense when you're not relaxed, and they don't like it." Stahl said her mother called her to say that she had found a teacher for her—to teach her how to smile. Stahl said she had a lesson and "had to find 'me' in there, and that took a long time."

Asked if working as an anchor made her respect the work that network anchors do, she replied that she had always respected their work; not because they read well, but because of the way they perform in a crisis: "A space shuttle disaster, the President's been shot—when they're thrown on the air and don't know the complete story and are flying by the seat of their pants. This is when they earn their money," she added. "The anchors remain calm and set the tone for the public so they don't panic."

# Summary

If you wish to report or anchor for radio and television, you must analyze your voice as soon as you can. One of your instructors may be able to tell you if you need help and where you can get it. If speech courses are not offered in your journalism program, seek out the speech department. Consider the help of a coach if you have some special problems with your voice or diction.

Remember that a regional or cultural dialect will not necessarily eliminate you from contention as a reporter or anchor. Many of those problems, if they can't be eliminated, can at least be modified sufficiently for you to work in the area where you were born and reared.

If you have a good voice, learn to use it properly. Get accustomed to reading your copy aloud before you go in front of a microphone. In addition to alerting you to grammatical errors or awkward phrases you may have missed, reading your copy aloud helps you discover that certain words and names in the copy are hard to pronounce. If so, add the phonetic spellings next to or above the difficult names and places. Last, reading your copy aloud gives you the opportunity to determine what words you want to emphasize and how you can use pacing effectively.

# Review Questions

1. Name some of the talents you must develop if you wish to become a radio reporter.
2. What additional talents will you need if you wish to report or anchor for television?
3. If you are having troubles of any kind with your voice, how soon should you get an evaluation?
4. If you have problems with diction, breathing, or dialect, what kind of help can you get?

5.   What are some of the approaches to solving voice problems?

6.   Two of the voice coaches quoted in this chapter say some of their techniques might be considered unorthodox. Discuss.

7.   The wire services offer some pronunciation assistance to their clients. What kind of help do they provide?

8.   Why is Paul Harvey so effective in getting and holding an audience's attention?

9.   Why do anchors mark their copy? What are some of the symbols they use?

# Exercises

1.   Read a few newspaper stories silently and then read them into a tape recorder. Make a note of the things you discovered were a problem in the copy only after reading it aloud. After making appropriate changes in the copy, read the story into the tape recorder a second time, and note any improvements.

2.   Write a one-minute radio script based on information from a newspaper or newspaper wire. Then read the script into a tape recorder. Listen to the recording, and make notes on anything that you did not like about your reading, such as inflection, breathing, pitch, or pace.

3.   Do a second reading, but this time mark your copy before doing so. After reading, note whether your delivery improved.

4.   Go through a newspaper or newspaper wire copy and find words that are unfamiliar to you. Look up the words in a dictionary for meaning and pronunciation and in a pronunciation guide if one is available. Write the words phonetically along with the rest of the sentences, and read them into a tape recorder. Then replay the tape for other members of your class, and note whether they understood the meaning of the words.

5.   After you have noted the words that fellow students did not understand, find synonyms for them and rerecord the sentences with the new words. See if the students understand the copy this time.

# **9** Finding the News

Most national and international news comes into a newsroom from the Associated Press (AP) wire service. Most local news comes from a combination of sources and activities, including the police and fire departments, the courts and various other municipal institutions, and community and business organizations. Local news also is generated by the routine follow-up of the leads and tips that pour into the assignment desk on a continuing basis from beat reporters, tipsters, and even non-news personnel who work for the station. This chapter and Chapter 16, "Collecting Information from Documents," examine all these news sources.

## The Wires

The term *wires* is still used to describe the services offered by news-gathering organizations such as the Associated Press and Reuters, a British firm. The word *wires* refers to the telegraph cables that were originally used to transmit the news to newspaper clients. Today, the AP feeds news to radio and TV customers, as well as newspapers. The news is distributed not by wires but via satellite to machines or computers. A few newsrooms still use the actual printers, but most radio and TV stations have converted to systems that allow the news to be fed directly into computers in the newsrooms and at the anchor desks. Writers, producers, and anchors can print out stories that interest them, and if they wish, the anchors can read the material live from the video screens at their desks.

Most small-market radio stations use the AP broadcast wire that transmits hourly summaries of the news. The broadcast wire is designed for those stations with little or no news operation. The broadcast wire is popularly referred to as the "rip-and-read" wire because that is the way these summaries are most often used at stations lacking staff to rewrite news copy. The stories are designed to be read without any rewriting.

Some radio and TV stations, usually in large markets, also subscribe to an AP newspaper wire, called the *A Wire*, which provides considerably more detail about national and international news than the broadcast wire because A-Wire stories are written primarily with newspapers in mind. The A Wire also moves many more stories than the broadcast wire. Because the A-Wire stories are written in newspaper style, however, they are virtually impossible to read on the air without a rewrite (see Chapter 6). So, there is little purpose in subscribing to the A Wire unless someone is available to rewrite the copy.

The AP also provides *splits* on the broadcast and main wires throughout the day and night. Splits are stories of state and regional interest sent to radio and TV customers from bureaus in your state and surrounding states.

In addition to the various wires, the AP also provides a variety of audio feeds via satellite, including news on the hour and the half-hour, special reports on the hour's major stories, and an hourly feed of actualities and natural sound. The AP also provides scripted national and international news, agricultural reports, business news, sports, entertainment news, special features, and a headline service designed for what the AP describes as stations with "a limited news appetite."

The AP also provides several photo and graphics services, including an interactive database that supplies thousands of head shots, maps, and images of breaking news and a high-speed, digital photo network that delivers color photos to TV stations.

## Television Satellite Feeds

Television stations also receive a steady stream of sound bites and reports via closed-circuit feeds, usually referred to as *newsfeeds*, by the networks and various independent producers. Although satellite technology has changed the way newsfeeds are transmitted, the networks have been feeding local stations with news for years. Other companies offer custom-made newscasts throughout the day.

Radio and TV stations also can buy satellite-delivered information about health and medicine, finance, weather, sports, consumer news, and numerous other subjects. Multiply the paid syndication services by 25 and you probably have a figure close to the number of organizations and companies that dump free information on satellites each day. The information is free because it's promoting an organization or a cause. Among those making use of satellites are associations representing the chemical, gas, sugar, and scores of other industries; the American Legion; the FBI; various religious and health-related organizations; public relations companies; and a variety of universities. Some of the free material is produced as a public service, but most is pure public relations.

## The Internet

Radio and TV stations rely heavily on the Internet for news and research; however, anything taken from the Internet must be used with caution and attri-

**Figure 9.1**
Vides News Editor Brian Waldrep and
Operations Manager David Koors of
WBRZ-TV, Baton Rouge, Louisiana, check
video being fed from a microwave truck.
(Photo by James Terry)

bution because a lot of the information is not reliable. (For more discussion on
the Internet, see Chapter 17, "Computer-Assisted Reporting.")

# Newspapers

Many broadcast news managers do not like to admit it, but they often rely on
newspapers as a source of news. Because they have much larger news staffs and
more room for news, newspapers often have stories that broadcast newsrooms
miss or do not bother to cover.

Some stations rely on newspapers more than others. Stations with enough
reporters to do a good job covering the local scene are less dependent on newspapers than are stations with small news staffs. Some stations are constantly
playing "catch-up" because they cannot compete with the newspaper's beat
system.

Broadcast newsrooms often find themselves trying to figure out ways to take
a good newspaper story and *advance* it. Advancing the story—finding some new
development to make it appear new or at least fresh—is often considered a justification for "borrowing" the information developed by the newspaper. It's
important to remember, however, that if a newspaper is the *only* source for a
story, it is ethically proper—and a necessary protection in case the information
is not accurate—to attribute the story to the newspaper. Remember also that

most newspapers copyright their material. Few papers object when their stories are broadcast, as long as credit is given. Some news directors take the position that once the accuracy of information first disclosed in a newspaper has been independently verified by the station, it is no longer necessary to credit the paper.

Although good broadcast news operations should rely as little as possible on newspapers for story ideas, papers should be mandatory reading for everyone in the broadcast newsroom. Broadcast editors and writers find that reading newspapers is often a good way to double-check the facts in a wire story. Also, it is not unusual for national papers such as *The New York Times* and *The Washington Post* to have details or new angles on a story that are not included in the wire versions.

## Monitoring Radios

Every newsroom should have radios that monitor police and fire department channels, which broadcast every fire or police call that is being answered in the station's immediate area. Someone should monitor the radios constantly. The station that ignores the radio gets scooped by the competition.

Scanning devices on radios can monitor police and fire channels at the same time. The scanners hop back and forth, pausing whenever anyone starts to speak. The chatter is difficult to hear at times, but with practice it becomes easier to decipher, particularly if you learn the special codes used by authorities. One of the most common systems used by police is known as the 10-code, which uses *signal codes* that vary from city to city. For example, in New Orleans, 10–55 means a police officer needs assistance. In Baton Rouge, that message is a signal 63. A robbery in progress in Baton Rouge is a signal 42, but in New Orleans it's a 65. Some cities, including New Orleans, use the state's criminal code numbers. A homicide is a signal 30, a driving while intoxicated (DWI) incident is 599, and a hit-and-run is 100. Because cities use different systems, you'll need to learn the codes when you enter a new market. They should be posted near or on the radio.

None of the information obtained from these radio scanners is ever to be used alone in writing a story for broadcast; the incidents must be checked out by phone. The police and fire reports often turn out to be unfounded or less serious than one might expect from the code. It is also a violation of Federal Communications Commission (FCC) regulations to rebroadcast any material heard on police, fire, or ham radio broadcasts.

## Making Phone Calls

Unless a station has someone on duty overnight, which is not that common except in large markets, the first member of the news staff to arrive at the station each day should call police and fire department headquarters. Large cities provide a special phone number and public relations staff just to handle the media. For the most part, however, reporters deal with the police and fire dispatchers.

News staffs, particularly in medium-sized and large markets, routinely make other telephone calls. Before and during rush hours, they check on auto traffic and commuter train and bus service to see if any major delays are present. During bad weather, such information becomes more critical. Trains and buses may not be moving. The roads may be treacherous. School officials may call in to report closings, and that information is important in *every* market.

During bad weather, the news staff also takes calls from the Parent-Teacher Association (PTA), the Rotary Club, the YWCA, the local theater group, and numerous other organizations that may cancel events because of the weather. The newsroom should have a complete list of emergency telephone numbers on rotary files, clipboards, or in the computer. The local gas and electric companies will have information on disruptions of service and potentially dangerous situations brought on by snowstorms, tornadoes, and earthquakes.

A serious snowstorm turns a routine weather report into a lead story. News staffs check with the local weather bureau at least every hour, and perhaps more often during a potentially disastrous weather situation.

# Stringers

Many stations—both radio and television—have working relationships with *stringers*, people who are not on the payroll but who are paid for stories that they develop, or who cover breaking news at night when no one is working at the station. Stringers often help a station avoid the embarrassment of missing a story that breaks overnight. Some stringers have their own camera gear, and some TV stations provide gear to stringers who are productive.

Many news directors also have arrangements with firefighters or police officers on duty overnight who agree to call the news director at home if an important story breaks. Some stations encourage viewers to submit stories shot on home video recorders if the stories have news value. Such video must be aired with extreme caution, however, because of the potential for deception, libel, and other problems.

# Tipsters

Most stations also encourage people to call with news tips. Some even pay for such information. It is surprising just how much news is generated this way.

All tips should be taken seriously. Many are about breaking news stories—a shooting heard from the listener's bedroom window or a fire spotted by someone walking the dog. Other tips come from people who are upset for some reason. It may have to do with something going on in local government or at the plant where they work. If possible, get the caller's name and phone number. Tipsters often refuse to identify themselves, but assignment editors should not make the mistake of thinking that most people who call a radio or TV station are cranks. Stations do receive a lot of crank calls, but newspeople must consider every phone call to be potentially important.

One of the news producers for a network investigative unit made the mistake of telling a tipster to "write a letter," which is one of the worst ways to deal with someone who calls with information about a story. Instead of writing a letter, the tipster called another network, which assigned a producer to check out the information. The story attracted national attention when it was broadcast. (The topic of tipsters is discussed further in Chapter 18, "Developing Sources.")

## Employee Input

Story ideas often come from people on the news staff—reporters, producers, anchors, desk assistants, and others—and some ideas even originate with secretaries and people in the mailroom.

People working in news seem to develop a sense that alerts them to news in all sorts of places. A producer waiting to cross the street near a bus stop suddenly got a blast of soot in her face. As she recovered, she noticed that a passing city bus continued to emit a steady stream of pollutants as it moved down the block. Standing next to the angry producer was a police officer. "Did you see that?" yelled the producer. "What?" replied the officer. "All that pollution!" The police officer looked a little confused by the observation and shrugged his shoulders as if to say, "So what?"

The producer could not wait to get to the newsroom to share her experience with the assignment editor. The editor listened intently and agreed that there might be a story. A couple of telephone calls later, the assignment editor strolled over to the producer's desk and said: "The reason that cop gave you a blank stare is because we don't have any laws that cover air pollution in this city." That was the start of a good series on pollution.

Everyone on the staff should be encouraged to develop story ideas. One news director uses the station's newsletter to encourage non-news employees to stop by the assignment editor's desk if they see or hear anything that might make a news story.

Assignment editors do listen to a lot of stories, and some of the stories do generate news, but assignment editors do more than just listen. They are responsible for collecting and organizing most of the source material that comes into a newsroom.

**Figure 9.2**  Assignment desk at WTVJ-TV, Miami. (Courtesy of
WTVJ, Miami)

Sometimes the assignment desk is small. There may be one person in charge
of assignments, and then only during the daytime. Assignment editors are found
mostly in TV newsrooms, but some large radio news operations in major cities
also employ them. At many radio stations, and some small TV stations, the news
director or perhaps an assistant news director functions as an assignment editor
but does not have that title. Large-market TV stations normally have at least two
assignment editors—one for the morning and one for the evening. In the largest
newsrooms, the assignment desk operates around-the-clock.

Almost everything starts at the assignment desk because that is where all
the information enters the system. Assignment editors are the "keepers" of the
news wires. They monitor the wires constantly, looking for stories that will be
of interest to producers who are responsible for putting newscasts on the air.
Some of these stories are assigned to reporters. Others are given to writers for
read stories or, perhaps, to be used for V-SOTs. Still others need follow-up by
the assignment editor. In a breaking story, that follow-up is immediate.

# Sounding the Alarm

A desk assistant is the first to hear the fire department advisory. It's obviously a
bad one. He tells the assignment editor, and she listens for about 15 seconds,

long enough to know that she has to get people moving on it. She calls the crew room. As she waits for an answer, she calls to the reporter who is listening to the radio: "Frank, let's go." Frank heads for the door.

By the time Frank reaches the microwave truck, the assignment editor has figured out exactly where the fire is and the best way to get there. She gives the information to the cameraman on the two-way radio and turns up the volume on the scanner. The producer of the six o'clock news notices all the sudden activity and is quickly informed that a reporter and a photographer are already on the way to a major fire.

On a fire story, especially in the middle of the afternoon, the microwave truck is used for a variety of reasons: to get some live reports on the air before the evening newscast, if warranted, and to go live from the scene during the newscast.

As soon as the truck arrives at the scene, the microwave rod is set up to make sure that a picture can be sent back to the station. A monitor is set up at the assignment desk, as well as in the master control room, where the actual feed comes in, so that the assignment editor will know if it's possible to get a live shot. The producer will also be waiting for that information.

Meanwhile, the assignment editor and her desk assistant are working the phones. The desk assistant says he caught something on the scanner about two hospitals—City General and St. Joseph's. Another reporter has been waiting at the assignment desk for orders, and now she gets them: "Go to City General Hospital." Another photographer is already sitting in the station's other microwave truck, waiting to roll.

And so it goes for the rest of the afternoon and into the late evening. A third reporter, who has been covering another story, is pulled off it by the assignment editor and sent to the second hospital. The assignment editor and her desk assistant get as much information about the fire and deaths and injuries as they can from the scanner and the telephones to support what the reporters are finding out at the scene.

Conversation is almost continuous among the reporters and those at the assignment desk as they all share this information. The assignment editor and the desk assistant also take notes for the producers and on everything from font information to the number of deaths and injuries and the status of the fire.

The assignment editor's desk is also the clearinghouse for exchanges between the reporters and the producers. After the first report is finished at the top of the six o'clock news, the producer may tell the assignment editor he wants an update in 20 minutes. That information is relayed to the microwave truck, and in a few minutes the producer is told: "You got it!"

As things settle down, a reporter checks in from the scene saying fire officials suspect arson and will hold a news conference in 20 minutes. There is an unconfirmed report that someone may already be under arrest. Next, the editor is on the radio with the crew at St. Joseph's, telling them: "Break down and get to Fire Department headquarters immediately for a news conference. Tell John [the reporter] that I will talk to him when you get rolling."

Meanwhile, the desk assistant has tried to get more information on the advisory. A call to fire department headquarters confirms the report on the news conference, but the official refuses to say anything about an arrest.

"Tell the producer," says the assignment editor, and the desk assistant takes off. Within minutes, the producer has the new copy on its way to the anchor desk. The newscast will be over before the news conference gets under way, but the anchor reads the new copy and promises the viewing audience: "We'll have details on the news conference at 11 o'clock and, of course, we'll break into our regular programming with any new details on the fire as soon as we receive them."

# Developing Story Ideas

Fires and crimes do get a lot of coverage on local newscasts, but assignment editors have to look for other, nonbreaking news to fill an hour or longer newscast. To accomplish this goal, they must be part journalist and part detective.

They must examine every wire story to see if any possible angle can be developed into a good local story. Chapter 6 mentioned how important it is to look for a local angle in national and international stories. This search is constant at the assignment desk. For example, if the unemployment figures out of Washington are bad, the assignment editor tries to develop a story about local effects. Have the local unemployment figures gone up too, or did the community do better than the rest of the nation? What are the opinions of the people at the unemployment office—those on line and those behind the desk? How are shop owners doing? If local unemployment has worsened, has it had an effect on their businesses?

What about inflation? If Washington reports an increase, how has it affected shoppers? The assignment editor might send a reporter to a supermarket. The manager might admit that prices have been going up, and you can bet the people at the checkout line will speak out.

The assignment editor also looks for ways to update a story. The fire story detailed earlier presents lots of opportunities. There will be interviews at the hospitals with the injured as their condition improves. The arson investigation will provide updates, and if someone is arrested, that would provide another update.

# Interaction

Assignment editors probably interact with more people than anyone else in the newsroom, which is why they are so essential to a good news operation. In the fire story, you saw the assignment editor's interaction with producers, photographers, and reporters. A close, harmonious working relationship must exist between those at the assignment desk and all these people. During a breaking story, the assignment editor must control the coverage of the story firmly from the start. The news director usually keeps a close eye on what is going on, but more often he or she allows the assignment editor to run the show.

When things are quieter, more dialogue is likely to take place between the producer and those at the desk. The producer often influences assignment decisions on nonbreaking stories. If the producer is not interested in a story, the assignment editor may think twice about giving it to a reporter, but many assignments have to be made before the producer even arrives in the newsroom. The producer has to accept the assignment editor's judgment in covering stories. Once reporters have been assigned to stories, the producer has to try to work most of them into the newscast. Otherwise, there would not be enough material for the newscast.

As you learned earlier, once reporters are on the road, the assignment editor keeps the producer informed about their progress. Some stories may not work and will be killed. A reporter may inform the desk that his story is not as strong as it first appeared and so will be shorter than anticipated. Another reporter may say her story will be longer. Producers must know all this in planning for the newscast.

Interaction with the camerapeople also takes much of the assignment editor's time and tact. A good relationship is vital. Generally, local stations assign just one photographer to a microwave truck. When a story is breaking, as in the case of the fire we just discussed, a station sometimes assigns a two-person crew (if an extra person is available) so that the photographer can shoot without worrying about setting up and monitoring the live shot. This is particularly true if the story breaks just before airtime. Some stations in large markets, and at the networks, have unions that determine the size of the crew.

An important part of the assignment editor's job during a breaking story, as you read earlier, is to get the reporter and crew to the scene as soon as possible. The assignment editor also needs to schedule reporters and crews so that they arrive on time for nonbreaking news conferences and other planned events. The assignment editor must provide accurate street and room numbers and the names of contacts.

Like many people in the newsroom, crews often work long hours and are under a great deal of pressure. They may miss lunches and dinners and be required to work overtime at the end of an already full day. Showing them the respect they deserve usually motivates tired crews more than do screams and demands. So, assignment editors, who are under a lot of pressure themselves, need to keep their cool. They also need to be organized.

# Insights

Assignment editors play a major role in determining what the newscast looks like. Although the producers make the final decisions about what goes into newscasts, they must rely on the assignment editor's judgment in the collection process. That process works best when it is organized.

Earlier sections of this chapter discussed the responsibility of the assignment editors to go over the AP wire carefully and to check the newspapers to see if something is going on that the wire might have missed. The assignment editors must also look through the *futures* file discussed in Chapter 6. The file contains information about news conferences and other events and feature stories that are set up in advance.

Once all this has been digested, the assignment editor must prepare a menu—sometimes called *insights* or *outlooks*—of all of the news possibilities for the day, along with evaluations and recommendations as to which stories should be assigned to reporters and which should be covered only by a cameraperson.

This document is distributed to the entire news editorial staff and discussed at a meeting, usually scheduled in mid-morning, that is attended by the news director, various producers, writers, and any reporters—especially beat re-porters—who have not already been sent out on stories. The meeting determines the "battle plan" for the day. As with any battle, it is impossible to predict the outcome. What appears to be news in the morning may not be so in the middle of the afternoon. That is the nature of news.

# Assignment Boards

In addition to the written assignment outlooks, the assignment desk staff must maintain an *assignment board* that lists all of the stories that have been assigned for that day. The board shows the names of the reporter and crew, the location of the story, the time it is scheduled and, usually, the time the crew is expected back. There also should be room for additional notes on the progress of the story.

A chalkboard or a white plastic board with dry erase markers is used so that changes can be made throughout the day. Because the board is usually located right behind or to the side of the assignment desk, it should be big enough so that producers, reporters, and others do not have to crowd around it to read the information. Keeping the board up to date is usually the responsibility of the desk assistants, who also answer the phones, dis-tribute copy to anchors and teleprompter operators, and perform many other chores that are asked of them as they gain experience working in a newsroom.

This job is one of the best ways to get started in broadcast news. Desk assis-tants who work hard and impress the staff and bosses soon find that they are given more responsibility, which may include writing an occasional story and going out on assignments with reporters.

# Summary

If news staffs didn't know where to look for news and how to gather it, there would be little news on radio and TV. Most collecting is done by assignment editors, while the gathering is done by the reporters.

The assignment desk is where most information enters the newsroom. The assignment desk staff monitors the news wire, the police and fire radios, and the telephones and receives an endless assortment of news releases by mail, wire, and telegram. Assignment editors also look for story ideas from reporters, particularly those with beats, as well as from stringers, tipsters, and other newsroom employees. The assignment editor, who may be the news director as well in some markets, makes the initial decisions about which material should be considered for coverage. He or she also assigns reporters and photographers to stories.

Assignment editors and news directors also rely heavily on the rest of the news team, especially producers. The producers select material and decide what goes on the air; they are responsible for the look of the news. Most newsrooms hold daily meetings to plan the newscast and maintain assignment boards to keep staff members apprised of their duties for the day. Broadcast news is a team effort. Without harmony and togetherness, the newscasts will not succeed, and the ratings will fall. That's bad news for everyone because when ratings fall, owners usually look for a new team. The team that works together will live to see another "sweeps."

# Review Questions

1. What is the name of the most widely used news wire service?
2. Which wire is used most often by small radio stations? Why?
3. What is the A Wire, and what kinds of stations usually subscribe to this service? Why?
4. What other kinds of products do the wire services offer radio stations? Describe them.
5. TV stations have access to feeds from the networks and other sources. How do they arrive at the TV stations? Explain how material is used.
6. Why are there special radios in broadcast newsrooms? How are they used? Are they important?
7. It is routine for many broadcast news staffs to make certain telephone calls each morning. What kinds of calls? Why are they important?
8. Who are stringers, and what do they do? Why are they important?
9. Explain why the assignment desk is an integral part of a news operation.

# Exercises

1. Part of the assignment editor's job is to look for updates on stories. Look at the wires or your newspaper, and pick stories that have potential to be updated. Explain how you would update them.

2.  The assignment editor is always looking for local reaction-type stories to national and international developments. Look at the wires and newspapers for stories that might provide local reaction. Tape a reaction from someone.

3.  If there is a news wire bureau in your area, visit the office, and write a report on what you observed. If there is not, visit your local newspaper office, and see how the wire is used by the staff. Then write a report.

4.  Visit a local radio or TV station and see who is monitoring the police and fire radio. Take notes on what you heard, and turn in a report.

# **10** Broadcast News Reporting

Good reporters first must learn to write, which is why the first part of this book was devoted mostly to writing. But just being able to write well does not guarantee that a person will make a good reporter. Many additional skills and abilities, unrelated to writing, are required.

Although print and broadcast reporters need many of the same skills, broadcast news reporters face challenges not encountered by their print counterparts, or even by broadcast journalists of the recent past. Electronic news gathering (ENG), which relies on videotape or digital equipment and microwave technology, places demands on TV reporters that were unknown when reporters filmed stories and had the luxury of writing their scripts while the film was being developed. Broadcast journalists today need to think faster and to prepare their reports more rapidly, often while the story is still going on around them. They also need to learn about the different types of assignments they are likely to cover and the best way to perform them.

The next several chapters describe these needs and offer suggestions for developing skills to meet them. This chapter begins with the basic skills required of successful reporters.

## Basic Skills

As noted in Chapter 1, the most important skill a reporter needs is accuracy. At first, this may not appear to be a skill, but being accurate requires a lot of attention-checking, and double-checking information demands concentration. Errors usually creep into copy when reporters become too relaxed. Nothing should be assumed or taken for granted. If information cannot be confirmed, it should not be used without some kind of attribution.

Reporters also must develop news judgment. They must understand what news is and be able to recognize that certain stories are more important than others. That skill sometimes takes time to develop. Later in this chapter, professional journalists offer their views and advice on what makes news and how you can develop news judgment. Reporters must also be curious, showing an interest in everything and everyone making news—whatever the reason.

Reporters must be concerned, sometimes alarmed, often angered, and always caring about the major problems that face the communities and world in which we live. Reporters often can do little to correct injustice or unfairness, or the misery, suffering, and critical problems of certain segments or groups in our society, but they should have a desire to do so. Their weapons are enlightenment and information.

Reporters must be determined and persistent in their search for facts and details. Reporters must be aggressive, walking a thin line between tenacity and belligerence. For many people entering journalism, some of these characteristics seem to come naturally, whereas others need to be developed. Let's look at these qualities in detail.

# Accuracy

The introduction to this book mentioned the importance of accuracy and the difficulties that arose in this regard during the O.J. Simpson murder trial, the JonBenét Ramsey murder case, and the Clinton-Lewinsky sex scandal.

Most of the blame for the inordinately high level of inaccurate reporting during these events was placed on (1) the record amount of media coverage; (2) the apparent need to be first with every bit of information, regardless of its value and questionable accuracy; (3) the new technology that encourages broadcast journalists to go live before they have sufficient time to think; (4) the manipulation of the media by a variety of entities, including but not limited to the prosecution, police, and the defense; and (5) the incredible, unprecedented use of unidentified and unreliable sources. The attitude during coverage of these stories appeared to be: "If the story is wrong, we'll correct it later . . . but let's air it before someone else does"—a certain formula for disaster.

## Election 2000: It's Better to Be Right than First

Before Election Night 2000 was over, the networks and cable news channels had to eat their words twice. First they called Florida for Al Gore, only to retract that call later. Then they declared Florida and the election for George W. Bush, only to also retract that call. Declaring Gore the winner in Florida came *before* the polls closed in the Republican-dominated Florida panhandle. That misstep may have cost Bush up to 10,000 votes, a Yale researcher told *Newsweek*.

But *CBS News* correspondent Dan Rather, appearing on CNN's "Reliable Sources," said that study after study show that no empirical evidence proves that projections made before the polls close affect the outcome of the election. Most of Florida is in the eastern time zone, except for the panhandle, which lies in the central time zone. So the polls there remained open an hour later. ABC officials noted that it was the only network that did not call Florida for Gore until after the polls closed in the panhandle, *The New York Times* reported.

Election night coverage was a humiliating experience not only for the broadcasters, who flip-flopped twice, but also for many newspapers that declared Bush the winner in their early editions, before it became clear that the outcome was still undecided. The situation was reminiscent of the *Chicago Daily Tribune* 1948 headline: DEWEY DEFEATS TRUMAN (which of course proved to be incorrect). Only this time, Gore called Bush to concede, and then later retracted his concession.

The first gaff came early on when the networks declared Al Gore the winner in Florida, with its crucial 25 electoral votes. But two hours later, the networks and the Associated Press began taking back their projections, stating that the vote was too close to call. It remained that way for several hours. At 2 A.M., it became clear that whoever won Florida would win the election. Sixteen minutes later, the Fox News Channel declared Bush the winner in Florida and hence the presidency. Within minutes, in lock step, the networks, CNN, and Reuters followed suit, but they were wrong *again.*

The AP didn't go along with the Bush win declaration, and at 2:37 A.M., it put out an urgent message stating: "The race was still up for grabs and it all came down to Florida." At 3:11 A.M., the AP put out an advisory that Bush's lead in Florida had dwindled to about 6,000 and warned that with the counting of two heavily Democratic counties to go, the lead could change. Shortly before 4 A.M., the networks were forced to retract their earlier prediction and began placing Florida and the national election outcome in the "undecided" category. More than a month later, the election was still undecided.

Election Night 2000 was "probably the worst moment in the 50-year history of television coverage of politics," said Bill Kovach, chairman, and Tom Rosensteil, vice chairman of the Committee of Concerned Journalists, in an op-ed piece in the *New York Times*. "Misleading coverage not only failed to report what happened on election night, but created . . . the suggestion of an election that was called back and might be stolen," adding, "when the truth is simply that a very narrow election is late on being decided."

Marvin Kalb, former network news correspondent and director of Harvard's Shorenstein Center on the Press, Politics, and Public Policy, said, in the past, the networks had been "remarkably reliable" in their calling of elections. But on Election Night 2000, Kalb added, "Television news flubbed its lines big time." Those comments appeared in op-ed pieces in the *Boston Globe* and *New York Daily News*. "These editorial blunders," he said, "quickly created a political crisis filled with uncertainties and suspicions."

Kalb further stated: "Americans, already skeptical about network coverage of politics, may now wonder whether they can trust the networks to be fair and accurate in their calling of presidential elections." He predicted that a congressional investigation into the way the networks cover elections would be initiated, which, he said, could "easily imperil" the editorial independence of the networks. Even before the election was decided, the chairman of the House Commerce Subcommittee on Telecommunications announced that it would hold hearings regarding the election coverage.

Why did the errors occur? Kalb said that the trouble lies in having one source of polling data. In years past, the networks each performed their own election research. But in recent years, to save millions of dollars each, they decided to use one service, the Voter News Service (VNS), to conduct research for all the outlets. "If VNS was wrong, all the networks would get and distribute the wrong information," Kalb said. VNS relied on interviews with voters at selected precincts as they left the polls, known as exit interviews, and actual vote counts.

Ironically, early during election night coverage, *CBS News* anchor and managing editor, Dan Rather, announced to his TV audience: "Let's get one thing straight, right from the get go. We would rather be last in the reporting returns than be wrong." And he continued: "If we say somebody carried a state, you can pretty much take it to the bank, book it that it's true." Of course, he had to eat those words later in the evening.

A few days after election night, Rather, appearing on CNN's "Reliable Sources," said: "We were wrong, we need to stand up and to take the responsibility for it." He added that "this is not an exact science, but *CBS News* has by far the best record in the business on election nights." In addition, Rather said, "we're taking steps to make sure it will happen as little as possible in the future," adding, "but it will happen."

He also said that, when making projections in an election, "one of the things we can do better is to underscore more often to the viewer that while we believe we're right, *making these calls . . . we can be wrong.*" "I think credibility is the most important thing we have. Accuracy is job one," Rather added.

*ABC News* correspondent Sam Donaldson, also appearing on CNN's "Reliable Sources," said: "We have egg on our face, no question about it," adding, "it's not a good system for all the networks to get their information from the same place." He said that much of the problem is caused by competition, the desire to be first. But Donaldson further said: "If we waited until all the votes are counted before declaring a winner, you'd say, 'Congratulations ABC' and the next time around no one would watch us because the other networks would beat us by projecting winners much earlier."

Some network executives acknowledged that the miscues resulted from faulty data and misleading returns fed into the VNS computers. Rather called for a 24-hour voting period and a uniform poll closing law that he said would "wipe out the possibility" of this happening again. The networks quickly launched investigations into what went wrong and how to prevent such a debacle from happening again.

Even before we knew who won the election, *ABC News* announced preliminary results of its investigation saying it will no longer call a contest in any state until all the polls have closed, the *New York Times* reports. And ABC said it will attempt to "insulate" its analysts from competitive pressure to call a state prematurely.

Issues raised by the election were heard in several Florida district courts, the state Supreme Court, and the U.S. Supreme Court. (More information on the U.S. Supreme Court is presented in Chapter 21, "More Ethical Issues.")

In the aftermath of the election coverage, Arizona State University journalism professor Stephen Doig wondered if the networks were right, in the first place, when they called Florida for Gore early on election night. Professor Doig completed a computer analysis of voting patterns in the election for the *Miami Herald*. He concluded that Gore would have beaten Bush in Florida if all the state's ballots for the presidency had been error free and completely counted. He said the networks' call for Gore, which was based on exit polling, "I suspect, was pretty accurate."

He believes that in the exit polls, the VNS found out who each person they interviewed voted for, but the machines missed some votes; however, Doig said, "I think [the networks] screwed up" by calling the election results before all the polls had closed. "[The call] might have affected the voting," he added. He was also critical of the networks for using the same research service. "Having more than one," he said, "allows the opportunity to see if others agree with you."

In a related matter, the *New York Times* ran a story headlined, "CBS Plans Changes in Election Night Coverage." In this article, the *Times* reports, *CBS News'* flawed decision on election night—calling Florida and the election for George W. Bush—could have been avoided if those making the call had been aware of their own correspondents reporting and the work of the Associated Press. CBS said it was making several changes as a result of its election night debacle. Among those changes, CBS (along with ABC and NBC) will not call a state's election results until all the polls in that state have closed.

## The O.J. Simpson Trial

Another classic example of broadcasting irresponsibility was KNBC-TV's report that DNA testing showed that Nicole Brown Simpson's blood was discovered on one of O.J. Simpson's socks found in his bedroom. Everyone connected with the case—the prosecution, defense, police, and Judge Ito—said the report was false. That assertion did not convince the television station, however; it reported the same story with some new false details the next day, causing the livid Judge Ito to consider discontinuing all TV coverage of the trial. An anchor for the station, questioned at a round-table broadcast, explained that "the source for the story had always been accurate in the past." Later, KNBC-TV did admit that its report contained some inaccuracies.

The report, unfortunately, was picked up throughout the nation. The headlines that night said something like "A bloody sock ties O.J. closer to the murders" or "Nicole Simpson's blood found on O.J. sock."

Those headlines point out a continuing problem in both the broadcast and print media. The people writing the headlines do not always understand the story as well as they should, and there often appears to be an attitude that says, "It's only a headline." Sometimes you have difficulty finding anything in the story that supports the headline. When the actual story that followed the headline was carried by a station in the author's listening area of Baton Rouge, Louisiana, there was no attribution until the end of the story. Meanwhile, all the details of the story were broadcast as fact. Viewers were led to believe that scientific tests showed that Nicole Brown Simpson's blood was found on one of O.J.'s socks. Ironically, months later, DNA experts for the prosecution would testify that Nicole Simpson's blood *was* found on one of O.J.'s socks; however, when KNBC-TV aired its report, those DNA tests had not yet been performed.

That was only one of several serious mistakes broadcast and printed by the media. Here are the worst of the others regarding that case:

Police had found a bloody ski mask.

The murder weapon was found on the plane that Simpson took to Chicago.

Simpson kept one of his hands in a bag during the flight to Chicago so no one would see he had an injury.

Police found a bloody golf bag belonging to Simpson.

Police have a shovel used to decapitate the victims.

Defense attorney Marcia Clark was videotaped at the crime scene 15 minutes before a warrant was issued.

Lawyer and Professor Charles Ogletree commented that so many stories were generated by the media "that it is difficult to say which ones are true or false." Howard Kirch, media writer for *The Washington Post*, accused those reporters covering the O.J. Simpson story of "second-hand journalism gradually turning rumor into fact."

The same situation was true in the tragic murder case of 6-year-old JonBenét Ramsey and the sex scandal involving the President of the United States and White House intern Monica Lewinsky. (These two cases are discussed more fully in Chapter 22, "Tabloid Journalism.")

The news coverage was not all bad, of course. A great amount of accurate and fair reporting took place during all of these events. Accuracy is essential in every story, not only in sensational murder trials and national scandals. And it does take a lot of hard work. Every detail in a news story must be checked and rechecked.

It does not matter how well a story is written or whether it has a clever lead or a snappy ending if it is not accurate in every detail. News managers have little patience with reporters and writers who cannot get the facts straight. Inaccuracy on a continuing basis can end a career quickly.

Names are particularly important. It was a time-consuming, painful job trying to sort out those who were injured and lost their lives in the 1995

Oklahoma City bombing and the high school shootings at Columbine High School in Littleton, Colorado, in 1999 and at other schools around the country. The names came slowly, as you would expect, because there was a great deal of confusion at the crime scenes. That confusion lasted for weeks in the Oklahoma bombing as rescuers looked for victims. That particular identification problem was enormous. Because of the devastation caused by the bomb, there was little remaining of some of the victims, making their identification a nightmare. Throughout that long process, it was critical for the media to report the names, and other details about the victims, with extreme caution.

Names not only have to be spelled right, but you must also know how to pronounce them, as was pointed out in Chapter 8. If you are on the air, you would not wish to be embarrassed by pronouncing a person's name incorrectly; and if you are writing for an anchor, you wouldn't want to embarrass that individual either. The chances are that if you do pronounce someone's name incorrectly, you will hear about it from the person or someone else.

No one is perfect, of course, and journalists do make mistakes. But the responsibility for accuracy demands that such mistakes be kept to a minimum. When they are made, they must be corrected as quickly as possible. (The news coverage of the Oklahoma City bombing is discussed in Chapter 11, "Reporting Assignments.")

# News Judgment

In the Introduction, the idea that news judgment is something "you are born with" was dismissed. It can be developed. But how?

First, perhaps news judgment should be defined, which isn't easy. Even professional journalists have difficulty explaining the term. ABC *Nightline* correspondent Jeff Greenfield says people have different news judgments, which he believes is desirable. He noted that *Nightline* anchor Ted Koppel is a "foreign policy freak" and tends to "see more value in an international story," whereas Greenfield himself is a "political freak."

Greenfield said that if a relatively unknown politician announced that he or she was running for president, Greenfield might suggest that it was time to examine the whole field of candidates, whereas Koppel might still prefer a foreign story. Greenfield commented: "Does that mean that Koppel is without news judgment? I think not. Does it mean that I am without news judgment? I think not."

Greenfield said news judgment can also be related to the audience you are trying to serve. "The editors of *The New York Times* and *The [Washington] Post* will see news differently," he said. "They each will ask, 'Is this a story my readers will care about and want to know about?'"

Greenfield cited as an example the story of Kimberly Bergalis, a woman who died from AIDS after being infected during oral surgery performed by her HIV-

**Figure 10.1**
ABC *Nightline* correspondent Jeff Greenfield. (Carol Halebian/Gamma-Liaison)

positive dentist. "Why is that a news story?" asked Greenfield. "Because something terrible happened to her. She never used drugs and never had sex of any kind. Yet, this beautiful young woman was dying of the disease."

The ABC correspondent said it was a news story for two reasons. First, he said, "We resonate to the story . . . it's a 'there but for the grace of God' story." Second, he added, "It raises a public-policy debate. Should medical professionals have to be tested for HIV?" Greenfield said that while people react differently to that story, news judgment dictates, "We've got to cover it."

*NBC News* correspondent Bob Dotson says that when he thinks of news judgment, he thinks of fairness. He believes reporters must ask themselves if there is more than one side to a story and try to present all sides. Dotson says he views ethics as an important part of good news judgment.

Former *CBS News* correspondent Richard Threlkeld believes news judgment is "in the eye of the beholder. If you are going to put on a newscast and want people to watch it," he says, "you have to give them stories that they ought to know—important developments overseas and how the mayor and governor are doing their jobs at home. They also want to know if there was a bad fire in the neighborhood. News judgment comes into play in giving the public the proper mix of things they should know and want to know."

Dotson says one of the best ways to develop news judgment is to learn from one's mistakes and try to avoid them in the future. He remembered working as a young newsman and being asked to do a story about the anniversary of Pearl Harbor. "I was only 22 at the time and didn't know a heck of a lot about Pearl

Harbor," Dotson recalled, "but I had a handout film that had sprockets on both sides of the film. I had a master's degree in cinematography," Dotson said, "but I forgot to check which side was up. So during the newscast the planes attacking Pearl Harbor came in upside down."

Dotson said that because he didn't know any better, he thought maybe the Japanese had actually done it that way. "But when the flag came on upside down I knew I was dead meat," said Dotson. "The news director always had a critique after the news, and he would tell you what you did wrong and often make you do it over again. Well," Dotson continued, "you didn't do that too often before you started thinking of ways to improve what you were doing."

*ABC News* correspondent Morton Dean says he developed news judgment "by just working in the field . . . by doing it and working with some very good people and learning from them. You have to pay attention to people around you, and if you are fortunate enough to have good, solid, professional people to work with when you start out, that's a great help. It's like being in a perpetual classroom." Dean adds: "It's important in this business to keep your eyes and ears open all the time. . . . You can always learn new things, not only about the world but about yourself. It's important to look at yourself and listen to yourself to pick up on whatever communication problems you have."

NBC correspondent Roger O'Neil notes that when he was a local reporter he "always paid attention to every network correspondent on the air." He "studied them, analyzed what they said and learned a lot."

Richard Threlkeld also says reporters always have to remember—regardless of their age—to be concerned about things that are of interest to people outside their age group. "Young reporters just starting out," he notes, "must realize that there are people out there who are over 35 and have different interests and concerns." Threlkeld adds that even he has to keep asking himself: "What are my daughters, who are in their 20s and 30s, interested in? What would they want to watch? The same goes for people who are my seniors. Is this a story that would interest them?" Threlkeld advises reporters to remember that broadcasting is "mass media, and that means everybody—little kids, and old people, and black and white and brown people. They're all watching, and they all deserve the best that you can give them."

# Curiosity

For curious people, one of the rewards of reporting is the joy of discovering things. Discovering something "first" is the best reward of all. But discovering information is not always as exciting as depicted on the TV programs based on broadcast news. To hold a network primetime audience, these programs must come up with some imaginative story ideas each week. In the real world, few reporters get caught up in the kind of sensational situations and intrigue depicted on sitcoms and TV dramas.

Most reporting assignments are fairly routine. Reporters spend a lot of time covering murders, lots of fires, plenty of elections, more news conferences than they would care to remember, accidents of all kinds, and hundreds of feature stories. That is the *real* world of broadcast news.

The fact that most reporters do not deal with crooked politicians, track down terrorists, or go to bat for someone on death row who they are convinced is innocent does not mean that reporting is dull. There is an endless assortment of stories to satisfy most people's curiosity, and there are opportunities to explore previously unknown subjects. Getting the answers, finding out about things— and learning and growing along the way—are part of the excitement of report- ing. These are some of the reasons why the profession is so compelling.

When reporters arrive at the newsroom for work, they never know what stories they will be covering, and that is an exciting concept for curious people. Most reporters will tell you that they could not imagine any kind of work that they would rather do. Former *CBS News* correspondent Betsy Aaron agrees: "It keeps you young. We're in this business because we are nosy, and curious, and angry and we want to change the world. If you lose this edge," she says, "then it's hard to put in the 90 hours a week and mess up your family life and the other things that go along with it."

# Concern and Caring

There is never a shortage of news about people who need help. People in many parts of the world are dying of hunger and disease. Thousands are dying as a result of evil and political strife in various countries. At home, unemployment, homelessness, and poverty continue to be major problems. Tuberculosis, a disease that at one time was thought to have been eradicated, at least in the United States, has again become a threat. AIDS is not only a serious medical emergency but a subject of national debate regarding whether the government is doing enough to combat the disease.

These are just a few of the tragedies and distressing stories making news. All such stories raise concern, as they should, for those hearing the news. Those reporting the news must be equally concerned. Part of the job of reporting such stories is providing information that may enlighten the audience. A radio or TV reporter may not be able to do much about the plight of civil war or famine victims except to report the story in a thoughtful and caring manner. In the case of domestic problems such as homelessness, AIDS, and unemployment, a reporter often can provide information that may help those affected deal with the problem or may call others' attention to it.

# Persistence

A good reporter hates taking "no" for an answer. Learning how to get people to talk to you when they may not want to is a skill. Getting them to tell you things they don't want to requires even more skill.

*ABC News* correspondent Barry Serafin says that he usually does take "no" for an answer when someone does not wish to speak with him, but he says that he also mentions in his report that the individual refused to be interviewed. Serafin says that the situation is different when a public official is involved. "Then, he adds, "I try not to take 'no' for an answer."

Serafin's colleague at ABC, correspondent Jeff Greenfield, has a similar view. "If it's a private individual who doesn't want to talk to you," he advises, "get out. But if it's a public or government official, you are entitled to keep banging on the door as much as you like. It's not a privacy issue."

Greenfield notes it takes a "combination of aggressiveness and guile" to get someone to talk when they are reluctant. He says he has had some success by telling people: "Look, I can't really force you to talk to me, but I am not out to prove a point or make a case. There is an issue at stake here, and your side is important to us. It is absolutely up to you whether you will talk to us."

Greenfield says he also makes this promise: "I'll give your side of the story fairly." He adds, "I then ask the person, 'Exactly what is it that you are most afraid to discuss with me?' Sometimes it works, and sometimes it doesn't."

# Aggressiveness

Most reporters seem to agree that they try to be aggressive without being obnoxious. They criticize reporters who shout and shove microphones into people's faces, demanding answers to their questions. Unfortunately, some news directors insist on such behavior—they expect to see microphones with the station call letters on the six o'clock news as much as possible even if the only voices heard on the microphones are the reporters'. News directors also listen to hear if their reporters asked questions, which is a reasonable expectation. But these scenes can get ugly. For decades, Hollywood filmmakers have portrayed reporters as rude and arrogant—and often stupid—in movie scripts. The Hollywood stereotype of the dumb reporter has been overdone but not entirely.

Most politicians, police officials, lawyers, and others who deal with the media on a daily basis are accustomed to a certain amount of badgering from the press. They would probably be disappointed and feel neglected if the news corps was not surrounding them when there's a story to tell. But the reporter who runs down the street after a newsmaker's car and shoves a microphone into the open window is out of line. More than one reporter has lost a microphone that way when the irritated person rolled up the window.

Reporter behavior is discussed in great detail later in the book when we take a closer look at some of the news stories already mentioned, such as the high school shootings and the JonBenét Ramsey murder case.

# Fairness

It is often argued that it is not possible for anyone to be completely objective. This may be true. Everyone has certain biases and prejudices, but reporters must learn to leave out their personal feelings when they start writing or delivering news. Objectivity for a journalist really means "fairness"; it means honestly giving both sides of an argument, controversy, or debate.

Reporters can tell when their report on a controversial issue has been successful because both sides of the issue accuse them of being partial to the other. Fairness was a major issue in the coverage of the Clinton-Lewinsky scandal and the JonBenét Ramsey murder investigation. As already mentioned, both stories are examined closely later.

# Diversity

Part of *fairness* also is learning to deal with diversity in a fair manner—accepting that all races are equal and should be treated equally whether it be in the newsroom or in a news story.

Earlier in the book, we explained that race should only be referred to in a crime story if the suspect is wanted by police. That's true, but to be of any use to police or to citizens who may run into the suspect, knowing that he is African American is of little use. Even if he is identified as a six-foot male with braided hair, that description would fit literally hundreds of blacks in a large community.

Keith Woods, a member of the Ethics and Diversity faculty at the Poynter Institute, says such vague descriptions of wanted persons are familiar to anyone who has ever watched the nightly news. He said that this sort of description passes for information in too much of American journalism today, part of a dysfunctional racial discourse that doesn't always mean what it says and seldom says what it means.

Woods recalled a sports headline that read: "Indians extend Boston's massacre" [after the Cleveland Indians defeated the Boston Red Sox]. This treatment may not have intended to evoke the racist stereotype of the savage American Indian, but it hurts just the same. Woods added that the mangled language of race is punctuated with descriptions that underscore ethnicity but describe nothing. He said it is "mired in euphemisms and the tortured, convoluted syntax that betray America's pathological avoidance of straight talk about race relations."

Woods said put it all together and you get stereotypes, dangerous misinformation, half-truths, and daily proof that when it comes to race, journalists are "chained to habits that defy the cornerstone principles of solid journalism." He noted that the word *minority*, a numerical term, is often used when the journalist actually has a specific racial group in mind, allowing for the ridiculous oxymoron, "majority minority." Poor, he noted, is euphemized as "disadvantaged" and often used as a synonym for people of color.

Woods gave as an example of the dysfunctional racial discourse he spoke of, this paragraph from an actual story:

> Incongruous as it seems, designer names that once were best known among the traditional preppy set are now the highly coveted *must have* items of black teenagers all over the country.

Woods asks us to consider the way race, class, and fashion are handled in that example from a story about teenagers' love affair with brand-name clothing. What, asks Woods, does "traditional preppy" mean? He says if you use the dictionary's definition (a student or former student of a private secondary school that prepares students to enter college), "preppy" and "black teenagers" would not be as incongruous as the writer says. More likely, Woods says, the writer meant "white and well-off" when she wrote "traditional preppy." Woods says the paragraph could be challenged for accuracy and completeness, two cornerstones of solid journalism.

He cites another example about a Florida woman shot in her jewelry store that said "her husband arrived and reported that the 28-year-old Vietnamese woman had been murdered." Why, asks Woods, is it relevant to identify the woman as Vietnamese? Woods says that maybe the woman was a Vietnam native working toward American citizenship. But he says that from the sentence construction, we don't know. The story did not provide the context that solid journalism demands. What we are left with, says Woods, is a story that singles out a person's race or ethnicity for no apparent reason.

Racial identifications do carry information about geography, bloodlines, and heritage but don't describe much of anything. Woods asks, for example, what does a Hispanic man look like? Is his skin dark brown? Reddish brown? Pale? Is his hair straight? Curly? Coarse? Fine? Does he have a flat, curved nose, or is it narrow and straight? Telling the public that he's 5-foot-8, 180 pounds, with a blue shirt and blue jeans says something about the person's appearance. But what do you add to that picture, asks Woods, when you say Latino?

Woods takes the question a step further: "What is black," he asks. "It's the color of pitch." But he notes that the word is used to describe people whose skin tones can cover every racial and ethnic group in the world, including white people.

Woods agrees that all racial and ethnic groups do share some common physical characteristics. But, he says, the media doesn't use the phrase "Irish-looking man," although red hair and pale skin are common Irish characteristics. And

Woods asks what image an audience might conjure if an anchor said the suspect appeared to be Italian or that police were looking for a middle-aged man described as "Jewish-looking." The point is, of course, that all Irish Americans don't look alike and neither do blacks. Why then, asks Woods, do we accept a description that says a suspect is African American. Woods points out, as we have elsewhere in the book, that unless the story is specifically about race, it has little descriptive value in a story.

Here are some excerpts from Woods' guide to fairer journalism:

When the scope of coverage shows communities in their fullest complexity— all classes, religions, races, ethnicities, men and women, gay and straight, all political persuasions—then there is greater chance that all groups will feel valued and will respect your organization.

How we refer to people or incidents can speak volumes to the public. Each adjective, phrase, or inflection, either verbal or written, has the power to signal to the audience that the reporter has a particular point of view. He warns about single-word descriptors—radical, hysterical, separatist—that are used as labels by one person or group against another.

Images shape impressions, and their effects, positive and negative, are long lasting; they work when they portray a diversity of people and offer a range of perspectives—they take the public where they might not ordinarily go.

The most abiding and most immediate values transmitted from journalists to their public arrive via the "play" a story gets; journalists tell people who and what is most important, which stories must be told now, and which can be relegated to the news briefs and the back pages. Play works best when all people are valued equally. Breast cancer stories get the same play as prostate cancer stories. Success and tragedy stories about people of color receive the same prominent play as those about white people.

There is more discussion on diversity—in the newsroom—in Chapter 25, "The Job Search in a Changing Industry."

# Staying Well Informed

Reporters cannot function well unless they are well informed. Being well informed does not mean just having a good education; it means taking the time to know what's going on around you. Journalists must constantly add new material to their knowledge. One of the best ways to stay well informed is to read.

Reading the news wire and the Internet extensively is an immediate way to know what is going on. Reporters should also read the local newspaper (or all of them if they work in a city with more than one) and at least one national paper every day. Weekly news magazines are a useful source of additional information, as are books, particularly nonfiction bestsellers.

It is also a good idea to observe the competition. Reporters who watch and listen only to their own station's newscasts miss an opportunity not only to find out what the competition is saying, but also, on occasion, to improve on their own techniques.

# Research

All good reporters do research because they want to know as much as possible about a story before trying to cover it. The Internet has made the research task tremendously easier than when reporters had to dig through libraries and morgues to find information. (Research is discussed further in Chapter 17, "Computer-Assisted Reporting.")

It is also a good idea to get on mailing lists. Many organizations are happy to add a reporter's name to their lists, and just getting on some mailing lists automatically places your name on many others. Much of the information distributed by these groups has limited news value because it is public-relations material, but it is useful for alerting you to the positions certain organizations take on issues. Many of the groups are dedicated to worthwhile causes. Almost all of them, and thousands of other organizations too, will have Websites.

# Manners and Sensitivity

Reporters often cover unpleasant stories. They are expected to interview people who are involved in a variety of tragedies—to talk, perhaps, to the parents or relatives of a homicide or accident victim. It is important for inexperienced reporters to learn how to handle such interviews with tact and sensitivity.

There have been so many bad examples of tactless interviews that the question "How do you feel about your daughter being murdered?" has become a stereotype of the insensitive reporter. It is an insensitive question. News directors should quickly discipline reporters who display such bad taste.

*NBC News* correspondent Bob Dotson says part of the problem is that "people don't want you there, and you don't want to be there." Dotson recalled covering a tornado story in Small Town, South Carolina, where several fatalities had occurred. "It was the day after the tornado struck, and we made sure that we got there before nine o'clock in the morning," recalled Dotson, "because anyone who is affected by a hurricane or tornado is not going to be at home later. They are either going to be at the hospital checking on loved ones or at the mortuary. So we got there before nine o'clock because the one thing people always do in tragic situations is come back and look for pictures. They don't care about stereos or TVs," Dotson noted, "but they are looking for pictures."

Dotson recalled that they found a man and his son digging through the rubble. "The son came up to us and jumped in my face, and rightfully so, and said, 'What are you guys here for . . . you're vultures,' and so forth. And I looked at him and said, 'You know it's Sunday morning, and there are a lot of folks getting up and asking themselves why . . . why did this happen?' And that is all I said, I didn't ask him a question. And then the father came over and he said to me, 'I'll tell you why.'"

"Well," Dotson said, "we started shooting what he had to say. But he became overcome with grief thinking about the loss of his wife and daughter, and he walked away. Then—because of the kind of person he was, and because he said he would tell us—he came back and finished the story."

Dotson said the story ran on *NBC News*, including the 10 or 12 seconds when the man walked away to compose himself and then walked back to the camera. "A week later I got a letter from him, and he said he had received thousands of letters from people around the country saying that he had helped them put tragedy into perspective, and he thanked me. And then I got a Christmas card from him. So," Dotson observed, "it doesn't necessarily mean that just because you are working on an emotional edge you are not going to be able to handle that situation properly."

He added that it is important in such situations to make it plain that you are representing yourself and not your company, and "If that means not having your camera rolling when you walk up, then so be it. If someone is experiencing great grief and doesn't want you there, fine, there's another story somewhere. But nine out of 10 times you can stay if you come along and talk to them as an individual first and don't ask questions—just commiserate. Then," Dotson added, "if they take a liking to you, someone will stop and tell you, and that's when you turn the camera on. But," Dotson stressed, "you never go up to someone who has great grief and act like a stereotypical journalist or you are going to go out on your ear, or worse."

*ABC News* correspondent Morton Dean says, "You have to think carefully about what you are going to ask. You can't rush into it. Ask yourself; 'What would make me react the best way if, God forbid, I were in a situation like this?' I sometimes say, 'This has got to be a terrible moment for you,' and I know there are people out there who, having heard that question, will say, 'No kidding, dummy, of course it's a terrible moment.'" But, Dean adds, sometimes those "dumb" questions have to be asked. He recalled that when he returned from reporting in the Persian Gulf, friends and even relatives often asked: "How could you people ask so many dumb questions at those news conferences? You know they are not going to answer a question about when the ground war is going to start."

Dean said his response was: "I've made a career out of asking dumb questions. I mean, that's our job—not to prove how smart we are but to elicit answers, and I think you sometimes have to ask what appears to be a dumb question. I am not out there to impress the audience that I have brilliant questions all the time. I am old-fashioned enough to believe that the idea is to get some news at the other end of the question."

As stated earlier, many Americans have a negative image of the news media. According to a Gallup poll conducted in November 2000, journalists ranked twenty-first out of 46 choices for honesty and integrity. TV reporters and commentators ranked twenty-second. The polls show that a large part of the people believe that the news media as a whole is biased and negative, influenced by powerful organizations, and unwilling to admit mistakes.

*CBS News* correspondent Mike Wallace also is concerned about the media's image. He noted that confidence in the news media "has fallen below confidence in the government." He said part of the reason for the mistrust of the press corps is that many people consider us "unnecessarily negative . . . insensitive . . . irresponsible . . . and arrogant." Wallace reminds us that back in 1971, a public opinion poll showed that Walter Cronkite was the most trusted man in America. Today, the trust of the media is at an all-time low.

Cronkite himself, who is not completely happy with the media, says that "newspapers and, to a degree, TV are doing a much better job of investigative reporting than they used to. With each of these [investigative] stories," he says, "we alienate a portion of the population. They fail to understand the importance of a strong, tough-minded press."

Cronkite says that if reporters do not do investigative reporting, "our democracy is in much greater danger than it would be even from an irresponsible press." He says it would be much worse if the press didn't have "the guts and determination" to report the truth. (The responsibility of the press—and sometimes the lack of it—is discussed further in Chapter 20, "Ethics and the Law," Chapter 21, "More Ethical Issues," and Chapter 22, "Tabloid Journalism.")

## Working with Colleagues

Reporting the news is a team effort. Getting along with colleagues is essential. Young reporters just beginning their careers should watch and listen to the seasoned staff members. Seeking their advice lets them know that they are appreciated. When that happens, there is little that they will not do to help a reporter, which is important when the reporter needs a cameraperson to skip lunch or a tape editor to spend an extra 30 minutes in the morgue looking for "just the right file footage" for a story.

It is also important to remember that reputations follow reporters from station to station. News managers like team players. They hire reporters who have demonstrated in previous positions that they are cooperative and eager to learn and grow.

## Summary

This chapter describes the skills and character traits of a good journalist. Although few reporters have all of the qualifications, the most successful ones strive toward them.

Here is a list of those skills and character traits:

| | |
|---|---|
| accuracy | good research habits |
| aggressiveness | news judgment |
| concern and caring | persistence |
| curiosity | sensitivity |
| fairness | |

Developing such skills will make your life, as well as your career, more interesting and rewarding.

# Review Questions

1. What is the most important skill required of a reporter?
2. News judgment is a difficult concept to express even for veteran journalists. How would you explain it?
3. Can news judgment be developed? Explain.
4. What other character and personality traits should a reporter possess?
5. How aggressive should reporters be when they are trying to get a story?
6. Reporters should always strive to be fair when they are covering stories. What does that entail?
7. Reporters are sometimes accused of being insensitive. How should reporters ask questions of someone who is involved in a tragedy?

# Exercises

1. Switch from station to station at the top of the local news, and note whether the stations are leading the news with the same or different stories. Which story would you have led with? Defend your choice.
2. Accompany a radio or TV reporter on a story, and observe how he or she handles an interview and works it into the story.
3. Interview a radio or TV reporter, and find out how he or she prepares for an assignment before leaving the newsroom.
4. Visit a newsroom, and find out what kind of research books, audio or video morgues, and computer resources are available for writers and reporters looking for background information. Turn in a report on your findings.

# **11** Reporting Assignments

Reporters spend most of their careers covering spot news, which dominates the contents of all radio and TV newscasts. Spot news includes fires, accidents, holdups, and other incidents that occur every day, with varying frequency, in every city and town in the nation.

As mentioned in Chapter 9, reporters learn about most spot news stories from the police and fire radio advisories. Tips from viewers and listeners can also provide the first word on a spot news story.

This chapter discusses the most common types of spot news stories, and Chapter 12, "Covering Planned Events," examines a variety of other typical assignments. The purpose of these two chapters is to describe the various types of assignments and to highlight the things that reporters must remember to do in covering them.

Most of the discussion focuses on editorial decisions. Remember, however, that television is a visual medium, and the success of reporting for television depends mainly on the pictures taken by camerapeople. Establishing a good working relationship with a cameraperson is also discussed in this chapter.

## Fires

The decision regarding whether to cover a fire usually is based on the amount of destruction it is causing. Sometimes a relatively small fire can have tragic results if it occurs in an occupied house, particularly in the middle of the night when people are asleep.

These considerations are on the news director's or assignment editor's mind when news of a fire first breaks. In a large city such as New York, there would not be enough reporters to cover other news if reporters were assigned to every fire. There are just too many of them. A cameraperson may be sent to cover a burning, empty warehouse, and the video may provide 20 seconds of footage on the six o'clock news. In the same city, such a fire may not even be mentioned on radio newscasts unless the blaze lasted for hours or caused some tie-up in traffic or injuries to firefighters. In a small town, a fire of any kind may be a major story and may need a reporter at the scene. A fire in a residential area is almost always news, regardless of the size of the community, once it has been determined that the dwelling is occupied and lives are in jeopardy.

Once at the scene, the radio and TV reporters look for the same kind of information: Have any injuries or deaths occurred? Are any people in the building? If it's an industrial building, what is burning? Is the material hazardous? How many firefighters and pieces of equipment are at the scene? How did the fire start? And finally, is arson suspected?

Reporters get most of this information from the fire official in charge. The official doesn't always know the answers to some questions, but they must be asked anyway. The radio reporter gets the answers on a tape recorder, and the TV reporter's cameraperson videotapes or beams the interview back to the station via microwave or satellite. Because of new technology, radio reporters also can go live from a scene without depending on the phone or two-way radio in the mobile unit. Using a cellular telephone, the reporter can move about at the scene and file the report whenever it's ready. By plugging a tape recorder into the phone jack, the reporter has the ability to go live with a previously recorded interview or to isolate an actuality for use in the middle of a live open and close (wraparound).

The radio and TV reporters at the fire scene also look for other people to interview—those who escaped from the building, those who might have seen the fire start or, in the case of fatalities, friends or relatives of those who died in the building. The radio reporter also records the natural sound of the fire and the battle to put it out, and the TV cameraperson does the same on videotape.

Station WISC-TV in Madison, Wisconsin, won a Radio and Television News Directors Association first-place award for spot news for its coverage of a most unusual fire. Here's the station's 10 o'clock news report on the fire, which was still in progress at the time.

| | |
|---|---|
| | (Beth V/O) |
| WIDE LIVE SHOT | An enormous four-alarm fire is still raging on Madison's east side, seven hours after it began. The warehouse owner came home from vacation tonight: |
| SOT | SOT |
| Kenny Williams | "I just can't believe it. It's taken |
| Warehouse Owner | a lifetime of work." |
| RUNS :03 | |
| TWO SHOT | (Beth O/C) |
| | Good evening, everyone. Dozens of firefighters are still trying to put out the |

**Figure 11.1**   A fire in this warehouse in Madison, Wisconsin, caused tens of millions of dollars in damage and kept broadcast news organizations busy for days. (Photo by Kathy Ozatko. Used by permission of *The Capital Times*.)

FILE TAPE #1009

fire at the Central Storage Warehouse on Cottage Grove Road.

(John)
And tonight they're having limited success.
The three buildings are the size of two football fields. Tonight two of them are ruined and dozens of firefighters are battling to save the third.

The blaze broke out when a forklift battery exploded in mid-afternoon. It set off what likely will go down in history as this city's costliest fire, in the tens of millions of dollars for the building alone. That doesn't count the 51 million pounds of food stored inside that is causing environmental concerns.

News Three's Joel DeSpain begins our coverage.

| | |
|---|---|
| Package<br>Font: Joel DeSpain<br>Reporting<br>Font: 4309 Cottage<br>Grove Rd. | (SOT) |
| | (Package outcue: Standard) |
| O/C TWO SHOT | John O/C<br>The fire isn't the only huge concern<br>tonight . . . |
| | Beth<br>There's also a big environmental impact,<br>and it deals with a river of food washing<br>down the street. |
| Key Live/Remote | News Three's Roger Putnam joins us<br>live with the story. |
| Remote | (Roger remote)<br>City crews are keeping waist-deep<br>grease from clogging city lines. |
| Package | SOT<br>(standard outcue) |
| Question after package | Roger, how are they doing battling<br>this melted butter and hot dog problem? |
| Roger remote continues | (Roger remote) |
| O/C | John O/C<br>At least two Madison-area companies<br>had products in the warehouse. Oscar<br>Mayer lost about four million dollars<br>worth of meats but says the loss won't<br>have much of an impact.<br>Certco, a grocery delivery company,<br>had frozen foods stored there—it's not<br>known how much. And Swiss Colony has<br>used the warehouse before, but it wasn't<br>confirmed that products were there<br>today. |
| O/C | (Beth)<br>Several accidents tonight as a result of<br>the fire, but nothing serious. |

V/O (NAT/SOT)                                    (V/O)
                                    Stoughton Road was blocked off for more
                                    than four hours. Debris from explosions
                                    at the fire was falling onto Stoughton
                                    Road creating a safety hazard. Dempsey
                                    and Atlas Roads were also congested.

WISC-TV continued its coverage throughout the night.

# Accidents

Accidents are another common type of spot news stories. Reporters cover a variety of accidents during their careers. When people talk of accidents, they tend to mean traffic accidents, which certainly do provide a lot of news. But many other accidents occupy a reporter's time as well: trains jump tracks, cranes fall at construction sites, children fall out of windows, small planes collide, and buildings collapse. Most of the time, such accidents—and many others—require reporter coverage.

Traffic accidents do get the most attention, however, even when they do not result in deaths or injuries. A chainlike collision involving a dozen or more cars on a snow-covered major highway is certain to attract reporters. Radio reporters know that drive-time audiences will be interested because of the effect such a pile-up may have on getting to and from work, and TV reporters and crews want to be at the scene for pictures and interview possibilities. TV audiences, at least in the minds of news directors and assignment editors, are fascinated by the sight of a dozen cars wrecked on a highway. Fortunately, most of those chainlike accidents produce more totaled cars than deaths and injuries. The drunk-driving accidents are the deadly ones, and reporters find little joy in covering them.

# Crime

The police radios chatter endlessly in all newsrooms. The information these radios provide sends reporters to many traffic accidents and also to the scene of holdups, gang battles, homicides, drug busts, and numerous other incidents that require police attention.

The crime that gets the most news coverage is homicide. Americans kill one another more than people in any other country, and most of these homicides seem to be reported on radio and TV newscasts. It is not unusual in a major city to have more than one homicide to cover at the same time. As macabre as it sounds, assignment editors sometimes have to decide which homicides to ignore and which to cover.

Reporters working nights in a large city often get "burned out" covering murders night after night. The scripts all tend to sound alike after a while.

Reporters talk to police in an effort to find out what happened and, more often than not, the word *drugs* is in the sound bite. There are sound and video of crying relatives, questions to witnesses, and shots of the body bags.

The O. J. Simpson murder trial was, of course, something unusual, and the media coverage was beyond comparison with any other homicide this century, as evidenced by the trial. The case was so unique because it involved a well-liked sports and entertainment celebrity who was married to a beautiful woman whom he allegedly abused physically. Simpson hired a so-called dream team of attorneys whom most Americans believed would win an acquittal or, at least, a hung jury. Later in the book, we take a look at the live TV coverage of the trial, which took nine months to try and only about three hours of jury deliberation to acquit Simpson.

Crimes other than murder are also news. The decision whether to cover other crimes, such as holdups and gang battles, depends mainly on the circumstances, the size of the market, and what other news is going on at the same time. In a large city, a holdup would only bring a reporter to the scene if people were seriously injured or taken hostage or if an enormous amount of money was involved. In a small community, even an injury-free holdup of a convenience store might attract a broadcast reporter to the scene.

It may sound obvious, but reporters must always remember that a person charged with a crime is considered innocent until proven guilty. The fact that someone is charged with a crime does not mean he or she is guilty; police make mistakes. It's up to a judge or jury to decide whether someone is guilty or not guilty. It is important to remember that many accused people walk out of court free.

Before the courts reach a verdict, a reporter must always say the defendant is "accused of" or "charged with." A reporter must never take on face value what a police officer or detective says at the scene of a crime. A reporter may be told that John Doe was stopped in his car and a pound of heroin was found in the trunk. It is irresponsible reporting to go on the air and say: "Police find a pound of heroin in a Center City man's car trunk. Details in a moment." The words *police say* or *police charge* are critical, even in a headline. The reporter must ensure that the defendant is treated fairly in any broadcast about a crime.

## Police–Media Relations

Most of the time, the media and police cooperate. Sometimes, however, police complain that the media do not treat them fairly. The now-famous Los Angeles case in which a video camera showed police officers beating motorist Rodney King received national media attention, and the acquittal of the police officers of the charge of using excessive force brought on riots in Los Angeles and other parts of the nation.

Before the trial, police charged that the story had received too much attention and that the media had smeared the entire Los Angeles police force because of the actions of a few. The media started looking more closely at the actions of police departments in other cities, and police in those cities started to feel that they, too, were attacked because of what happened in Los Angeles. The result was an overall strain in relations between police and reporters. But journalists have a job to do, and what happened in Los Angeles deserved the media attention it received. Whether it was blown out of proportion is debatable.

While police and the media usually *do* get along, police can make jobs tough for reporters who do *not* "get along" with them. Tempers are lost sometimes, but the Hollywood detective movie stereotype of the police and reporters constantly at one another's throats is much overworked. Many detectives and reporters become friends because of their working relationships, and those relationships are invaluable.

# The Courts

Those arrested by police wind up in criminal court unless the defendants are younger than 16 years old, who are then handled by the juvenile courts. Domestic relations courts also get some cases involving marital disputes.

A second court system, the civil courts, handles noncriminal matters—civil suits between individuals, between individuals and corporations and other institutions, and between two or more companies. These suits, for the most part, are about money. Someone wants payment for damages. It could be for libel, an unpaid bill, shoddy workmanship, an auto-accident injury, or numerous other reasons.

Federal courts deal with matters that in one way or another involve the federal government or federal laws.

This section concentrates on the courts that most reporters cover—criminal and civil.

## Criminal Courts

Depending on the state, city, or town involved, a variety of court procedures take place before a defendant comes to trial. In small communities, a defendant may appear first before a justice of the peace, or he or she may appear in a county court. The defendant could be released on bail or remanded to jail to await a court hearing. In minor cases, a judge may hear the case and render a verdict, unless the defendant requests a jury trial.

In cities, the defendant usually is brought first to a police station, where he or she is *booked*—formally charged, photographed, and fingerprinted. Depending on the time of day of the arrest and booking, the defendant appears in court the same day or the next, where he or she enters a plea and is released on bail or sent back to jail to await arraignment and the setting of a trial date. More serious crimes are sometimes turned over to a grand jury, which examines the evidence and decides whether the accused should be indicted and stand trial or be released.

If the defendant is a celebrity, radio and TV reporters usually cover the court appearances, even if the charge is relatively minor. More serious crimes—such as rape or homicide—draw a crowd of reporters. As noted earlier, because so many killings take place in large cities, radio and TV reporters virtually ignore many of them. Assignment desks send reporters to homicide arraignments only if there is something unusual about the killing or if the defendant or victim is well known.

In smaller cities such as Richmond, Virginia, and Baton Rouge, Louisiana, which have unusually high numbers of homicides in proportion to their size, almost every homicide is big news. Each one gets complete coverage, along with a reminder of the standings: "The city's 64th homicide of the year was reported tonight."

## Reporter Access

Although many courts are easing restrictions on cameras and recorders in court-rooms, many still bar such equipment. When they are allowed, access is usually obtained on a pool basis. Some courts allow reporters with cameras and tape recorders to question lawyers, prosecutors, defendants, and others in the corridors, whereas others restrict the media to remaining outside the courthouse.

Good reporters attend the court hearings and trials even if the equipment is barred. They take detailed notes on what goes on for use in their reports. The reporter not only looks for important remarks and choice quotes from the judge, prosecutor, defense counsel, and witnesses but also makes note of facial expressions and other signs of emotion. If it's a jury trial, the reactions of the jury members are particularly important because they may give some clue about how the case is going.

When cameras are not allowed in the court during an important case, an artist is usually assigned along with the reporter to render sketches of the principal figures. Chapter 19, "Specialty Reporting," has more discussion about cameras in the courtroom.

## Civil Courts

When people believe that they have been damaged in one way or another by individuals, professionals, or companies, they may seek redress by suing in civil court. The suit may be for libel, malpractice, failure to live up to a contract or to pay a bill, or divorce (just to name a few). The loser in civil court usually ends up paying money. No one goes to jail as they once did when debtor prisons existed; however, refusal to pay court-ordered alimony or child support would be considered contempt of court, and that could put the guilty party in jail.

Radio and TV newsrooms do not assign reporters to many civil court trials or hearings because most of the cases tend to be dull and relatively unimportant; however, an unusual malpractice case involving millions of dollars or a class action suit against an automobile company for allegedly building an unsafe vehicle attracts broadcast media to the courthouse. Reporters also cover civil cases when celebrities are seeking damages for libel or are involved in a scandalous divorce or paternity suit.

As far as reporting assignments go, the rules are the same as those for covering the criminal courts. Attend the hearings and trials, take notes (particularly if you can't use equipment inside), and try to speak with both sides outside the courthouse.

# Demonstrations

The right to demonstrate is a freedom enjoyed by all Americans, and hundreds of thousands of us, maybe more, take advantage of this freedom each year. Radio and TV reporters do not cover every demonstration, but if the organizers know their business, they can almost always orchestrate a demonstration to guarantee media coverage. Regardless of the nature of the demonstration, the primary responsibility of the reporter is to avoid being "used."

With the possible exception of issues of civil rights and U.S. involvement in the Vietnam War, the battle over abortion has brought out more protesters than any other controversy. Americans on both sides of the issue are dedicated to their cause, and they spend a great deal of time defending, or trying to close, abortion clinics. The picture and sound possibilities are always good at such demonstrations, so a high percentage of them get radio and TV coverage. The right-to-life demonstrators are likely to have their children in tow and an assortment of picket signs accusing abortion clinics of murder; often they may be carrying a fetus in a jar. The pro-choice advocates have their share of signs and are extremely vocal in pleading their case that a woman should have control over her body.

Reporters cannot allow themselves to get caught up in this frenzy. Once the media arrive at the scene, the crowd gets louder and more agitated; the arrival of the TV cameras brings the noise to a peak. If you see this happening, wait until the crowd gets back to normal or near normal. Turning the camera off, and moving away from the crowd for a few minutes, is often effective.

The reporter should find a spokesperson in the group and get a statement. It is not the reporter's role to debate the merits of the controversy with the individual. The reporter should also knock on the door of the clinic and try to talk with someone inside.

**Figure 11.2**  Reporter Christine Devine of KTTV-TV in Los
Angeles conducts an interview during the rioting that followed
the acquittal of the police officers charged in the beating of
Rodney King. (Photo by Mikiholo)

Often, both sides show up at the same site. That makes the reporter's job
of being fair even easier. Remember that regardless of what the demonstration
is about, the reporter must always get the views of both sides.

# Riots

Demonstrations sometimes get out of hand and turn into riots. And sometimes
riots just break out on their own—in prisons, among workers involved in a strike,
or on city streets following a racial incident. The most sensational rioting in
recent years followed the verdict in the Rodney King trial in California.

There are special rules for covering such events. The most important one is
that reporters should never put themselves or the crew in unnecessary danger.
It is impossible to determine, or even guess, what an unruly mob will do, and
it could just as easily as not turn its anger on the media.

Nighttime is particularly dangerous. Camera lights invite trouble, and most
news directors tell their crews not to use them. Today's cameras do a credible
job with just streetlights. News managers suggest that crews use telephoto lenses
if the situation shows the least sign of becoming dangerous.

Helicopters have eliminated some of the danger from covering potentially
explosive situations. All seven VHF-TV stations in Los Angeles had helicopters in

the air videotaping the looting and rioting that followed the Rodney King trial verdict.

# Disasters

Webster's dictionary defines a *disaster* as "an occurrence causing widespread destruction and distress." Hurricanes and tornadoes often produce disasters. A plane crash or the sinking of a vessel is also a disaster, if many lives are lost. Most certainly, the bomb that killed 168 people in the Oklahoma City federal building was a disaster.

Some reporters never experience a disaster; however, those reporters working in tornado or hurricane areas and in cities with major airports will probably cover one eventually. The horror of disasters creates an emotional and trying experience for reporters.

Although it's often difficult, reporters covering a disaster must get the facts straight. That may sound obvious, but because of the magnitude of a disaster, a lot of confusion ensues. All sorts of people will be talking to reporters, and it is often difficult to tell which version is accurate. A reporter must check and double-check all information. If something sounds suspicious, it should be reported with specific attribution. If there are two versions of casualty figures, for example, the reporter should give both figures, with attribution, and advise the audience of the discrepancy. This approach is better than trying to guess which figures are accurate and running the risk of having to make a correction later. The key point: When in doubt, be cautious.

Covering the Oklahoma City disaster was, of course, complicated by the criminal aspect of the bombing. Reporters spent as much time, probably more, trying to keep up with the police and FBI investigation of the bombing as they spent trying to sort out the number of dead and injured.

## Oklahoma City Bombing

A broadcast journalist who was in the middle of the news coverage of the bombing says it was "like Pearl Harbor" in that it scored a direct hit on the hearts of Americans and prompted a surge of sympathy from around the world. Bill Perry was working for the Oklahoma PBS network when the blast occurred. He said that unlike Pearl Harbor, modern news technology allowed information from the blast to be distributed within seconds of its devastating detonation.

Perry said that when the yellow Ryder truck exploded at 9:02 A.M. on April 19, 1995, all of Oklahoma City's network-affiliated stations were beginning their morning meetings to plan the day's news coverage. All of the stations are clustered in the same area of the city, about eight miles from the bomb site, and when the explosion occurred, everyone in the newsrooms heard and felt it.

According to Perry, the CBS affiliate, KWTV, already had two crews downtown for other stories, and the helicopter was warming up to go to Kansas for a spot news story. That chopper was redirected to the federal building, and the station had pictures of the site quickly. The news director, Joyce Reed, said her photographers take cars and gear home from work, and most of them were headed in to the station when the bomb exploded. Many of them, she said, went directly downtown. Others picked up reporters and headed for the scene.

Two other stations, the NBC affiliate KFOR and the ABC affiliate KOCO, also sent choppers to the scene, but the FAA quickly closed the air space, and no other aerial images could be obtained for a month, until demolition crews collapsed the building completely. All the news reports and pictures after the first hour were taken from the ground.

A reporter for WKY radio, Billie Rodely, said he was driving downtown when the blast occurred. He said he jumped out of the car and started running when he suddenly realized there was glass everywhere. Rodely said he was still several blocks from the scene and continued running until he got about a half block away. That's when he saw the bombed-out building. Rodely said he was shocked at what he saw. Nobody knew what happened, he said, "the blood was incredible." Rodely said he saw things up in the trees that he never reported. He said the other reporters who got there early were the same way. "It wasn't necessary to talk about body parts and tissue," he added.

One of Perry's colleagues, reporter Charles Newcomb, said his first view of the bombing scene far exceeded what he had expected to encounter. "We were a half mile away from the building," Newcomb said, "and it already looked like a war." He said bricks and broken glass were everywhere.

As microwave links were established, reporters at the scene and anchors at the studios were reporting over raw videotape of the bombed-out building. Susan Kelley, the news director at KOCO, recalls that some photographers struggled at first with whether they should be shooting footage of the scene or helping the victims. Photographers would later say that they continued shooting because there was such a strong response by medical personnel that they thought they might just get in the way. But Kelley said that crews still helped even while doing their job, whether it was loaning people a cell phone or literally giving them the coats off their backs because someone was cold.

KFOR news director, Melissa Klinzing, said that within two minutes of the explosion, the station was getting calls from around the country from stations wanting video. She said they uplinked their local coverage for NBC stations, and that eliminated a big headache. She said: "What we sent up was exactly what everybody wanted, and most of them re-broadcast it as it came down." Klinzing said that at one point when she was in the control room, she looked at the various monitors and saw that her station's video was on not only on the Oklahoma City station but also on CNN and NBC at the same time.

KTOK is located only about three miles from downtown and had the largest radio staff in the city, but the station's coverage was complicated by the fact that the bomb exploded on the same day they were relocating all their offices and studios to other floors in the highrise building where the station is located. As if that was not enough trouble, the staff was ordered to evacuate the building even though there was no bomb threat at that location. Because the FBI occupied the top three floors of the building, it was evacuated.

News director Jerry Bohnen said all of the office personnel left the building, as ordered, and security guards also tried to get the broadcast staff to leave. "The security guard was telling me to leave while I was on the air," Bohnen said. Three on-air people remained on the floor, and everyone else in the building left.

Bill Perry says all the stations apparently had disaster plans, but none of them used them. KFOR's Klinzing said a plan on paper in such a situation isn't the important thing. "If each person in the news machine doesn't know what their role is at that point," she said, "you've lost the coverage battle." Jim Palmer, news director at WKY radio, agreed. "There can be no plan for something of this magnitude," he said. "What it takes," he added, "is relying on your experience and an ability to avoid panic. You assess your capabilities, get on the air, and do what you've got to do. It's live radio."

Bill Perry says that all of the stations received an immediate outpouring of help from the community and within the stations. He said newsrooms were quickly augmented by volunteers from management, sales, promotion, and all other departments. For the most part, he said, they answered the phones so newspeople could do their jobs. Klinzing said you couldn't predict who would show up to help. "There were people here who I had fired, and they came back to help and stuck around for a week with no pay."

At KOCO, a photographer from Seattle who had arrived in town for a job interview landed at the airport right after the bomb went off. He went to the station and volunteered to help out on live shots and stayed for a week with full approval of his station. It was some time before the man was interviewed for the job, and he got it.

Perry said that's the way it all began—what was probably the longest local newscast in broadcast history. It would be five days, he said, before any of the Oklahoma City stations played a commercial or aired anything but around-the-clock news coverage. Perry further stated that "as the hours ticked by and the bombing became a worldwide news constant, a parking lot two blocks from the federal building mushroomed into an international media village as each news-gathering entity searched for its own angle to the story."

"But for those first critical hours of the catastrophe," Perry said, "the story belonged solely to the staff members of local radio and TV." He added that the performance by all these newspeople "is why Oklahoma City is not only known as the site of *the big bomb* but also as a city fully capable of top-notch broadcast coverage of a story of epic proportions."

Bill Perry, who provided this description of the early news coverage of the disastrous bombing in Oklahoma City, is a former News Director at NBC and

ABC television affiliates. He's currently Executive Producer of Documentaries for the Oklahoma PBS network.

# Tragedies

A tragedy is a form of disaster but on a smaller scale. For the friends and relatives of a couple and five children who were killed in a fire, however, the event is no less a disaster. For reporters, tragedies are often more difficult to cover than full-blown disasters because they become more personal. Regardless of how tough a reporter thinks he or she is, the sight of five small body bags being removed from a burned-out building has a strong emotional impact. Reporters can cry, and sometimes do, alone. They must, however, report such stories as dispassionately as possible and move on to the next one. For some, the emotion is too strong; more than a few reporters quit as a result.

## *Violence*

It sometimes seems as though violence is an inescapable part of our lives. In one form or another, violence touches on the lives of many thousands of Americans each year. And when we escape such horror, it appears that we often miss it narrowly or know some friend or relative who is a victim of it.

There have been many reports about violence and television, and sometimes it seems as if the two words are synonymous. The debate about too much violence on TV has been continuing for more than two decades. Although most of it deals with violent entertainment and the impact such programs have on children, there is great concern among journalists and nonjournalists that television news also shows too much violence.

News directors defensively point to society and argue, as we pointed out earlier, that the world is violent and journalists are just reporting what is going on. Much of that argument is valid, but critics maintain that too much emphasis is placed on violence in the news and that it is not necessary to report every violent incident, as it sometimes appears to TV viewers.

News directors counter that they do not cover all violence, and if they did, there would not be enough room in the 30-minute newscast to cover any other news. It is true that in many large markets, particularly, there may be multiple murders on any given night, and as the author recalls from his days as an assignment editor in New York City, reporters often covered murders almost every night of the week. I recall one reporter complaining that she was going to go crazy if she had to cover one more murder during the week. There were 571 murders in New York City in 1999, and Chicago had 645. Even in smaller markets, like Louisiana's capital city, Baton Rouge, there were 53 murders in 1999, an average of about one a week. Sadly, we live in a violent world, and the

**Figure 11.3**   The federal building bombed in Oklahoma City. (AP World Wide Photo)

United States is more violent than the rest of the world's nations, at least in crime-related violence.

This section examines the problem of violence in the news and how journalists try to deal with it—not only the reporting of it but also how they handle the often gruesome details of the crime, those who commit the violence, and the often-forgotten victims.

The 1990s were violent years. Much of it was brought about by wars in the Middle East, Europe, and Africa, and that violence is covered elsewhere in the book. This section deals with domestic violence, much of it about the shocking series of school shootings that occurred from 1997 to 1999.

## Schoolyard Shootings

The school violence began in Pearl, Mississippi, in October 1997, when a teenager killed two students and wounded seven others at a high school. Two months later at a high school in West Paducah, Kentucky, a 14-year-old student killed three students and wounded five others. Then on March 24, 1998, in Jonesboro, Arkansas, two boys, ages 11 and 13, shot to death four girls and a teacher and wounded 10 others.

A month later, on April 24 in Edinboro, Pennsylvania, a 14-year old boy shot and killed a science teacher in front of students at a graduation dance. A month later, on May 19 in Fayetteville, Tennessee, a high school senior fatally wounded a student in the school parking lot. Only two days later, in Springfield, Oregon, a 16-year-old killed his parents and then went to Thurston High School, where he killed two students and wounded 25 others.

The final school shooting tragedy in the series was the deadliest. On April 20, 1999, two students at Columbine High School in Littleton, Colorado, shot and killed 12 students and a teacher before turning the weapons on themselves. It was the worst such school violence in the nation's history.

The impact of these tragedies on the nation was overwhelming. The incidents also tested journalists' ability to deal with juvenile violence at a level never experienced before. The magnitude of the violence also brought media coverage of an unequaled level to the communities in which the tragedies took place. National media gave the stories saturation coverage. Some of it continues even today as anniversaries serve as reminders of those grim days and give cause for revisiting the stories.

Much of the news coverage of the school shootings has been praised but, as might be expected, many examples of bad journalism were also witnessed.

Most of the analysis of news coverage centered on the most violent of the shootings—Jonesboro, Arkansas and Littleton, Colorado.

*Media Invade Small Community*

Approximately 200 journalists invaded Jonesboro, Arkansas, in the days after the tragedy. Before the week was out, CBS had dispatched 17 reporters and support staff to the scene. CNN had 30 people there, and ABC and NBC added another 37.

One of those who analyzed TV coverage of the Jonesboro shooting was Ed Turner, a Freedom Forum Senior Fellow and Editor-at-Large for CNN. Turner is a former Executive Vice President for the Cable News Network. Turner said that in covering the Jonesboro shooting, television scored few major hits, but it didn't commit any major blunders either. He said the nightly newscasts were thorough, if lacking real depth. He added that the morning talk shows provided informed, interesting guests, but the magazine shows generally were disappointing.

Turner said that the local and regional late-night coverage, while less sophisticated and polished, was nonetheless solid in almost all respects. Turner said the network evening newscasts did not delve deeply into the broader issues of gun control, parental responsibility, and school responsibility. He said NBC allotted the most time to the story, and its coverage seemed the broadest.

Turner praised the relatively small staff of TV station KAIT in Jonesboro, which, he said, produced solid reports on what happened. He said the reports

**Figure 11.4**   SHOOTING: LITTLETON, COLO, 20 APR 99—Columbine high school students run from the school after gunmen opened fire on terrified students, killing up to 25 people before taking their own lives April 20, police said. Jeff Stone, sheriff of Jefferson County, said the gunmen, students at the school, were found dead in the library on what he called a "suicide mission." (Reuters/Gary Caskey/Archive Photos)

were "often long on emotion but did not embarrass, mislead, or inflame." He said that in a sense the station served as a place where the community could grieve and that the newscasts undoubtedly were appreciated for their sensitive tone.

The CNN Editor-at-Large concluded that the quality of TV journalism ranged from average to good. Turner's analysis was part of a report prepared by the Freedom Forum, examining Jonesboro's coverage. It was part of a series examining fairness in the news media. As part of its investigation, the Freedom Forum collaborated with the College of Communication at Arkansas State University and the *Jonesboro Sun*. They invited residents of the community to a "speak out." Approximately 300 people showed up to share their thoughts and, in some cases, to criticize the media coverage. Some said journalists were intrusive, invaded the privacy of victims, and relied on children as news sources.

*Criticism of Media*

The Freedom Forum report said that many citizens believed that the media were too quick to draw conclusions about the character of life in a rural, southern town—a perception that was deeply resented as a stereotype. In the weeks that followed the town meeting, the Freedom Forum sent a team of reporters to Jonesboro to check out the comments made by those at the meeting. Robert H. Giles, a Senior Vice President of the Freedom Forum and director of the Free Press/Fair Press project, said the team of reporters spoke to victims and their families and reporters and editors involved in the story and "tracked down reports of inappropriate behavior by individual journalists."

The Freedom Forum reporters sent to Jonesboro said that virtually everyone they interviewed gave most reporters relatively high marks for accuracy and fairness, taste, and sensitivity. But the investigators said the roughly 10 percent of the reporters who "pushed too hard" or behaved callously are the ones who are remembered. They noted that people who were interviewed remembered the conduct of the media, rather than the content of their reports. The Freedom Forum report said it found few instances of misinformation in news reports, and almost all of them came early on, when the story was first breaking.

Jonesboro Police Chief Floyd Johnson had mixed reactions to the reporters who came to his community. He said that before the shooting, he thought he'd seen it all in terms of the media because when he was a sheriff in 1968 he dealt with the media when a tornado struck Jonesboro and killed 34 people. But he admitted he was wrong. He was not ready, he said, for the wave of journalists who turned up after the shooting. "For the most part," he said, "when you were dealing with a reporter one on one, they were very sympathetic, seemed to have a lot of sympathy for the folks." "But," he added, "I would have to compare them with a bunch of animals whenever they all get together with their cameras." He said: "They'll run into each other, run over you, park in streets, and block others."

Although inaccuracies in reporting the story apparently were few, one broadcast said that Shannon Wright, the teacher who was fatally shot as she protectively draped her body over a student, had died when she actually did not die until many hours after the erroneous report. Still other reports incorrectly said the woman was pregnant.

The husband of the hero-teacher, Mitchell Wright, also had mixed views about the media. He said that he is convinced that photographers climbed his fence and tried to get into his yard one night and that a TV crew set up a camera across the street from his house, focusing a camera on his front door. Wright said a neighbor warned the crew that if they did not get their equipment out of the road he was going to run over it.

Wright did commend the media for their constant referrals to his wife as a hero. He consented to interviews with ABC and NBC to talk about his wife. But he said a CBS representative tried to pressure him into doing another interview against his will, claiming that it would not be fair because he had talked to other networks. The CBS representative allegedly tried to sway Wright by saying that her boss was going to be upset with her if she didn't set up the interview.

Another resident of the town, Gretchen Woodward, says she was hounded by two reporters who accosted her when she left her house, demanding to know if she was Mitchell Johnson's mother and refusing to leave when she told them she had nothing to say to them. The woman said the reporters hid in her yard through the night and that she had to call police at 1 A.M. and again at 3 A.M. to get them off her property.

A sheriff said he had many complaints about media peeking through windows and knocking on doors. He said that some people claimed that if residents opened their doors some crews would walk in and reporters would start asking questions, saying that "they're live on 'Action News' or what have you."

The Freedom Forum report also said that some people were approached by news organizations with offers of money for exclusive interviews. The sheriff said one offer was for substantial cash payments to deputies monitoring the cell-blocks if they would take a picture of the two boys in custody. The sheriff said he warned his deputies that if they took the pictures, or allowed them to be taken, they would be fired.

The mother of one of the children killed in the shooting, Suzann Wilson, said she only got upset once with the media, when a photographer stepped out in front of the hearse on its way to her child's funeral to take a picture. The woman had requested that no cameras of any kind be at the funeral. She said when they got to the cemetery there were hordes of reporters and cameras at the graveside, some hanging from trees. But both Wilson and Michael Wright agreed that some news coverage of their loved ones helped with the healing process.

Analysis of media performance during the other school shootings was similar to those in Jonesboro. For the most part, it appears journalists acted responsibly, but there were some "bad apples."

There also were some interesting contrasts. For example, in the Columbine school shooting, the residents of the community appeared more willing to talk to the media, often searching out reporters and producers for an opportunity to discuss the tragedy. "It was bizarre," said KUSA-TV's Ginger Delgado. "When in your life," she asked, "have you seen so many victims and families come forward? So willing to talk." She said maybe students and families just accepted the axiomatic wisdom of our talk-show culture: talking heals pain.

Delgado said that many of these sources were teenagers who "seemed so self-possessed, looking directly into the cameras, spouting pithy sound bites." She said they soon learned to query reporters: "Are you national or local?"

One of the students who narrowly escaped the bullets but saw the tragedy close-up, Bree Pasquale, was one of those who apparently found relief in talking about the attack. She described to reporter Delgado how one of the gunmen "put a gun to my head and asked if we all wanted to die." She said: "I just started screaming and crying and telling them not to shoot me." "The shooter turned to another girl," Bree said, "and shot her in the head in front of me, and he shot the black kid because he was black." The KUSA interview with Delgado was broadcast over and over again on CNN and NBC.

*ABC News* correspondent Judy Muller, who was pulled off a story suddenly in New England and dispatched to Littleton, says she also was surprised when people involved in the tragedy were willing to talk to her. In her memoir, *Now This* (Putnam Publishing Group, 2000), she recalled striking up a conversation with a woman who was standing by herself near the school library and discovering that the woman was a teacher. Muller said that even as she was empathizing as a former teacher and mother, she identified herself as a reporter and somehow, as she put it, "I found the courage to ask her if she could talk to me on camera." The woman frowned, looked down at the ground, and then agreed to do the interview. Muller said it was not the only time during her stay in Littleton that she was surprised that people were willing to talk to her. Muller said it seemed to her that people, almost in a mass wave of catharsis, were unfailingly polite in their responses to reporters as they shared their experiences.

Throughout the week that followed the shooting, soaring network news audiences pumped up ratings for school-shooting specials such as *Dateline* on NBC and ABC's *20/20*. That Thursday night's edition of *48 Hours*, which included the interview with Bree, marked the first time that the CBS news magazine ever beat NBC's *ER* in the ratings.

Writing in Brill's *Content*, contributing editor Jon Katz called the media coverage of the Colorado shooting and its aftermath "grotesque, even outrageous." He said journalism, even its most serious practitioners, accepted and transmitted the idea that two students turned to mass murder because they played nasty computer games or had access to Internet bomb-making sites. Although approximately 20 million Americans, mostly kids, are into video and computer gaming, Katz said this idea was so widely disseminated and discussed by journalists that most Americans actually came to believe it.

The week after the massacre, a Gallup poll showed that more than 80 percent of Americans agreed that the Internet was at least partly responsible for the Columbine killings. "And," asked Katz, "who could blame them?" CBS's *60 Minutes* devoted an entire segment to this question: "Are video games turning kids into killers?"

Katz noted that hundreds of newspapers and TV stations ran stories linking computer games, Websites, and other "aberrant, abnormal, or weird behavior to mass murder." Katz added that these messages were almost guaranteed to panic parents and students and stampede educators into overreaction. "Instead of being a force for truth," Katz observed, "many in the media became transmitters of hysteria."

Veteran reporter Bob Steele, director of the ethics program at the Poynter Institute for Media Studies, praised media outlets that looked at the broader issues in the shootings as well as the violence. He said opening up the coverage of the shootings to include the broader aspects of the nexus of children and violence is key. Stephen Gorelick, a sociologist who teaches communications and journalism at the City University of New York, said journalists should give the public as much information as they can in such situations, without feeding the public desire for salacious material.

*ABC News* correspondent Judy Muller recalls that the first morning after the shooting, she was assigned to do a profile of the victims, what she described as "a reporter's worst nightmare: asking impossibly intrusive questions in order to get seemingly impossible answers, aimed at summing up a life in a matter of seconds, and all this against terrible deadline pressures." Muller says she and her producer started the day with a feeling of dread. She said there had been no official word yet on who the victims were, so they had to try to find out who they were and ask someone, a family member or friend, what they were like.

Muller found her assignment "emotionally wrenching." She recalled how she and her crew went to the school library where parents were waiting to hear whether their children were safe. She said she watched the faces of the parents as they searched the list that had been posted telling which students had been located and which were still inside the school. At that moment, Muller said, I was not a reporter, I was a parent. "I could no more have walked up to one of those people, who clearly were experiencing one of the worst moments of their lives, and ask them questions than I could have driven a knife into my own heart."

Muller said her camera crew stood back from the scene, filming quietly and from a distance, but she knew that it also was hard for them because they, too, were parents. "But," the correspondent added, "we had to do our jobs, to tell the story to a nation that waited, horrified, for the facts of yet another school shootout."

*Why Such Killings?*

LynNell Hancock, director of the Prudential Fellowship for Children and the News, and an assistant professor at the Columbia University Graduate School of Journalism, says that journalists dealing with high school shootings "should just get the facts out first and not try to weigh in with 'why' so much." On that note, James Garbino, director of the Family Life Development Center at Cornell University, says that the real reasons—the "whys"—are often difficult to pinpoint and sometimes just not possible to decipher. He said the media need to explore many possible "whys."

Sometimes those trying to find out the causes of the shootings focus on guns. The media was often accused of using the gun issue to explain many of the shootings; however, Garbino notes that journalists cannot ignore the role that guns play in youth violence. He says that granting too much attention to the opposite view that "guns don't kill, people do" is also a mistake.

Garbino says that journalists also should avoid referring to schoolyard shootings as "senseless" acts of violence. He said school shootings do "make sense inside the head of the kid who did them." In fact, he added, most of these kids commit these acts as a culmination.

### Don't Forget the Victims

Most analysts of the school shooting coverage agreed that while discussions of motives of the killers cannot be excluded, it's important to give a significant amount of coverage to the victims. One observer pointed out that in tragedies such as school shootings, a whole town or community is affected, not just the victims. Bob Haiman, a Freedom Forum Media Studies Center fellow, agrees that stories detailing the grief of families and the community are important. He said that other stories dealing with fund-raising for victims, counseling sessions, and vigils also are of value. As the editor of the *Jonesboro Sun* put it, "the victims are not just the 25 people who were shot. Everybody is in pain."

### Was the Reporting Excessive?

A negative view of the media coverage of the school shootings came from James Glassman, a fellow at the American Enterprise Institute. He called the news coverage "inordinate," saying that the media chose "to blow individual incidents in small towns into national crises."

Richard Wald, Senior Vice President of *ABC News*, thinks that the communities involved in such tragedies tend to have a higher regard for the work of local media than the networks. He said: "If you live in the community and watch the local news and read the newspaper, there is a tendency to view [those reporters] as being more sensitive." The national media is viewed, more often than not, as outsiders.

*ABC News* correspondent Judy Muller says that when she and her crew drove up to the school parking lot in Littleton, her worst fears of media excess were realized. She found the following scene: "Sprouting like overturned toadstools in the mud, satellite dishes pointing at the sky as far as the eye could see, part of a media encampment that was growing by the hour." Muller says she thought to herself, "Surely we can find a better way to cover these stories in the future, perhaps pooling our efforts to the point where no family would be requested to speak more than once." Muller says such ideas "pop up after each of these shooting incidents but are quickly forgotten as those media outlets weigh anchors and sail away to other troubled waters."

Some analysts believe that in the news coverage of high school shootings, too much emphasis may have been placed on discussing whether schools are safe, creating fear among Americans about their own children's safety. According to the National School Safety Center, schools are relatively safe. One survey notes that teens are far more likely to commit suicide than homicide with guns.

Sid Bedingfield, Vice President of CNN, agrees that school violence has to be put into perspective. "Finding balance in any crime story," he said, "is important." He said you have to look at the many schools where the children are safe.

Another controversy that arose out of the school shootings was the identification of the young people who did the shooting. Many news organizations have long-standing policies of not identifying juveniles until it is determined that they will be tried as adults. But some exceptions are made, and decisions often can be influenced by what other members of the news media do.

*ABC News* says it chooses to release the names of minors accused of crimes on a case-by-case basis. In the shooting cases, ABC said it released the names when relatives of the suspects made statements to the media. CBS said that while it does not usually identify minors allegedly involved in crimes, "the boys had been identified by other news outlets, including their hometown newspaper and TV station, before we were going on the air." CNN and NBC spokespersons made much the same argument for releasing the names.

At the conclusion of its report on how the media performed during the shooting coverage in Jonesboro, Arkansas, The Freedom Forum offered the following "lessons for the media":

1.  Be wary of unsubstantiated information. Anything not observed by a reporter should be scrupulously attributed.
2.  Avoid demonizing or glorifying suspects or victims.
3.  Correct errors promptly and prominently in full detail.
4.  Obey the law, don't trespass on private property, and respect the privacy of those involved.
5.  Appreciate the value of veteran journalists who know the community and who have built relationships over the years based on trust.
6.  Remember that when a disaster or tragedy occurs, coverage should reflect the fact that the entire community may feel victimized, not just those directly affected.
7.  Understand that viewers are better able to handle the grim details when they are reported in a larger context of sympathetic and extensive coverage that embraces the experience of the entire community.
8.  Don't hype an already powerful story or tell it in florid language.
9.  Avoid drawing quick conclusions, making unsubstantiated assumptions, or creating stereotypes.
10. Never misrepresent yourself or engage in deception to get the story.
11. Report on what went right and what worked when government and the public responded to a major, newsworthy event.
12. Remember that trust is the bedrock in the relationship between the news media and the community. It enables public officials to deal openly with the media by providing information that allows the story to be told quickly, completely, and accurately. Trust also helps the community understand the purpose, needs, and duties of the news media.

### Violent Stories Also Cause Stress for Journalists

Some news managers said that during and after the coverage of the school shootings they suggested to reporters and other staff members that they might wish to take advantage of station-provided counseling. The horror of the story took its toll on many journalists.

Covering tragedies can create immense psychological stress for journalists, according to the *American Journalism Review* (AJR), and sometimes it makes sense to get help. AJR cited one example of an *Arizona Republic* reporter, Katrina Bland, who was transfixed by a Polaroid photo attached to a police file showing a small pink coffin containing the body of an 8-month-old child who had been killed by an adult. In a story that she wrote about the tragedy, Bland wrote that the coffin was the size of a dresser drawer. Later, the reporter said that the photo of the coffin surfaced in her dreams, in which she would spot the doll-sized coffin at her office, in a convenience store, or nestled among her belongings in a drawer at home. The reporter said the nightmares triggered more such sleep-halting dreams about young children burned, beaten, and sexually molested. When the dreams persisted, Bland finally turned to a crisis counselor.

Writing about Bland's experience in AJR, Sherry Ricchiardi said the reporter's dreams pointed out the dilemma for journalists confronting horror, whether in a police file, on highways, or at house fires or the bombed ruins of a federal building. The AJR writer noted that although such coverage can create intense psychological stress, the standard newsroom script calls for stoicism. She said admitting to emotional fallout collides with the detached, dispassionate demeanor on which the profession prides itself.

Chris Cramer, President of CNN's international news division, says "some journalists do shy away from the stress issue and 'pooh-pooh' it, fearing being exiled as some kind of wimp." Ricchiardi says some journalists apparently fear that if they admit to any mental trauma, it may be viewed as weakness or even spark editors to pull them off important projects. Psychiatrist Frank Ochberg finds that surgeons and journalists have most strongly resisted outside help.

Coverage of automobile accidents and other emergencies often falls to rookies, according to Ricchiardi, and to deal with the stress, a Journalism and Trauma Program was established at the University of Washington in Seattle. According to program director Roger Simpson, the program aims to inoculate journalism students via role-playing and discussion. "I guess it's like a vaccination," he says. "If you do this in the classroom, it may be somewhat easier at a crash."

Although some journalists apparently are seeking psychological help for the effects of frequent exposure to tragedy, others such as Michael Sorkin of the *St. Louis Post-Dispatch* decided to try to avoid such trauma. After several years of covering corruption and murder in East St. Louis, Sorkin asked his editors not to tap him for any more "blood stories."

## The Waco, Texas, Conflict

On February 28, 1993, the U.S. Bureau of Alcohol, Tobacco, and Firearms (BATF) launched the largest assault in its history against a small religious group, near Waco, Texas. The raid was a disaster: Six Branch Davidians and four agents were killed. That tragedy was then followed by a 51-day standoff. Then, the U.S. Justice Department approved a plan that sent tanks carrying CS gas (O-chlorolbenzalmaloronitrile) into the compound where Branch Davidian leader David Koresh and his followers were holding out. After the gas was shot into the building, a fire broke out and all 74 men, women, and children were killed.

The tragedy provoked much criticism against both the Justice Department and the BATF. But the media also was accused by some for allowing itself to be manipulated by government agencies, for not being aggressive enough in trying to put the conflict into perspective, and for not giving the public sufficient information about the Branch Davidians, who were blamed from the start by the government as a dangerous "cult" that was responsible for triggering the assault on the compound that took so many lives.

Some of the criticism against the media was that it was too quick to accept the government's explanation for the standoff and never made a serious effort to explain the Branch Davidians' side of the story. The media was charged with going along with the orchestration of public relations by government officials and not trying harder to talk to Davidian leaders.

Finally, the media was criticized for accepting the conflict as just another "cult" story about people who were strange, different from most, and probably dangerous. Before the Waco tragedy, the American people were unaware of the Branch Davidians, and even those living near the compound said they knew little or nothing about the religious sect. But after the compound went up in flames, the Davidians were known to millions around the world.

Public opinion polls in the United States showed little sympathy for the Davidians but substantial support for the actions of federal agents in handling the siege.

*Was News Coverage Fair?*

In the book *Armageddon in Waco*, Anson Shupe and Jeffrey K. Hadden say the absence of public criticism of the federal agents' behavior is not surprising because from the onset, the mass media substantially reported the story without much scrutiny of the details of the raid and siege as these were presented to them in government press briefings in Waco. Shupe and Hadden, who have written extensively on religious sects and cults, say that in presenting the story largely without criticism, the media contributed significantly to legitimating the government's role and portraying the federal agents as properly assuming responsibility for abused and endangered children; with responsibility for bringing to justice a band of criminals who had assembled an enormous cache of illegal weapons; and finally, portraying the agents as guardians of a community at risk from the followers of the fanatical and dangerous cult leader and his brainwashed followers.

**Figure 11.5** "The Mount Carmel compound near Waco, Texas, is shown engulfed in flames on April 19, 1993. The FBI on September 2, 1999, released a newly discovered videotape of an agent obtaining approval from his boss to fire flammable tear-gas canisters during the deadly assault on the Branch Davidian compound." (Reuters/Gerald Reed/Schumann/Archive)

In the same book, James T. Richardson charges that the media have contributed directly to development and promotion of the anticult ideology. But, he adds, the media cannot be blamed for the specific way the tragedy developed. "The several authorities in charge, from beginning to end," he writes, "must be held responsible for the many bad judgments and misguided plans that were developed before, during, and even after the fire at the compound." But, Richardson notes that a key element of the strategy taken, particularly by the FBI, was to exercise total control of the media. He said the authorities treated the media simply as a resource to be allocated and used as desired and as a nuisance to be dealt with severely if they refused to comply.

*Government Control of Media*

Some reporters at Waco said there was more government control during the conflict than they had ever experienced during their careers. Richardson, who has written extensively on new religions, says that federal officials made an early decision that reporters would not be allowed access to Koresh and his followers.

A total ban on communication with those inside the compound was established, and reporters, of whom there were hundreds, were moved progressively back from the front lines until they were some three miles from the compound. Richardson charges that the government agencies used the media for their own ends, inhibiting and restricting information and preventing any sympathetic account from the residents in the compound. He noted that the FBI was upset at one point when Koresh called CNN directly and cut all phone lines except the one they wanted kept open.

Richardson says that when reporters did try to get closer than the three-mile limit, they were treated harshly. Some were summarily arrested, thrown to the ground, handcuffed, and taken to jail. Shelly Katz, a *Time Life* photographer, said that in more than 30 years, "I have covered everything from wars to riots but was never restrained as I was in Waco." Richardson says that Koresh and his followers knew they were losing the media war, for they continually requested access, sometimes even unfurling homemade banners from bedsheets saying: "God Help Us, We Need Press."

Koresh's attorney, Dick de Guerin, told a Freedom of Information conference that it now seems plausible that had the media been allowed better access to the Branch Davidians, it might have resulted in a different outcome.

*Could Media Involvement Have Changed the Outcome?*

But Richardson charged that this would have had the effect of humanizing Koresh and his followers and that would have undercut the authorities' seemingly official policy of demonizing the religious sect. Richardson said the media might even have served as third-party negotiators with Koresh, not an unprecedented occurrence in such situations. But, notes Richardson, none of this happened. Instead, FBI tactics and Koresh's reactions to them moved the situation tragically toward the conflagration that occurred. Richardson concluded: "The effort at managing and controlling the media was virtually a total success, but the *operation* itself was a complete failure: most *patients*, including the children, died."

James Wood, editor of the *Journal of Church and State*, observes that "if the state had intervened elsewhere in the world against a religious group as it happened at the Branch Davidian compound, it would have been reported in the U.S. as an act of oppression."

# Keeping in Touch

The news director and the assignment editor always must know what's going on "out there." If, for example, a demonstration is getting out of hand and is turning into a riot, the newsroom must be told. Any changes in stories, even routine ones, should be reported. Nothing irritates an assignment editor more than a crew and reporter who "disappear."

A reporter must keep the newsroom informed as much as possible about the status of a story. Is it running late? Is it falling apart? Is the video poor? All of these things and more must be shared so that those working on the newscast in the newsroom know what to expect. They also have the right to expect the reporter and crew to return early enough so that the story can be edited and aired on time. The team in the field should decide on a cutoff time—the time at which they must stop shooting and start to pack up their gear and head for home.

# War Reporting: The Rules Have Changed

CBS News *60 Minutes* correspondent Ed Bradley, who was wounded while covering the Vietnam War, described it as a "tough time because . . . people are dying and being maimed all around you." He said the guy who was standing two feet from him was killed. But, he added, in an interview with the *RTNDA Communicator*, "I forged friendships I have today. One of my closest friends is a cameraman I worked with in Vietnam and Cambodia."

What is it like to be a war correspondent? That all depends on which war and who's fighting. The rules can be different from country to country. Sometimes reporters are well respected and at other times they are considered targets or pawns.

Nancy Durham of the Canadian Broadcasting Corporation (CBC) is a war correspondent, foreign correspondent, and a self-described "one-woman band." She's based in London, from where she's dispatched to trouble spots around Europe and elsewhere. She told *Brill's Content* that her beat is "ordinary people in a mess." That beat has brought her to the Balkans, including Kosovo, more than 10 times in recent years. It's hard enough for a reporter and cameraperson to cover a war together, but somehow Durham is able to do it all by herself. Most broadcast news organizations are reluctant to send people overseas because of the cost. But with the one-person band, such as Durham, they can cover a war on the cheap. NBC London Bureau Chief Karren Curry told *Brill's Content*, "[Durham is] pretty much what the future of broadcast journalism is."

*New York Times* reporter Deborah Sontag told what it was like to be assigned to the Middle East as the year 2000 drew to a close. In her article, "From Peace to War, The Dubious Privilege of Living on Two Sides of a Chasm," she wrote:

> "Etonayim," we tell the Israeli soldiers at the blockade, "journalists." It's our password. Sometimes respected, sometimes not. "Meshuga!" one young soldier told me, circling his index finger by his temple as he waived me through to Ramallah with his gun. "You're nuts". . . .

Tom Gjelten, diplomatic correspondent for National Public Radio, reported from war zones in the former Yugoslavia, the Middle East, and Central and South

America in the 80s and 90s, and has won the Overseas Press Club, George Polk, and Robert F. Kennedy Journalism Awards. He's "suspicious" of anyone attracted to war reporting "just for the thrill or adventure of it. . . . Cowboy types tend to be unreliable."

Gjelten goes on to say that, in combat, "You're not working phones and you can't do much research. . . . You're truly on your own, away from editors and the normal reporting structure." Gjelten adds that you must be "a self starter." It requires a tremendous amount of ingenuity and lots of enterprise.

Most journalists will never be required to cover a war or other military action, so offering advice on how to do so might not seem necessary. The journalists who reported from Vietnam and Korea and during World War II would probably say there is not much advice they could give now, other than the obvious about reporting accurately and objectively, because the "rules" have changed. They changed in Grenada and even more drastically in the Persian Gulf during Operation Desert Storm.

Historically, war correspondents have been permitted to walk onto beaches with U.S. Marines and to sit in the belly of a bomber flying on a mission over an enemy target if they wanted to risk their lives in such endeavors. Many did, and some died. That kind of reporting allowed the people at home to know first-hand how the war was progressing and what was happening to their loved ones. But during the Vietnam War, the first war to be brought into American homes via television, Americans saw more dramatically than ever before what war was really like. They would eventually see, despite the efforts of the military and various administrations to keep it from them, that the U.S. was losing the war.

Many generals and politicians still blame the media, particularly television, for causing the withdrawal of U.S. forces from Vietnam. Many journalists maintain that the military learned a lesson in Vietnam: never again to allow the media the kind of unrestricted access they were permitted in Vietnam.

The invasion of Grenada was virtually complete before the media were allowed to report from the island. National security was cited as the reason for the secrecy. As for Desert Storm, Doug Ramsey of the Foundation for America Communications said there were "two great victories in the Gulf War: the allies decisively defeated the Iraqi military and the American military decisively defeated American news organizations."

Ed Fouhy, a 25-year network news veteran, said that as a result of Vietnam, the military not only instituted pool coverage of wars, but they also "sent their officers to charm school, and to make sure the briefers were people with stars on their shoulders—not bars as they were in Vietnam." Fouhy said the Pentagon made a political decision to control information.

Jeffrey Marks, the chairman of the Radio and Television News Directors Association, said the military engaged in "news management." He said: "We were maneuvered away from the stories we wanted to cover. Trips into the field were orchestrated to show only what the military wanted America to see and hear. . . . Reports were censored for reasons of pride, not security."

NPR correspondent Deborah Amos, who reported from the battlefield, said the ability to report was "personality driven." She said: "If you had a decent public affairs officer, it got done. If you had an officer who was suspicious of the media, then your life was hell." Former *CBS News* anchor Walter Cronkite told Congress that "with an arrogance foreign to the democratic system, the U.S. military in Saudi Arabia is trampling on the American people's right to know."

A group of news organizations was so disturbed by the censorship that occurred in the Persian Gulf that it filed a suit in U.S. District Court in New York against the Defense Department, charging the department with imposing unconstitutional restrictions on the media during the Gulf War.

Former *CBS News* correspondent Robert McKeown (now with *Dateline NBC*), who was the first journalist to report live from the front lines on the night the ground war began and the first reporter to report live from Kuwait City (arriving even before allied troops), said there was "greater manipulation of the press than there had ever been before." But he said it didn't affect his reporting a bit because he and some others "decided to be illegal from the beginning and not to be part of the press restrictions and pool."

McKeown said, however, that the censorship affected the networks overall and the war was covered "to only a fraction of what it should have been, given the technology." McKeown was able to scoop many of his colleagues because he was equipped with a mobile satellite dish. He said CBS decided to invest millions of dollars in the rolling dishes because it wanted to beat the opposition when the ground war began. He said the network ran into delays of four or five days in getting material broadcast during the air war, and they "wanted to make sure that wouldn't happen when the ground war started."

McKeown disputed the Pentagon's claim that pool coverage was necessary because of national security. He said that he saw many things in the desert that could have presented a security problem if he had reported them, but that he didn't even though he had the ability to go live at any time.

McKeown further said: "It is not our job to compromise national security. The system always has been built on a system of checks and balances and a responsible press. A responsible TV reporter would not report stories that jeopardized national security, and we didn't."

CNN's Peter Arnett, a Pulitzer Prize winner for his reporting of the Vietnam War, was the subject of much controversy for his reporting from Baghdad after all other Western correspondents were forced out of the Iraqi capital. Arnett's reports were censored by the Iraqis, which troubled many people who felt his reports could not be trusted and might help the enemy.

In defense of Arnett, *New York Times* TV critic Walter Goodman said that Arnett "was doing what any journalist would do." He noted that the other networks would also have liked to have had a reporter in the city if they could have managed it.

Goodman further added: "The notion of American correspondents reciting reports approved by the enemy is uncomfortable, but noncoverage is not an

**Figure 11.6**   Christiane Amanpour of CNN reports from Lebanon.

**Figure 11.7**   Former *CBS News* correspondent Bob McKeown reports from Kuwait during the Gulf War. (AP/Wide World Photos)

attractive alternative. The best the journalist can do in enemy territory is to make plain to viewers and readers the conditions under which he or she is permitted to operate and try to slip in more information than the minders have in mind."

The TV critic stressed that while he could not fault Arnett for staying in Iraq, "the question nags" whether he and other reporters in Baghdad "adapted too readily to their host's scenario, whether they might not have found more ways to talk to viewers over, behind, beneath, and around those friendly minders."

# Beats

During their careers, reporters cover most of the types of spot news stories just discussed. Some reporters may have one particular type of story assigned to them as their *beat*. Unfortunately, not too many radio and TV newsrooms use the *beat* method of reporting, which was developed by—and is still a tradition at—newspapers. Most broadcast managers argue that they do not have the budgets necessary to assign reporters to beats. They note that news is only a small percentage of what is viewed on television every day, while newspapers devote most of their attention to it. Many people believe broadcast news suffers because it does not have enough beat reporters.

The networks and some large-market stations, however, do have beat reporter-journalists assigned to special areas such as the environment, medicine, and business. A firm believer in the beat system is Marty Haag, former Vice President of News and current consultant for the A.H. Belo Corporation, which owns five TV stations, including KHOU in Houston and WFAA in Dallas. Haag, who also consults for Audience Research and Development (AR&D) and is a "personal" Peabody Award winner, strongly recommends beat reporting to his clients. Some of the beats he suggests are business, technology, growth, religion, and education.

WFAA's beat reporters used to devote all of their time to beat reporting, but now they and the other beat reporters for stations in the Belo group split their time between beat and general assignment reporting. Haag says he believes in the beat system because "the world is too complicated. The beat reporter knows what he's writing about; you have someone who is familiar with the players." Haag says the beat system also allows a TV station "to compete with newspapers. We don't want to be clipping stories out of the newspapers and then covering them," he says. "We want to be ahead of them, not behind them."

Another believer in the beat system is Ed Godfrey, News Director of WAVE-TV in Louisville; however, his station's reporting staff numbers only 11, half the number Haag has in Dallas. Of course, Louisville is much smaller than Dallas. Godfrey, a former president of the Radio and Television News Directors Association, has beat reporters cover city hall, the state capitol, medicine, and consumer news. He says beat reporters give a news operation two important advantages: They can enterprise stories and cultivate sources.

But Godfrey says there are some disadvantages to beat reporting. Sometimes, he says, the reporters "get too close to their beats and wind up with stories not interesting to a general audience or get too close to their sources and can lose their objectivity." But he quickly adds that the advantages of beat reporting "far outweigh the disadvantages."

In Phoenix, KTSP-TV News Director Dave Howell wishes he had "the luxury of enough reporters to work on beats full time." His newsroom, he says, is like most: "You wind up with a hybrid, part general assignment and part beat reporter." KTSP does employ a full-time health reporter because, Howell says, research shows that more people are interested in health than in any other area except the weather.

Beat reporting is discussed further in Chapter 20, "Specialty Reporting." Both general assignment reporters and beat reporters need to be concerned with two aspects of broadcast reporting: advancing the story and avoiding the pack.

## Advancing the Story

If news were a commodity, it would be a bad investment because it doesn't last long—it's perishable. So, reporters must keep looking for new angles to try to update, or *advance*, the news. Chapter 4 discussed the need to update the lead of the story so that the news sounds fresh even if it is not.

Updating a story—putting a new lead on it—is only part of what is involved in advancing a story. A new lead reporting, for example, that the death toll in an air disaster climbs from 100 to 115 does advance the story, but it is a rather routine update. In the more traditional sense, this story could be advanced if, for example, the cause of the crash was determined or it was suddenly discovered that a famous person was on the plane. The story also could be advanced if a reporter learned that this particular type of aircraft had been involved in a series of similar crashes in recent months or if a reporter discovered that the FAA was about to ground all planes of the same make.

## Avoiding the Pack

Good reporters are always looking for an unusual angle for their stories. Sometimes it is difficult to report a story differently from other reporters because the lead seems so obvious; however, finding a new twist to a story is what distinguishes some reporters from the rest of the pack.

*ABC News* correspondent Morton Dean says he tries to get "an edge" on his colleagues by doing research before he goes out on a story. "I try to get as much background and history as I can," says Dean. "I try to find my own sources. I

**Figure 11.8**   The newsroom at WFAA-TV, Dallas. (Courtesy of Don Wall, WFAA-TV)

try to make an extra phone call. One way or another I try to find a nugget of information that might give me an edge."

*Dateline NBC* correspondent Robert McKeown notes that "good reporters aren't to be found" in the pack. They are out seeking people other than officials. He also says it's important to "know the beat and become familiar with it so that you sound like you know what you are talking about when a story develops. You should have a sense of what is really happening."

## Establishing Rapport with the Cameraperson

The beginning of this chapter mentioned that a good relationship between a reporter and cameraperson is essential. Here are some suggestions and observations on how to establish that relationship.

*ABC News* correspondent Morton Dean says it is always a good idea "to discuss with the cameraperson what you are looking for, what your expectations are, and what you plan to do with the story."

Former *CBS News* correspondent Robert McKeown (now with *Dateline NBC*) gives much of the credit for his successful reporting during the Gulf War to his cameraman, David Green, and his satellite technician, Andy Thompson. McKeown and his crew had a high-tech mobile unit that allowed them to set up a transmitter that sent a live TV signal to a satellite, which relayed the signal some 23,000 miles to CBS studios in New York. McKeown says most people are not aware of the cooperative effort that goes into the news that they see on their screens.

*NBC News* correspondent Bob Dotson tells reporters to look for help and advice from the cameraperson. "They should have a shorthand, kind of like what a married couple would have," he says. "If you have this sort of camaraderie, the cameraperson is going to think, maybe for the first time in his life, that somebody thinks what he's doing is important."

Dotson credited Tom Zannes, a freelance cameraman for NBC, for the outstanding video used in Dotson's excellent package about a woman trapped in a cavern in Carlsbad, New Mexico. (The script for this package appears in Chapter 5.) Zannes was in the cavern with the team that was exploring it for the *Encyclopaedia Britannica* when a member of the team slipped and broke her leg. When Dotson arrived at the scene to cover the story, Zannes was still in the cave. Dotson said Zannes was allowed to remain there during the rescue because he is a world-class caver and because "he knew when to take pictures and when to put the camera down and help with the rescue."

Former *CBS News* correspondent Ben Silver says that if there is not a close working relationship between the reporter and the cameraperson, each may go off in a different direction, and they won't end up with a good product. "If you want camerapeople to get good video for your story," he says, "they have to know where you're going with the story."

Silver, now professor emeritus at Arizona State University, says reporters should remember that camerapeople often have journalism backgrounds and have good ideas too. "Two sets of eyes are better than one," he says, "and three sets of eyes are even better." Silver notes that when reporters are working on a story, strangers sometimes approach them with information. "Listen to them," Silver advises. "They may have seen something you and the cameraperson missed because you were busy doing something else. You always have to keep an open mind."

# One-Person Band

If you start out in a small market, which is where most young people right out of college do begin their careers, you may not only be reporting the news. You may be shooting it as well. To save money, more and more small stations—and even some bigger ones—are hiring people who can "do it all."

Thanks to lighter cameras, digital technology, and tighter budgets, some stations are employing people who know how to write, report, and handle a camera in the field. At some stations, those same people edit the stories when they return to the station. Many of the people who are working alone seem to enjoy the freedom of doing everything by themselves. Does the quality of the product suffer? Probably, but those writing the checks often are willing to accept less if it costs less. On the positive side, it means that there may be more opportunities for young people who have learned the basic skills—writing, reporting, and videography.

Michelle Kosinski, the bureau chief in Salibury-Piedmont for WSOC-TV in Charlotte says working alone helps her get better stories. "It's just me and my camera," she says, "so people tend to tell me more. They feel closer to me." Kosinski says she writes her story while she shoots. "There's a beauty in seeing something and making it look the way you want it to look."

Lisa Goddard, who worked on her own in Myrtle Beach, South Carolina, before moving on to another reporting job, agrees. She liked having control over her packages. "You can shoot based on how you want to write," she says. But Goddard admitted that being alone was difficult when she had to do stand-ups. She said that for the first two weeks on the job she kept cutting off her forehead.

Peter Landis, News Director at NY1, the 24-hour cable news operation, has 23 people who both shoot and report. He says economics force newsrooms to do more with less. He asks: "Why pay for two people to do the job one person can be trained to do?"

# Convergence

In addition to the comeback of the "one-person band," another trend in broadcast news is *convergence*. With convergence, reporters cover a story for one medium, do the same story for other media owned by the same company, or they may simply share information. As with the "one-person band," convergence is also dictated by economics. One person does the job that used to be handled by two or three. In addition to saving money, advocates maintain that convergence results in a better product.

Here's how it works: A television reporter's company also owns other media in the same market, such as a radio station, a newspaper, or a Website, or all of the above, in the same market. The reporter writes his story for television, then does radio and newspaper versions of the same story. Or the newspaper reporter could start the ball rolling, and the process can involve other media, such as cable and the Internet.

Just as the "one-person band" is not new, neither is a marriage between different media. While these concepts are not new, they're developing at a "much more rapid pace than ever," according to Barbara Cochran, president of the Radio and Television News Director's Association (RTNDA). Some examples of convergence in which news organizations share personnel and resources are as follows:

- In Tampa: WFLA-TV, the *Tampa Tribune*, and Tampa Bay On Line (TBO.com)
- In Chicago: WGN radio, WGN-TV, and the *Chicago Tribune*
- In Cedar Rapids, Iowa: KCRG radio, KCRG-TV, and the *Cedar Rapids Gazette*

• In Orlando: the *Orlando Sentinel* shares content with the Florida Cable News Channel

Not only are different media owned by the same company converging, but media owned by different companies are also forming partnerships, although limited ones, in which they tap into each other's expertise. Some examples are NBC and the *Washington Post* and their Internet resources; CBS and the *New York Times*; and WBZ-TV and the *Boston Globe*.

How serious is the endeavor? In Tampa, a television station, newspaper, and Website are working side by side in a brand-new $40-million complex devoted to convergence, reports the *RTNDA Communicator*. "They share news tips, resources, and reporters in a convergence effort far more ambitious than anyone else has ever tried," reports the *Communicator*. The company, Media General Inc., has built a $40-million, four-level, state-of-the-art news complex devoted to convergence, called the News Center.

The Gazette Company of Cedar Rapids, Iowa, is also considering building a news plant devoted to convergence, says Chuck Peters, the company's Chief Operating Officer. Peters says the company has already converged six different subsidiaries into two. One entity includes radio and television. While the broadcast and print people are committed to sharing information, the news director and newspaper editor exercise independent judgment, but cooperate where they can, says Peters. Although the business side of the company is also involved in convergence, "we don't blur lines between news and advertising," he said.

At the News Center in Tampa, editors from the various media sit next to each other on the assignment desk, which is the "nerve center" of the converged operation. A camera is set up near the *Tribune* newsroom. It enables newspaper reporters to tell about stories they covered during the television newscasts.

Rick Ragola, president of WFLA, told the *Communicator* that convergence combines the immediacy of the Internet, the urgency and emotion of television, and the depth of the print media. How is the concept working in actual practice? Some worry that quality suffers when reporters spend so much time shifting gears as they prepare stories for the various media. Another criticism is that a reporter who serves more than one medium can't cover as many stories as a reporter who serves just one medium. *Tampa Tribune* reporter Lisa Greene told the *Communicator* that presenting her story on more than one platform gives her greater reach, but she fears it takes time away from reporting on other topics.

And there are other problems with convergence: Reporting for print and radio and TV require different skills. Print reporters must learn how to integrate pictures and sound into a television story and how to perform in front of a camera. Broadcast reporters have to learn to write for the print media. And still photographers must learn how to tell a story with motion pictures and sound.

That's no easy task. It's much easier for videographers to take still pictures than for still photographers to handle a motion picture camera.

One newspaper reporter said convergence has improved his writing, forcing him to be more concise when writing for television. A television reporter says she can write concisely for television and use more depth in the newspaper version of the story and still greater depth—or at least length—in the Internet story.

The Internet version often includes not only the complete stories used on the air and in print but also facts edited out of the broadcast and print versions of the story, or "outtakes" as they are referred to in broadcast parlance. With convergence comes greater impact, or exposure. Stories that might normally appear only on television, for example, with convergence might also appear in the newspaper, on the radio, and on the Internet. Convergence enables the viewer or reader to go to the Internet for more details on the same story.

So, if you are planning to go into broadcast news, here's a word to the wise: In addition to broadcast journalism courses, take courses in print reporting and even the Internet. You may have to work in all three mediums. A print reporting course not only helps you master a different medium, but because you're required to do more reporting and writing in print than in broadcast reporting courses, it also greatly adds to your reporting and writing skills.

Shortly after America Online (AOL) absorbed CNN-Time Warner in 2001, CNN announced a layoff and redefined the role of its reporters, according to the *Wall Street Journal*. Both actions were designed to cut costs. Reporters were ordered to learn how to use lightweight digital cameras and editing equipment. In addition, they would also be expected to file their stories on the Internet at AOL and on CNN radio. So, the question was asked, were convergence and the "one-person band" hitting the big time? Convergence seemed to be in, as was at least a modified form of the "one-person band."

Top CNN executive Eason Jordan was quoted as saying: "Correspondents whose expertise is TV reporting must know how to write for interactive and provide tracks for radio and deliver them as needed." The *Wall Street Journal* quotes another executive as saying that CNN hopes to be a big content provider to AOL and the AOL-owned Netscape. And, he said, the merger provides "significant cross-promotional opportunities" because AOL reaches 27 million homes. Jordan said deploying compact digital cameras and editing equipment "will allow us to deploy smaller reporting teams of one or two people, at times when it makes sense." Adding that "larger teams will be with us for some time to come."

Reporters were less than excited about doing camera and editing work. Legal correspondent Greta Van Susteren was flabbergasted, the *Wall Street Journal* said. "I would certainly like to learn to do it, but I'd like to learn to speak French," she added. "For this reason, they don't ask me to do makeup in the makeup room, I don't think they'll ask me to do this."

# Quality Suffers

James Rosen, a former one-person shooter-reporter, sometimes referred to as a video journalist, says "I loved shooting but hated the *schlepping*." He recalls when he was working for News 12 in the Bronx, he once covered a college graduation speech by Bill Cosby and had to park 10 blocks away. He says he left the tripod behind and blew his stand-up. "The quality of the piece suffers," he added, "when you work alone." Rosen says he was grateful for the challenge and opportunity to learn the skills. Rosen is now a Washington correspondent for Fox Newschannel and has a photographer, editor, producer, and makeup person.

Steve Sweitzer, News Operations Manager at WISG-TV in Indianapolis, doesn't think that video photographers should be worried about losing their jobs. He says the photog's job may be redefined somewhat, but there is still plenty for two people to do when out on a story. "Two minds are still better than one," he adds. Sweitzer says news operations that value quality will hire pros to operate the cameras and get the most out of the equipment. That feeling is shared by Jim Disch, director of news and programming for CLTV in suburban Chicago. "We prize our photography," he says. "We use tripods unless we're running after something." And he adds that he believes the station will best serve its viewers by hiring both photographers and reporters.

Jack La Duke, New York state bureau reporter for WCAX-TV in Burlington, Vermont, has been going solo for 35 years and loves it. But he admits it is not a perfect way to cover the news. He says you are shooting the interview and thinking about the questions, listening, and asking follow-up questions while worrying about the focus and the batteries. He says he enjoys working alone, but it's not for everybody.

Some critics also raise safety issues about working alone. In breaking news, the reporter often watches the photographer's back and helps protect that person from danger. Sweitzer notes that good reporters stand right next to the photographer. Other news directors worry about theft of equipment when only one person is doing the job. Still another news director was concerned about stand-up shots, which he described as "often god-awful when only one person is trying to shoot and talk at the same time."

Despite the criticism of "one-person bands," Michael Rosenblum, a former producer at *CBS News*, is busy training them. His consulting firm has trained more than 1,000 people to be shooter-reporters in the past 10 years.

For young people in school, we advise you to learn how to do it all as well as you can, not necessarily because you may have to do everything in your first job but because if you know how to write, shoot, and report, you will know what everyone else in the team has to know. That background will make you better at your job, whatever that job may be.

# Summary

Most reporting jobs in radio and television are general assignment positions. Reporters with these jobs cover everything they are told to cover, but most of their stories are spot news stories. Spot news deals with everyday breaking stories—fires, accidents, crimes, disasters, and so on. Some stations and the networks use beat reporters, who are assigned to specific topics, such as education, politics, and health.

Whether you cover general assignments or a beat, remember that good reporters learn how to advance a story, how to find new information to keep a story fresh, and how to find a new angle from which to develop a story.

# Review Questions

1.  What are spot news stories? Give some examples.
2.  What factors are considered when deciding to cover a crime or a fire?
3.  Journalists must be especially careful with stories about defendants in a criminal case. How is that done?
4.  Why does an assignment editor or news director decide to cover some court cases and pass up others?
5.  What precautions should reporters and crews take to ensure that a demonstration is covered fairly?
6.  What precautions should reporters and crews take in covering a riot?

# Exercises

1.  Arrange with a news director or assignment editor to follow a reporter when he or she is assigned to a breaking news story. Report on what happened at the scene and how the reporter covered the story.
2.  Attend a pro-life or pro-choice demonstration, and report on how the media covered the story. Make note of the radio and TV reporters who covered the demonstration and monitor their wraps and packages to see if the reports were balanced and fair.
3.  Check the local newspaper(s) to see how the demonstration was covered by print reporters. Write a report comparing the print and broadcast coverage.
4.  Monitor a local TV newscast, and see how many spot news stories were reported. What other types of stories were in the newscast?

# **12** Covering Planned Events

There are literally thousands of corporations, politicians, special-interest groups, nonprofit organizations, government agencies, and other individuals and groups looking for exposure on network and local newscasts. Assignment desks are inundated with news releases and telephone calls from public-relations firms and publicists working for these various groups. Many stations also have a special public-relations wire in the newsroom that allows organizations to get their releases to the assignment editor more quickly. And, of course, most of these organizations have Web pages on the Internet where newsrooms can reach them and vice versa.

Every one of these publicists tries to persuade the assignment staff that there is something special or important about the product, company, issue, or individual they represent. The assignment desk rejects most of these news releases and telephone calls for a variety of reasons—usually because they are too commercial or have little or no news value, or because there just isn't enough airtime available to go around. But some of these releases and telephone calls alert the assignment staff to events that are important and warrant coverage.

## News Conferences

Gathering a crowd of journalists with tape recorders and cameras in one room is a triumph for anyone working in public relations. The number of journalists who attend such news conferences depends on what is being "sold." Make no mistake about it, that is what we are talking about—"selling."

It makes no difference whether the news conference is called by a government official, a Broadway producer, a major corporation, or the Red Cross; each news conference has a message to sell to the American people. For example, the district attorney may call a meeting with the news media to announce the arrest of several organized-crime bosses. The arrest is news, of course, but the district attorney also wants to let everyone know what a good job she and the department are doing.

The Broadway producer is betting that the media will turn out to hear about a new show because the release just happens to mention that the chorus line will be there in full costume.

The Red Cross is hoping for the best but knows that it may have difficulty getting reporters to show up at its news conference to discuss a blood shortage because it's not likely to provide good pictures for television or exciting sound bites for radio. The conference may get a 20-second read story on the six o'clock news. You might wonder why a blood shortage is not considered an important story. It is, but it probably will get more attention from newspapers than from radio and television. It just isn't a "good" broadcast story, a point of view that elicits a lot of criticism of broadcast news, much of which is justified.

That same morning, General Motors is holding news conferences in the convention center in your city and in various key locations throughout the country to display its new line of cars, including, as its news release boasts, a compact car that gets 50 miles to the gallon. As you might expect, every radio station, TV station, and newspaper, as well as several magazines, will send reporters, and the story will make most local and network newscasts.

How do reporters get ready for news conferences? Let's look at a reporter preparing for the conference being held by the district attorney. Depending on the sophistication of the newsroom, the reporter starts with the clips and video

**Figure 12.1** Setting up for a news conference. (Photo by James Terry)

morgue, which may be computerized, to see what's available on the arrested organized-crime figures. If there is video of them, she asks for it to be pulled. She reads carefully any clips on the arrested men and checks the Internet and Websites for local newspapers. Before she leaves for the news conference, she also might make a quick check with other reporters in the newsroom to see if they have any additional information they gathered while covering other stories involving the men.

The reporter and her cameraperson arrive at the news conference early because it will be crowded and she wants to get a good position for the camera and herself. When the conference begins, the DA reads a prepared statement. The cameras and tape recorders will be rolling, although little of the statement—and maybe none of it—will get on the air. The question-and-answer period following the opening statement usually produces the best sound bites.

The reporter keeps notes on the opening statement, in any case, so she will know where the best bites are if she decides to use any of them. She does the same when the question-and-answer period begins, keeping track of the time when the best comments are made. While she was reading the clips in the newsroom, the reporter noticed that the organized-crime leaders were arrested five years before. The DA—the same one—got a conviction, and the men were sentenced to 5 to 10 years in prison. The reporter hopes that no one else beats her to the question she is ready to fire at the DA: "How come these guys aren't still in prison? It's only five years since you grabbed them and put them away the last time." The question would surely be provocative; perhaps the answer would be one of the highlights of the news conference. In all likelihood, the DA would respond with something like, "I just convict them; ask the judge and the parole board why they are back on the street so quickly." The DA, who had been critical of the judiciary on several other occasions, provided anchors with the headline, "DA Criticizes Judges and Parole Board."

Sometimes it is important to ask tough questions. News conferences should not be just a forum for those calling them. It's also important to ask follow-up questions, particularly when the individual holding the news conference is evasive or unclear. Techniques for asking good questions are discussed in Chapter 15, "The Interview."

Many broadcast reporters like to interview individually the person holding the news conference when the conference is over. *ABC News* correspondent Morton Dean says he does this if he doesn't hear what he wants during the news conference or if he wants to go in a different direction. "Otherwise," he says, "I'll pull a bite from the news conference."

Reporters often call in advance to arrange an interview with the person *before* the news conference. Some people agree; others refuse because they know it sometimes irritates other members of the media. This is particularly true when the reporter is still conducting the interview when the rest of the news corps arrives in the room. Other broadcast reporters, seeing what's going on, tell their camerapeople to set up and start shooting. Suddenly, there's a mini-news conference going on before the regular one starts. Such occurrences are particularly offensive to the print reporters, who must then wait for the scheduled news conference to begin. Once the broadcast people have their interviews, it is not unusual for them to pack their gear and be on their way, leaving the person holding the news conference with just the newspaper people. Many broadcast reporters cover news conferences this way because their assignment editors tell them to be in and out of the news conference quickly so they can move on to other stories.

Doing an interview before a news conference has its risks. Another reporter may know something important that the early reporter missed in the one-on-one; or a confrontation may occur when one of the print reporters asks an embarrassing question that catches the news conference host by surprise. The early reporter who came and went will not have this confrontation on tape.

# Local Government

The work of city and town government is extremely important, but it also can be one of the dullest assignments radio and TV reporters must cover. The problem for broadcast reporters is that the deliberations of the city council, the board of supervisors, and other local officials often take hours. The debated issues, however, often affect many people. An increase in local taxes, a curfew for teenagers, or a company's effort to locate a waste disposal plant in a community brings out a big crowd and lots of journalists. Because such meetings can go on for hours and days, what do radio and TV reporters do?

Let's suppose that the Centerville town supervisors are considering an out-of-town company's offer to build a waste-burning incinerator in the town. The company claims that the facility will employ 100 people and that it will be completely safe. Centerville could use another 100 jobs. Basically, Centerville, a dairy-farm community of about 5,000 people without much industry, is hurting financially; however, these people are farmers because they appreciate the earth and clean air, and they are suspicious of anyone or anything that might damage the environment. A local newspaper has already reported that the company wants to burn medical waste.

More than 100 people show up at the high-school auditorium to hear exactly what the company has in mind. There is a radio station in town but no TV station. A TV reporter from a nearby city shows up along with a local radio reporter and print journalists. TV cameras and tape recorders are rolling as town officials introduce a spokesperson and an engineer from the waste-disposal company. After some lengthy statements by the two representatives—complete with charts and statistics—a heated debate begins. The broadcast reporters take detailed notes, keeping a record of who is speaking and when. A local real estate agent says the plant would hurt property sales. "People escape the city to get away from pollution. They won't buy here if you build the plant," the agent says.

A parent questions the effect of toxic fumes on the town's children. The company official tries to reassure the crowd, which clearly is reacting negatively to the idea of building this plant in town. "There is absolutely nothing dangerous about anything we will be burning," the spokesperson says.

A man stands up holding a newspaper clipping. "Wasn't your company cited for not burning things right in the Carolinas?" he asks. "This story says your company left a real mess around and you were burning all sorts of dangerous things improperly."

The company official tries to explain away the story, saying, "We had a few workers who weren't doing their jobs the way they should have, but they've been replaced and things are all squared away now."

The man with the paper is still standing. "And this story says that you only employ about a dozen workers at that Carolina plant. You claim the plant here would mean 100 jobs for our town."

The debate went on for two hours, but the story prepared by the TV reporter would probably last no more than 90 seconds, maybe a little longer if the meeting took place on a slow news day. The local radio reporter would devote more time to the story because the issue is big news in Centerville. The radio reporter might do a special in-depth wrap-up of the meeting in addition to some one-minute wraparounds during newscasts throughout the day. There is no local daily newspaper, only a weekly, so the townspeople are anxious to hear as much as they can on the debate.

The cameraperson with the TV reporter picked up the heated debate and stopped shooting during the dull periods. After a while, a cameraperson develops a sense for knowing when to start and stop shooting a story like this one. Because the cameraperson knows that less than a minute of sound bites will make the news, it is unnecessary to shoot continuously.

After shooting the highlights of the debate, the reporter and cameraperson moved outside and interviewed some people as they left the building. Everyone they spoke with was opposed to the incinerator. In an effort to be as fair as possible, the reporter continued interviewing until she finally found a man who said he was "keeping an open mind on the matter" until he heard more. "If there really would be an extra 100 jobs," he said, "I'd want to think about it."

The reporter decided they had enough material. She would have liked to do a separate interview with one of the company representatives, but there was no time. The debate had continued for almost two hours, and the ride back to the station would take 40 minutes. She decided to use part of the official's remarks for balance and to include some of the debate along with the interviews she conducted outside the building. She also decided to use some of the crowd shots to go along with the sound bites. The company had provided her with a video of the South Carolina plant.

The reporter opened her package with a sound bite—a *cold* open—as follows:

| | |
|---|---|
| SOT Woman yelling at meeting | SOT runs :04<br>"I'm not going to let you put anything in my backyard that's going to poison my children!" |
| V/O Crowd debating<br>NAT SOUND UNDER | V/O<br>This woman was one of almost 100 people who showed up at a meeting in Centerville tonight to listen to a proposal that would establish a waste-burning incinerator in this predominantly dairy farm community of five thousand people. |
| SOT MAN TALKING IN CROWD. HE'S WAVING A NEWSPAPER. | SOT :12<br>"I don't trust your company. This story says your company left a real mess around and you were burning all sorts of dangerous things improperly . . ." |
| V/C SHOTS CE S.C. PLANT | The company that this man is referring to is the Medvac Waste Disposal Corporation out of Greenville, South Carolina. And there have been published reports that Medvac was fined for not properly disposing of medical waste at its plant outside Greenville. |
| SOT<br>FONT:BOB SMITH<br>CEO, MEDVAC<br>WASTE DISPOSAL | SOT :06<br>"We did have some trouble for awhile, but we've corrected all those problems." (protest from crowd) |
| V/C ANGRY CROWD | (V/O)<br>There was no doubt about the sentiments of most of the people assembled here tonight. These are farm people and the environment—the land |
| Video of farms and rolling hills | they work and the air they and their cows breathe—is precious to them. But many young people have left the farms and are desperate for work in Centerville. Medvac claims it would hire |

|                                      | 100 people at the incinerator it wants to build. |
|--------------------------------------|--------------------------------------------------|

SOT ANGRY MAN

SOT :08

"And what about these 100 jobs you're talking about? This story says that you only employ about a dozen workers at that Carolina plant."

V/O CROWD LEAVING
HALL

V/O

The debate lasted almost two hours and we only found one man who had anything positive to say about the proposed plant.

SOT O/C TWO SHOT

SOT :05

"Well, if it's true that the plant would bring 100 jobs to town, I'd want to think about it."

V/O VIDEO OF TOWN
OFFICIALS AND OTHERS
TALKING OUTSIDE HALL

V/O

Town supervisors told Medvac that they would have a decision for them within 30 days. But from the tone of tonight's meeting, it seems unlikely that the project will be approved. This is Laura Wright reporting from Centerville.

This package is a good example of the proper way to cover a local government meeting. Unfortunately, many local reporters cover such stories from the back of the meeting room or on the steps of city hall. In such stories, the opening shot shows the reporter and then the camera moves from the reporter to the members of the city council or other governing body. In dull fashion, the camera pans from one member to another while the reporter voices the report. There usually are no sound bites in the story, just the voice of the reporter and the nameless faces and voices of the town officials. Former *CBS News* correspondent Ben Silver calls such reports "video clichés."

To avoid such uninteresting stories, the reporter covering local government meetings should find out in advance what is going to be discussed and select the most interesting subject and, if possible, one that lends itself to video footage. For example, let's consider a story about the extension of sewers to a certain part of town. Before the debate, the reporter and cameraperson should go to the location, take pictures of the area, and speak with some residents. Some

**Figure 12.2** "Texas Governor and Republican candidate George W. Bush and Democratic presidential candidate Vice President Al Gore talk during their presidential debate at the University of Massachusetts in Boston, October 3, 2000." (Reuters/Jim Bourg/Archive Photos)

might like the sewer idea, but others might oppose it because it would mean higher taxes.

Now when the reporter attends that public meeting and reports that the town supervisors voted to extend the sewer system, she can say, "Earlier in the day we spoke to some residents of that area, and here's what they had to say." The taped comments and video of the area make better news than pictures of the reporter announcing the supervisors' decision and shots of the members voting.

# Political Campaigns

Covering politics can be one of the more interesting stories that reporters cover, although sometimes the politicians themselves are less than inspiring and the issues sometimes not very stimulating. Also, covering politicians can be frustrating because the candidates often skirt the real issues and get into name-calling and personality assassination. Compounding the problem is that the public is often indifferent to politics, ranking the subject fairly low, below topics such as education, crime, and the environment.

A group at Harvard University measured voter interest in the 2000 presidential campaign and found that two-thirds of the public were paying little or no attention. This apparent indifference of the public to such an important subject that impacts so keenly on their lives presents a real challenge for journalists—to make their coverage of politics as interesting and stimulating as possible. And covering politics is not just an assignment for top journalists covering the race for the presidency.

People are running for some political office just about everywhere. Most reporters find themselves covering a political campaign early in their career. Even relatively small communities hold elections—for mayor, sheriff, town supervisor, and numerous other positions. Reporters also cover the campaigns of candidates for the state legislature, for Congress, and for the presidency when those candidates visit the area.

The most important requirement for reporting on politics is remaining neutral. Regardless of how reporters feel personally about the candidates, they must maintain their objectivity. Assignment editors and news directors are not going to ask reporters what their politics are when they're assigned to cover the campaign of a state assemblyperson. The reporters are expected to report fairly, without any bias, even if they think poorly of the candidate. On the other hand, it is not unusual for reporters to find that they like some candidates after they have been on the road with them; however, reporters need to watch that this admiration doesn't creep into their scripts. When it does, the reporter might not even be aware of it, but sometimes it is visible to the audience and other journalists.

*ABC News* correspondent Barry Serafin says it is a challenge sometimes to hide personal feelings when assigned to cover one candidate. "After a while the candidate will be calling you by your first name and so will his wife. It is particularly difficult to maintain your objectivity," says Serafin, "when you like the person. It's not so bad," he adds, "if you don't like him because all your training automatically comes into effect and all the safeguards drop down. If you like him it's harder but you absolutely, positively have to keep that arm's length—that journalistic objectivity."

Serafin recalled covering Ronald Reagan during two campaigns. "I got to know him better than any other candidate, and afterwards I was happy when some of the people around him said, 'We didn't always like the stories you did, but we think you were fair. We never thought you cheap-shotted us.'" Serafin said, "I decided that if after two campaigns they didn't like every story I did and thought I was fair, then I probably didn't do a bad job."

ABC *Nightline* correspondent Jeff Greenfield also notes that a reporter runs the risk of getting to like the candidate he or she is following and sometimes "has a professional reason for wanting the candidate to do well, including taking him to the White House with him." Serafin says, however, that that danger has

**Figure 12.3**  Ted Koppel with Vice President Al Gore. (Photo by Maria Melin, ©2000, ABC, Inc.)

been minimized because the networks now tend to rotate their political reporters.

## Putting Comments into Perspective

When covering a candidate during a campaign, a political reporter should not just parrot the candidate's speeches. If the candidate says the same things every place he or she goes, it would be appropriate for the reporter to point that out. It would be equally important for the reporter to note when candidates change their positions on the issues depending on the kind of group they're addressing.

The reporter should also tell the audience things about the location of the speech and the crowd. Was the candidate speaking in a predominantly Republican or Democratic area? Was the crowd mostly white-collar or blue-collar? Obviously, if the candidate was Republican and she was addressing a crowd in an affluent area of the city, her reception could be expected to be warmer than in a ghetto. Likewise, the opposite could be expected if the candidate was a Democrat.

The crowd's reaction is important. Was it enthusiastic or relatively quiet? Was the crowd large or small? If the weather affected the turnout, that should be noted. Did people challenge the candidate's remarks? Did they seek out the candidate to shake his or her hand?

Former CNN correspondent and anchor Bernard Shaw suggests that the broadcast media should be doing more to put political statements and claims into perspective. He questions whether radio and TV stations really want to stop "attack ads." He notes that millions of dollars in ad revenue are at stake and that sales departments "are loaded with people who have never seen an ad they didn't like. But isn't there a higher calling? A higher need?" asked Shaw. He adds that attack ads have become news stories, and it is the responsibility of news directors to point out the distortions and to expose candidates who "work harder at ducking than discussing issues."

Shaw also suggests that the news media should let candidates know that the voters are not more interested in a "staged picture than a thousand words of discussion of issues on their minds." He speaks of the "arrogance of the candidates and their managers and their media manipulators who fly into an airport, speak for five minutes, pose for pictures for 10 minutes, and get back in the plane and move on to another location."

Shaw says that when a candidate does that, there is nothing wrong with leading the newscast that night by saying, "Democratic candidate Tom Harkin thought enough of San Jose voters to spend 22 minutes at the airport today before going on to a Los Angeles fundraiser tonight. The senator said nothing he did not say before, but he did note that our weather was the best he had seen in days."

Shaw cites another way to put a political story into perspective:

The President took his election campaign to the Centerville nursing home for the elderly today, promising that he would not allow Congress to tamper with Social Security. But when he left, the President used a side door and his motorcade went the wrong way on a one-way street, apparently to avoid some two thousand unemployed workers whose benefits had run out.

Shaw says audiences are "keen for those kind of reporting distinctions. They need them for perspective on the sleights of hand that they are subjected to by politicians lusting for votes but lacking in so many ways."

Shaw also attacks some "sins" committed by politicians, citing as an example the arrogant refusal to answer reporters' questions on the issues. "But worse than the candidate's refusal to answer the question," he says, "is the news media's complicity by generally failing to point out and underscore that the politician did not answer the question."

Shaw says that every time this happens it reinforces "the politician's misguided belief that he can get away with it and voters don't care." The former CNN anchor believes it's time to stop the exploitation of the news media by politicians. "If what politicians are saying and doing is not news, why put it on the air?" he asks.

Some stations are to be commended for examining politicians' paid campaign spots and analyzing them for content and inaccuracies and pointing out flaws in them when appropriate.

# Feature Stories

Covering hard news—whether spot news or planned events—is the "meat and potatoes" of broadcast journalism, whereas feature stories are the "dessert." Those are the stories that often bring a smile and sometimes a tear to our faces.

*CBS News* correspondent Charles Osgood is a master of the feature story. He says he gets many of his ideas from unimportant-sounding stories on the wires. For example, he once found a three-line story about the Navy's considering a change in the rank of admirals. Osgood said: "You just suck the rest of it out of your thumb." His thumb gave us this:

> The U.S. Navy wants to establish a new rank to distinguish one-star rear admirals from two-star rear admirals. They thought about it and thought about it and the proposed name for the new rank that they've come up with is "Rear Admiral Lower Half." Now if President Reagan approves "Rear Admiral Lower Half" then "Rear Admiral Lower Half" it will be. Let's consider if this is such a good idea.

> Military ranks are sort of baffling to the layman to begin with. We all know that generals and admirals are big deals, but there are many gradations inside the general and admiral category; and these are not always what you would think they would be. Major outranks a lieutenant, but a lieutenant-general outranks a major-general. A very model of a modern major-general only has two silver stars. A

**Figure 12.4**
*CBS News* correspondent Charles Osgood. (Courtesy of Charles Osgood/CBS News)

lieutenant-general has three. Both of them are outranked by the just plain general who has four silver stars. All three are addressed as "general" and so is the brigadier-general who has the one star. These are a dime a dozen at the Pentagon, as are admirals, of course. And there are different kinds of admirals, too. The admiral who corresponds to a four-star general is called an admiral. The admiral who corresponds to a three-star or lieutenant-general is called a vice admiral. And the one who corresponds to a major-general is called a rear admiral. The next naval rank down corresponding to a brigadier or one-star general is now called a commodore.

The U.S. Navy has now decided that its commodores should be admirals too, just as the Army's brigadiers are generals, and so the Navy has proposed a new rank called "rear admiral lower half." You would address such an officer as admiral so-and-so, not rear half so-and-so, by the way. The abbreviation for the new rank—they have thought of everything—would be "R.A.D.M. lower half," not "R.A.L.H.," as you might think. Too bad, because then if your first name was Ralph you could be R.A.L.H. Ralph. Sort of like Major Major Major in *Catch-22*.

I'm sure "Rear Admiral Lower Half" is very nautical and a great naval tradition and all of that, but what I question is whether "Rear Admiral Lower Half" brings the right sort of image to mind. The concept of rear is already somewhat puzzling, since the aft section of a ship is not called the rear, but the stern. There are a lot of stern admirals. Some of them are rear admirals and some are not. Once our attention has been called to a rear, it seems an unfortunate added indignity to specify that one is referring specifically to the lower half thereof.

How about you? Would you rather be called a commodore or a rear admiral lower half? Commodore is a little dated, admittedly. Even the Hotel Commodore isn't called the Commodore anymore. No, it isn't the Hotel Rear Admiral Lower Half either. It is now the Grand Hyatt Hotel. How about grand hyatt for the name of a new rank? Instead of rear admiral lower half so-and-so, the officer would be grand hyatt so-and-so. Grand hyatt has a certain brassy Gilbert and Sullivan flair to it. "Captain Jones, you're being promoted to the rank of grand hyatt." None of that stuff about rears and lower halves. You see what I mean?

Osgood said the nice thing about writing such stories is that "you don't have to know a lot . . . I go to the almanac and find the different ranks in the Army and

Navy and how they correspond to one another. I don't know that stuff," he added, "but you can get your hands on it easily and it's right there in the newsroom."

Features also receive a lot of attention on NPR's *All Things Considered* and *Morning Edition*. Reporter Cokie Roberts wrote and produced a feature about Congressman Morris Udall for "Morning Edition." Here's the way the anchor led into the report:

ANCHOR:    One of the most respected and best-loved members of the House of Representatives is expected to announce his resignation today. Arizona Democrat Morris Udall has been suffering from Parkinson's disease for many years but in January a serious fall incapacitated the 68-year-old Congressman, leading to his likely resignation. NPR's Cokie Roberts reports:

ROBERTS:    Mo Udall came to Congress 30 years ago as a reformer out of the West, ready to take on the structures and seniority of what was then a hidebound House of Representatives. He leaves as a senior statesman who earned the admiration and affection of his political friends and enemies through his hard work and, especially, through his humor. Mo Udall is not only a very funny man himself, he is a connoisseur and custodian of American political humor, compiled a number of years ago into a book.

(sound bite)

UDALL:    I was doing a chapter the other day on politicians' mixed metaphors and bloopers. I'll share a few with you today as a sort of preview if I can push the book a little bit (laughter). I'll start with Gerry Ford, who said in that famous speech on the House floor, "If Lincoln were alive today he would be turning over in his grave." And somebody said, perhaps it was I, "we honor Lincoln because he was born in a log cabin which he built with his own two hands." (Laughter)

ROBERTS:    The occasion of this spate of storytelling was Udall's 1984 announcement that he would not run for president again. He said the presence of other liberals in the race made his candidacy unnecessary but, in fact, Udall was already suffering from the Parkinson's disease that has made the last several years so difficult for him. The decision not to make the run was a tough one because Udall had long before been attacked by the political malady of presidentitis. He went for the White House in 1976 but after coming in second in seven straight primaries, Udall concluded that he drew more

**Figure 12.5**   Cokie Roberts reporting for ABC during the 1996 election. (©1998 ABC, Inc.)

laughter than votes, causing columnist James Kilpatrick to declare the Arizona Democrat too funny to be president. That eventually became the title of Udall's book, which was finally published in 1988. When NPR's Scot Simon interviewed the Congressman on his collection of political anecdotes, Udall—as usual—praised John Kennedy and Adlai Stevenson as the masters of the political quip.

(sound bite)

UDALL: Stevenson had a natural sense of humor—a sense of the ridiculous. A good example: Stevenson went to one of the women's colleges up in New England and made a big hit and as he was leaving this woman shouted, "Great going, Governor Stevenson, you got the vote of every thinking person." And he said, "It's not good enough, I need a majority." (laughter)

ROBERTS: It could have been his own story. Udall was never able to attract a majority for president or for a House leadership position, although he ran for Speaker in 1989 and for majority leader in 1971. But he did wage a successful attack on the House seniority system, pushed through a landmark campaign finance bill, and as chairman of the Interior and Insular Affairs Committee he shepherded several major environmental measures through Congress, including the Alaskan Lands Act. Udall succeeded legislatively by pulling together sometimes impossible coalitions, often using humor as his thread. To Udall, the ability to amuse was essential for a committed politician.

(sound bite)

UDALL: Politics used to be entertainment. If you lived in a little town in South Carolina 100 years ago, you never saw a presidential nominee on TV or otherwise. They were names in a news-paper and when the politicians came to town, they were expected to make two-hour speeches that would entertain the troops, and now we have speech writers and gag writers in great profusion. The mere act of hiring a gag writer says I don't understand myself and the issue enough to make people laugh legitimately, I have to hire somebody to give me a false line.

ROBERTS: Today's generation of politicians, lamented Udall in his book, "is less seasoned, more serious, richer, and less humorous. The ability to deliver a riveting speech, rich in substance and leavened with humor and anecdotes, is a declining art in Washington today." It would have died a lot faster had Mo Udall not been here for the last three decades, savoring his stories and telling his tales.

(sound bite)

UDALL: I grew up between the Navajos and the Apaches. I worked on Indian problems all my life and the Indians really appreciate this story: a politician goes to an Indian village and gathers the Indian voters around and says, "You like me, you vote for me, and we get schools and hospitals for little Indian

children." And they shouted, "Gooma, gooma." And he said,
"You vote for me and we will put gas heat in every tepee."
And they shouted, "Gooma, gooma." And the chief said, "You
white man great friend of Indian, you must come down to the
corral where we are going to give you an Indian pony. But,"
he said, "be careful you don't step in the gooma, gooma."
(laughter)

ROBERTS:     (music under) Arizona Democrat Morris Udall, retiring today.
I'm Cokie Roberts.

Features also are a basic part of local TV news, and to a lesser degree, to network
TV news. Every local news producer schedules a variety of features throughout
the newscast to give it balance. (More discussion on that subject is presented in
Chapter 21, "Producing.")

# Summary

Reporters spend much of their time covering planned events. Unlike spot news,
which is unpredictable, most planned events are known about by the assignment editors days and weeks in advance. These events fill part of the newscast
almost every night. A good percentage of planned events are news conferences.
Because news conferences are called by people trying to "sell" something,
reporters must be prepared to ask tough questions; they cannot allow themselves to be used.

Other common planned events are those provided by the workings of government—town and city council meetings and, in state capitals, meetings of the
legislature. Research is important. Reporters must be familiar with the issues
under discussion and be ready to ask intelligent questions about them. Planned
events are not always exciting; they often have few or no picture opportunities.
They are, however, an important part of covering the news, even if they wind
up as a 20-second voiceover.

Another type of nonbreaking story is the feature story. Feature stories give
reporters more opportunity to display their creative talents. Every reporter has
his or her favorite type of story, but you must remember that you have to learn
how to cover them all, not just the colorful and exciting ones.

# Review Questions

1.  Name some of the planned events that broadcast reporters cover.
2.  How do assignment editors determine which planned events they will cover?
3.  What are the chief reasons that people and organizations call news conferences?
4.  How does a reporter prepare for a news conference?

5. What is the best way for broadcast reporters to cover a town or city council meeting?
6. What is the worst way to cover such a meeting?
7. What are the most important things to remember when covering a political campaign?

# Exercises

1. Cover a city council or town meeting with a tape recorder or video camera. Prepare a wrap or package.
2. Attend a news conference, and prepare a wrap or package.
3. Attend a morning news meeting at a TV station, and write a report on how decisions were reached on which stories would be covered that day.

# **13** Reporting Live

Chapter 10 mentioned some of the differences between broadcast reporting and newspaper reporting. This chapter discusses one of the most profound differences—the ability of broadcast reporters to deliver live reports. This chapter offers some suggestions for handling the special pressures and responsibilities that reporting live places on broadcast journalists.

Reporting live from a mobile unit has always been routine for a radio reporter. Immediacy has been radio's big advantage. Since the early days of radio, Americans have been accustomed to getting the first news of an important story from that medium. Often, the news has come from a radio reporter at the scene.

Radio has lost some of its advantage as new technology has made it possible for television to put a live signal into homes almost as quickly and easily as radio does. Radio continues, however, to be first in reaching a large portion of the listening audience—those traveling on the highways.

## **Organizing Thoughts**

Because they broadcast live so often, radio reporters learn early in their careers how to organize their thoughts quickly. They also develop the skill of ad-libbing. Radio reporters are often expected to report from the scene of a breaking story for much longer periods than their TV counterparts because radio is normally not under the same time limitations as television. It is much easier to interrupt a music format on radio with a breaking story, for example, than it is to interrupt a soap opera on television. Lost advertising revenue is far less expensive for a radio station than for television, and it is much easier for a radio station to make up lost commercials.

The best way to organize material for a live report is to use a reporter's notebook. This device is particularly handy because it fits into a handbag or jacket pocket. Always take more than one pen or pencil. (In freezing weather or pouring rain, a pencil works a lot better than a pen.)

**Figure 13.1** WTVJ-TV Reporter Ed O'Dell and Cameraman Pedro Cancio rush to the scene of a story in Miami. (Courtesy of WTVJ-TV, Miami)

In anticipation of going live from the scene, broadcast reporters must keep notes on a variety of happenings. First, they must keep track of important comments that are made, whether during a news conference or a one-on-one interview. They must note exactly when the remarks were made so they can be located quickly on the videotape or audiotape. Some reporters take courses in speedwriting; others develop a system of their own. Experienced reporters learn that they cannot get so involved in taking notes that they lose control of the interview. They make entries only when comments are important enough to be used as a sound bite or in the narration that will surround it. TV reporters who have a camera with a time code recording system that shows the actual time of day that each scene is recorded only have to note the time when they hear something important.

Reporting live presents different problems for radio and TV reporters. For starters, radio reporters work alone, whereas TV reporters have at least one and sometimes two people with them in the microwave truck.

The production of the live report also is handled differently by a TV reporter than by a radio reporter. Sometimes the news conference or individual interview is microwaved back to the station while it is in progress. An associate producer or a writer at the station may monitor the feed and make notes. When the feed is over, producers can quickly confer with the reporter on which sound bites he or she wishes to use and then instruct the tape editor to cue them up. The reporter then does a live open from the scene, and the sound bites are played from the station. The reporter returns after the bites to do a live close.

It is also possible to do everything from the mobile unit. New technology allows TV crews to record and edit video in the truck, add the reporter's narration, and actually play the story from the truck without using any of the support equipment at the station. This type of sophisticated equipment is usually found only in large markets.

Another major difference between reporting live for radio and TV is obvious: The audience does not see the radio reporter. It does see the TV reporter, which adds some complications. The radio reporter can get comfortable in the front seat of the mobile unit, cue up her tape, spread her notes out, and concentrate on delivering her narration without worrying about anyone seeing her. Meanwhile, her TV colleague may be memorizing his script so that he is not constantly looking at his notebook during his time on camera.

Let's examine a typical live report filed by a radio reporter from the scene of a fire:

> Two people are known dead in a fire that swept through an apartment house on Rose Avenue in the suburban West End community of Center City. Fire Chief John O'Hara says he doesn't know if everyone else in the building escaped.

> (sound bite)

> "We think everyone but the one couple got out of there, but it's too early to tell. So far no one has reported anyone missing, so we are hopeful."

> (reporter)

> The dead have been identified as Barbara Swift and her husband Robert. It's believed the fire started in their apartment shortly after midnight and spread to the rest of the building. So far, there's no

information on what caused the fire, which was brought under control about an hour after it started. More than two dozen people were in the building. One woman who escaped, Val Hills, said she is happy to be alive:

(sound bite)

"There was so much smoke, that's what scared me the most. When I heard some shouting, I got up and I knew there must be a fire. Fortunately, I was able to get to the stairs and get out."

(reporter)

Some 50 firefighters and 10 pieces of equipment are still at the scene. Some of the firefighters are still hosing down the building and others are going through the debris just to make sure no one else is in there.

Once again, two people are dead in this Rose Avenue fire in the West End. It's believed that everyone else escaped from the building. This is Frank Sneed. Back to you, Bill.

Meanwhile, a TV station was carrying this story from its reporter at the scene via microwave. The story opens up with the reporter on camera and the fire scene behind her:

| | |
|---|---|
| O/C Heather | Two bodies have been removed from this burned-out apartment building on Rose Avenue, and it's not yet known if there were any other fatalities. |
| | The fire started around midnight in one of the apartments and spread quickly through the rest of the building. Earlier, we spoke with a couple who escaped from the burning building. |
| SOT | SOT |
| Font: Frank Lewis | "We were asleep when we heard shouting and jumped out of bed. I could smell smoke. I grabbed some trousers and my wife tossed on a robe and we got the hell out of there." |
| Font: Laura Lewis | "I was scared stiff. I'm just happy to be alive." |

O/C two shot

(Heather)
With me now is Fire Chief John O'Hara. Chief, do you think everyone is out of there?

(Chief)
"Well, we're hopeful. So far no one has reported anyone missing so that's a good sign. But you never can be sure."

(Heather)
Do you know how the fire started?

(Chief)
"Well, we think it started in the apartment of the couple who died in the fire and then spread to the other apartments, but so far we aren't sure how it started."

O/C tight shot of Heather

(Heather)
Thank you, Chief.
The couple who died in the fire have been identified as Barbara and Robert Swift. There was no other information available about them.

V/O
Shots of building and firefighters wetting it down

Shots of smoldering building

V/O
As you can see, this building is completely gutted, and if everyone else got out alive it would be amazing. Apparently some two dozen other people were in the building. About 50 fire-fighters have been battling the blaze. They brought it under control around one o'clock—about an hour after it began. Some of the firefighters have been moving slowly through parts of the burned-out building in an effort to determine if anyone could have been trapped inside. Meanwhile, other firefighters continue to hose down the smoldering remains of the building.

O/C Heather                                                    O/C
                                            Once again, two people dead and
                                            apparently everyone else escaped from
                                            this apartment complex on Rose Avenue
                                            in the West End section of the City. This
                                            is Heather Nelson, KTHU News.

After the radio and TV reporters finished their live reports, they would probably be asked a few questions by the anchors. Sometimes it is possible for the
anchors and reporters to confer in advance on what questions the anchors will
ask. The reporters often try to field whatever questions come their way without
any advance preparation. That's when ad-libbing ability is important.

# Ad-Libbing

Certain methods can help reporters improve their ad-libbing ability, or speaking without a script. Word association is one common method used by reporters
to make sure they do not run out of things to say during a live remote. Many
reporters write down a list of key words or phrases in the order in which they
want to cover their material. When they exhaust all the information dealing with
a key word, they move to the next one on the list until they have covered everything. Good ad-libbing reporters need only that one word or phrase to keep them
going, which is important because reporters are often forced into remote situations that require a considerable amount of ad-libbing.

*ABC News* correspondent Barry Serafin says the best way to learn how to
ad-lib is by doing it. He says he never thinks about reporting to an audience of
20 million people but concentrates on the idea that he is conversing with a single
person in a "natural and human manner." Serafin praises *ABC News* anchor
Peter Jennings' ad-libbing ability on what Serafin calls a "we're not sure what's
going on here folks" kind of story.

Serafin notes that Jennings is not afraid to say, "Well, we're not quite sure
where we are going here, but we'll let you know when we are, and in the meantime I'm going to do this." "Jennings doesn't try to be a superman—he tries to
be calm and composed," says Serafin. "He lets the audience know he's following the story with them—that he's human." Serafin adds: "The main thing about
ad-libbing is not to sound perfect . . . Don't try to tell what you don't know. Don't
speculate."

# The Challenges of Electronic News Gathering

A great way to prepare for the world of electronic news gathering (ENG) is to
do radio remotes. It is easier for TV reporters to handle the challenges of live

**Figure 13.2**   ABC anchor and correspondent Peter Jennings on the set of
*World News Tonight With Peter Jennings*. (Michael O'Neill/ABC News.
© 1999 ABC, Inc.)

television if they have a radio background, but not as many reporters are making
the transition from radio to television as in the past.

Most TV reporters now start their careers in television, and they have to
learn how to do remotes from the start. During the transition from film to videotape and microwave in the mid-1970s, many TV reporters found it difficult to
make the adjustment. They were accustomed to having 45 minutes or more to
write their scripts while the film was being developed. The only time TV
reporters went live was when the station or network bought a telephone line,
and that was reserved for important occasions. Many TV reporters were unable
to handle the pressures of going live and thus changed jobs.

Former *CBS News* correspondent Betsy Aaron made the transition but
recalls the luxury of the film days when a reporter might have from 3 o'clock
in the afternoon until airtime to write a script. "You had time to think," she said.
"The time for reflection and making phone calls about your story has disappeared. The deadline is always immediate," she added, "and often the product
suffers."

Serafin also recalls making the transition: "In the days of film you couldn't
be changing, writing, and producing the piece 10 seconds before it ran." Serafin
remembered going live at the end of the Falklands War when an angry demonstration started outside the palace in Buenos Aires. "Because of technology,"

Serafin said, "I was really forced at the last minute to make some editorial decisions about what was going on. Was it just a little spasm of public opinion or was it the beginning of the end of the government . . . or none of the above? I had to report to a network audience [without really knowing the answer] and it was difficult."

*ABC News* correspondent Morton Dean agrees. He says it is "scary" when you have to go live and you are not quite sure what is going on. "I think that is the most difficult part of this business—covering a breaking story live," Dean says. You are often out there 'naked' and you have to resist the pressure to give information that you're not certain of and to give your own personal thoughts as opposed to what's really going on." Dean says he's often asked to give his opinion about "what is going to happen" at the scene when he really does not know.

Dean recalled his reporting experience in the Gulf War when he was going live, and Iraqi Scud missiles were zooming overhead, and people were putting on their chemical outfits, and troops were running around with guns and taking their positions. "It's really very difficult to keep your wits about you," he said.

When asked if he was ever uncomfortable about his live reporting during the Gulf War, Dean said only to the extent that he developed a habit that may be considered bad in television: saying "I don't know" when he really doesn't know. "I think there's a terrible temptation to be glib," said Dean, "and just talk nonstop and maybe not say anything. You must have the courage to say 'I don't know,' and some people think that's a sin when you are on television."

Dean said there are times "when your mind is not working that quickly . . . and you have to feel secure enough to say 'I'm not sure about that' . . . or 'I have to think about that.'" He also said there have been times when he refused to go live, telling his producer he really had nothing to say.

Aaron is concerned that some people in the field are so involved in the technology that they do not care about what reporters are saying. The result, she says, "is that you have people who will say 'only time will tell' in a hundred different ways. They say it very smoothly, but they don't know how to say anything else. They don't know what they're covering, or why, or the history or implication . . . They just know it's a great picture and they make air. Sometimes," she says, "dead air is better than making air."

ABC *Nightline* anchor, Ted Koppel, says that the ability to go live often gets in the way of good journalism. "Putting someone on the air while an event is unfolding is clearly a technological tour de force, but it is an impediment, not an aid, to good journalism."

Koppel also recalled that when he was in Vietnam, "we focused far more on the journalism and far less on the distribution mechanism." He said satellite transmission had become an option, but "only in the rarest instances." Most of the time, he added, the film had to be shipped to the States. "You write differently when you know that your piece won't make air for another day or two."

The same concerns about technology were expressed 12 years earlier by the late veteran newswoman Pauline Frederick of NBC. She noted that technology has "given our profession marvelous tools with which to work. But, the question that should forever confront us is whether in our eagerness to use these instruments, the import of the message may become confused with the messenger, who could be perceived as trying to make and shape the news."

Former *CNN News* anchor and correspondent Bernard Shaw also raises some questions about the new technology. "We can fire up, and fly in or roll in portable satellite earth stations, slap on a wireless mike, report live, and not wait for tape at 11. We have digital this and digital that, telephones that connect to a satellite, fiber optics in the wings, and technology that will provide even smaller satellite dishes and antennas that will fit in an oversize briefcase. But," asks Shaw, "how are we using this stuff?"

Shaw goes on to suggest several situations that raise the question of whether broadcast news technology offers balanced and fair reporting. "If in covering a nation at war, a correspondent shows pictures of devastation without pointing out that the host government is severely restricting the movement of reporters and showing only what that government wants shown, is the crucial element of perspective for the viewer or listener well-served?" asks Shaw. "If there are no pictures to videotape and no sounds to record but only shreds of information gained from listening and observing, is expensive live capability that impressive?" he asks. "If you are a reporter covering a protest around a nuclear power plant and you have the cameraperson shoot, say, 50 demonstrators tight so that it looks like 500 demonstrators, and if the reporter decides not to interview a plant spokesman because it's too close to satellite feed time, has that technology yielded better balance and a fair report?" asks Shaw.

All the correspondents agree that ENG has increased the risk of inaccuracy. As stressed in earlier chapters, nothing is more important for journalists than accuracy. Reporting live to a community, to the nation, and often to the world carries with it a tremendous responsibility. There have been some notable cases of live reports that gave inaccurate accounts. For example, it was reported that presidential aide James Brady had been killed during the assassination attempt on President Reagan in 1981; in fact, Brady survived his traumatic head wounds.

As with any story, but particularly when covering a story live, reporters must check and double-check their information and must rely heavily on attribution when the slightest possibility exists that the information may not be accurate.

# Keeping Cool

The Scud attacks during the Gulf War demanded a lot of "cool" on the part of network reporters. Some correspondents were reluctant to leave the roofs until they were ordered to do so by anchors and network officials. The matter-of-fact, low-keyed reporting of CNN correspondents Peter Arnett, John Holliman, and Bernard Shaw from a hotel room in downtown Baghdad was certainly one

**Figure 13.3**
Former CNN correspondent
Bernard Shaw reports from the
scene during the Gulf War. (1992
CNN. All Rights Reserved.)

of the highlights of the Gulf War reporting. The trio said that watching the air
raids on Iraq from their hotel windows was "a little like watching a fireworks
display." To their credit, their calm and responsible reporting could have been
compared to the way they might have handled an assignment at the Statue of
Liberty during a Fourth of July celebration.

Peter Arnett, in particular, kept things in perspective, discouraging speculation about what was and was not going on when it was obvious that such
speculation would have served no useful purpose.

The only time a correspondent seemed to lose composure was when some
technical problem prevented the reporter from being heard or seen during the
middle of a missile attack. Technical problems are often the cause of reporters
losing their cool during less dramatic live reports.

All of us have seen a TV reporter in trouble during a live remote. The scene
usually goes something like this: The reporter is standing in front of a camera
getting ready to report live and something goes wrong with the ear-piece system
that allows the producer or cameraperson to speak with the reporter. The
reporter ends up looking mystified because she does not know whether she is
on the air. A cameraperson may be trying to signal what's going on, but sometimes this person is also in the dark. A worst-case scenario is when the reporter
actually says, "Are we on?" when in fact she is.

Sometimes these mishaps can be avoided if a TV monitor is available for
the reporter. That way, the reporter would know if she is on the air without
having to wait for verbal instructions. These situations are trying for reporters,
who understandably do not like to appear foolish in the eyes of the audience,
but the TV audience has become so sophisticated that it tends to ignore such
mishaps or, at worst, to chuckle a little over the breakdown in communications.
It's best for reporters to accept the fact that mistakes are going to happen and
equipment is going to malfunction.

# Memorizing and Delivering Live Reports

Some reporters have an amazing ability to memorize scripts. For most reporters, however, memorizing one minute of copy presents a problem. Because all TV reporters are asked to do live reports, they must either develop the ability to memorize their material or use some tricks to help them. Most stations and networks have no problem with reporters glancing down at their notes during live reports, particularly during a breaking story. It's less acceptable, however, especially in a routine live report outside a city-council meeting or the mayor's office, to see a reporter's head bobbing up and down every few seconds to read notes.

Former *CBS News* correspondent Ben Silver says it sometimes helps "to just throw the script away." Silver recalls: "I was having trouble memorizing the close to a story and I must have done it 10 times when the cameraman finally said, 'Give me the script.' He took the clipboard from me and I did the close without any problem."

# Changing Lens Shots

On particularly long, taped standups, some reporters have the cameraperson change the shot during the delivery. The opening camera shot might be wide as the reporter delivers the first part of the standup. Then, the reporter can pause while the cameraperson moves in for a tight shot. The reporter then delivers the second half of the script, and the audience is unaware that any break in the delivery occurred. The two shots have to be drastically different to avoid a *jump cut*—the jerking of the head that would be seen if the camera shots were too much alike.

# Summary

The biggest challenge that most broadcast reporters face is reporting live. Radio reporters have always faced that challenge because they could be on the air from the scene of a breaking story in minutes with the use of a two-way radio. TV reporters relied on film for their coverage until the 1970s, when two technologies were developed: small, portable videotape cameras (minicams) and microwave. Reporters suddenly lost the luxury of preparing their reports while they were traveling back from the scene of a story and while the film was being developed. Suddenly, reporters found that with microwave technology, they were often asked to go on the air immediately, while their videotape was being rewound and edited or cued up within minutes of being shot. They discovered that most of their thinking time had disappeared.

These developments brought about not only new challenges but also new risks. When thinking time is reduced, the chance of inaccuracy is increased. As a result, TV reporters have two concerns: (1) to collect information and sort it out quickly, and (2) to ensure it is accurate. The immediacy of the new technology also requires that reporters learn to ad-lib, making their improvised speech look easy and comfortable.

# Review Questions

1. New technology permits broadcast news reporters to go live from almost any part of the globe with short notice. But these technological advances also place new burdens and responsibilities on journalists. Explain.
2. Before the arrival of microwave technology, TV reporters used to have more time to collect their thoughts. Why?
3. Good organization and note taking are important when a reporter covers a story live. How can these skills be developed?
4. Reporters who hope to be successful reporting from the scene of a breaking news story must develop certain skills. What are they?
5. How can reporters improve their ability to memorize and deliver live standup reports? Explain.

# Exercises

1. Cover some event in the community, and then arrange for another student in the school's broadcast lab to videotape your standup report on the story you covered. After you have given your report, have the other student question you on tape. Return to the lab, and watch the tape.
2. Cover a news conference with either an audiocassette player or video equipment. If you are using an audiocassette player, pick a sound bite and cue it up so that you can play it over the phone in the middle of a wraparound. If you are using a video camera, do an open and close at the scene without preparing a script. Return to the lab, and insert a sound bite between the open and close that you recorded at the scene.
3. Have another student read a lengthy story to you from a newspaper. Make notes as he or she reads the story. Study your notes for two minutes, and then record a report either on audiotape or on video. Play it back for other students and your professor, and ask for an evaluation.

# **14** Putting the Television Story Together

When reporters leave the newsroom on assignments, they never know how their stories will turn out. The producers and assignment editors may be looking for a package—a story that includes one or more sound bites, the reporter's narration, and video. Sometimes they must settle for less, however, because the story itself turns out to be less important than they originally thought or because the interviews are not strong or the video is weak. When that happens, the story often becomes a voiceover-sound on tape (VO/SOT), or is relegated to the simplest type of picture story, a voiceover (V/O).

There also are times when the assignment editor knows in advance that a story is not worthy of a package. A cameraperson may be sent on a story without a reporter just to shoot video and natural sound. The producer will be made aware of that situation and will plan on covering that story in the newscast as a VO/SOT or V/O. This chapter discusses these types of television stories.

## The Package

A TV newscast is mostly made up of packages. That's because, if they are done well, packages have all the elements that bring a story alive: good pictures, interesting sound bites, and a well-written script. As mentioned, if any of these elements is weak, the story may be downgraded or kept short. In other words, the quality of the video and the sound bites often determines the length of a package. But even great video and excellent sound bites do not always guarantee a long package. It depends on what else is going on in the news that day. Even on slow days, packages rarely run longer than a couple minutes.

### *At the Scene*

Good organization is essential in putting together a successful package. Reporters try to decide quickly how they are going to produce the package. They may not have every detail pinned down, but they generally decide on some fundamentals, such as whether they are going to do the open, the close, or a transition in the middle on camera. If one of these on-camera options may be needed, it should be shot just in case.

## Taking Notes

Good organization requires good notes. *NBC News* correspondent Bob Dotson says he uses his notebook "like a pilot's checklist." He says he never finds the creative part of reporting to be a big problem. "I always find that the obvious is overlooked, like I forgot to get the wide shot or I forgot to ask the mayor whether he was going to run for another term."

Dotson notes that as soon as he knows he is going to do a story, he starts putting little boxes in his notebook with "thoughts, ideas, pictures, anything" he thinks he may need. "And then I scratch off what I don't need as I go along," he adds, stressing, "I do not leave a story until I have checked all the boxes that I do need so I don't overlook anything."

## Opening the Story

NBC correspondent Roger O'Neil says: "If I can't get you with the first pictures and the first sentence, I've lost you. So, I may spend several hours writing the first sentence, and the rest falls into place."

That luxury of time, however, is usually available only to network correspondents. Reporters at local stations would soon be looking for other jobs if they took two hours to pick their first shots and lead sentences. O'Neil's comment does, however, point out how important it is to get a good lead and strong video at the top of a story.

O'Neil notes that the first sentence is dictated by the first pictures, and the first pictures are dictated by the best pictures. "I can write a story a hundred different ways," he says, "but I'm going to find the best pictures and find a sentence that fits those pictures."

## Good Pictures

O'Neil takes issue with those who believe that words are more important than the pictures. He says those who believe that the script should be written first and the pictures added to support the words "should be in the newspaper business. We're in the business of pictures," he adds, "not the business of words."

He notes many reporters "fail to tell the story with pictures and then fill in the words" because they believe they don't have enough time to look at the pictures. "That's an excuse," O'Neil says. "I never write a script until I have looked at the pictures."

O'Neil's former colleague, *NBC News* correspondent Bob Dotson, also looks at his pictures before he writes. He described how he and his editor worked on the Carlsbad Cave rescue story (see Chapter 5) in a recreation vehicle that was equipped with editing equipment: "We spun through the tapes as they came up, and I would make log notes . . . in the left-hand column of the script. What I start to do is tell the story visually in my mind—this is what happened, this is where it went, and this is how I finish it. Once I've got that set in my mind, I can sketch that out pretty quick."

Dotson said it then was relatively easy to go over to the right side of his script and write what viewers will not be able to see. "The problem with writing your script first and then trying to paste the pictures to it," he said, "is you end up with wallpaper and it doesn't flow. Suddenly you have a paragraph and no pictures to cover the paragraph."

Dotson said that even when he worked as a local reporter and had to do a couple of stories a day, he still chose his pictures before writing his script. He said it's a "little like learning jujitsu. You learn the system and philosophy of how to approach a story and learn how to do it quickly and well. If you 'write your pictures' first, your story is going to stand out from all the others [reporters] who don't."

*60 Minutes* correspondent Ed Bradley believes TV news has been "driven too much by pictures and what's available in telling picture stories rather than information." *60 Minutes*, because of its format, relies on a lot of "talking heads" and, Bradley says, "there's nothing wrong with a talking head . . . as long as it's shedding some light on something." Most television reporters and producers find talking heads to be dull and replace the face with video relating to the story. When Bradley was reminded that *60 Minutes* is full of talking heads, he responded: "God bless talking heads."

## Good Writing

Former *CBS News* correspondent Richard Threlkeld noted that all good reporters have something in common—they are good writers. "If you are a good writer," he said, "you also must be a good reporter."

Threlkeld believes that to be successful as a TV reporter you "almost have to relearn what you have been taught in school when you had to do term papers and put all your thoughts down on the printed page for people to read." Threlkeld said that it might be obvious that television is a different medium from others but, unfortunately, "this doesn't sink into the brains of most broadcast journalists."

Threlkeld noted that everyone works differently; for example, according to Threlkeld, *CNN News* correspondent Bruce Morton gets "everything together in his head and then he'll sit around for a bit and then he will simply write a script about as fast as it takes me to tell it to you." Threlkeld said the late Charles Kuralt "agonized more," whereas he himself is somewhere in between: "I get all the pictures together and all the printed material I need, and then I write fairly fast."

As for the debate on which is more important, the words or the pictures, Threlkeld said both are important. But, he adds, "I think what most reporters in TV fail to see—and never do see with some exceptions—is how important pictures are to writing." Threlkeld said that while it's important to write well—in a conversational and colloquial style—the pictures, in most cases, must come first. "When you look at them, you must ask yourself 'how can these pictures tell the story?'"

The end result of all this, said Threlkeld, is that reporters end up "underwriting. And most of the best prose in both broadcasting and print is underwritten." Then, like so many others, Threlkeld reminds us that "one of the finest writers of this century, an old journalist named Hemingway, was a master at underwriting." He adds: "If you can underwrite and let the pictures tell the story, you are ahead of the game."

*ABC News* correspondent Morton Dean says his approach depends on the story. His approach differs, for example, if he's working on a story and reporting from the scene or has a chance to come back to the studio to work on it. "My preference," he notes, "is to look at the footage and then write the script and make the pictures and sound work for me and interject myself only when necessary."

Dean says that when reporters work with a complicated story, they sometimes can't limit it just to the pictures they have. He notes: "You sometimes have to write material for graphics or include standups. You may have information that is essential to the story that you must get into your script one way or another."

Charles Kuralt said: "I believe in never writing a line without knowing exactly what picture I am writing to; so when the script is finished, the story is edited—at least in my head." Kuralt said that during his "On the Road" series, his cameraman Izzy Bleckman "knew never to shoot anything unless I was there taking notes, because we shipped the film unprocessed with the narration, and never even saw it until it was on the air." Kuralt added: "This worked fine, as long as I was there to imagine the shot as Izzy was making it, so I could be sure to work it in."

The following is the script Kuralt wrote in Strafford, Vermont, and sent to his editor at CBS in New York. Along with the narration, he provided directions on the left side of the script and a separate *dopesheet* telling the editor what was on the film. Kuralt said all this detail proves that the "hardest part of every story is putting it together on paper."

| | |
|---|---|
| pan village Kuralt SOF | This one day in Vermont, the town carpenter lays aside his tools . . . the town doctor sees no patients . . . the shopkeeper closes his shop. Mothers tell |

| | |
|---|---|
| . . . to Kuralt on camera SOF | their children they'll have to warm up their own dinner. This one day, people in Vermont look not to their own welfare, but to that of their town. It doesn't matter that it's been snowing since 4 o'clock this morning. They'll be here. This is town meeting day. |
| people walking up hill to town meeting | Strafford, Vermont, has grown to a population of 536 since it was chartered by King George the Third in 1761. Its first town meeting was held in the freedom days, March 1779. And every March for 175 years, the men and women of Strafford have trudged up this hill on the one day of the year |
| . . . and pan with one group up to town hall as people pass sign | which is a holiday for democracy. They walk past a sign that says, "The Old White Meeting House. Built in 1799 and consecrated as a place of public worship for all denominations, with no preference for one above another. Since 1801, it has also been in continuous use as a Town Hall." |
| snow outside, pull back from window to high, wide shot of hall<br><br>Brown voice under | Here, every citizen may have his say on the question. The question is, will the town stop paying for outside health services. The speaker is a farmer, an elected selectman—David K. Brown, and Farmer Brown says "Yes." |
| Brown on camera . . .<br><br><br><br>faces of people listening<br><br><br><br><br><br>Brown on camera again | BROWN SAYS: "I'll tell you the selectmen have had some, what I consider unsatisfactory service from them. Last year, we had an individual in town that was in a very deep depression and he did not have any immediate family in town and they called upon us to do something about it, and we went and he was trying or thinking about committing suicide. So we called the Orange County mental health, and this |

was I believe on a Friday night. They said they'd see him Tuesday afternoon. And if we had any problems, take him to Hanover and put him in the emergency room. Now I don't know if we should pay $582.50 for that kind of advice."

others on feet, voice under

They talked about that for half an hour, asking themselves if this money would be well or poorly spent. This is not representative democracy. This is pure democracy, in which every citizen's voice is heard.

moderator

"ALL THOSE IN FAVOR, SIGNIFY BY SAYING 'AYE.'" "AYE." "ALL THAT ARE OPPOSED" "NAY" "I'M GOING TO ASK FOR A STANDING VOTE. ALL THOSE IN FAVOR, STAND PLEASE."

As they stand

It is an old Yankee expression, which originated here, in the town meeting, and has entered the language of free men: "Stand up and be counted." And,

moderator prepares
to announce

when the judgment is made, and announced by James Condict, maker of rail fences and moderator of the meeting, the town will abide by the judgment.

he does

THERE ARE 100 VOTES CAST . . . 61 IN FAVOR AND 39 AGAINST. IT THEN BECOMES DELETED FROM THE TOWN BUDGET.

faces in meeting as
somebody speaks voice
under about street lights

This is the way the founders of this country imagined it would be, that citizens would meet in their own communities to decide directly most of the questions affecting their lives and fortunes. Vermont's small towns have kept it this way. Will or will not Strafford, Vermont, turn off its street lights to save money?

| | |
|---|---|
| man in audience | PAPER BALLOT! PAPER BALLOT! ANY MEMBER HAS THE RIGHT TO DEMAND A PAPER BALLOT! IS THAT SECONDED? DOESN'T HAVE TO BE SECONDED! |
| moderator | "PREPARE AND CAST YOUR BALLOTS FOR THIS AMENDMENT." |
| line of people coming up . . . . . . handing paper ballots to deputy sheriff<br><br>CU's hands and ballots<br><br><br>Ballots being counted. We see "Yes" and "No" | If any citizen demands a secret ballot, a secret ballot it must be. Everybody who votes in Vermont has taken an old oath, to always vote his conscience without fear or favor of any persons. This is something old, something essential. You tear off a little paper, and on it, you write "yes" or "no." Stafford voted to keep the street lights shining. |
| Somebody takes a piece of pie<br><br>woman dishing up beans (little woman standing beside line of taller people)<br><br>wood in stove WS meeting | There is pie, baked by the ladies of the PTA. There are baked beans and brown bread, served at Town Meeting by Celia Lane as long as anybody can remember. Then, a little more wood is added to the stove, and a dozen more questions are debated and voted on in the long afternoon. What is really on the menu today is government of the people. Finally came the most routine of all motions, the motion to adjourn. |
| moderator and crowd | ALL THOSE IN FAVOR SIGNIFY BY SAYING "AYE" (LITTLE AYE). ALL THAT OPPOSE (BIG NAY) . . . THEN WE DON'T ADJOURN AND THE NAYS HAVE IT. |
| somebody else on feet talking, voice under people out of building into snow . . .<br><br><br>. . . downhill . . . | It is heady stuff, democracy. They wanted to go on enjoying it for a while in Strafford today. When finally they did adjourn, and walk out into the snow, it was with the feeling of having preserved something important, something more important than their street lights—their liberty. |

...and camera pans to village      Charles Kuralt, CBS News, On the Road to '76 in Vermont.

**dopesheet**

SOF

Roll 1—Kuralt open, people arriving, about 200 feet.

ALL REMAINING SOF ROLLS ARE PUSH ONE STOP ASA 250

Roll 2—400 SOF—Registering to vote at Town Meeting, Strafford, Vermont . . . call to order by Moderator James Condict . . . pledge of allegiance . . . voting in booths, presidential primary . . . WS room over moderator's shoulder . . . faces . . . one of the selectmen, David K. Brown, farmer, reports on town budget . . . more faces.

Roll 3—400 SOF—crocheting red white and blue sweater . . . Selectman David Brown says Mental Health gives poor service . . . debate on $1,179 for Community Health Services . . . etc.

Roll 4—400 SOF—Ayes and nays can't be distinguished . . . which leads to a standing vote . . . announcement of vote: 61–39 against spending the money . . . nice intercut of wandering child being snatched away from front of room by mother . . . debate on street lights, $1,900 budget item. Farmer Jerry Smith (with beard) says one shines in his eyes at night . . . etc.

Roll 5—400 SOF—On street light question, call for a paper ballot on whether to cut street lighting in half. Details of balloting, hands CU, etc., then counting paper ballots and announcement of result, 59 yes, 82 no, so motion to reduce street lighting defeated . . . break for lunch, pies in foreground . . . home-cooked baked beans and brown bread being dished out by Celia Lane, who has served baked beans at the Town Meetings since anybody can remember . . . high shot of room with eating going on . . . neighborly floor-level eating and chatter . . .

Roll 6—400 SOF—More chit-chat during lunch break . . . janitor feeds more wood into the stove . . . high shot thru window of snow falling, pull back to meeting, repeat several times . . . counting ballots from above . . . faces in audience . . . Gile S. Kendall, farmer, selectman reelected . . . people coming forward to vote, faces in and out of frame.

Roll 7—400 SOF—Vote for second constable. Bob Nutting defeats Lois Smith and Gerald Smith . . . faces in crowd, rack focus young face to old face, etc. discussion of reappraisal of property values . . .

Roll 8—400 SOF—More reappraisal discussion. Girl, pull back to feeding fire. Jerry Smith makes a "You don't need government agencies in Vermont" speech . . . discussion of $750 appropriation to senior citizens center in neighboring town . . . and of radio for car of "civil defense" director . . . voting down adjournment! Sign: "The Old White Meeting House. Built in 1799 and consecrated as a place of public worship for all denominations, with no preference for one above another. Since 1801, it has also been in continuous use as a Town Hall." with people coming and going in front of sign. People leaving, pan down steeple. People down hill and pan to village. Empty town hall after they've all left.

Phil Scheffler, a senior producer for *60 Minutes*, says Kuralt had a "particularly fine eye. He saw things others didn't and saw them very clearly. That's also why he was such a good reporter." Scheffler says the thing that struck you about Kuralt's writing was "how simple it is. It's unadorned. He was able to create a very clear picture in your mind as to what he'd seen."

## Organizing the Story

One of the most frustrating orders for most reporters is "keep the story short." *NBC News* correspondent Roger O'Neil says he finds it more challenging to do a short story than a long one. O'Neil believes that the key to writing a tight script is *organization*. He says he is often accused of being "cold or mad at people, or the world," because he is quiet on the car trip back from a story. "I am quiet," O'Neil says, "because I'm thinking about the pictures I saw the photographer take—trying to arrange those pictures in my head. I am quiet because I am thinking about what I have to do when I get back to the station."

O'Neil says too many reporters do not take advantage of that trip back to the station. "They don't think about what they are going to do with the story until they sit down at the typewriter," he notes. "Then they complain they don't have enough time to tell the story because they haven't thought it out."

Reporters certainly should be using that time in the car to organize their thoughts, and it helps to have interviews on audiotape. Every broadcast reporter should carry an audiocassette recorder for this purpose. It is not necessary to have a good-quality recording because the audiotape will not be used for broadcast, only to help the reporter select sound bites. This tip is a great timesaver.

*NBC News* correspondent Bob Dotson says he uses the car ride both to and from the scene to get organized. "The minute I know that I am going to do a story," he notes, "I start thinking in terms of how I am going to develop it, what questions I would ask, where I would go from point A to B." Dotson adds that on the way back from the scene he listens to the audiotape and selects the sound bites long before he returns to the studio.

## Selecting Sound

Dotson says that in addition to good sound bites, he is always looking for good *natural sound*—what a novelist might call mood setters. "What you are really doing in TV is not showing or telling but trying to have people experience what it is like. Sound can help you experience it, and sound can bring your audience back to the TV screen because so much of what we call news just washes over us all the time. But if you stop talking, and you hear a rooster crow, people are going to turn to see the rooster. They will put down the spoon, stop eating dinner, and come to the TV set."

As for sound bites, Dotson says, "I always use sound as an exclamation point. I do not use sound to explain. There just isn't enough time to let the subject explain. In a minute and a half, you have to use several voices to tell all sides of the story. So you, as a professional writer, give the basic information and use the sound bite for emphasis."

Dotson gives this example: "You have a sound bite from someone talking about a picnic. The person says, 'We're going to have a picnic on Friday at one o'clock and we are going to have a band there and it's going to be a great time and we hope you all will come and it's sponsored by the Kiwanis Club.' You take the bite, which is really like an exclamation point—'We're going to have a great time'—and you, as a professional writer, fill in the information that leads up to the sound bite. And the sound bite proves what you just said."

## Working with the Video Editor

Dotson compares video editing with rewriting. "It's like a catcher on a baseball team. That's the backstop, and all the other things you have done during the process of putting that story together can either be lost or saved in the editing room. Sometimes the fantasies you had as you were writing your story can be saved by the editor. That's where you are putting it all together—your sound and pictures and words—and editors have to be very hard on the process." They must say: "These symbols move the story forward, and these symbols you put in the basement and show your parents later on, because we don't have time for them."

Dotson adds: "I always look at a news story as a kind of good jazz ensemble. At some point there is a trumpeter, and at some point there is a drummer, and each person has his soul and it's important sometimes that they all play together. That's the same way with a story, and the editor helps reinforce that."

# The Voiceover

In a voiceover (V/O), the newscaster or reporter reads copy as the video appears on the screen. Normally, voiceovers are not long because they are usually used to break up a series of packages or to give the anchors some exposure. The following is the script for three short voiceovers used in a newscast produced by WBRZ-TV in Baton Rouge, Louisiana:

| | |
|---|---|
| Two shot O/C<br>Margaret and Andrea | (Margaret)<br>Updating some of the other stories making news across the nation . . . authorities in Newport News, Virginia, are investigating an accident involving an Amtrak train. |
| Roll Sony V/O<br>Video of derailed train | (V/O)<br>A dump truck collided with this train at a railroad crossing. The force of the collision sent the engine and all five passenger cars off the tracks. |
| Video of injured people | The driver of the truck died in the accident . . . about 50 people on the train were hurt, but not seriously. |
| Wipe to Sony<br>Video of plane wreckage<br><br>Font: Blevelt Falls<br>Lake Lilesville, N.C | (Andrea V/O)<br>And divers in North Carolina are searching for the bodies of nine people who died when a military transport plane crashed into this lake in North Carolina. |
| More video of wreckage | The victims were stationed at Fort Polk. They were on a training mission. So far, the cause of the crash is unknown. |
| Wipe to Sony<br>Kennedy and wife shaking hands with people in Dallas<br>Kennedy motorcade in Dallas<br>Video of people on lawn as Kennedy motorcade goes by | And a citizens' group called Public Citizen is demanding the National Archives release nearly 200 autopsy photos and X-rays of President Kennedy.<br><br>A bill in Congress would require the release of documents pertaining to |

the assassination, but excludes the
autopsy material to protect the Kennedy
family's privacy.

ON CAMERA TAG                                    (Andrea O/C)
                                         A spokesman for this citizens' group
                                         says the materials should be public
                                         record.

Most newscasts use voiceovers along with read stories to fill in the time around
packages; voiceovers seldom run longer than 20 or 30 seconds. The first
voiceover in the example ran 24 seconds; the second ran 16 seconds; and the
third ran 27 seconds. They were separated by *wipes*, an electronic technique
that slides one video picture off the screen and replaces it with another—in this
case with the opening video of the next story.

The use of the word *Sony* in the left column lets the director know that the
video material is in the Sony tape decks. The director's copy of the script would
indicate by number which deck plays which tape during the newscast.

# The Voiceover-Sound on Tape

As discussed earlier, when a voiceover is used to lead into a sound bite, it is
called a V-SOT or V/O-SOT. Here's an example of a V-SOT script:

                                                      Newscaster
V/O
Video of police                          Central City's fight against crime got
officers at graduation                   a boost today with the graduation of
Video of female                          45 new officers from the police
graduates                                academy. Among the officers—eleven
                                         women. One of them is Ann Black,
Video of Black                           and she had her own cheering
and family                               section: her mother and father, her
                                         husband, and her three-year-old
Video of Black                           daughter, Sally. Black's father also is
holding daughter                         a police officer.

SOT: 05                                            (SOT/Ann Black)
                                         "It's just a wonderful time . . . to finally
                                         be on the force, like my dad, and to
                                         have everyone I love here to cheer me
                                         on . . . it's just great."

At this point, the anchor could return on camera to do a *tag* to the story or go
back to a *voiceover*, as is the case here:

```
                                              ANCHOR
V/O
Video of graduates            The 45 new officers will not have too
tossing hats in air           much time to celebrate. They report for
                              duty in the morning.
```

V-SOT stories are usually used when a reporter was not assigned to do a package or the producer decided that the material was not strong enough, or of enough interest to the audience, to warrant the time necessary for a package.

# Reporter Involvement

Many news directors want to see their reporters' faces in their stories. They encourage reporters to appear on camera either at the end or in the middle of their packages. The theory is that the audience should think of the reporters and anchors as "family," and the more on-air exposure these family members get, the better management likes it.

NBC correspondent Roger O'Neil says: "It's stupid for network and local stations to require standups just to get their reporters on the air." The always outspoken O'Neil adds: "It's ludicrous to take good pictures away just to put some ugly reporter's face on the air." ABC's Morton Dean and former *CBS News* correspondent David Culhane agree. Both say they like to stay out of their stories as much as possible, preferring instead to let the pictures and other people's words tell the story.

The best reason for a reporter to appear in a story is to help explain it. Some reporters would argue that should be the only time a reporter is seen on air. On occasion, a reporter can help the viewer better understand a situation by appearing on camera in the middle of the story. Such a standup bridge is sometimes useful in tying together two parts of a complicated story, but it can also be disruptive when a reporter suddenly breaks up the flow of the story for no practical reason.

Some of the worst examples of reporter involvement occur when the reporters become a part of the story. Unfortunately, many news directors have no problem with reporters sliding down hills during a snowstorm or eating a hot dog at a street festival or lifting weights at the opening of a new health spa. The late Charles Kuralt, in his book *A Life on the Road*, wrote this about reporter involvement:

> With respect to my own appearances on camera, we have adopted the
> Tricycle Principle. We were somewhere in the Midwest, watching the local
> news on the TV set in the bus before going out to supper. There was a feature
> about a children's tricycle race, cute little toddlers pedaling away and
> bumping into one another, an appealing story pretty well-filmed and -edited.

Izzy said, "You know what? Before this is over, the reporter is going to ride a tricycle?"

"Oh, no" I said. "That would ruin the whole thing."

Sure enough, the reporter signed off in a closeup with a silly grin, the camera pulled back to show that he was perched on a tricycle, and he turned and pedaled clumsily away, making inane what had, until then, been charming. The anchorpeople came on laughing to sign off the show.

The Tricycle Principle is simple: "When doing a tricycle story, don't ride a tricycle." The story is about children, dummy, not about you. Keep yourself out of it. Try to control your immodesty.

Some TV audience members think such reporter involvement is cute, however, and that's enough for many news managers. On the other hand, most news directors I've spoken with agree with Kuralt. They will tell you that they discourage such behavior and want reporters involved in their stories only when there is a legitimate reason. For example, it would not be inappropriate for a reporter to demonstrate how to use a new at-home device that measures blood pressure. Doing so could be the best way for the reporter to explain how the new device works.

# Summary

One thing reporters find exciting about their job is that they rarely know what's going to happen when they get to work or how the story they've been assigned to cover will turn out. The sound bites may be fascinating and the video colorful, so that the story becomes a good package. But covering news also has its frustrations. An interview may be weak, or some promised video opportunities may not materialize. The story then becomes a voiceover-sound on tape or a voiceover.

Good organization and notes improve the chances that a package will be a success. Reporters should not try to predict the outcome of the story they're working on, but rather should know as much as possible about the subject and the players involved in their assignment when they leave the newsroom. Before they leave the scene, reporters should be certain that they have covered everything they need.

# Review Questions

1. Discuss the differences between read stories, voiceovers, voiceover-sound on tape, and packages.
2. Discuss some of the considerations that determine which of the described techniques in this chapter are used to tell certain stories.

3. What are the most popular ways to open and close a package? Discuss the merits of each technique.
4. What do most top broadcast news reporters say about the relative importance of pictures and words in packages?
5. Richard Threlkeld says that all good reporters have something in common. What is it?
6. What factors determine how long a package runs?

# Exercises

1. Pick a story out of the newspaper or from the wires, and write a 20-second voiceover. Record the voiceover at your school lab.
2. Pick another story that has some quotes, and script a 30-second V-SOT.
3. Prepare a package about a feature story. Limit it to one minute and 45 seconds and include two talking heads. If your school has the equipment, produce the package.

# 15 The Interview

One basic method used by reporters to gather information is the interview. Newspaper, radio, and TV journalists use different techniques, but they generally all try to achieve the same end: to find out as much newsmaking information as they can from the person they are interviewing. In broadcast jargon, the interviewee usually is referred to as the talking head, or simply the "head."

Newspaper reporters have the luxury of going into depth in their interviews. Because radio and TV reporters have limited time on the air, they have less time to conduct their interviews. Therefore, they must be selective in their questioning and must be well prepared. This chapter discusses techniques for conducting successful interviews.

Lesley Stahl, co-editor of *60 Minutes* and former chief White House correspondent, was asked if there were any questions that she would never ask and she replied "delving into officials' personal lives." She added: "I've never been convinced that the way a person conducts his personal life has a direct bearing on how he's going to conduct whatever office he's been chosen to fulfill."

*TV Guide* once described Stahl as "a watchdog with perhaps a streak of pit bull somewhere in her ancestry." When asked why more reporters do not ask difficult questions, she said some think they're in a popularity contest with the public and the most important thing is that the audience like them. She added: "You're not going to win a popularity contest if you ask questions like, 'Are you a crook?'"

## Preparing for the Interview

Reporters should always research the subject and find out as much as possible about the person to be interviewed. Good places to start your investigation are the radio or TV newsroom clip files and audiotape and videotape libraries. Some news organizations also have access to computer database services such as LEXIS-NEXIS, which indexes national and some regional newspapers, the wire services, and more than 100 magazines and journals.

**Figure 15.1**
Lesley Stahl, *60 Minutes*
co-editor and *CBS News*
correspondent. (Photo
Patrick Pagano/CBS
PHOTO ARCHIVE)

Reporters also must decide before the interview what kind of information they want. Interviews are not always expected to produce news. Some are designed to solicit emotional responses, such as those conducted for a human-interest story. Other interviews are attempts to find out more about the news-maker or, perhaps, his or her family. Reporters might seek such information if, for example, the interviewee had been appointed to some public post or as head of the local hospital.

If a reporter is interviewing the winner of a congressional seat, she is going to be looking for information that is different from what she sought the day before when she interviewed the mother of quadruplets. The reporter will want to ask the congresswoman-elect about her priorities when she gets to Washing-ton, why she thinks her campaign was a success and, perhaps, whether she believes her victory indicates some sort of national trend. When the reporter spoke to the mother of quadruplets, she asked questions about the problems of taking care of four babies, about whether the house is big enough to accommodate the family, and so on.

# Phrasing Questions Carefully

Many people interviewed by reporters are shy by nature or intimidated by microphones and cameras. Many others just seem to measure their words carefully. In order to prevent one- and two-word responses, reporters must phrase their questions so they are impossible to answer with a "yes" or "no" or by just a shake of the head.

If you ask a person, "Do you like farming?" you are bound to get a "yes" or "no" answer, but if you ask "What do you like about farming?" you should get a sound bite. If you ask a witness to an auto accident "Did you see what happened?" you might, again, end up with a one-word response. If you ask "What did you see?" you'll most likely get a longer response. Children are particularly likely to give "yes" or "no" answers, so ask them open-ended questions and be patient.

# Avoiding Leading Questions

Do not lead the interviewee toward giving a particular response. Some of the best reporters are sometimes guilty of this bad habit. During the Gulf War, a nationally known TV reporter asked a Bush administration official if he was "upset" after viewing pictures of an air raid that showed heavy destruction to a civilian target. The reporter herself clearly *was* upset by the pictures, and phrasing the question in that manner was a disservice for two reasons: (1) it probably influenced many viewers' feelings about the video, and (2) it put the administration official in an uncomfortable situation. If he had said he was *not* upset, he would have appeared callous; if he had said he *was* upset, he might have sounded critical of the military, which may or may not have been fair or accurate. The reporter allowed her personal feelings about the air raid to influence the question. It was a leading question. She should have asked the administration official, "What did you think about those pictures?"

# Listening Carefully

Reporters should arrive at an interview with a list of questions that they intend to ask the newsmaker; however, they also must develop a keen habit of listening carefully to the answers and asking follow-up questions. Many inexperienced reporters are so intent on asking their prepared questions that they fail to listen to the answers. They often do not realize that their previous question was not answered fully, or at all. Sometimes, to the embarrassment of all, the reporter asks a question that already has been answered. The astute newsmaker—often anticipating the reporter's next question—sometimes adds additional information to an earlier response. The rude awakening comes when the reporter asks another question on the list and the newsmaker says, "I just answered that."

To avoid falling into such traps, the reporter should put the list of questions to one side and refer to them only when necessary. *CBS News* correspondent Ed Bradley says he always has a list of questions but does not get locked into using it. He says that if he's interviewing someone and that person moves to a subject farther down on his list, he goes with the interviewee because he can then go back and pick up where he was.

The *60 Minutes* correspondent notes that some reporters "come in with an agenda, a list of questions, a predetermined mindset as to where the interview is going to go; they don't hear what it is that people say." He believes listening is important because too many reporters have "a tendency to try to fill space . . . instead of listening to what it is that a person says." Bradley advises interviewers to allow some silence and let the person fill it instead of trying to fill it by themselves.

Another effective technique is to establish direct eye contact with the person being interviewed. It's easier for reporters to concentrate on what people are saying if they look them right in the eye. This habit also establishes good rapport. Maintaining eye contact with newsmakers lets them know that the reporter is listening and interested. If the reporter's eyes drift toward the list of questions, or to the cameraperson, the newsmaker might take that as a signal that he or she has said enough and wait for another question even though he or she might not have finished answering the previous question.

## Warming Up the Head

Reporters differ on just how much they should disclose to the interviewee, the head, about the line of questioning before the interview starts. The advantage of *warming up* the head is that it gives the person time to collect his or her thoughts, usually ensuring a smoother interview. Without a warm up, the interviewee might be caught by surprise. The person might say, "I had no idea you would ask that; I really don't know the answer" or try unsuccessfully to fake an answer. Warming up an interviewee also tends to put the person more at ease. A relaxed head usually provides a better interview.

Sometimes, however, reporters do not want the interviewee to know the questions in advance because they plan to ask questions about a controversial topic designed to catch the person by surprise. There is no rule against warming up the interviewee, but some reporters are opposed to it. Almost all agree that it should be restricted to situations in which the reporter is looking for noncontroversial information. For example, a reporter would not warm up the head if the questions dealt with charges claiming the person misappropriated funds during an election campaign.

# The Tough Questions

Susan Morris, who teaches at the University of Pittsburgh and conducts workshops on interviewing techniques, believes that "no one enjoys asking embarrassing questions. It's uncomfortable and difficult." But she adds: "I've learned that a certain toughness is required. While excessive pressure can destroy an interview, it's important to keep in mind that you are there to get answers, not to create a good impression. After the interview," she points out, "you have to write a news story, not a press release."

Morris also says it helps to blame the tough questions on other people. For example, questions can be phrased as follows: "Today's newspaper reports that . . . What is your response?" or "Some of your critics say . . . Could you clarify the situation?" She says that "by attributing the charges to another source, you make it clear they are not coming from you personally."

*60 Minutes* co-editor Lesley Stahl established a reputation over the years, particularly when she was a White House correspondent, of asking tough questions. She says her attitude is that public officials in our system are obliged to explain and justify their policies, decisions, and actions. She says she is proud of being tenacious. "I liked being called tough. But," she added, "I also was being called impolite and I didn't like that." She says the pressure of the clock is why so many interviewers get the reputation for being discourteous. Stahl said the time is being eaten up (by the interviewees' filibustering) and you're still on question two. "It's a constant balancing act between moving it along and being rude."

*TV Guide* once ran a picture of Stahl sneering with a line saying, "Her questions range from sharp to stinging." Stahl says she developed a lot of her interviewing skills when she was anchoring *Face the Nation*. She says she and the producers would try to guess what the newsmaker might say to various questions, then fashion comebacks. Stahl said she never went on the air without a thorough blueprint. The trick, though, she added, was not to stick with the blueprint but to use it as a backup security system that would leave her free to listen and point out when a question was ducked. Stahl said that many officials actually took lessons in how to avoid answering, how to wriggle out from under tough questions. Stahl says administration officials often admitted that their goal in coming on *Face the Nation* was to escape without making any news.

# The Surprise Questions

*CBS News* correspondent Mike Wallace is probably the reporter most identified with surprise questions—those that catch the interviewee off guard. Wallace's

seemingly relaxed, easygoing style tends to disarm the individual he's questioning. His look of apparent bewilderment and confusion should, by now, warn
interviewees that Wallace is ready to spring a trap, but the people he interviews
keep taking the bait. The scene is familiar: There's a pause while the individual
tries to figure out how Wallace knew enough about the person or the subject
matter to ask the question that now must be answered.

Is such interviewing fair? John Spain, former station manager for WBRZ-TV
in Baton Rouge, Louisiana, who has a distinguished record for investigative
reporting, says, "I try to be honest and fair, but I'm not obligated to tell someone
we are investigating everything we have come to talk about. If we did, he probably wouldn't do the interview."

Spain says that if the individual says he or she will only talk about certain
subjects, then Spain has to decide if he still wants the interview. "But most people
will talk to you," says Spain, "because they don't think they have done anything
wrong and everything will be OK as long as they can tell their side of the story.
They do, and that's when we ask them the tough questions that they didn't know
we knew."

Spain said the long-standing rule followed by lawyers is: "Don't ask any
questions unless you already know the answers," which also applies to reporters.
"We go as well prepared as we can," he says.

Spain adds that people "generally underestimate our knowledge, resources,
and ability to look into their actions. Why," he asks, "do people continue to talk
to *60 Minutes*? It's because they totally underestimate what the media has been
able to obtain in terms of research and background."

## Questions to Ask Before the Interview

In a noninvestigative situation, the main reason for interviewing people is to get
information that is generally not known to the reporter and the public. Once the
cameras and audio recorders are rolling, reporters shouldn't spend time asking
people how long they have been employed, where they were educated, whether
they are married, or whether they have any children. If that sort of information
is important, it should be learned informally before the actual interview begins.
You might want to include such information in the introductory sentence of your
story, but you would rarely waste valuable air time with video- or audiotaped
responses on these subjects. The recorded questions and answers should be
restricted to those that gather information about what the newsmaker knows or
thinks about an idea or issue or, perhaps, to those that capture emotions.

## Keeping Control of the Interview

Sometimes, reporters inadvertently allow newsmakers to take control of an
interview. Politicians are particularly skilled at manipulating interviews. For

**Figure 15.2**
Mike Wallace reports for CBS's weekly
news show *60 Minutes.*

example, some politicians take a couple of minutes to answer a question, whereas others ask reporters how long a response they want and then give an answer of exactly that length. Because politicians and others accustomed to working with broadcast journalists know that reporters think in terms of sound bites, they usually try to express their views in about 12 seconds to make sure their answers are not edited.

A problem arises when the newsmaker takes too long to respond. The choice then is either to interrupt or to allow the head to finish the answer and then re-ask the question, saying, "That was great, but could you cover that same ground again in about half the time?" Most often the individual is happy to comply, which simplifies the editing process and results in a more natural-sounding response. Editing a sound bite down from a minute to 20 seconds sometimes alters the speaker's inflections.

Some newsmakers try to mislead reporters. They avoid answering some questions and skirt around others. Unless challenged, newsmakers often dominate interview situations. If the head doesn't answer the question or gives only a partial answer, the reporter should try to follow up. The newsmaker often then gives largely the same answer phrased differently. The reporter then needs to decide whether to ask the question a third time, or perhaps to say to the newsmaker, "I'm sorry, but you still have not answered my question." When the response is, "That's all I'm going to say on the subject," that in itself makes a statement. The reporter might then note in the story, "When pressed to answer the question several times, he refused to elaborate on the original answer."

# Asking Enough Questions

It takes time to develop the skill of knowing when you have asked enough questions during an interview. Reporters just entering the field tend to ask too many questions, usually because they are understandably insecure. As reporters gain experience, however, they usually start to develop a feel for when they have collected enough information.

Because time is precious to a broadcast reporter, asking too many questions means that the reporter spends more time than necessary at the scene or on the phone. That leaves less time for working on other stories and complicates the editing process.

Successful reporters who have researched the topic and the newsmaker know when they have just the right amount of material on tape. Because they have an idea of what information they hoped to hear, they know which sound bites they will probably end up using, and they also have a fairly accurate idea of how long those bites will run.

Experienced broadcast journalists often know immediately after the interview is over how they are going to put their stories together. With practice, reporters develop a habit of mentally processing information, sound bites, and pictures in a way that allows them to organize their material quickly.

# "Did I Forget Something?"

The pressure of conducting interviews quickly can sometimes cause reporters to miss important information. It is often a good idea for the reporter to ask the interviewee if he or she would like to add anything or to ask candidly if the reporter might have missed anything important. It is surprising how often the response is, "Well, as a matter of fact, I probably should tell you . . ."

# Off the Record

One frustration of being a reporter is being told: "I'll discuss that with you only if you promise not to use it." When the tape recorders and cameras are turned off, the newsmaker sometimes reveals what turns out to be the best part of the interview. That information—even if it is off the record—is often useful to reporters because it can put them on a trail that might lead to other people who will reveal the same information for the record.

Reporters *must* honor any off-the-record agreement. A reporter who breaks that promise is guilty of a serious breach of ethics. This long-held tradition was tested in January 1995 on the CBS news magazine, *Eye to Eye*, hosted by Connie Chung. During an interview with 68-year-old Kathleen Gingrich, the mother of the House Speaker, Newt Gingrich, Chung "tricked" Mrs. Gingrich into admitting that her son once referred to First Lady Hillary Clinton as a "bitch."

Chung did not actually tell Mrs. Gingrich that they were "speaking off the record," but it was close enough to cause a major debate among journalists. During the interview, Chung asked Mrs. Gingrich what the Speaker thought of President Clinton. "What has Newt told you about President Clinton?" was the actual question, and Mrs. Gingrich responded "Nothing. And I can't tell you what he said about Hillary."

That remark was too good to be true, and Chung could not resist following it up, as any good reporter would do; however, the ethical issue came into play when Chung told the elderly woman: "Why don't you just whisper it to me, just between you and me." Some people maintain that when Chung said "just between you and me," she made an off-the-record contract with Mrs. Gingrich even if she did not use those specific words. Mrs. Gingrich took the bait and whispered, "[Hillary Clinton's] a bitch. About the only thing [Newt] ever said about her. I think they had some meeting, you know, and she takes over." Chung asked, "She does?" and Mrs. Gingrich continued, "Oh, yeah, but with Newty, she can't."

A large segment of the journalism community and journalism educators believe that Connie Chung should have known better than to ask Mrs. Gingrich to share this information with millions of Americans when she thought she was having a "just between you and me" discussion. As bad as Chung's behavior was, however, it was not nearly as irresponsible as the actions of the show's producers. The so-called whispered conversation between Chung and Mrs. Gingrich was actually amplified in the control room, so there was no doubt what was said. But the real travesty came later when the executives in control of *Eye to Eye* decided not only to leave the offensive remark in the taped interview but also promoted it on CBS before the program actually aired.

Commenting on Chung's tactics, the *Sacramento Bee* asked: "Remember when CBS covered news?" The paper said that Chung obviously "set up Mrs. Gingrich . . . and Hillary Clinton was done a great disservice."

Chung defended herself by claiming that Mrs. Gingrich should have known better than to make the comment because of the obvious cameras, lights, and microphones; however, the *Sacramento Bee* said that even if that was true, "such a blatant abuse" of the off-the-record arrangement that was implied "mocks the process." The paper added: "As it is, reporters are ranked with used-car salesmen and ambulance-chasing lawyers . . . thanks, Connie, for enhancing our stature within the tar pit."

The *Bee* said that it's not that Chung does not know better because "she has been at the game too long and she got where she is because she's good. . . . It's distasteful to see her so willing to cross the line between news and entertainment."

The *Denver Post* also picked up on CBS's decision to edit 90 percent of the Gingrich interview but to leave in the "bitch" remark. The *Post* said the CBS crew was in Mrs. Gingrich's home for eight hours and ended up with only two hours of videotape. The paper added: "If CBS's and Connie Chung's integrity were worth anything, [editing] should have [eliminated] the 'bitch' remark." The Dean of Northwestern's Medill School of Journalism, Michael Janeway, agreed. The former editor of the *Boston Globe* said: "It brings 'alleged' news journalism to the level of gossip and it's unprofessional."

*CBS News* President Eric Ober defended Chung, which came as no surprise, but those who watched Ober move up the ranks at CBS as a journalist, news director, and station manager for many years before becoming president of the network, questioned his sincerity. He said: "Mrs. Gingrich's comments may have been unfair, but CBS News does not believe withholding those comments would have been appropriate."

A Boston University journalism professor, Caryl Rivers, said Ober's comments were "garbage. It was a good quote," he said, and CBS "ran with it because it was a good quote." Columbia University journalism professor, Stephen Isaacs, said Chung "goofed badly. When you say, 'This is between you and me'—that's a contract. It doesn't matter whether there's a camera rolling or not." The *Houston Post* agreed: "It's a rule of reporting that when you tell a source that what he or she tells you will be kept in strict confidence, regardless of how you phrase that assurance, you keep your word."

There were many Chung supporters, however. Michael Olesker, writing in the *Baltimore Sun*, rhetorically asked if Chung had got Mrs. Gingrich to say something she shouldn't have. "Absolutely," he wrote, "that's the job of any reporter." John Freeman, writing in *The San Diego Union-Tribune*, says that even if Chung did trick Mrs. Gingrich into making the "bitch" comment, that the correspondent had every right to ask the question. "It's her job to ask tough questions," wrote Freeman. "Was CBS wrong to air the interview? Not at all."

## Chung's Demise

It wasn't long after the controversy that Ober announced that Chung's *Eye to Eye* program would be discontinued and that Ms. Chung would be dropped from *The Evening News*, which she had shared with Dan Rather for almost two years. Poor ratings appeared to be the primary cause for her demise, but other factors, such as the Gingrich episode and criticisms about Chung's performance in general, seemed to be involved.

Ober said the Rather-Chung combination just was "not working." An unnamed CBS executive was quoted by Mark Gunther of Knight-Ridder as saying that "there is not enough room for two anchors on a 22-minute program that tries to pack in lots of news."

CBS added Chung to the anchor's desk because Rather's ratings were dropping, and it hoped that Chung would attract more women viewers to the newscast. But two years later, the ratings were still not that good. Chung blamed the ratings for her dismissal from the newscast, saying she was "taking the fall" for the newscast's failure. She added: "I don't think there's any justification for it."

Writing in the *Dallas Morning News*, columnist Ed Bark wrote that Chung was unable to navigate the terrain between "serious journalist and tabloid gadfly." Bark noted that some of her interview coups with people such as Tonya Harding, Heidi Fleiss, and Faye Resnick were used as "ammo against her by both CBS News management and TV critics."

But according to Ed Kelley, the managing editor of the *Daily Oklahoman*, he believes Chung's appearance in Oklahoma City during the bomb blast disaster "probably cost her her job." Kelley said that Chung landed the on-site anchor position at the bomb scene over vacationing co-anchor Dan Rather and "further damaged an already strained relationship with good journalism." He added: "Her on-air questions to rescue officials sounded condescending to many Oklahoma City residents and she had to publicly apologize."

Arguing the other side of the controversy, business executive Nancy Woodhull says that "female journalists have become scapegoats." She says that when they are hired to increase ratings—and they don't—"the guy who gave you the poor ratings in the first place stays and the female . . . is canned like Connie Chung."

Chung has bounced back, however. She's an anchor-correspondent for *ABC News*, working on *20/20* and *Prime Time Thursday*.

# Curbing Nods and Smiles

Television reporters must be concerned about their facial expressions and head movements during an interview, particularly in a studio situation when two or more cameras are being used. Limiting this natural tendency is also important in field situations when listening shots of the reporter (called *reversals*) are being taken for editing purposes. It's permissible for reporters to smile or to nod their heads in agreement during an interview about a noncontroversial subject; however, when the issue is controversial and involves a subject with more than one point of view, a reporter cannot be shown expressing agreement or disagreement. A smile or frown or nod could send a wrong signal to an audience. The question of credibility and objectivity immediately comes into question.

For example, to protest the Gulf War, some students managed to get onto the CBS *Evening News* set with Dan Rather. To Rather's credit, he ignored the whole incident and went on with the newscast; however, at one affiliate station that replayed the incident, the anchor shook her head in obvious disgust as she came back on camera. She compromised her objectivity. Regardless of how she personally felt about the invasion of the CBS studio, she should have kept it to herself.

# The Phone Interview

Radio reporters have the option of conducting many of their interviews on the phone. TV reporters use the phone only as a last resort because interviews without pictures are weak.

One disadvantage of the phone interview is that it's sometimes difficult to know when the newsmaker has finished giving an answer. Unless reporters listen carefully, they might interrupt the answer before it is complete, which sometimes makes editing the sound bites difficult. When you realize you might have missed something, apologize and ask the person to repeat the answer.

Phone interviews should only be used when it is impossible to interview the individual in person. It sounds unprofessional to conduct an interview on the phone with the mayor or someone else in your city or town when you could hop in a car and go to the person's office. Phone interviews are most effective when used to reach newsmakers in another part of the country or overseas. Such interviews demonstrate to the audience that the station is making a special effort to cover the news.

# Checking Facts

Some responses during an interview may not sound right. If that happens, reporters should tell the newsmaker that something is puzzling them or that they do not quite understand the answer. If the answers still do not sound true or are confusing, the reporters should check the information as soon as possible. Reporters could try contacting other sources who might have the same information or doing some research in the newsroom files, the library, or computer databases. If the information cannot be verified, reporters should explain that in the story. For example:

> The head of the Newtown Power Company said there had never been an accident at the plant in the two years since it opened until today, when four people were seriously injured. We were unable to reach a union representative to verify the statement.

# Some Other Tips

Susan Morris of the University of Pittsburgh has these other interview suggestions:

1. Develop a technique of asking short questions that get right to the point.
2. Phrase the questions without apologies and in a matter-of-fact manner. Avoid beginning a question with "I hate to ask you this, but . . ."

3. Pause between questions even when dealing with less volatile subjects. You are likely to get more thoughtful answers.
4. If a person is hedging, take time to explain what the information is being used for. Explain that you do not have an editorial position.

# Summary

To conduct a good interview, you must prepare for it. Do some research to find out as much as you can about the person you will be interviewing. Decide on the kind of information you want, and choose your questions accordingly.

Remember to listen carefully during an interview. Make sure your questions are answered to your satisfaction. If they aren't, say so, and follow up on your questions. Don't be used. Try to maintain control of the interview. If you permit it, the interviewee will often take over. Keep to your objectives; don't let the head go off on tangents.

Finally, the most important thing to remember about interviews is that they are not necessarily a reliable source of accurate information because those being interviewed want to be perceived in the best light. Often, interviewees are hiding something from you. Within reason, you should try to find out what they're hiding and be sure to check all facts they do disclose.

# Review Questions

1. Why must radio and TV reporters be more selective than their newspaper colleagues in choosing questions to ask in their interviews?
2. How should you prepare for an interview before you leave the station? Give some examples.
3. It's always a good idea to prepare a list of questions for an interview, but there also are dangers. Explain.
4. How should you phrase questions to make sure you get complete answers?
5. What kind of trouble can reporters fall into if they do not listen intently to the person they're interviewing?
6. Discuss the pros and cons of warming up the person you're interviewing.
7. Discuss tough and surprise questions.
8. What are the advantages and disadvantages of off-the-record comments?
9. Why must reporters be aware of their body language during an interview?

# Exercises

1. Interview a faculty member in a department other than your own. Before doing so, however, find out as much as you can about the individual, and turn in those notes along with a story based on your interview.

2.  Introduce yourself to a student whom you've never met, and conduct an interview. Write a story or produce a package about the person.

3.  Read through your local newspaper, and pick someone in your community who is in the news. Interview the person, and then produce a wraparound report or package.

# 16 Collecting Information from Documents

Although the interview is the most common method of gathering information, it is not always the most reliable. Most spot news stories—fires, accidents, natural disasters, crime—usually can be covered with a few quick sound bites and video that support the reporter's story. But if the story is more complex or interviews fail to provide all the answers, reporters must look to other sources of background information. This chapter explores the many documents available to reporters to provide such information.

## Public Records and the "Sunshine Laws"

One freedom people enjoy in a democracy is the openness of society. Very little goes on in public life that is not recorded in one way or another. At times, however, those in public office attempt to cover up some of their activities. They can, and often do, complicate the reporter's efforts to uncover information. Persistent journalists are often able to circumvent such attempts at secrecy by examining public records. Reporters also have another strong weapon—the Freedom of Information Act (FOIA).

Congress passed the FOIA in 1966, allowing the public access to records held by federal agencies of the executive branch. Since then, all 50 states have passed similar laws that permit the public to examine most records maintained by state and local governments. The freedom of information laws have been dubbed the "sunshine laws" because they are designed to shed light on the workings of government; however, that light hasn't always shined brightly. Government agencies often refuse to disclose public records to private individuals or to journalists. The federal government, for example, has often claimed that revealing certain information would threaten national security. The issue was usually not the nation's security but information that would prove embarrassing to the agency or bureaucrat involved.

With that in mind, Congress amended the FOIA in 1974 and 1976, requiring federal agencies to release documents to the public unless the agencies could show some valid reason for not doing so. Nine exemptions were added to the FOIA, but the ones used most pertain to national security and foreign policy, advice and recommendations made within a federal agency, unwarranted invasion of privacy, files dealing with criminal cases that are current or pending, and trade secrets.

Because state "sunshine laws" vary, reporters seeking information from a state or local government office must examine that state's law before filing.

## Filing an FOIA Request

The first thing a reporter must do when seeking government information is determine which federal agency has the information being sought. Sometimes, a telephone call to the agency is enough to produce the information. If not, the reporter must then file an FOIA request in writing. The request should be written on the news organization's letterhead, and it should include the following:

1. An opening sentence making it clear that the letter deals with a Freedom of Information Act request.
2. An offer to pay reasonable fees for reproduction of records. (Some news organizations prefer to list an amount they are willing to pay, say $50, rather than use the term "reasonable amount.")
3. A request that the fees be waived because the information would benefit the public. (An optional statement indicating how the information would be beneficial increases the likelihood of the waiver being granted.)
4. A specific description of the documents being requested, including the actual titles of the documents, if they are known.
5. A reminder that, by law, the agency has 10 days to provide the information requested or to explain why it is denying the request.
6. Some reporters like to inquire whether any other government agencies have requested the same information. This "fishing expedition" sometimes provides some unexpected information that's helpful.

It is a good idea to send the letter by certified mail and to request a return receipt. The envelope should indicate "FOIA Request" or "To the Attention of the FOIA Officer."

Although the FOIA states that the agency has 10 days to respond to the request, it also allows the agency to take more time as long as it informs the reporter. Many agencies assign a number to the request, which should be used in any future contacts with the agency. A telephone call to the agency sometimes speeds up responses. If the agency does not reply within a reasonable time—two or three weeks—the reporter should send another letter, again reminding the agency of the time limits.

If an FOIA request is denied, the requester can file an appeal with the agency, which must be answered within 20 days. If that fails, the reporter can go to court to try to obtain the information—a costly and often lengthy endeavor; however, the threat of a lawsuit sometimes can convince an agency to release the information.

FOIA requests filed by investigative reporter Mark Lagerkvist of News 12 Long Island are reproduced in Figures 16.1 through 16.6, on pages 279–286.

The information obtained by Lagerkvist required an exchange of 10 letters with the New York State Department of Health; however, the correspondence made it possible for him to break a story about certain health maintenance organizations (HMOs) that reward doctors who do not refer patients to specialists, hospitals, and other providers.

Lagerkvist said a family physician in one major HMO can "earn" more than $50,000 a year in bonuses by restricting referrals. "These 'bargains' may compromise the medical decisions that affect millions of Americans and their access to health care services," writes Lagerkvist.

The News 12 Long Island reporter worked six months on the secret deals of HMOs. The result was a four-part series and half-hour documentary revealing that 11 of Long Island's 12 HMOs reward doctors who limit referrals or penalize those who do not. Because of space constraints, only one part of the four-part series is reproduced in this book (see pages 271–278).

Lagerkvist won first place in the National Press Club Consumer Journalism award competition for the series. For earlier reports, he won major national journalism awards from United Press International (UPI), Investigative Reporters & Editors (IRE), and the Scripps-Howard Foundation. He has also received more than 30 regional and state awards from the Associated Press (AP), the Radio and Television News Directors Association (RTNDA), and a variety of major press clubs. During his 20-year career, he has enjoyed equal success as a television and newspaper reporter.

Lagerkvist said the one thing that concerned him most about the HMO story was that patients rarely were informed of the financial incentives that doctors received. He also noted that patients were not warned about how the arrangements could affect the judgment of their physicians.

You will notice that Lagerkvist's script format is just the opposite of the traditional split page—the technical information on the left and the narration on the right. Because Lagerkvist's stories are all prepackaged, this script is used only by the reporter in putting the story together; it's not used by a director in the control room. It is not shown on the teleprompter, which, of course, could not handle a script in which the narration appears on the left side.

```
HMO #1
Lena Lange of Deer Park        Lange
had cancer . . . She says
her doctor told her no
test was needed . . .
LANGE: "You know, they        Lena Lange
```

were playing with my
life . . ." (:03)

HMO patient

(BLIP)
Hazel Taus of East Islip
was in danger of going
blind in one eye . . . She
says her doctor said the
condition was not
serious . . .

*HMO-47/13:18
H. Taus

TAUS: "They would let me
lose the sight in my eye
rather than give me a
referral . . ." (:03) (BLIP)

Hazel Taus
HMO patient
HMO-39/12:51

As a newborn, Luke Kube
had a serious infection . . .
Doctors told the family not
to worry . . . But by the
time Luke received the
care he needed, it was too
late . . .

Luke Kube

D.KUBE: "I think it could
have been totally avoided
by a simple blood test."
(:04)

Diane Kube
HMO patient's mother
HMO-41/19:19

(BLIP)
These are more than just
three isolated cases of
questionable medical care
. . . They are clues to a
hidden danger that may
affect you and millions of
other  Americans . . .
Under the guise of health
care reform, many doctors
can profit by restricting
the care their patients
receive . . . And for
patients, the bottom line
may be deadly . . .

STANDUP

| | |
|---|---|
| (FLATLINE) | |
| On Long Island, more than a half-million patients belong to HMOs, health maintenance organizations . . . But few are told of the secret deals between HMOs and their doctors . . . For six months, News 12 investigated those deals . . . We found that 11 of the 12 HMOs on Long Island reward doctors who limit the cost of medical care provided to their patients . . . | Clinic footage

Graphic #1 w/font |
| In some HMOs, doctors may earn bonuses by keeping their patients away from expensive tests and medical services . . . In other HMOs, doctors may be financially penalized for sending patients to specialists or hospitals . . . | Graphic #1 w/1st effect

Graphic #1 w/2nd effect |
| RELMAN: "It's certainly unethical. And I think it ought to be made illegal. I think arrangements of that kind ought to be against the law because it provides powerful economic incentives for doctors to act in an unprofessional way." (:15) | Arnold Relman, M.D. N. Engl. J. Med. HMO-15/5:25 |
| News 12 discovered those incentives can change a doctor's income by 10,000, 20,000 or more | U.S. Healthcare charts |

than 50,000 dollars a
year . . .

HIMMELSTEIN: "Patients          David Himmelstein, MD
ought to know that when         Harvard Medical School
they don't get to see a         HMO-23/1:27:05
specialist, the doctor
makes more money. They
ought to know exactly
how much money that is."
(:09)

Instead, patients know          HMO-doctor contracts
little or nothing about
these deals . . . There are
no laws requiring New
York HMOs or doctors to
tell patients about the
incentives . . .

J. KUBE: "The brochures         James Kube
make it sound like the          HMO patient's father
service is excellent. But,       HMO-42/36:55
of course, they don't
mention anything about
bonuses or kickbacks or
whatever it might be."
(:07)

The Kube family belonged        HIP I.D.
to the Health Insurance         (footage or graphic)
Plan of Greater New
York—better known as
H-I-P or HIP . . .
With nearly one million
members, it is the state's
largest HMO . . .
HIP is a non-profit             HIP docs at work
company . . . But the care
is provided through
for-profit groups of doctors
that work exclusively
for HIP . . .

JAMPOL: "It's a very
close and symbiotic
relationship." (:03)

Jesse Jampol, M.D.
HIP
HMO-35/2:56

HIP offers bonuses to the
medical groups . . . It is a
cash incentive for the
doctors to limit the
amount of hospital care
that patients receive . . .

HIP docs at work

JAMPOL: "When the group
meets or beats its targets,
it is entitled to get a
portion of the savings."
(:07)

Jampol SOT
HMO-36/19:10

The bonuses can equal up
to 10% of the doctor's
income . . . A doctor with
a $100,000 salary can
make an extra $10,000
a year . . . The key is to
keep HIP patients out of
the hospital . . .

$$$ graphic
w/fonts

J. KUBE: "I can't believe
they get paid bonuses for
stuff like that." (:04) Like
most HMOs, HIP does
not tell patients about its
private deals with doctors
. . .

J. Kube SOT
HMO-42/36:25
HIP at work

LAGERKVIST: "Is there
any direct disclosure of
that?"

Jampol SOT
HMO-36/32:19

JAMPOL: "No, there isn't.
That's an internal
functioning of the plan . . ."

JAMPOL: "I don't see
that it would do anybody
any good."

HMO-36/32:44

J. KUBE: "I wouldn't have taken the insurance if I had known that at the time." (:04)

J. Kube SOT
HMO-42/36:10

Seven years ago, Luke Kube was born at Syosett Community Hospital . . . The parents soon realized something was wrong with their newborn son . . .

STANDUP
at hospital

D. KUBE: "I noticed he was jaundiced. And I mentioned it to the nurse, and she said she would check with the doctor and have the doctor come and look." (:06)

D. Kube SOT
HMO-41/2:25

But without test or treatment, Luke was discharged from the hospital by an HIP doctor . . .

Luke Kube

D. KUBE: "I think they should have done the blood test before we left the hospital . . ." (:02)

D. Kube SOT
HMO-41/18:46

During the next week, Luke's condition did not improve . . . According to the parents, a doctor at this HIP center was reluctant to send Luke back to a hospital for the test . . . After two office visits and several phone calls, the Kubes finally refused to take no for an answer . . .

HIP clinic at
Ronkonkoma

D. KUBE: "At that point, I had to insist that they do this test because I couldn't take him home that way anymore." (:09)

D. Kube SOT
HMO-41/13:16

The hospital test showed that Luke's blood contained dangerously high levels of a toxic pigment called bilirubin . . . In newborns, too much bilirubin can destroy brain cells . . .

Blood test shots

The Kubes believe that's why Luke has cerebral palsy . . . The infection was not treated until their son was 10 days old . . . And now he is unlikely to ever lead a normal life . . .

Luke Kube

J. KUBE: "With a simple blood test, I think this whole situation could have been avoided . . ." (:06)

J. Kube SOT
HMO-42/32:04

HIP and the doctors refused to comment on this case . . . In court, the doctors denied any blame . . . But they paid a large malpractice settlement to pay for Luke's future needs . . .

Luke Kube

HIP denies that its bonus system compromises the medical care its doctors provide to patients . . .

Jampol B-roll

JAMPOL: "We have in place a number of mechanisms to make

Jampol SOT
HMO-36/27:22

sure the patient gets the appropriate care." (:06)

And HIP contends it only gets more complaints because it has more patients than other HMOs . . .

JAMPOL: "I don't think that the number of complaints against HIP are unusual."

Jampol SOT
HMO-36/35:32

But according to state records, HIP gets more than its share of complaints . . . One-fourth of the HMO members in New York belong to HIP . . . Yet last year, HIP was cited for two-thirds of all HMO violations and deficiencies issued by the state health and insurance departments . . .

Complaint files

If this looks bad on paper, you should see it in real life . . . And how it affects real people—like Luke Kube and his family . . .

Luke Kube & family

D. KUBE: "This is the way he is. And 'what if'? I can't think about 'what if' anymore . . ." (:06)
HMO-41/23:29

D. Kube SOT
HMO-41/23:29
D. Kube SOT

Lagerkvist said the HMO investigation could not have been done without public records. He said that some of those records were found with the help of the FOIA, but "we also got some without using the law. They give us certain documents," he said, "because they know that we can get them . . . so they give them to us."

**NEWS**
**12**
**LONG ISLAND**

One Media Crossways
Woodbury, New York 11797

Telephone: 516/496-1766

April 28, 1994                    *TRANSMITTED BY FAX*

Don McDonald
FOIL Officer
NYS Dept. of Health
Albany, NY

Dear Mr. McDonald:

Under the provisions of the state Freedom of Information Law, I am seeking access to the following records:

All Statements of Deficiency and Plans of Correction from 1990 to present for the following Health Maintenance Organizations: Aetna, ChoiceCare, CIGNA, Empire, HIP, Managed Health, Metlife, Oxford, Prudential, Sanus, Travelers and U.S. Healthcare.

Please call me at 516/496-1299 when the files are available for review. Upon review, I may request photocopies of certain records.

Sincerely,

Mark Lagerkvist

c. Peter Slocum

**Figure 16.1** FOIA request filed by investigative reporter Mark Lagerkvist of News 12 Long Island.

**STATE OF NEW YORK**
**DEPARTMENT OF HEALTH**

Corning Tower     The Governor Nelson A. Rockefeller Empire State Plaza     Albany, New York 12237

Mark R. Chassin, M.D. M.P.P., M.P.H.                      May 3, 1994                      Paula Wilson
  Commissioner                                                                            Executive Deputy Commissioner


        Mark Lagerkvist
        NEWS 12 - Long Island
        1 Media Crossways
        Woodbury, New York 11797

        Dear Mr. Lagerkvist:

                              RE: 94-05-023

            This will acknowledge receipt of your April 28, 1994 request for
        copies of documents under the Freedom of Information Law regarding
        SODs/POCs from 1990 to the present for select HMOs.

            We have forwarded your request to appropriate Department program
        units to identify documents that are responsive to your request and
        which can be made available under the provisions of the New York State
        Freedom of Information Law.

            We estimate that it will take approximately 20 days to complete
        your request or determine the availability of documents responsive to
        your request.

            A fee of $.25 per page has been established by the New York State
        Department of Health for photocopies and/or data printouts.

            When the information or documents have been obtained, we will
        call and make an appointment for you to come in for access. When you
        come in for access, you should arrange to make the copies yourself and
        make payment that day.   At that time, you can also look over the
        documents we had previously copied for you regarding FOIL #94-04-200.

                                        Sincerely,

                                        Donald Macdonald

                                        Donald Macdonald
                                        Records Access Officer

**Figure 16.2**   Response to Lagerkvist's FOIA request from New York State Department of Health.

One Media Crossways
Woodbury, New York 11797

Telephone: 516/496-1766

May 24, 1994                              *TRANSMITTED BY FAX*

Donald McDonald
Records Access Officer
NYS Dept. of Health
Albany, NY

Dear Mr. McDonald:

Under the provisions of the state Freedom of Information Law, I am requesting access to
certain contracts between HMOs and primary care providers.

I've previously discussed the logistics of this request with Elizabeth McFarland, Bureau
of Alternative Delivery Systems. And in an attempt to avoid an unnecessarily
burdensome request, I am narrowing the scope to the following HMO/primary provider
contracts:

HIP: Three recent contracts between HIP and its primary physician-group providers in
Nassau or Suffolk counties.

SANUS: Three recent contracts between Sanus and primary care providers for the
HMO's "Sanus 65" Medicare plan in Suffolk or Nassau counties. Plus two recent
contracts between Sanus and primary care providers for its "commercial" plans in Suffolk
or Nassau counties.

MANAGED HEALTH: The most recent contract between Managed Health and CHP, its
sole group-provider.

U.S. HEALTHCARE: Three recent contracts between USHC and primary care providers
in Suffolk or Nassau counties.

Page - 1

**Figure 16.3** Lagerkvist's follow-up letter seeking additional information under the FOIA.

HEALTHNET (EMPIRE): Three recent contracts between Empire's HealthNet and primary care providers in Suffolk or Nassau counties.

AETNA: Three recent contracts between Aetna and primary care providers in Suffolk or Nassau counties.

CHOICECARE: Three recent contracts between ChoiceCare and primary care providers in Suffolk or Nassau counties.

CIGNA: Three recent contracts between Cigna and primary care providers in Suffolk and Nassau counties.

METLIFE: Three recent contracts between MetLife and primary care providers in Suffolk and Nassau counties.

OXFORD: Three recent contracts between Oxford and primary care providers in Suffolk and Nassau counties.

PRUCARE: Three recent contracts between PruCare and primary care providers in Suffolk and Nassau counties.

TRAVELERS: Three recent contracts between Travelers and primary care providers in Suffolk and Nassau counties.

In all, this request encompasses a sample of three dozen HMO/primary care provider contracts. My original idea was to request access to all HMO/provider contracts, but my conversations with Ms. McFarland led to this proposed compromise.

Please call me at 516/496-1299 to let me know when some or all of these records are available for inspection. If you have any questions or suggestions, please don't hesitate to call.

Sincerely,

Mark Lagerkvist
News 12 Long Island

**Figure 16.3**  continued

**STATE OF NEW YORK**
**DEPARTMENT OF HEALTH**

Corning Tower    The Governor Nelson A. Rockefeller Empire State Plaza    Albany, New York 12237

May 27, 1994

Mark R. Chassin, M.D. M.P.P., M.P.H.
*Commissioner*

Paula Wilson
*Executive Deputy Commissioner*

Mark Lagerkvist
News 12 - Long Island
One Media Crossways
Woodbury, New York  11797

Dear Mr. Lagerkvist:

RE: 94-05-176

This will acknowledge receipt of your May 24, 1994 request for access to documents under the Freedom of Information Law.

We have forwarded your request to appropriate Department program units to identify documents that are responsive to your request and which can be made available under the provisions of the New York State Freedom of Information Law.

We estimate that it will take approximately 30 days to complete your request or determine the availability of documents responsive to your request.

A fee of $.25 per page has been established by the New York State Department of Health for photocopies and/or data printouts.

When the information or documents have been identified, you will be advised of the cost and how payment should be made.

Sincerely,

Donald Macdonald
Donald Macdonald
Records Access Officer

**Figure 16.4**    Response from New York State Department of Health to Lagerkvist's second FOIA request.

**LONG ISLAND**

One Media Crossways
Woodbury, New York 11797

Telephone: 516/496-1766

June 10, 1994                          *TRANSMITTED BY FAX*

Donald McDonald
Records Access Officer
NYS Dept. of Health
Corning Tower - Room 2230
Albany, NY

RE: 94-05-023

Dear Mr. McDonald:

I appreciate your office's effort to provide access to the requested records
during my visit to Albany this week. However, it appears that a large portion
of the records were inadvertently omitted from disclosure.

My request dated April 28 included "all Statements of Deficiency and Plans
of Correction from 1990 to present" for 12 HMOs (copy attached).
However, after careful review, it is apparent that I was only provided access
to the SODs and POCs that resulted from the Department's periodic
inspections.

Overlooked were the SODs and POCs that resulted from complaints received
by the Bureau of Alternative Delivery Systems. As part of #94-05-023, I
expect access to those records without the delays of processing a new FOIL
request.

Page - 1

**Figure 16.5**  Lagerkvist's letter to New York State Department of Health complaining that he did not get
all the records he requested.

Cynthia Weber Glynn of BADS suggested that I could access a regional subset of the "missing" SODs and POCs at the Department's office in New Rochelle. At this point, I would consider that to be an acceptable solution. If that is not acceptable to you, I am willing to inspect the full set of complaint-initiated SODs and POCs when I return to Albany for request #94-05-176.

I do appreciate your office's efforts and hope that you will give this matter prompt attention. If you have any questions, comments or suggestions, please call me at 516/496-1299.

Sincerely,

Mark Lagerkvist
News 12 Long Island

c. Peter Slocum

**Figure 16.5** continued

**NEWS**
**12**
**LONG ISLAND**

One Media Crossways
Woodbury, New York 11797

Telephone: 516/496-1766

June 10, 1994                         *TRANSMITTED BY FAX*

Cynthia Weber Glynn
Bureau of Alternative Delivery Systems
NYS Department of Health
Corning Tower - 19th Floor
Albany, NY

Dear Cynthia:

Thank you for taking time to meet with me earlier this week. Your
input and assistance were greatly appreciated.

As we discussed, I am seeking statistical information from BADS
for 1993 on the number of complaints, the number of substantiated
complaints and the number of complaints that resulted in
Statements of Deficiency for each of the 12 HMOs that serve Long
Island.

Those HMOs are: Atena, BCBS HealthNet, ChoiceCare, Cigna,
HIP, Managed Health, MetLife, Oxford, PruCare, Sanus, Travelers
and U.S. Healthcare.

Page - 1

**Figure 16.6**  Lagerkvist's additional follow-up letter requesting more information under the FOIA.

Once again, thanks for your help. When the information is available, please call me at 516/496-1299.

Sincerely,

Mark Lagerkvist
News 12 Long Island

Page - 2

**Figure 16.6** continued

Lagerkvist conducted other investigations on HMOs in Florida and New Jersey. "Over the years," he said, "I learned about secret deals and conflicts of interest in HMOs, and my news director wanted to see if we could duplicate what we did elsewhere." As investigative reporters are quick to tell you, if you can find out about the "bad guys" in one market, there's a good chance you can find them in other communities. Lagerkvist did.

But he said it was "like pulling teeth. Everyone was uncooperative . . . it took weeks and months to get information from them . . . the HMOs did not want to discuss anything." He said the New York State Department of Health did give him some basic information filed by HMOs, but they also "held back a lot."

Lagerkvist said that sometimes he visits the government agency to look at their files to find out what they have. In this case, Lagerkvist drove from Long Island to Albany, the state capital, and after conversations with officials, he realized they had not given him everything he wanted.

"In some cases," Lagerkvist said, "they were not keeping records because they did not think it was important to do so." The reporter cited an example in which the Department of Health told him that it did not keep records of contracts between HMOs and the doctors they hire. Lagerkvist said: "Sometimes you

**Figure 16.7**   Mark Lagerkvist, investigative reporter for News 12 Long Island. (Courtesy of News 12 Long Island)

can learn a lot from the fact that they don't keep certain records." He added: "It tells me that they are not monitoring the deals because they don't think it is significant enough to merit their attention."

Although he was not able to see signed contracts between the HMOs and doctors, the Department of Health did provide Lagerkvist with blank contracts that indicated that "deals" were being made. With that information and other public records, Lagerkvist was able to confront HMO officials and found out more details on the arrangements they were making with physicians, which became the focus of the reporter's investigation.

## Supporting Video

As is often the case in investigative reports, finding enough good video can be a problem, but Lagerkvist said he was happy with the way the story looked visually. He said: "We didn't have any video of doctors huddling in corners making deals . . . no secret cameras . . . but you can't let the video dictate what we do. If we did," he added, "that would be pandering."

So, what did Lagerkvist do? He relied on a lot of generic footage of doctors at work in the HMOs without showing any closeups, which could cause legal problems (see the section "False Light" in Chapter 20). He also used some graphic material; however, the most important element, he said, was creativity. "If you tell the story right," he said, "you can get the video to work. If the story is important and compelling . . . and you have good, clean, and concise sound bites, it will all come together naturally."

When asked if the HMO story had caused any changes in the system, Lagerkvist said not as yet, but he suspects the "other shoe has not dropped." He said there was a tremendous amount of requests for tapes of the series, and some of those requests came from local and state legislators. Lagerkvist was quick to point out, however, that while it is nice to bring about change and to win awards for such reports, the "bottom line is to serve and inform the people . . . to provide a public service by telling them things that they did not know before."

Another FOIA request filed by producer Chris Szechenyi, who was with WRC-TV in Washington, D.C., at the time, made it possible for him to break a story involving the unreliability of defibrillators (i.e., high-tech medical equipment designed to shock a failed heart back to life). The producer discovered that during a six-year period, such equipment malfunctioned 512 times. He also discovered that the product made by one company, Physio Control Corporation, a subsidiary of Eli Lilly, accounted for 442 of those malfunctions. The company has about 80 percent of the defibrillator market. Szechenyi decided to find out all he could about Physio Control Corporation. He filed an FOIA request with the Food and Drug Administration (FDA). By law, medical-device manufacturers must report deaths to the FDA within 15 days if there is a reason to believe that the deaths were caused by a medical device.

Szechenyi said he thought about doing a story about faulty medical equipment after Congress held hearings regarding problems with heart valves. "I was aware that there was a database for all that information provided to the FDA on malfunctioning equipment by hospitals and manufacturers. But when I went to the government's National Technical Information Service (NTIS) to check on the information, I found thousands of pages of reports. I knew there was no way to successfully gather all the information and come up with any intelligent evaluation. I realized I needed a computer to collate the information to find out which devices were causing the most problems."

Szechenyi then discovered that for $350 NTIS would provide a computer tape that would give him the information he needed. He also realized that he would need help to decipher the tape and thus joined forces with the Missouri Institute for Computer-Assisted Reporting (MICAR). The investigation took four months, and when it was over, Szechenyi and WRC-TV produced a four-part series on medical-equipment problems. The probe was not limited to the Physio Control Corporation. Szechenyi said the defibrillator failures are "only a fraction of the [death] toll caused by a variety of defective medical devices." The investigative team discovered that there were 3,328 deaths and 52,000 injuries associated with medical devices during a six-year period. Szechenyi said: "We discovered that pacemakers, ventilators, heart valves, and other devices designed to save lives are in fact losing lives."

Szechenyi noted that the story, which won the National Headliner Award in 1991, could not have been done without the information produced by the FOIA. Computer technology was also important to the investigation. Since 1984, the FDA has entered into its computers the investigation of more than 100,000 cases of medical-equipment failure. For each case, the computerized record contains the name and address of the manufacturer, the kind of medical device that was involved, a description of the problem, and a statement detailing whether the device merely malfunctioned or caused an injury or death. The record also states whether the FDA has finished its investigation and whether the device was determined to be at fault.

Szechenyi said that computer analysis "is only the first step in the reporting process. Once you have identified a product that is causing problems, you have to find out if there were any recalls." Information about recalls can also be obtained from the FDA under the FOIA. The recall notices say what's wrong with devices, how many were distributed, and what the company is doing to correct the problem.

Szechenyi said FDA inspections of a company's plants also are available under the FOIA. He noted that "it paid to be friendly" with the FOIA officer at the FDA field office in Seattle, who sent a stack of documents only three weeks after Szechenyi made the request. The producer said he got about 600 documents from the field office; it also waived all fees.

Szechenyi said that "behind the statistics and records are tragic human stories, and court records are the best source to find the victims." He also got results by contacting some top litigation lawyers. "I found one lawyer who handled a medical-equipment malfunction case," Szechenyi said, "and he told me about other attorneys who had similar cases, and that's how we got the human stories used in our reports."

## A Neglected Tool

Szechenyi says that he avoids using the FOIA, if he can, because filing a request is so much trouble. Perhaps that is why few journalists use the FOIA. Only a small percentage of broadcast journalists have filed FOIA requests. Actually, prisoners and businesses have used the FOIA more than any other group. Although some information obtained through FOIA requests can be found in other places, there are times, as Szechenyi admitted, when there is no way to do the story without the FOIA.

## The Privacy Act

Some members of Congress were concerned that the FOIA would impinge on one of Americans' most treasured freedoms—privacy. In 1974, Congress passed the Privacy Act in an attempt to protect individuals from unwarranted invasion of their privacy. The act forbids the government from disclosing information in its files pertaining to individuals. Many journalists, however, argue that the government uses the act to keep important information from the public.

# Government Reports

Ironically, while the government often fails to disclose certain information to the public, it publishes volumes of manuals and directories that are important sources of information for journalists. Sometimes, the information found in these government publications is as embarrassing as the material an agency does not disclose.

The government publications found at public and university libraries that are particularly useful to journalists are the reports issued by the General Accounting Office (GAO)—a congressional agency. The GAO issues more than a thousand reports per year, and its recommendations to Congress often provide interesting and sometimes provocative story ideas for journalists. The now famous stories about the Pentagon paying 20 and 30 times what it should for hammers and other basic tools came from GAO reports.

Other government publications that are useful to reporters include the following:

*The Code of Federal Regulations*—which describes how laws and regulations are enforced.

*The Congressional Record*—which offers a daily report of congressional debate and other business. It also lists most agencies and high-ranking government officials, including members of Congress, of its various committees, and of the judicial and executive branches.

*The Federal Regional Directory*—which lists federal offices that have records on local programs and activities involving the government.

*The Federal Register*—which gives a daily account of federal-agency activities and executive orders from the White House.

*The Federal Regulatory Directory*—which describes the 15 major regulatory agencies and lists the more than 60 lesser-known regulatory bodies. It also lists the names of top officials.

The U.S. Bureau of the Census publications—which provide statistical information on almost every aspect of life in America.

*The U.S. Government Manual*—which outlines the responsibilities and organization of the federal government. It includes all types of valuable information, including addresses, phone numbers, and names of officials at various government branches.

*The Washington Information Directory*—which provides additional nongovernment sources not shown in the Government Manual.

All of these publications—and a great many more—are also housed in Government Depository Libraries located throughout the United States and on many university campuses.

## Business Publications and Indexes

Reporters working on complex or investigative stories about business can find a variety of useful publications in the library, including Dun & Bradstreet's directory of companies worth a million dollars or more. *Standard & Poor's Register of Corporations* is also useful because it not only lists the corporations but also includes background information on major business leaders. Reporters looking for information on specific products use the *Thomas Register of American Manufacturers* series.

Magazines and newspapers also write about business and industry. The most respected of these sources are the *Wall Street Journal*, *Forbes*, *Fortune*, and *Business Week*.

## Trade Publications

The story of American industry is also told in hundreds of magazines and publications available in libraries. Many of these publications are biased because they speak for the industry they represent. Nevertheless, reporters often find useful information in such publications, which can provide leads for reporters seeking industry spokespeople. Trade publications are also an important source for information on what position various industries are taking on an issue.

# Database Services

We have made numerous references in this book to the information explosion—the so-called information super highway—which has had a major impact on all types of communications. It already is a boon to journalists. The Internet, in particular, has invaluable tools for searching all types of subjects.

Many libraries have computerized the catalogue of the information that's housed in them, which makes locating the information much faster. Many libraries subscribe to database services such as LexisNexis, InfoTrac, and others that index hundreds of newspapers, magazines, academic and scientific journals, and trade publications.

Many broadcast newsrooms that acquired computers for word processing, assignment lists, producer rundowns, and various other news activities also subscribe to database services, particularly LexisNexis, the largest and broadest of all the services. LexisNexis is also available at 75 percent of American colleges and universities.

In addition to its retrieval service, you can get assistance from a "live person" 24 hours a day and you can consult with specialists in law, finance, and taxation free of charge. LexisNexis offers thousands of sources of news and business information, including many that appear in full text. It includes virtually all the major newspapers, wire services, CNN, and major networks. Foreign newspapers and wire services also can be accessed.

Reporters routinely use LexisNexis for the following tasks:

- background and document stories
- identify contacts and experts
- formulate interview questions
- verify facts obtained in interviews and news conferences
- verify quotes for accuracy
- obtain quotes they missed
- see how others covered the story
- develop different angles
- obtain story ideas
- gather statistics

## *Great for Running Stories*

Retrieval services like Lexis-Nexis are a major help in covering stories such as the O. J. Simpson trial and the Oklahoma City bombing. The company provided complete transcripts of both the trial and sidebar conferences (between the attorneys and Judge Ito) within an hour after the morning and afternoon sessions. Reporters also were able to research prospective witnesses before they took the stand and read case law cited by the lawyers.

After the Oklahoma City bombing, reporters were able to quickly access a history of bomb attacks in the United States and obtain lists of experts on bomb attacks and building blasts. LexisNexis also provided texts of FBI news briefings and President Clinton's news conferences.

Investigative reporters also use the retrieval services. Reporter David Farrell of the *Detroit News* said that after gathering extensive information on the service, he uncovered a network of dummy corporations with the sole purpose of depositing checks authorized by two top police officials. Farrell's story generated a full-scale investigation that resulted in prison sentences.

So why not use the Internet, which is free, instead of LexisNexis? LexisNexis is more focused, easier to use, and much faster than the Internet, says company spokesman Phil Romba.

# Other Public Files

Reporters have another useful method of locating information, particularly information about individuals' government files. Governments at all levels maintain files on numerous activities that happen within their borders. When a baby is born, or when someone dies, or is married or divorced, or registers a car or opens a liquor store, or buys a piece of land or is arrested, or sues somebody or opens a restaurant, someone issues a document that is kept on permanent record. Anyone who wishes to do so may look at and copy such documents.

## Police Records

The amount of information that reporters can obtain from police records varies from community to community. Reporters who establish a good rapport with a police desk sergeant often get the information they want with little trouble. Technically, any information on the police log or blotter should be available to reporters. Without a good rapport, however, it sometimes takes the threat of court action to get the information. The records include the name of the individual, the date of the arrest, the charges, and the disposition of those charges. Once a person is behind bars, that information is normally available where the individual is being held.

## Court Records

Information about the court cases most reporters deal with—criminal and civil cases—is available at a court clerk's office. In a civil case, anyone can obtain information about the complaint or petition brought by the plaintiff. The com-

**Figure 16.8**
*NBC News* correspondent Roger O'Neil.
(Courtesy of Ray Farmer/NBC News)

plaint usually describes what the defendant has allegedly done and why the plaintiff wants the court to award damages.

In criminal cases, reporters also have access to the charges brought against an individual. The records list the name of the complainant, most often a police officer, and the name of the defendant. The records cite the charge and describe what allegedly occurred that led to the arrest and court action. Reporters soon learn that it's a lot easier, and quicker, to find these records if they are on a first-name basis with the court clerks.

## Birth and Death Records

The facts of a person's birth often can be important to a reporter. A birth certificate lists the names of the parents, the date of birth, the name of the doctor who delivered the child, and the name of the hospital. Death certificates also provide information that may be important to a story. They show the cause of death and the date and time it occurred; however, such records are not always public. If an individual left a will that involved real estate, reporters may also obtain a copy of the death certificate attached to mortgages and deeds found at the property tax office.

Being friendly and showing respect often make it easier to find some of these records or, perhaps, to get a quick look at those that are not supposed to be open to the public.

## Licenses

Nearly every community issues licenses of many kinds, and sometimes knowing who received a license can be important to a newsperson. In a large city, little goes on in business that does not require some sort of a license—even selling hot dogs on the street. Such licenses list the name and other personal information about the grantee. Such information would be valuable, for example, if a reporter was working on a story about a junkyard that was an environmental or safety hazard.

The licensing of guns has been an ongoing issue throughout the nation. Because there is no national gun-control law, the ability to check on people who may own guns depends on where the reporter is doing the checking. New York has strict gun laws; Virginia does not. In 1995, Virginia passed a law making it legal to carry a concealed weapon. This bothers many people who live just across the border in the nation's capital, which has one of the worst crime and homicide records involving guns in the world.

Driver's license records and car registrations are also easily available in some states and can be obtained with a minimum amount of coaxing in most others if the reporter can provide a good reason for wanting the information.

Many professional people, such as doctors, architects, and engineers, also must hold licenses. The state agencies or boards that issue those licenses have biographical information, including education and the applicants' specialty.

## Land Records

The property tax office can provide a lot of information to an investigative reporter. It has records on who pays the taxes on property and, presumably, but not always, on the owner of the property. The records also reveal the former owners' names and the purchase price of the property, as well as who holds the mortgage on the property, if there is one. The names of the real-estate brokers and lawyers who were involved in the sale are also indicated. This information might be important to know if, for example, a reporter was checking on a city judge who seemed to be lenient with drunk drivers and it was discovered in the property tax records that the judge was living in a million-dollar home in the suburbs.

## Financial Records

It is easy to check a person's financial record. Many people, except perhaps reporters looking for such information, believe that it's too easy to find out how Americans handle their finances. Reporters need only ask the station's business office to call TRW or some other credit bureau, and the person's computer-produced financial record will be on the reporter's desk in minutes. The record shows credit histories for 10 years or more, the names of those holding mortgages, where individuals shop, and whether they pay their bills on time. The report also shows any bankruptcy declared during the past 10 years.

Anytime an individual moves and establishes credit of any kind, the new address is recorded, which can be useful to a reporter trying to find the person. Other firms provide a person's new address as long as the reporter supplies a Social Security number.

**Figure 16.9**   Morton Dean anchors *World News This Morning* and news breaks in *Good Morning America* from the caucuses in Iowa on February 12, 1996. (© 2000 ABC, Inc)

## Tax Records

Tax records are among the most difficult documents to obtain. Reporters do, from time to time, obtain information about a person's tax returns from the Internal Revenue Service (IRS), but almost always as the result of a leak initiated by someone inside the agency. Some reporters manage to develop sources inside the IRS, but it is not easy.

## City Directories

The city directory is often helpful if you want to find out where a particular individual lives. The directory lists a person's name, address, spouse, children, employment, and several other useful pieces of information. The directories are particularly helpful when a reporter is trying to talk to relatives of someone who is in the news.

Telephone books are also useful; they would be the first place to look when trying to locate someone if you know the town or city in which he or she lives. In some communities, the telephone company also prints telephone books that list people and companies by their addresses. They are extremely useful, for example, if a major fire breaks out on the 1500 block of Main Street. There are listings for all of the phones on Main Street that are not restricted, so all the reporter or assignment editor has to do is try to locate a phone near the 1500 block. A call to a phone listed at 1550 Main Street, for example, might find someone who can see the fire from an apartment window. It's then simple to put the person on the air while he or she describes the fire and answers the reporter's questions.

## Summary

Unfortunately, many radio or TV news organizations do not give their reporters enough time to use the various information sources described in this chapter. Reporters spend most of their time working on breaking news stories. Investigative stories require a lot of research time and are expensive to produce. Most stations want at least one story a day from their reporters, which doesn't allow much time for checking court records or filing FOIA requests.

If you do have an opportunity to work on stories that require in-depth research, the information in this chapter should be extremely helpful. The FOIA is an important asset if you want to examine the actions of government at any level—town, city, state, or federal. The library at your college or university has numerous documents that will reveal more about the federal government, how it works, and what mistakes it makes. The report of the GAO, a congressional watchdog, and the Congressional Directory are also useful.

You should also familiarize yourself with the various business publications, indexes, journals, and magazines in your library and learn about the ability of the Internet and databases such as Lexis-Nexis, which have cut reporter research tremendously.

This chapter also describes how to use the various government files maintained by police and the courts, tax and land offices, and bureaus that keep records on births, deaths, licenses, and numerous other activities.

## Review Questions

1. What is the Freedom of Information Act?
2. Why is it so important to journalists?
3. Does the FOIA apply only to the dealings of the federal government?
4. List the different points that should be made in a letter requesting information under the FOIA.
5. Journalists can learn about the government and how it operates through various records and publications. List some of the most important ones, and explain how they are useful.

6. How can computer databases be useful to reporters?
7. What kind of information can reporters obtain from police and court records?

# Exercises

1. Suppose that you are filing an FOIA request with the Defense Department because you have a source that claims that when he worked for the Acme Tool and Dye Company in Centerville, a government contractor, as many as 60 percent of the products produced in the plant were rejected for various reasons. Prepare the FOIA request.
2. Pick three corporations among the Fortune 500 list, and find out the names of the top officials who run them. Also list any other companies that are owned by one of these parent corporations, and find out the names of any corporations or individuals who own a substantial number of shares in a parent company.
3. Use a database service to find out how many articles were published last year about Dan Rather. List the names of the publications along with the titles of the articles and the dates they appeared.
4. Visit the local courthouse and find out the names of those who were convicted of drunk driving during the past month.

# 17 Computer-Assisted Reporting for Broadcast

*By Brant Houston (Copyright 2000 by Brant Houston)*

In the past decade, computer-assisted reporting (CAR) has become part of many journalists' day-to-day work and aided those journalists in creating high-impact, public-service stories.

CAR is the acquisition and analysis of electronic information and databases. It is the natural extension of using hard-copy (paper) documents, and many records described in Chapter 16, "Collecting Information from Documents," have become electronic.

Although journalists need training to use CAR, the result—once they have had the training—is that they become proficient at finding, filtering, sorting, and analyzing public records. In the past, journalists might have taken days to look at a few hundred records; now they can examine tens of thousands of records in a few hours.

A few years ago, CAR was a skill reserved for a few expert reporters and research librarians, but it has now been rapidly integrated into deadline, daily, and beat reporting. For example, many journalists routinely use databases and the tools of CAR whenever covering a plane crash.

With knowledge of CAR, a journalist has a distinct advantage over the competition. The journalist with CAR skills can bring more depth, context, and credibility to a story. CAR often provides a journalist with an exclusive story. In addition, the explosion of public information on the Web, the simplification of software, and the increased speed in computer processing permits a CAR journalist to outdistance others on breaking stories.

This chapter provides an overview of the basic tools of CAR and the kinds of stories that broadcast journalists have reported with the help of these tools. This chapter also refers to the books and online resources that offer much more detail about research on the Web and on performing data analysis.

# The Three Basic Tools

The three basic software tools of CAR are online resources, spreadsheets, and database managers. These three are not exclusive, and often a CAR journalist employs all three while working on a story.

Online resources include the Internet and commercial databases. Reporters use them to find people, background businesses, monitor discussion groups on special topics, and acquire relevant data for a story. The effective use of the Web is a critical skill because, as everyone knows, it's possible to "surf" for hours without results. Equally important is the focused use of commercial databases because of the potential high cost of their services.

With spreadsheet software, such as Microsoft Excel, a reporter can quickly calculate, sort, and filter electronic data. Tabular data (i.e., data in columns and rows like a stock table or sports rankings) can be efficiently downloaded into a spreadsheet from the Internet. A reporter also can easily enter data into a spreadsheet. Reporters often use spreadsheets to examine budgets, salaries, population figures, and housing costs.

A database manager (e.g., Microsoft Access) lets a reporter quickly search, summarize, and compare public records. Although a database manager is more difficult to learn to use than a spreadsheet, it is a powerful tool. A database manager can search hundreds of thousands of electronic records for a specific item, summarize those records to determine if patterns exist, or compare separate files of information to find records that match. Broadcast reporters have used database managers to discover the day of the week that public employees most often call in sick, to identify dangerous bridges and dams, or to find teachers who are also convicted felons.

# Online Resources

Commercial databases are available online and on CD-ROMs. (Never forget to check the local library for what might be available for free on CD-ROMs.)

For online pay services, many journalists use Lexis-Nexis, which has news stories and many legal resources. They also buy Autotrack services from Database Technologies or CDB Infotek services to get information about corporations or individuals that is not on the Web or that is not easy to find on the Web. But until a journalist becomes skilled at searching commercial databases, it is wise to ask an experienced research librarian for help rather than waste time and money.

Regardless of how the information is obtained, a journalist should know what information is offered through these services. Nora Paul, an expert researcher, provides a valuable review and comparison of commercial services in her book *Computer-Assisted Research* (4th edition, 1999, Bonus Books and The Poynter Institute for Media Studies). This book is a good starting guide to what is available at different commercial databases and on the Web.

## Search Engines and Guides

The Web can be frustrating for a journalist, especially if he or she is utilizing search engines (automated indexers of Web pages) that return hundreds or thousands of "hits" when a journalist enters one keyword. Tom McGinty, training director for Investigative Reporters and Editors, Inc., gives one of the simplest pieces of advice on search engines: Read the help files. Those help files will teach you Boolean logic, which involves narrowing or widening your criteria through the words "and," "or," and "not" (see Figure 17.1).

Many reporters find the Web subject indexes (particularly Yahoo.com) and the directories offered on the home pages of the search engines to be more helpful. Better yet—because they are aimed at journalists—are the "homegrown" guides created by journalists. The Reporter's Desktop, www.reporter.org/desktop, authored by Duff Wilson of *The Seattle Times*, and the Net Tour, www.ire.org/training/nettour, offered by the National Institute for Computer-Assisted Reporting, authored by McGinty and Sarah Cohen of the *Washington Post*, are efficient places to start (see Figure 17.2).

## Finding People

Many Websites offer ways to find people's addresses and phone numbers. Most of them are like a reporter's tip sheet, however, in that they give possible answers, but they must be checked out and verified—like everything on the Web. If a journalist can't find a person by looking at the service www.switchboard.com, then he or she could try Yahoo's People Search at

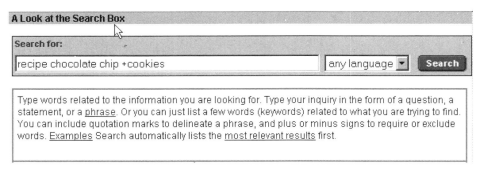

**Figure 17.1**  Altavista.com (a commercial search engine) provides a clear description of how to look for a recipe with its "search box."

Bookmarks
Location: http://www.ire.org/training/nettour/
Instant Message
Internet
Lookup
New&Cool
NICAR `Net Tour
A Strategy Guide with Starting Points

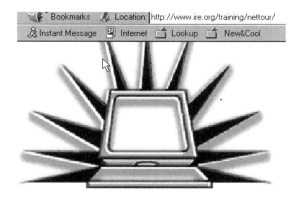

**Figure 17.2**
The welcome screen for the Net Tour Website.

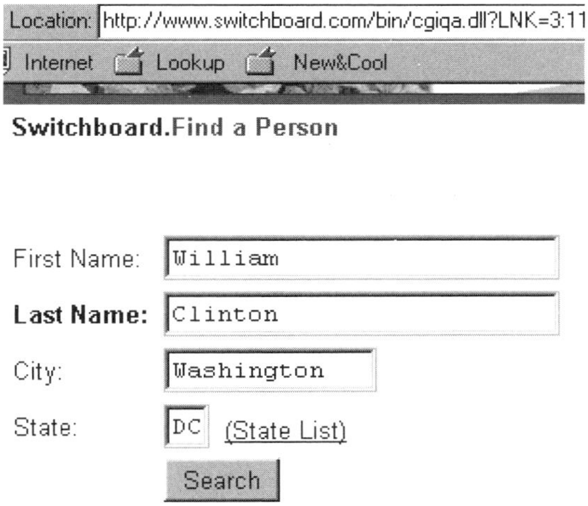

Location: http://www.switchboard.com/bin/cgiqa.dll?LNK=3:11
Internet
Lookup
New&Cool
Switchboard.Find a Person
First Name:
William
Last Name:
Clinton
City:
Washington
State:
DC
(State List)
Search

**Figure 17.3**
Entering a search for President Clinton on www.switchboard.com.

www.people.yahoo.com, or one of the many other "people finders" available, such as www.whowhere.lycos.com. For example, a search for President Clinton at www.switchboard.com is shown in Figure 17.3.

The service returns his basic information that in the year 2000 he lived on Pennsylvania Avenue, but no further information is provided. (Although it does appear he is a Switchboard user. Note the asterisk in Figure 17.4.)

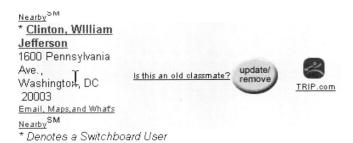

**Figure 17.4**   The results for a search for President Clinton on www.switchboard.com.

## Backgrounding Businesses

The Web has become an excellent resource for conducting research about businesses. First, many businesses have their own Websites on which they reveal much about themselves. Second, you can find basic business information at services like Switchboard.com with maps to the business locations. Third, businesses must file information with the government. Many states are placing corporate records and licensing records up on their Websites.

If a company has publicly traded stock, then they appear on a site all journalists should use routinely—the U.S. Securities and Exchange Commission Website, www.sec.gov, where filings by companies are kept in a database called "EDGAR" (see Figure 17.5).

The EDGAR site contains information that tells you about the companies' earnings and losses, subsidiaries, lawsuits, officers, strategies, and many other useful bits of information. Journalists often go to other sites, including www.hoover.com (as in vacuum cleaner, not the dam or president), which gathers extensive information about businesses.

## Information on Disasters

The Web also plays a crucial role for journalists covering disasters. Whether you're looking for information on bombs, explosions, hurricanes, or floods, both breaking news and context are available. Many journalists log on electronic discussion groups to get material and tips they may not hear at the scene of a catastrophe. After the Oklahoma City bombing, many journalists learned about the rise of "militia groups" by reading e-mail postings to newsgroup discussions. Both the Web and in-house databases have become a standard resource when covering airplane crashes.

Andrew Lehren, who does the CAR work for *Dateline NBC*, has not only used CAR for in-depth projects, but also has demonstrated the effective use of

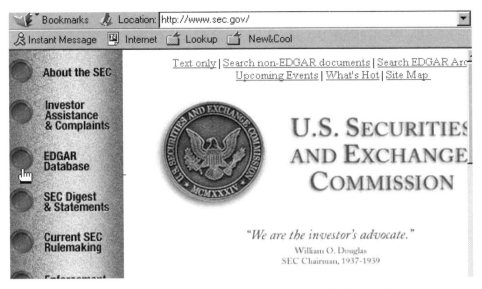

**Figure 17.5** The welcome page for the U.S. Securities and Exchange Commission Website.

databases on deadline or for quick-turnaround stories. When TWA Flight 800 went down over Long Island in 1998, Lehren, who at that time was database administrator at the National Institute for Computer-Assisted Reporting (NICAR), swiftly showed the fallacy of the theory that the plane had been shot down by a Stinger missile. Lehren found the altitude of the plane when it exploded and then went to a Website that had information on Stinger missiles, which revealed that those missiles could not reach that altitude.

More recently, Lehren did work on the crash of John F. Kennedy Jr.'s plane, using both online resources and aviation safety databases. Lehren analyzed data from the National Transportation Safety Board. He said the data provided "a wealth of information about those who have died" in Piper Saratoga planes.

In an article for NICAR's newsletter, *Uplink*, Lehren said the data "allowed comparisons of crashes involving instrument-rated versus visual flight-rated pilots." Kennedy was only visual flight-rated. Lehren also analyzed service difficulty reports for planes from the Federal Aviation Administration (FAA), including air-worthiness directives, ownership records, registration records, and Aviation Safety System records.

While this sounds like a tremendous amount of material to check, Lehren said he worked with *Dateline* producers and correspondents to come up with breaking news and relevant information in the two days immediately following the crash.

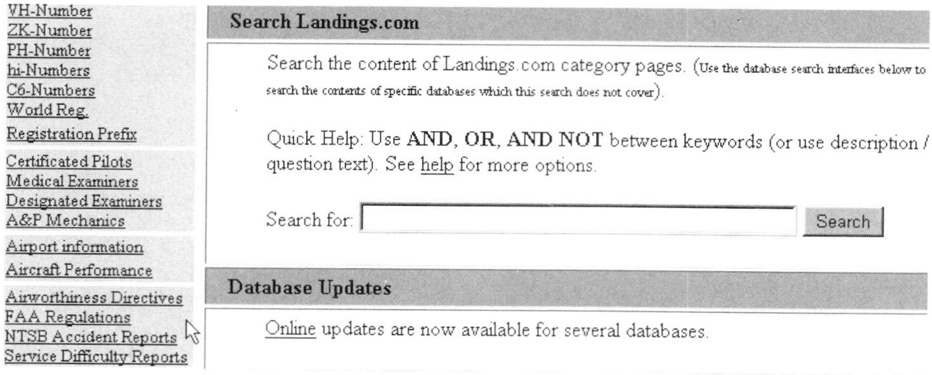

**Figure 17.6**    The search screen for the Landings.com Website.

Lehren also noted that an important lesson from this story is not to rely solely on Websites, but to make sure to have complete databases already in-house. He said several critical Websites were down or missing crucial reports and records at the time he was conducting research about the JFK Jr. plane crash.

One of the best starting points for air safety is a site called www.landings.com, which provides a gateway into many databases (see Figure 17.6).

Notice the reports available pointed out by the cursor in Figure 17.6. These are the reports that Lehren examined, but Lehren also had ordered and received complete datasets before the crash and had learned how to analyze them. Journalists must be prepared ahead of time to cover an event on deadline.

## Covering Beats

Many reporters check daily on Websites that relate to their beats or topics they cover. For example, a journalist reporting on Congress would make http://thomas.loc.gov a daily stop. That site carries extensive information on legislative bills and other information on Congress. To keep track of campaign contributions, the interested journalist would also check the Federal Election Commission site, www.fecinfo.com, to keep track of campaign contributions, and other nonprofit sites, such as The Center For Responsive Politics at www.crp.org. Broadcast journalists with CAR skills download information often on campaign finance to monitor and report independently on local politicians and their supporters.

A journalist interested in the environment and health would check the Environmental Protection Agency site, www.epa.org, and the nonprofit Natural Resources Defense Council site, www.nrdc.org. These sites contain information on pollution and efforts at cleanup. Reporters can also go to these sites to check on the environmental records of local companies.

If a journalist were keeping track of crime, he or she would routinely check the Federal Bureau of Investigations (FBI) site, www.fbi.gov, and the Bureau of Justice Statistics site, www.ojp.usdoj.gov/bjs, for perspective and to look for trends and possible stories. Crime data is often downloaded and entered into a spreadsheet to calculate percentage increases and decreases in the kinds of crime.

## Downloading Databases

A journalist should routinely download information from Websites. For example, journalists should regularly obtain information about their states and local communities from the U.S. Bureau of Census site, www.census.gov, and have that information on hand for stories. This site is a good place to find data for a multitude of stories, and it makes much of its data easy to download.

A search for median incomes for families of four in each state led to this location at the Census Website, shown in Figure 17.7. This information is in a particularly friendly format—an HTML (hypertext markup language) file that

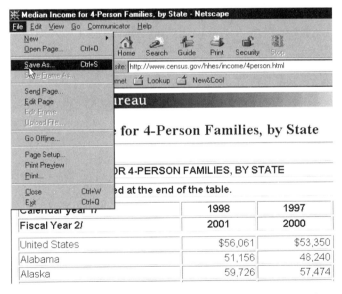

**Figure 17.7**  A table of information is being downloaded from the U.S. Census Website by going to "File" and clicking on "Save As."

can be readily opened by Microsoft Excel. (We will return to this file in the spreadsheet section of this chapter.)

# Spreadsheets

Spreadsheets can help a journalist monitor changing information, look at salaries and budgets, analyze crime statistics, and track population figures. A journalist can quickly perform calculations with a spreadsheet because a spreadsheet can copy and apply the calculation to other numbers. A spreadsheet also can store the information, unlike a calculator, for later use.

Journalists often need to add a column of numbers such as salaries. With a spreadsheet, a journalist can type in a series of numbers and add them up with a formula. The spreadsheet makes this possible to do by giving every number an address like a map. The address is composed of the letter of the column and the number of the row in which the number itself is located.

In the example in Figure 17.8, the formula "=SUM(A3:A11)" was typed in A13. That formula means that all the numbers from A3 to A11 are added. Notice both the total and the formula that was typed to get the total. (The formula is just above the cursor in Figure 17.8.)

This capability is especially useful when a journalist is adding up hundreds of numbers. A spreadsheet has many ways of speeding up calculations, but one of the most valuable is the ability to copy a formula. If all the salaries in Figure 17.8 were to be increased by 5 percent, the total salary after the increase could be calculated by multiplying the number in A3 by 1.05 as shown in Figure 17.9. (The 1.05 gives the previous salary plus the 5 percent increase.)

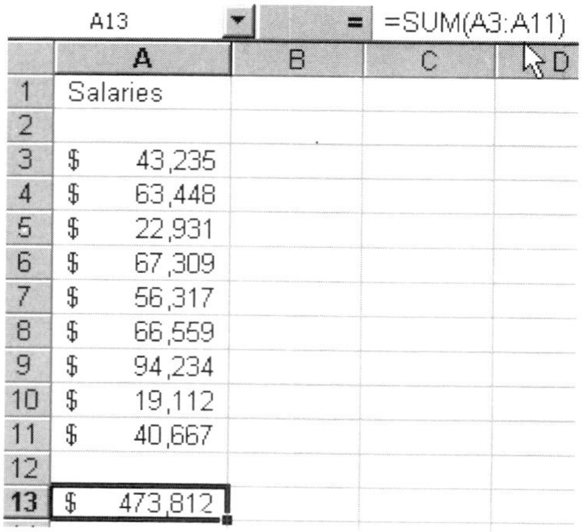

**Figure 17.8**
Adding figures in a Microsoft Excel spreadsheet.

| | A13 | ▼ | | = | =SUM(A3:A11) |
|---|---|---|---|---|---|
| | **A** | | B | C | D |
| 1 | Salaries | | | | |
| 2 | | | | | |
| 3 | $ | 43,235 | | | |
| 4 | $ | 63,448 | | | |
| 5 | $ | 22,931 | | | |
| 6 | $ | 67,309 | | | |
| 7 | $ | 56,317 | | | |
| 8 | $ | 66,559 | | | |
| 9 | $ | 94,234 | | | |
| 10 | $ | 19,112 | | | |
| 11 | $ | 40,667 | | | |
| 12 | | | | | |
| **13** | $ | 473,812 | | | |

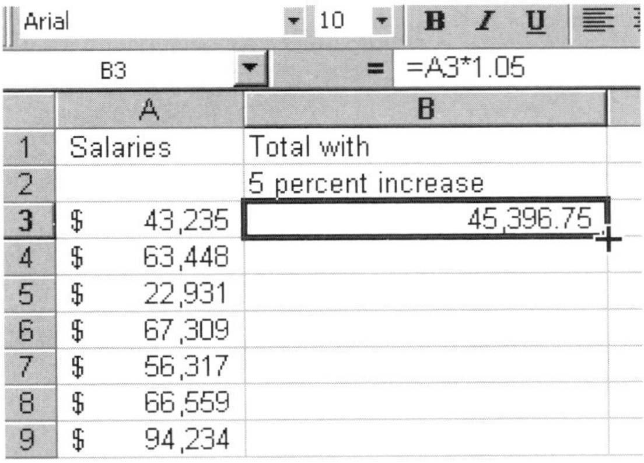

Arial 10 B I U

B3 = =A3*1.05

| | A | B |
|---|---|---|
| 1 | Salaries | Total with |
| 2 | | 5 percent increase |
| 3 | $ 43,235 | 45,396.75 |
| 4 | $ 63,448 | |
| 5 | $ 22,931 | |
| 6 | $ 67,309 | |
| 7 | $ 56,317 | |
| 8 | $ 66,559 | |
| 9 | $ 94,234 | |

**Figure 17.9**
Performing a percentage increase formula in a Microsoft Excel spreadsheet.

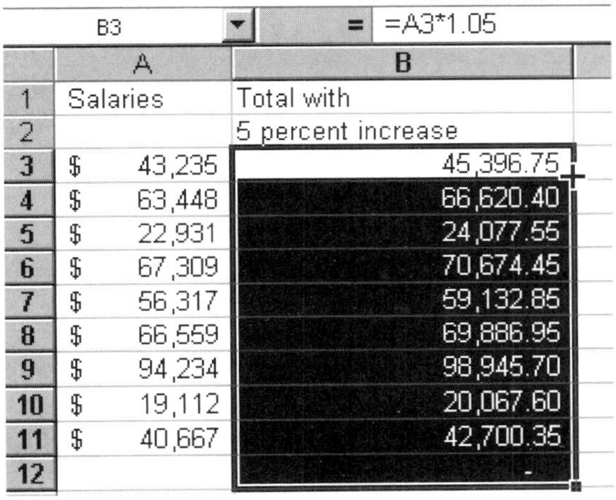

B3 = =A3*1.05

| | A | B |
|---|---|---|
| 1 | Salaries | Total with |
| 2 | | 5 percent increase |
| 3 | $ 43,235 | 45,396.75 |
| 4 | $ 63,448 | 66,620.40 |
| 5 | $ 22,931 | 24,077.55 |
| 6 | $ 67,309 | 70,674.45 |
| 7 | $ 56,317 | 59,132.85 |
| 8 | $ 66,559 | 69,886.95 |
| 9 | $ 94,234 | 98,945.70 |
| 10 | $ 19,112 | 20,067.60 |
| 11 | $ 40,667 | 42,700.35 |
| 12 | | - |

**Figure 17.10**
Duplicating formulas throughout a column in a Microsoft Excel spreadsheet.

Note both the formula and the number in B3. Also, note that the cursor has been turned into a narrow cross when placed in the lower right-hand corner of B3. By double-clicking on the narrow cross, the formula automatically is copied down the column. This shortcut saves journalists (or anyone else, for that matter) an incredible amount of time (see Figure 17.10).

## *Using Downloaded Data*

A journalist often doesn't have to type in numbers, but can download them from the Web or receive them on a diskette. Let's look at the downloaded U.S. Census Bureau data on the incomes of four-person families in the United States.

| E15 | ▼ | = | =D15/C15 | |
|---|---|---|---|---|

| | A | B | C | D | E |
|---|---|---|---|---|---|
| 1 | Census Bureau | | | | |
| 2 | | | | | |
| 3 | **Median Income for 4-Person Families, by State** | | | | |
| 4 | | | | | |
| 5 | | | | | |
| 6 | | | | | |
| 7 | MEDIAN INCOME FOR 4-PERSON FAMILIES, BY STATE | | | | |
| 8 | Footnotes are located at the end of the table. | | | | |
| 9 | Calendar year 1/ | 1998 | 1997 | Change | Percentage |
| 10 | | | | | change |
| 11 | United States | $56,061 | $53,350 | $2,711 | 5% |
| 12 | Alabama | 51,156 | 48,240 | $2,916 | 6% |
| 13 | Alaska | 59,726 | 57,474 | $2,252 | 4% |
| 14 | Arizona | 49,397 | 47,133 | $2,264 | 5% |
| 15 | Arkansas | 44,471 | 38,646 | $5,825 | 15% |
| 16 | California | 55,209 | 55,217 | ($8) | 0% |
| 17 | Colorado | 63,428 | 58,988 | $4,440 | 8% |
| 18 | Connecticut | 75,534 | 72,706 | $2,828 | 4% |

**Figure 17.11**   Creating a composite spreadsheet for data analysis in Microsoft Excel.

When the file is opened in a spreadsheet, rows and columns can be deleted or added. Then calculations can be done to put the data in perspective. In the worksheet in Figure 17.11, the increase from 1997 to 1998 has been calculated and copied for every state. The percentage change also has been calculated. Note that the increase in Arkansas (15 percent) was higher than in other states. The formula for that calculation (D15/C15) can be seen at the top of the worksheet.

To see the many other uses of Excel for journalism, we refer you to Chapter 3 in *Computer-Assisted Reporting: A Practical Guide*, by Brant Houston (2nd edition, 1999, Bedford/St. Martin's Press).

# Database Managers

A database manager takes more time to learn than a spreadsheet, but it is a powerful tool used by businesses and government agencies and now more often by journalists. With a database manager, a journalist can search tens of thousands of electronic records, summarize the records in seconds, and compare or match those records to records in another file.

## Searching

To search in a database manager such as Microsoft Access, a journalist must "query" the database. A query can be done by filling out the equivalent of a form and specifying the criteria by search—very much like using a keyword on an Internet search.

Journalists often use databases for political campaign finance records. In this example, contributions in 2000 to U.S. Senator John Ashcroft, a Missouri Republican, were downloaded from the Web and placed in Microsoft Access. The data included the name of the contributor, the amount contributed, the contributor's city and state of residence, and the contributor's occupation. Note the names of columns of information in Figure 17.12.

One routine search that can be applied to this database is to see which contributors are not from Missouri. Rather than scanning through the data, a "query form" can be used to find everyone not from Missouri. The query form also allows a journalist to select which columns, known as "fields," to look at. In Figure 17.13, the columns for name, amount, and state have been selected from the possible choices above, and the criteria "not MO" (meaning not from Missouri) has been typed in the state column.

The result when the query is "run" is a list of non-Missouri contributors, as seen in Figure 17.14.

## Summarizing

A query in a database manager can also powerfully summarize data. Although it can be helpful to find individual contributors, trends can be spotted by obtaining total contributions from each state that is not the home state of the candidate.

Figure 17.15 shows an example of such a query. In this case, the contributions are "grouped by" each state and then totaled with the word "sum." The result is also sorted by the highest amount to the lowest amount (in descending order).

| individual contributions : Table | | | | | | |
|---|---|---|---|---|---|---|
| NAME | DATE | AMOUNT | CITY | STATE | ZIP | EMPLOY/OCCU |
| ABERNATHY, DEBORAH | 10/14/99 | 500.00 | JOPLIN | MO | 64801 | SOFTWARE |
| ABILHEIRA, ELIAS | 5/3/99 | 1000.00 | ENGLISHTOWN | NJ | 07726 | SCHOEFELD AND |
| ABLES, | 1/24/00 | 250.00 | OLATHE | KS | 66061 | PHYSICIAN |
| ABRAMOFF, JACK | 6/22/99 | 1000.00 | WASHINGTON | DC | 20006 | PRESTON GATES & |
| ABRAMOFF, PAMELA | 6/22/99 | 1000.00 | SILVER | MD | 20901 | HOUSEWIFE |
| ABSHEER, LARRY | 4/13/99 | 250.00 | ST LOUIS | MO | 63119 | MISSOURI ATHLETIC |
| ABSHEER, LARRY | 6/30/99 | 250.00 | ST LOUIS | MO | 63119 | MISSOURI ATHLETIC |
| ABSHEER, LARRY | 11/23/99 | 200.00 | ST LOUIS | MO | 63119 | MISSOURI ATHLETIC |

**Figure 17.12** Excerpt from a campaign contribution database created in Microsoft Access.

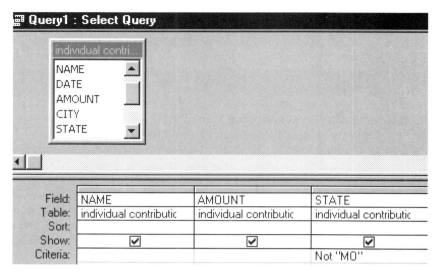

**Figure 17.13** Excerpt from the query form for a Microsoft Access database.

**Figure 17.14**
Results of a query run on a campaign contribution database in Microsoft Access.

Query1 : Select Query

| NAME | AMOUNT | STATE |
|---|---|---|
| ABILHEIRA, ELIAS | 1000.00 | NJ |
| ABLES, | 250.00 | KS |
| ABRAMOFF, JACK | 1000.00 | DC |
| ABRAMOFF, PAMELA | 1000.00 | MD |
| ACCARDO, NATE | 1000.00 | KS |
| ACKERMAN, | 500.00 | MI |
| ACKERMAN, EDITH | 1000.00 | PA |
| ADAM, P | 1000.00 | KS |
| ADAMANY, FRED | 1000.00 | IL |
| ADAMANY, FRED | 1000.00 | IL |
| ADAMS, MILDRED | 1000.00 | OR |
| ADAMS, MORGAN | 200.00 | CA |

The result of "running" this query shows that the largest amounts from out-of-state contributors came from Kansas and Texas (see Figure 17.16).

With this information, a reporter can now start asking why contributors from another state would give so much to Senator Ashcroft's campaign.

## Comparing and Matching

The ability to compare and match information from different files is the third major advantage of a database manager. The database manager can make

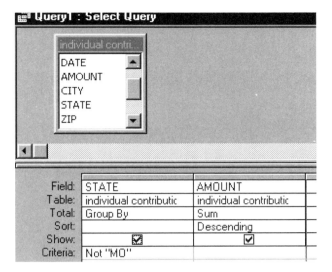

**Figure 17.15**
Excerpt of a summary query in a Microsoft Access database.

| STATE | SumOfAMOUN |
|---|---|
| KS | 195975 |
| TX | 116663 |
| CA | 76727 |
| IL | 70200 |
| VA | 62850 |
| NY | 57900 |
| PA | 57350 |
| MI | 50100 |

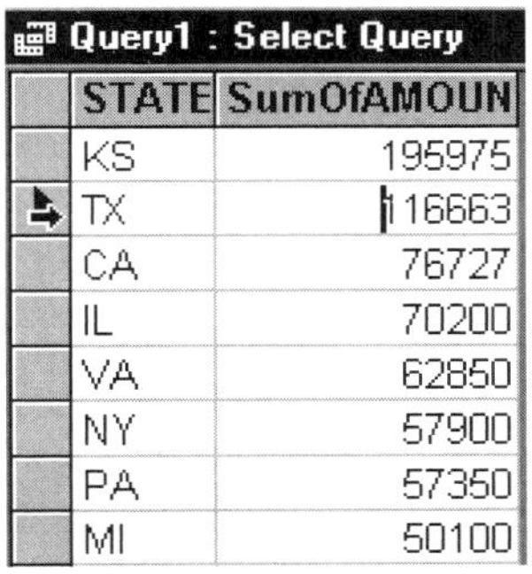

**Figure 17.16**
Results of a summary query run on a campaign contribution database in Microsoft Access.

matches depending on one or more criteria. In enterprise stories, journalists generally have to rely on several criteria to find possible matches.

In a query, matches of files of school staff and convicted felons would probably look like Figure 17.17, where the first names, last names, and dates of birth are matched to find possible felons working in a school system. The lines between the two files in the query are created by clicking on one column header and dragging it to the similar column header in the other file.

## *Building Your Own Database*

Sometimes there is no data available, only hard copy. In this case, broadcast reporters have successfully built their own databases and entered data into

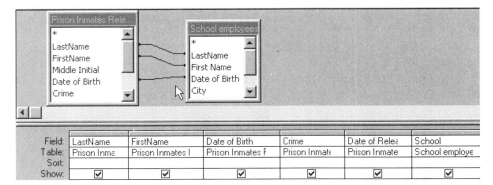

**Figure 17.17**   Excerpt of a query comparing school staff and convicted felons in a Microsoft Access database.

| Field Name | Data Type | Description |
|---|---|---|
| Lastname | Text | Employee's last name |
| Firstname | Text | Employee's first name |
| Salary | Number | Amount of sarly |
| Date of Hire | Date/Time | Date employee was hired |
| Title | Text | Job title of employee |
| Department | Text | Department in which employee works |

**Figure 17.18**   A "design view" window for building a Microsoft Access database.

them. One classic story was done by Karl Idsvoog and Corky Johnson when they worked for WCPO in Cincinnati. They constructed a database on time and attendance records of county election employees in Ohio. The reporters entered the data and found that Friday was not only the most popular day for employees to be absent, but that employees were often absent on that day.

It is not difficult to construct a database and enter data. In Microsoft Access, a "design view" window allows a journalist to give names to columns and decide what kind of data—text, numbers, or dates—can be entered into the database (see Figure 17.18).

## Acquiring Data

The federal government has an electronic Freedom of Information Act (FOIA), and most state and local governments have similar acts or laws that permit the distribution of electronic information in the same manner as the distribution of hard-copy information.

When seeking electronic databases, however, a journalist needs to obtain some technical information. This includes a record layout (which looks like the database design in Figure 17.18), the format or language the data is in, the size of the data in megabytes, the number of the records, and the kind of medium (e.g., diskette, CD-ROM, computer tape) in which it will be delivered.

# CAR Stories

Broadcast journalists have reported hundreds of news stories, many of them dramatic, using these techniques. Some CAR stories particularly lend themselves to high impact because the data can be summarized with a single shot, chart, or interview.

In 1999 in Atlanta, WSB-TV and *The Atlanta Constitution-Journal* joined forces and found almost 3,000 convicted criminals working in Georgia schools. Using the Georgia Open Records law, the station and newspaper obtained a database of school employees and of criminals. With the guidance of long-time CAR practitioner David Milliron at the *Constitution-Journal*, they matched names and dates of birth between the two databases and then used social security numbers to confirm the matches. To give the story a human angle, they began by focusing on the case of a football coach.

Here's a transcript of the beginning of the story:

PART 1
LEAD:

Channel Two Action News has learned that teachers or teachers' aides in several metro area school systems have felony convictions on their records—and yet we found them still working directly with students.

These are just a few of the nearly three thousand school employees statewide we found with felony and misdemeanor records.

One is at a metro school already embroiled in a controversy involving charges against the head football coach.

[1] (*ANCHOR*)
>>Channel Two's Richard Belcher has spent months investigating the backgrounds of teachers throughout the metro area.

He's here with the results of his Whistle Blower Two special assignment.

Toss:
(*RICHARD*)
≫When the head football coach at Dekalb County's Avondale High School was arrested on charges of sexual assault on a student, it turned out that Billy Ray Smith had already been criminally prosecuted.

Another story that cross-referenced two files to create a disturbing finding involved dangerous Emergency Medical Technicians (EMTs). At WBNS-TV in Columbus, Ohio, Paul Adrian, a CAR specialist, compared a database of all certified EMTs in Ohio to a database containing drunk-driving convictions in the state and another database of prison inmates. Adrian and his colleagues found 82 certified medics who had three or more drunk-driving convictions and a smaller group that had serious felonies.

State law prohibited people with alcohol problems or who had serious felonies from becoming medics, but officials did not check the backgrounds of applicants—despite a state law requiring background checks. WBNS-TV began its piece by looking at one medic, Jeffrey Crain, who had drunk-driving convictions and disciplinary problems. It continued by building its case:

And Crain is not the only medic getting DUIs on a regular basis. The I-Team found 6 EMTs in Ohio who have 5 drunk driving convictions . . . We discovered 3 with 6 DUIs . . . And when we asked the computer . . . How many medics have received 3 or more DUIs? The answer . . . 82.

One out of three of them does currently have a valid driver's license.

And it doesn't stop there.

Our analysis also uncovered five people, able to get their EMT certification, who have been convicted of killing somebody on the road.

The story resulted in the removal of some EMTs from their jobs and a revamping of regulations.

## Resources Needed

To start making use of CAR techniques, a reporter needs only a good personal computer with software that includes a Web browser, a spreadsheet, and a database manager. The reporter should begin with smaller stories as he or she works on building up CAR skills. The reporter also should find a colleague who is interested in these techniques and who is willing to check the calculations and queries done by the reporter.

For ideas about how to use CAR techniques, the reporter can check the Resource Center of Investigative Reporters and Editors, Inc., www.ire.org/resourcecenter, where examples of hundreds of stories that have used CAR are electronically indexed and copies of those stories can be ordered.

# Summary

The use of CAR techniques has been steadily rising among both print and broadcast journalists. The techniques can be employed on most stories and add more context and depth to those stories. In some cases, CAR techniques allow journalists to come up quickly with new information on breaking stories.

Journalists need training to make sure that they understand how to apply these skills with accuracy, but they should not be afraid to use tools that improve their credibility.

# Review Questions

1. What are the three basic tools of computer-assisted reporting?
2. For what kinds of tasks should a spreadsheet be used?
3. What tasks does a database manager perform?
4. Name two Websites that help journalists find people or research information about businesses.
5. Name four Websites from which journalists can download information.

# Exercises

1. Find information on your community from the Environmental Protection Agency Website regarding pollution.
2. Go to the Census Website and find data about your community. Download data relating to population estimates and open them in a spreadsheet. Calculate the change from one year to another.
3. Enter five salaries in a spreadsheet. Using a formula shown in this chapter, calculate the total of those salaries.
4. Download campaign contribution information on a local congressman and identify the highest contributor.
5. Find five examples of broadcast stories that used CAR techniques.

# **18** Developing Sources

The fact of being on the air attracts people who want to provide information for news stories. As reporters and anchors become known and respected by their audience, they receive telephone calls and letters about a variety of subjects. Some are letters of praise; some are complaints. Also included among those calls and letters are some news tips. Some of the most important stories aired by radio and TV stations come from tipsters. Others come from sources cultivated at public agencies and insiders at corporations and other institutions. This chapter discusses how to develop relationships with such sources.

## Tips

Stations that establish reputations for doing investigative stories are more likely to get tips than others. Astute news directors encourage tipsters, often setting up private telephone lines just for that purpose. Most calls involve breaking news—fires, accidents, crime—but sometimes the caller has information that leads to an investigative story.

Tips are usually the result of stories that were reported earlier by the station. For example, a story about a politician using public funds for a personal trip to Las Vegas may attract calls from viewers who know about similar trips by other politicians. Who makes such calls, and why? The calls and letters are often from people who have been working closely with the wrongdoers. They may be annoyed because of the misuse of public funds, because they lost their jobs, because of jealousy, or because of a long-standing grudge. The caller then becomes a source who might provide additional information on other stories or the names of additional sources. The way the phone conversation might go is: "I don't know all the details, but I can give you the name of someone who can, as long as you don't reveal my name." The phrase "don't reveal my name" is key to developing and keeping sources.

# Confidentiality

The fastest way to lose a source is to break a promise of confidentiality. Few sources give reporters sensitive information without a promise of secrecy. Once a reporter gives that promise, it must be respected, regardless of the consequences. A reporter's right to protect sources has often been tested in the courts, and reporters do not always win. On rare occasions, reporters have gone to jail or been fined for refusing to disclose a source.

Before entering into such an agreement with a source, reporters must analyze what they are agreeing to keep secret. Reporters disagree, for example, on whether it's a good idea to offer confidentiality to those who admit that they are actively involved in crime. Some reporters say they agree to such a pact if that's the only way to break the story. Other reporters say they would never enter into such an agreement and warn those sources that if they disclose any information about criminal behavior on their part, the reporters will not guarantee secrecy. *Washington Post* columnist and investigative reporter Jack Anderson says, "We will give immunity to a very good source as long as the information he offers us is better than that which we've got on him."

If a reporter promises to keep a source secret and that promise is broken, it can be costly. The U.S. Supreme Court ruled in 1991 that news organizations cannot break promises of confidentiality to news sources. The landmark decision was the result of a suit brought by a public-relations consultant in Minnesota after two newspapers in that state broke their promise of confidentiality. The plaintiff, Dan Cohen, was working for gubernatorial candidate Wheelock Whitney when he agreed to give the *Star Tribune* of Minneapolis and the *St. Paul Pioneer Press Dispatch* information about a shoplifting conviction of Marlene Johnson, a candidate on the opposing ticket. *Pioneer Press Dispatch* reporter Bill Salisbury and *Star Tribune* reporter Lori Sturdevant had promised Cohen confidentiality. Their newspapers decided, however, to withdraw the agreement and identified Cohen in the stories. He was fired from his job with a large advertising agency the next day.

The lawyers for the newspapers argued that the public had the right to know who had disclosed the derogatory information about the candidate and argued it was the newspapers' First Amendment right to publish Cohen's name. The Court voted 5 to 4 that Minnesota law requires "those making promises to keep them," and that the newspapers had no right to break their promise of confidentiality.

Salisbury said the Cohen case "may permanently change the relationship between reporters and anonymous sources. It should discourage editors from breaking reporters' promises, thus making sources feel more confident that their names will be protected." Salisbury said the ruling also "chips away at the press's First Amendment protections, and it invites more lawsuits over broken promises." Cohen was awarded $200,000 for breach of contract.

# Accuracy of Sources

A reporter should never use a source as a basis for a story until the information is checked for accuracy. Verifying a story is not always easy, especially when a reporter is working under deadlines. One of the best ways to ensure that a story is accurate is to find several other sources who will disclose exactly the same information. This is known as double- or triple-sourcing. Some reporters insist on finding at least some sort of printed documentation before they broadcast a story. If pushed, a source will often provide such documentation or reveal where it can be found.

Most station managers have a policy that requires reporters to disclose their sources or documentation to at least one person in authority at the station before they are allowed to broadcast the investigative material. Failure to provide such safeguards invites disaster. The classic reporting example cited in every text-book—and in every newsroom—is the Janet Cooke incident in which editors at *The Washington Post* failed to check a story about a child addicted to drugs. The well-written story won a Pulitzer Prize. Unfortunately, the profiled child was a composite of children the reporter had met, not an actual person, and the newspaper had to return the prize. Janet Cooke was fired, and *The Washington Post* changed its policy on checking its reporters' sources. The late distinguished investigative reporter Clark Mollenhoff warned that "few informants are totally reliable, even though they may believe they are telling the reporter the full truth." He said the information taken from a confidential source should be used only as a lead to records, documents, or other sources that can be quoted by name.

In their book *Investigative Reporting*, authors David Anderson and Peter Benjaminson write that it is sometimes a good idea for reporters to "talk to other reporters" about a source before investing a lot of time in documenting a story. They note that other reporters might already be familiar with the source, and the story he or she has to tell, and might have already "researched and debunked the information." They also say: "Nothing is quite as discouraging as working for days on a top-notch investigative piece only to discover that another reporter is typing out a final draft while you are still looking for the phone booth your source called from."

# Gaining Confidence

Reporters who find good, reliable sources and prove to them that they will protect their confidentiality usually find that those sources will continue to provide information, sometimes for many years. Self-esteem is often one motive for tipsters, and feeling good about being involved in the breaking of a story often encourages them to find new items. Smart reporters tell their sources that they are providing a service to the community. This allows sources to see themselves as part of a team, and they will actively look for new information to provide to their colleague at the radio or TV station.

# Making Friends

Other good information comes from "friends" whom reporters cultivate in offices where records and documents are housed and, particularly for crime-beat reporters, at police desks.

Experienced reporters also suggest that "hanging out" at restaurants, coffeehouses, and bars where politicians and city and county employees gather is another good way to develop friendships and new sources. These sources begin to accept you as one of them, and if they have any stories to tell or have heard some interesting rumors, they may share them with you.

# Leaks

Information from an unidentified source in the government, political, or corporate world is known as a *leak*. As with sources who provide tips, government insiders, for one reason or another, reveal information of a sensitive nature to the press with the promise of confidentiality. Such insiders could be White House staff members, assistants to members of a state assembly, or someone in a mayor's office who wants the media to know something about an individual or about an action that is being planned or debated behind closed doors. Leaks from grand jury deliberations during the White House scandal involving President Clinton and intern Monica Lewinsky were commonplace, and police leaks played an important role in the often unprofessional media coverage of the JonBenét Ramsey murder case. (Both of those cases are discussed further in Chapter 22.)

One of the most celebrated leaks in recent years involved the nomination of Supreme Court Justice Clarence Thomas. Just before the Senate was to vote on Thomas's nomination, the press was leaked a story that Anita Hill, who once worked for Thomas, had told federal investigators that he had sexually harassed her. As a result, the vote was delayed as the Senate Judiciary Committee extended the hearings.

Two reporters, Nina Totenberg of National Public Radio and Timothy Phelps of *Newsday*, reported the information. The leak sparked a national debate within Congress and among Americans, who found themselves divided on the propriety of such information being leaked to the media. There were new calls for the plugging of such leaks and suggestions of penalties for those who were found guilty of perpetrating them.

Phelps and Totenberg were subpoenaed by a special Senate counsel, who attempted to discover the source of the leak. When both reporters refused to

**Figure 18.1**
Nina Totenberg, legal affairs
correspondent for National Public
Radio, testifies before a congressional
committee during the Clarence Thomas
confirmation hearings. (Photo by
Michael Geissinger)

identify their source, the counsel attempted to gain support for some action against them, such as a contempt citation, but he failed. Senators apparently were not anxious to test First Amendment rights by compelling the reporters to disclose their sources.

Totenberg said she "simply wasn't going to tell" who gave her the information and that she was "prepared to go to jail" rather than reveal who leaked the information to her. In an interview with Professor Emeritus Ben Silver of Arizona State University, Totenberg noted that she did not identify Anita Hill by name until Hill agreed to be interviewed. Otherwise, Totenberg said, "I would not have done it. I don't think you can trust an accusation as long as it remains anonymous."

When asked how she felt about reporting such allegations, Totenberg said: "It's more than just reporting an allegation; she [Hill] turned out to be a credible witness, although I can't vouch for the truth of the allegation."

Totenberg said her mail "is full of allegations," but unless she can verify them, she doesn't broadcast them. "You can't fully corroborate all the time," said the NPR correspondent. She said that was true in the Anita Hill case, but she eliminated the problem by speaking with a person she considered credible, Susan Hoerchner. She said Hoerchner, a judge on the California Workers' Compensation Appeals Board, told her that Hill had made the same sexual harassment allegation against Thomas eight years earlier during a conversation she had with Hill. Hoerchner said that she and Hill had met when they were students at Yale University. Hoerchner later gave the same information to the Senate Judiciary Committee.

Leaks, of course, have been a way of life in Congress and probably in every administration since the creation of the U.S. government. Most Washington observers both in and out of government agree that it is impossible to stop leaks. There is also a common point of view that leaks, for the most part, provide a service to the American people. A leak from a source believed to be in the Nixon administration, the so-called Deep Throat, led to the Watergate scandal that resulted in the downfall of President Richard Nixon.

As for the leak involving Clarence Thomas, former *CBS News* correspondent Richard Threlkeld said he may be "getting jaded" as he gets older. He noted that "one man's leak is another man's essential release of timely information. The Republicans were mad because a Democrat apparently leaked information about Anita Hill. But," Threlkeld pointed out, "some years ago during Abe Fortas' contentious removal from the Court, Senator Strom Thurmond's office leaked information about him, and his misdoing, to the press, and that made him leave the Court." Threlkeld asked: "What's wrong with that? Senator Thurmond, I am sure, would call that timely release of essential information, so I'm not that concerned about leaks." Threlkeld concluded: "There always have been leaks and there always will be. . . . There are no gaskets in the faucet of public information that would stop them."

**Figure 18.2**
Anita Hill is sworn in at the Clarence Thomas confirmation hearings. (AP/Wide World Photo)

**Figure 18.3**  Supreme Court Justice Clarence Thomas during his confirmation hearings. (Reuters/Bettman)

## Trial Balloons

A different type of leak is the *trial balloon*. In this case, the leak has the endorse-ment of the White House, the mayor, or some other government official or agency. The trial balloon tips off one or more people in the media about some controversial action the department or official is thinking of taking. The purpose of the trial balloon is to measure reaction in advance not only from the people but also from the media, lobbying groups, and others. If the trial balloon is greeted with strong opposition, then the official or agency could quietly forget the action it had contemplated. On the other hand, if there is no loud protest, or the planned action is received with enthusiasm, the action probably would proceed as planned.

## Authoritative or Informed Sources

When sources of information cannot be substantiated by ordinary means, reporters often attribute the information to a spokesperson, or authoritative or informed sources. There are times, for example, when correspondents at the White House, State Department, and Pentagon obtain information from gov-ernment officials that may only be used with the understanding that the source is not to be named. So reporters who wish to use the information must say, "a spokesman at the Pentagon or a source at the State Department revealed today."

Reporters who do not wish to use such vague attribution would be unable to use the information.

Most people in the radio and TV audience take such attributions for granted, assuming that if the reporter is quoting a spokesperson the story is probably true. Often it is, but there's no guarantee. The use of the term *informed sources* and *unidentified sources* was almost as much of a scandal in the media coverage of the Clinton-Lewinsky scandal as the scandal itself. That topic is discussed in great detail in Chapter 22, "Tabloid Journalism."

# Background Briefings

Government officials often give information to reporters but insist that neither the officials nor the agencies they represent be identified. These meetings are called *background briefings*. If reporters wish to use the information revealed at such briefings, they must attribute it, again, by using phrases such as "official sources" or "well-informed sources."

# Summary

Developing good sources and keeping them confidential constitute the backbone of effective reporting. This chapter focuses on the importance of maintaining relationships with sources. Most reporters honor confidentiality agreements, and some have even gone to jail rather than disclose their sources. They knew if they had revealed their sources, they would have lost their credibility and effectiveness as journalists.

It is equally important to know whether your sources are reliable. It is essential to check and double-check the information they provide; never use information from only one source as the basis for a story. At the same time, don't dismiss information without thoroughly checking to see if it could be true.

If you agree to keep information off the record, make sure you do, otherwise it will be the last time that person gives you any information. Also remember that when you do agree to keep something off the record, start looking for sources you can quote for the record.

# Review Questions

1. What motivates people to give tips to a radio or TV station?
2. Explain why you would or would not broadcast information provided by a tipster.
3. Discuss some ways to develop sources.
4. What is a leak? Give an example.

5. What is a trial balloon?
6. What does "off the record" mean?

# Exercises

1. Suppose that you are a TV assignment editor and you receive a call from an individual who claims she saw the mayor meeting with a well-known mobster. Describe in detail how you would handle the situation.

2. Suppose you are a news director for a radio station. You get a call from a student at the local university who says he has been dealing in narcotics but wants to quit. He says he will tell you the whole story about drugs on campus, but you have to keep his identity secret. Do you agree and put a reporter on the story? Explain your decision.

3. An individual has been leaking information to you for several years and has always been reliable; however, she now tells you a story about corruption that could bring down the city administration if it is true. Do you tell anyone else at the station what you have been told? Do you disclose your source? Explain in detail.

# 19 Specialty Reporting

## Investigative Reporting

Some journalists believe that the term *investigative reporting* is redundant—that all reporting is investigative. There is some truth in that statement. Earlier chapters in this book have been devoted to the techniques that all reporters use, such as Chapter 15, "The Interview," Chapter 16, "Collecting Information from Documents," and Chapter 18, "Developing Sources." It is true that reporters ask questions and do some research for just about every story, but little in the way of actual investigation takes place, and, in probably 90 percent of the stories we hear and watch on radio and television, not much investigation is required.

It is not investigative reporting to ask a fire chief if the cause of a fire was arson. Likewise, it is not investigative reporting to ask a police detective if the double homicide he's investigating was drug related. And, for good or bad, aren't those two of the most common questions asked by reporters during the course of a day or week, at least in most large communities? We are not claiming that this is the way it should be—that's another debate—but it is reality; however, there is a great need for investigative reporters to deal with the 10 percent of the stories that most of us are not even aware of.

The best investigative reports reveal information that otherwise might not be revealed to the public and often involve information that some individual or group either in government or industry might be trying to hide. Sometimes the stories produced by such investigations may be contrary to the versions set forth by government or business officials trying to conceal the truth. The very best investigative reports—the kind that often win the coveted Pulitzer Prize—effect some change in the way government or private industry does business.

As mentioned earlier, we have gone into great detail throughout the book about how to prepare for such reporting. The most important things to learn are basic reporting, how to dig out information, how to develop sources, and how to use the sunshine laws.

One of the most celebrated investigative reports was the Watergate investigation by *The Washington Post* in 1972 that began as an apparent routine break-in of Democratic Party offices in the nation's capitol. It ended in the resignation of President Richard Nixon and brought fame to the lead reporters on the investigation, Carl Bernstein and Bob Woodward.

In recalling how they uncovered one of the most sensational scandals in political history, Woodward and Bernstein stressed that what they did in Watergate was the most basic, empirical police reporting of the kind you first learn when you get into the business or even that you learn in journalism school. They said they went about the Watergate story "the same way we would do any other story we were assigned to—we knocked on a lot of doors."

The reporters said they started at the bottom, talking to secretaries, clerks, chauffeurs, administrative assistants, and gradually worked their way up. Woodward and Bernstein said that part of the post-Watergate myth is that investigative reporting is a "highly refined pseudoscience, different and apart from the rest of journalism."

Bernstein is among those who question the use of the term *investigative reporting*. He said that maybe *saturation reporting* is a better term. He described that as "a commitment of resources that would enable us to gather every fact, conduct hundreds of interviews, if necessary, and really learn our subject before we jump into print or go on the air."

Earlier in the book, two investigative reports were cited that involved the use of freedom of information laws (Chapter 16, "Collecting Information From Documents"), one by investigative reporter Mark Lagerkvist dealing with health maintenance organizations (HMOs) paying doctors bonuses not to refer patients for special medical treatment when they need it; and a second report by Chris Szechenyi concerning medical devices that are supposed to save lives but often didn't because they were defective. A third investigative report, which follows, about an Olympics scandal in Salt Lake City was the product of a tip, a subject that was discussed in detail in Chapter 18.

## The Salt Lake City Scandal

In the previous chapter, we referred to tips and how they often can lead reporters to important stories. A tip brought the most important story of his career to Chris Vanocur, a reporter for KTVX-TV in Salt Lake City, according to Alicia C. Shepard's story in the April 1999 issue of *The American Journalism Review*.

Vanocur had worked as a reporter for the Salt Lake City TV station for about eight years. His beat was politics, but it was not politics that brought him fame— it was the Winter Olympics. It all started with a letter that someone sent to him. Just who sent the letter has not been revealed, but it was addressed to a young woman whose father was an influential member of the International Olympic Committee (IOC), which in 1995 chose Salt Lake City as a host city.

The woman identified in the letter, Sonia Essomba, had been receiving money for two years for tuition at American University in Washington, D.C.,

**Figure 19.1** Reporter Chris Vanocur, from KTVX-TV in Salt Lake City.

along with rent and expenses. But the letter that ended up in Vanocur's hands said that assistance was about to end. The author of the letter was David Johnson, the second in command at the Salt Lake City Organizing Committee to bring the Olympics to Salt Lake City.

Johnson was informing Essomba that it was no longer possible to continue the scholarship program because of budget restrictions. The letter made mention of a check that was enclosed for $10,114.99, which was described as a final payment. That letter touched off the biggest corruption scandal in the history of the Olympics, and Chris Vanocur, son of Sander Vanocur, the former Washington reporter for ABC and NBC, broke the story.

The airing of the letter on KTVX-TV launched a media frenzy that would dominate the news not only in Salt Lake City but in most of the nation. It also touched off new investigations by a variety of journalists around the world that made it an international news story. As the Vanocur report mushroomed in Salt

Lake City, officials disclosed that Essomba had received more than $108,000 from the Salt Lake City Olympic Committee and that the Committee had spent more than $1 million on 24 of the 114 IOC members to ensure that the Utah city would win the Winter Games in 2002.

Salt Lake City Olympic officials gave IOC members free credit cards and spent almost $20,000 to take three couples to the 1995 Super Bowl. The city also loaned $30,000 to one member of the IOC and, incredibly, even paid for plastic surgery to remove the bags under the eyes of another IOC member. Although rumors had been circulating that Salt Lake City was offering incentives to IOC officials to bring the games to the city, none of it was documented until Vanocur's report aired.

Within months of Vanocur's report, journalists in other parts of the world would soon discover that payoffs had been made by many officials in cities trying to attract the Olympic Games. For example, Nagano Olympic officials had spent $22,000 on each of 62 IOC members in order to bring the 1998 Winter Olympics to that Japanese city. But, again, there's no telling when and if this international scandal would have broken if it had not been for the tip—the letter someone sent to Vanocur.

After getting the letter, Vanocur got on the Internet and started searching. He said he had no idea who Essomba was or what he was dealing with. He typed in the name Essomba and got some hits, including one reference to a doctor in Africa, who was an IOC member. Vanocur said he had heard stories about scholarships, and he began thinking that the Sonia referred to in the letter he received probably was a relative of an IOC member. Vanocur said he then called the Salt Lake City Olympics Committee and arranged for an on-camera interview for the next day. During that interview, committee spokesman Frank Zang confirmed that Sonia was the daughter of the IOC member and that the committee had, indeed, been paying part of her tuition.

Vanocur returned to KTVX and prepared a story for the 10 o'clock news, revealing the letter about Essomba. It was the lead story, of course. Vanocur said that the city's Olympic Committee was paying thousands of dollars to a close relative of somebody who voted on whether or not Salt Lake City should get the Olympics.

The city's newspapers picked up Vanocur's story the next day, and then a host of new revelations was exposed, including a bombshell release from the president of the Salt Lake City Olympic Committee saying that nearly $400,000 in financial aid or scholarships had been given to 13 individuals over a seven-year period. Six of those people were relatives of IOC members. Ultimately, an international scandal that started with a 95-word letter that landed on Vanocur's desk ballooned into thousands of print and video stories and four separate investigations.

Within Salt Lake City's Olympic Committee, four board members have re-signed, the president and vice president are gone, and other administrative officials are on leave. Ten IOC members either resigned or were expelled, and in Salt Lake City four Olympic Board members resigned.

As for Vanocur, he says: "For me there's a little bit of drama with the story, how a somewhat small-town reporter gets a hold of a letter that ignites a scandal. A guy who does modest good work over the years. It's kind of nice for me," he says, "to semi-step out of my father's shadow. He's kidding me now about being known as Chris Vanocur's father."

Here's the script for the first broadcast that Vanocur prepared on the Olympics scandal:

| | |
|---|---|
| On Camera<br>Anchor Kimberly | Tonight, disturbing new questions about the financial dealings of the Salt Lake Olympic Committee, and that's our top story. |
| Anchor Randall | News 4 Utah has learned that Salt Lake Olympic organizers have quietly been spending thousands of dollars to pay the college tuition costs of relatives of International Olympic bigwigs. |
| Kimberly | Chris Vanocur is here with a News 4 Utah exclusive investigation. Chris . . . |
| Vanocur (live on set) | This is a letter Salt Lake Olympic folks probably didn't want us to get. It raises very serious questions about how Olympic money is being spent and even about how Salt Lake got the Olympic bid. |
| Vanocur package 1:45 | This confidential letter was drafted in 1996 by a senior Salt Lake Olympic official. It's written to a Sonia Essomba and reads: "Under the current budget structure, it will be difficult to continue the scholarship program with you. The enclosed check for $10,114.99 will have to be our last payment for tuition. |
| Sound bite: Frank Zang,<br>Spokesman, Salt Lake<br>City Olympic Committee | "I think this is just an example of a program that we had going to help third world countries and to provide people with education opportunities." |
| Vanocur | But, in fact, Sonia Essomba, this Salt Lake Olympic official later conceded, is not a needy third world student, but actually the daughter of a prominent |

surgeon, Rene Essomba, who just happened to be an influential African member of the International Olympic Committee.

Vanocur stand-up

In other words, our Olympic Committee was paying thousands of dollars to a close relative of somebody who voted on whether or not Salt Lake should get the Olympics.

Sound bite: Stephen Pace
Utahns/Responsible Public Spending

"This looks like, walks like, and quacks like a bribe being paid out of a publicly guaranteed organization."

Vanocur

But Olympic officials say this was all private money and that there was nothing improper.

Sound bite Frank Zang

"Do you think that raises any red flags? Well, these were activities 2 or 3 years ago, when this organization was known as a bid committee."

Vanocur

But look at the date on this letter, September 1996, more than a year after Salt Lake got the bid. And according to several highly placed Olympic sources, Sonia Essomba was not the only relative of an I.O.C. member to receive large tuition scholarships.

Sound bite: Frank Zang

"There were scholarships from other countries around the world. I do not know what all of their connections were with respect to their national Olympic committees."

Vanocur on set

So, tonight, two lingering questions are: Exactly how much has been spent on other people's tuition, and is the practice still ongoing. What are the answers? We don't know. The answers are in the Olympic budget, which has been seen by only a handful of Olympic officials. That's why tomorrow, News 4 Utah will officially ask to be given access to all of the Olympic budget.

# Environmental Reporting

The growing concern for the environment in the past decade has encouraged broadcast news managers to allocate more news to the subject. In many newsrooms, the environment is still covered by general-assignment reporters, but more and more news managers are hiring broadcast journalists who have become familiar with environmental problems. Knowledge of the subject can be acquired in college, but reporters often gain their expertise simply by taking the time to learn about the complex issues.

Numerous periodicals deal with every aspect of the environment, and reporters intent on learning about environmental issues should spend many hours in the library reading these publications or should subscribe to them. A wide variety of environmental seminars also are offered throughout the country by private and government groups. The Environmental Health Center issues a newsletter; "Greenwire" is a news service offering stories about the environment; and the Society of Environmental Journalists provides help and resources for journalists trying to improve their knowledge of environmental issues. The Radio and Television News Directors' Association (RTNDA) often discusses the environment at national and regional meetings. Helpful computer databases, such as the Toxic Release Inventory, which stores information on 366 toxic chemicals, are also available.

CNN correspondent Debra Potter, who covers environmental stories, believes that no beat is more important. She says: "Broadcasters owe it to their audiences to cover the subject because it touches viewers and listeners where they live." Potter says communities throughout the nation are wrestling with environmental issues such as waste disposal and water quality. She notes that polls show that Americans believe that the environment is one of the five most important issues facing the nation.

She stresses that environmental reporters who know and understand the issues—who know where to look and which questions to ask—get a jump on environmental stories. She also notes that environmental issues are difficult to explain and that environmental reporters must act responsibly "by not raising false hopes or unfounded fears."

Bob Engleman of Scripps-Howard newspapers says that covering the environment is like covering any other complicated, important issue. He advises following these steps:

1. Learn the issue.
2. Maintain skepticism.
3. Seek out all viewpoints.
4. Ask probing questions.
5. Report the story as accurately and as fairly as possible.

*ABC News* correspondent Jeff Greenfield says that unless reporters covering the environment completely understand the various aspects of the story, they would be "better off not doing it at all." He believes that if reporters misinform people about politicians, they do not cause too much damage. "But," he adds, "if you falsely report to the community that children are at risk because of something in the schools, or the land, or water, you have done much harm." At the same time, Greenfield notes that reporters who fail to inform the public about a real risk do even greater harm.

The editor of the *Freedom Forum Journal*, Craig Le May, says environmental reporters must "look at what local industries are doing—how they make and transport products, how they do business." He also warns reporters that much of the environmental information available is from press releases, which are not reliable.

Le May says that reporters must search through all the public relations and make sense of the issues. He notes that the rule for cultivating sources is the same as for other types of assignments: "Get the best people and find out what they have at stake in what you are reporting." He warns, for example, that researchers at universities are often funded by organizations with a fixed point of view, so reporters have to be skeptical of their findings. Le May also urges reporters to beware of trade groups that "masquerade as environmental organizations." He notes that the National Wetlands Coalition sounds like an environmental group, but it is actually a lobby group for the largest oil, gas, and utility companies.

Robert Logan, the director of the Science Journalism Center at the University of Missouri, also urges reporters to be "skeptical of everybody. Everyone is selling something," he warns, "even if they are not into making money." Logan says reporters should remember that the investigative rule "Follow the money to get to the bottom of something" is bad advice for environmental reporting. He suggests instead: "Follow the best scientific evidence first, and then look for the money."

Here's a report from environmental reporter Don Wall of WFAA-TV in Dallas on the possible dangers of electromagnetic fields:

on cam/2-shot

((CHIP))
ARE ELECTROMAGNETIC FIELDS
PRODUCED BY POWER LINES . . .
DANGEROUS TO YOUR HEALTH?

((TRACY))
THE PUBLIC UTILITY COMMISSION
OF TEXAS HAS RELEASED THE
RESULTS OF A 3-YEAR STUDY THAT
SAYS PEOPLE WHO LIVE NEAR POWER
LINES HAVE NOTHING TO WORRY
ABOUT.

turn to box: a
current danger

((Tracy turn box))
BUT EVEN T-U ELECTRIC SAYS
MORE RESEARCH NEEDS TO BE DONE.
CHANNEL 8's ENVIRONMENTAL
REPORTER DON WALL EXPLAINS IN
THE FIRST OF HIS TWO-PART SERIES,
"A CURRENT DANGER."

sot
supers on tape
runs: 4:14
SCENE FROM

FRANKENSTEIN

SOT

(THUNDER AND LIGHTNING . . .
POWER EXPLODING AS THE
CURRENT PASSES INTO THE
MONSTER.)

IT WAS THE POWER OF
ELECTRICITY THAT GAVE LIFE TO
FRANKENSTEIN'S MONSTER.
(it's alive, it's alive . . .)

(WIDE WITH CHILDREN
WALKING IN FRONT OF
POWER LINES . . .
GRAPHICALLY FIELD
EMANATES FROM
POWER LINES)

IN A LESS SPECTACULAR, BUT
NO LESS DRAMATIC WAY,
ELECTRICITY GIVES POWER TO OUR
DAILY LIVES. AND EVERYTHING
THAT CARRIES ELECTRICITY EMITS
AN ELECTROMAGNETIC FIELD—AN
EMF—WHICH OUR BODIES ABSORB.

S: DON WALL, WFAA
TV, FORT WORTH
(AT NIGHT, HOLDING
TWO FLUORESCENT
BULBS)

THIS IS WHAT WE MEAN BY AN
ELECTROMAGNETIC FIELD.
I'M STANDING UNDER A
TYPICAL 138,000-VOLT POWER
LINE, LIKE THOSE THAT RUN
THROUGH MANY NEIGHBORHOODS, AND
THE EMF IS STRONG ENOUGH TO
ILLUMINATE THESE FLUORESCENT
LIGHTS.
THERE ARE NO PLUGS, AND NO
CORDS. THE POWER TO LIGHT THESE
BULBS IS IN THE AIR.
AND THERE ARE STUDIES WHICH
CLAIM THAT EMF EXPOSURE IS
DANGEROUS.

SOME STUDIES LINK PROXIMITY TO POWER LINES WITH CHILDHOOD LEUKEMIA.

ANOTHER STUDY SAYS EMF'S MAY CAUSE BRAIN CANCER.

THE FINDINGS ARE CONTROVERSIAL AND SCIENTIFICALLY SOMEWHAT UNCERTAIN. MANY RESEARCHERS BELIEVE POWER LINES ARE PERFECTLY SAFE.

BUT THERE IS NO DOUBT THAT PEOPLE WHO LIVE NEAR POWER LINES ARE EXPOSED TO GREATER EMF LEVELS THAN PEOPLE WHO DON'T.

S: PLANO

THESE THREE WOMEN WALKING— ALONG THE BLUEBONNET TRAIL— THINK EMF'S FROM POWER LINES MAY HAVE CAUSED THEIR SONS' BRAIN TUMORS.

("OBVIOUSLY, BY BUILDING THIS PATH UNDER THE POWER LINE, SOMEBODY'S ASSUMING THAT IT'S PERFECTLY SAFE?")


"I'M NOT SURE THAT ANYONE TOOK IT INTO CONSIDERATION, FRANKLY."


9 CHILDREN WITH BRAIN TUMORS HAVE BEEN DIAGNOSED IN THE HIGHPOINT AREA OF PLANO, A CLUSTER OF DISEASE THESE MOTHERS HOPE WILL BE STUDIED.


KRIS ALBERTA'S FAMILY LIVED IN A TOWNHOUSE RIGHT NEXT TO THESE POWER LINES.


("YOU WERE OUT HERE ALL THE TIME?") "QUITE A BIT. I USED TO WALK THE DOG OUT HERE. MY SON WOULD COME OUT HERE AND HE RODE HIS BIKE, JOGGED."

HER 16-YEAR-OLD SON, DUSTIN, WAS HEALTHY, UNTIL THEY MOVED HERE. A YEAR AGO, HE WAS DIAGNOSED WITH BRAIN TUMORS; HE DIED IN MARCH.

S: KRIS ALBTERA

"BEING HERE FOR TWO YEARS, IT'S A POSSIBILITY THAT IT COULD HAVE CONTRIBUTED OR CAUSED HIS BRAIN TUMOR, AND NO, I DON'T FEEL SAFE WALKING UNDER HERE, OR ANOTHER. WHEN I SEE PREGNANT WOMEN OR YOUNG CHILDREN UNDER HERE, I DON'T THINK THEY ARE SAFE."

THAT'S HOW SUE FARROW FEELS TOO. SHE AND HER SON PLAYED IN THIS PARK SEVERAL TIMES A WEEK WHEN HE WAS SMALL.

9-YEAR-OLD DUSTY HAS HAD 6 OPERATIONS RELATED TO HIS BRAIN TUMOR. FOR NOW, HE'S DOING WELL.

BUT HIS MOTHER SEARCHES FOR ANSWERS.

S: SUE FARROW

"HE'S A YOUNG KID. HE'S EATING GOOD FOOD, HE'S NOT OUT POISONING HIS BODY IN OTHER WAYS. THERE HAS TO BE SOME TYPE OF AN OUTSIDE INFLUENCE THAT COULD TRIGGER, OR PROMOTE, OR SET OFF A TUMOR." ("AND YOU THINK IT COULD BE POWER LINES?") "POSSIBLY YES."

THESE WOMEN BELIEVE SIGNS SHOULD BE POSTED, WARNING PEOPLE OF POTENTIAL EMF DANGERS FROM POWER LINES.

KRIS

"I DON'T WANT ANY OTHER CHILD, OR ANY OTHER PARENT, TO GO THROUGH WHAT WE DID, IF IT CAN BE AVOIDED. AND THIS I SOMETHING THAT COULD BE AVOIDED."

(SEE AERIAL OF POWER
LINE NEIGHBORHOODS
IN TARRANT COUNTY)

DR. JOEL GOLDSTEEN AGREES. HE'S
AN URBAN PLANNER AT THE
UNIVERSITY OF TEXAS AT ARLINGTON.

HE'S DONE A STUDY OF
TARRANT COUNTY THAT SAYS
ROUGHLY 70,000 PEOPLE ARE
POTENTIALLY AT RISK FROM
OVERHEAD LINES.

GOLDSTEEN SAYS UNTIL THE
RESEARCH ABOUT POTENTIAL
DANGERS IS CONCLUSIVE, CITIES
SHOULD NOT BUILD JOGGING PATHS OR
SCHOOLS AND CHILDREN SHOULD NOT
BE ALLOWED TO PLAY UNDER OR NEAR
POWER LINES.

S: DR. JOEL GOLDSTEEN
UNIV. OF TEXAS
ARLINGTON

"YOU CAN'T DO THAT. YOU
CAN'T CONTINUE BUSINESS AS
USUAL. CITIES THAT ARE DOING THAT
ARE DOING A DISSERVICE TO THEIR
RESIDENTS AND THEY ARE ACTING
UNETHICAL AND UNPRINCIPLED."

AND, FOR NOW, IT REMAINS AN
EMOTIONAL ISSUE—PERHAPS EVEN
MORE THAN A SCIENTIFIC ONE.

SUE FARROW

"YOU TALK ABOUT EMOTIONAL
MOMS. WE MAY BE EMOTIONAL.
MAYBE THAT'S WHAT IT'S GOING TO
TAKE TO GET PEOPLE AWARE TO
COME OUT AND SPEAK ABOUT IT."

T.U. ELECTRIC DOES NOT BELIEVE
POWER LINES ARE HARMFUL, BUT
THEY AGREE THAT MORE RESEARCH
NEEDS TO BE DONE.

AND THEY SAY THERE ARE THINGS
YOU CAN DO TO MINIMIZE YOUR
EXPOSURE TO ELECTROMAGNETIC
FIELDS. MORE ON THAT TOMORROW.

# Business Reporting

Many radio and TV news organizations regularly program business news; some even offer daily business programs. Other organizations that do not set aside time for business segments in regular news programs still may have someone on the staff who covers business news. Business specialists need to understand the complex issues of business and finance. These issues include mergers and takeovers, the savings-and-loan scandal, the ups-and-downs on Wall Street, and interest rates and trade deficits.

Students thinking about a career as a business reporter should take courses in economics, marketing, and other business-related subjects and, perhaps, consider graduate work in business. An MBA degree carries a lot of weight with many news managers.

As always, research is a necessity. Broadcasters specializing in business reporting should read periodicals such as *Barron's*, *Business Week*, *The Economist*, *Forbes*, and *Fortune*. *The Wall Street Journal* is the bible for the business world. Similarly, *The New York Times*, *The Washington Post*, and their counterparts in other large cities have excellent business columns and reports that business specialists should follow.

Many good trade publications are also devoted to business and industry. Although many of these publications have biases that the reporter must consider, they should by no means be discounted. They are full of information that helps reporters learn about industries and new systems, techniques, and products.

The business reporter uses the same basic techniques as a general-assignment reporter—developing good sources and cross-checking information for reliability. Covering business is a little like covering politics. There's a lot of speculation, and a good reporter soon learns to be skeptical about any predictions concerning the economy, interest rates, and the stock market.

Reporters thinking about specializing in business news should remember that the opportunities are not as great as in some other specialties, such as environmental and medical reporting, because radio and TV stations do not normally spend as much airtime on business subjects as on these other issues. This lack of coverage results partly because many news directors think that except for the Dow Jones averages, most business news is either too dull or too complicated to explain to the public. At the same time, many stations that do have business reporters say they get good feedback from the public on business news.

# Health and Medical Reporting

Health and medical subjects rank high in interest among radio and TV audiences for obvious reasons—we all want to remain healthy. Reporters with a knowledge of health and medical issues are assets to news managers. Most large news staffs have someone assigned to a medical and health beat. Many broadcast news producers regularly include health and medical stories in newscasts. Reporters do not have much trouble selling producers on a good medical story. Likewise, depending on the size of the market, good health and medical stories are usually not difficult to find.

Because they are public-relations conscious, hospitals and research centers often bring stories involving their facilities or research to the attention of radio and TV newsrooms. Listeners and viewers also provide tips on medical-related stories, usually when someone close to them has been involved in something good or bad at a medical facility. Many tips concern malpractice, but some involve lifesaving techniques and appealing human-interest stories about children waiting for organ transplants and the generosity of people who contribute hundreds of thousands of dollars to make the surgery possible.

Objectivity is always an essential part of all reporting, but sometimes medical reporters must be particularly sensitive about their reports because providers often appear to be in the wrong. Doctors are accused of charging too much or refusing to accept Medicaid patients. Hospitals are criticized for turning away some patients and price gouging others. Many of these stories are true, but reporters must examine both sides of any issue. Reporters sometimes discover that hospitals are on the verge of financial collapse because of rising costs and heavy investment in equipment. They find that the government is slow in paying Medicare patients' bills and is often unrealistic when deciding on the amount doctors can charge.

Good medical reporters look for positive stories about doctors and hospitals to balance the negative ones. If and when reporters find they are beginning to dislike the medical profession as a whole, it's probably time for them to start looking for another beat. Health and medical reporters also cannot allow themselves to be duped. They must constantly ask tough questions about the medical establishment and whether it is meeting the needs of the American people.

Science and health-related courses in college help journalism students prepare for medical reporting. These students also should read the many health and medical magazines that are available. Teaching-hospital libraries also have stacks of journals from major research centers. Although these resources are provided primarily for medical students, persuasive reporters usually have no difficulty gaining access to the journals once the staff is convinced the reporters are not malpractice attorneys.

Here's an example of a medical story by former CNN medical reporter Dan Rutz about chronic fatigue syndrome.

O/C                                              Anchor
                                    The Centers for Disease Control has
                                    completed a study of chronic fatigue
                                    syndrome. As Dan Rutz tells us, this

mysterious ailment apparently is more common than experts had believed.

Rutz V/O
Doctor is
examining patient

V/O
People with chronic fatigue syndrome fight an illness with no known cause. Many shuffle from doctor to doctor in search of care and understanding.

SOT
Font: Dr. Richard
Prokesch

SOT
"For many years, it was thought that these people were crazy and that this really is not a disease . . .
and now I think a lot of people are believing that there is something, probably more than one thing, that is causing it."

V/O
Gunn at computer

Computer screen

Over-the-shoulder shot
of Gunn at computer

V/O
Walter Gunn and others from the Centers for Disease Control sampled patients' records and interviewed people diagnosed with chronic fatigue syndrome. The researchers disqualified everyone with a history of any other disorder, such as depression, that might have caused or contributed to their symptoms.

SOT

Font: Walter Gunn
Centers for Disease
Control

SOT
"We were quite surprised that about 26 percent of fatigued people referred to us did in fact meet the case definition. We didn't expect to find it to be more than five percent originally."

V/O
Full Screen Fonts

*Severe Prolonged Fatigue
*Other Diseases Ruled Out

V/O
To be counted, patients had to have sustained at least six months of fatigue severe enough to have cut their activities at least by half. All other possible causes had to be

| | |
|---|---|
| *Chronic Flulike Symptoms | ruled out by test or examination, and patients had to have had the flulike symptoms associated with the disorder. |
| O/C Standup | O/C<br>The survey in Atlanta and three other cities reveals far fewer cases of chronic fatigue syndrome than activists claim. The CDC admits that the estimate is low but nevertheless considers it valuable in proving to skeptics that the disease is for real. |
| V/O<br>Mary Niebling<br><br>Niebling sitting at sink while she washes dishes | V/O<br>Mary Niebling runs a chronic fatigue support group when she feels strong enough to attend.<br>Numbers are important to Niebling, who pushes for more research into a cause and cure for her chronic mystery. |
| SOT<br>Font: Mary Niebling | SOT<br>"I have lost everything that means anything to me, my marriage, my children, my home, my career, my finances, my intellect." |
| V/O<br>Neibling entering doctor's office<br><br>Doctor examining Niebling<br>Nat sound | V/O<br>Since there is no test for chronic fatigue syndrome, public health officials say it is hard to come up with an accurate count. Doctors are seeing more people like Mary Niebling, and the CDC receives from one thousand to three thousand calls a month from people who think they have it too. Dan Rutz, CNN Medical News, Atlanta. |

# Consumer Reporting

Pollsters tell us that most Americans are more concerned about their economic situation than they are about their health. People without jobs often do not worry about their health until they have no money to pay their medical bills. So, news stories that affect a consumer's pocketbook are popular with audiences and news directors.

Consumer reporters have fertile fields to till—shady business operators, inferior products, overpriced services, undelivered goods and services, and many others. They do not have to look far to find their stories. They hear from listeners and viewers by the hundreds, many who have been victimized or swindled in one way or another.

The consumer reporter often has to try to correct the problem, but those reports can be tacky. We see a reporter talking to a person who has been unable to get a rug that she ordered 90 days ago. The dealer keeps promising that it will arrive any day and keeps breaking the promise. Then the "action reporter" takes over, and the next thing you know the person gets the rug (and a cameraperson is probably there), and the dealer promises it will never happen again.

Consumer reporting works best when the reporter investigates serious problems and scams that affect a lot of people. Reporters provide a real service when they alert the audience to beware of a company that guarantees consumers credit cards for a fee and then doesn't produce; a home-siding company that's tricking retired couples into paying double what they should to repair their homes; or a garage that charges customers for unnecessary repairs.

Consumer reporters also provide other services to the public. They often report on new products that may be useful to the physically disabled, a new low-cost prescription service for senior citizens, or the best way to discover low-cost airfares. They also are at their best when exposing serious "ripoffs," as in this report from consumer reporter Jack Atherton of WTVJ-TV in Miami:

| | |
|---|---|
| KEL/EXCLUSIVE | WHEN YOU BUY A NEW CAR . . . JUST HOW NEW IS IT? TROUBLE-SHOOTER JACK ATHERTON HAS (2 |
| TWO BOX | BOX) EXCLUSIVE NEW DETAILS . . . AND ADVICE ON HOW TO BEWARE! |
| TAKE JACK LIVE . . . | (TAKE JACK LIVE) KELLY, THE INITIAL COMPLAINT WE GOT WAS ABOUT A FORD TAURUS . . . BUT NOW WE'RE HEARING THAT LOTS OF NEW CARS MAY BE OLDER THAN YOU THINK. |
| TAKE ENG INSERT . . . CG/ EXCLUSIVE | (TAKE ENG INSERT) THIS HIALEAH DOCTOR SPENT A WHOLE YEAR HUNTING FOR A NEW |

CAR UNTIL HE SAW A MAGAZINE AD FOR THE TAURUS SHO.

CG/DR. WILLIAM WAGNER
FORD CUSTOMER

DR. WILLIAM WAGNER, A FORD CUSTOMER, SAYS:
"WHAT FINALLY MADE ME DECIDE WAS THAT THEY HAD IMPROVED THEIR 5 SPEED MANUAL TRANSMISSION."
"THEY ADVERTISED THAT?"
"YES."

CG/HOLLYWOOD

CG/LAST WEEK

ACCORDING TO DR. WAGNER'S DEALER, HOLLYWOOD FORD, THAT IMPROVEMENT WAS A NEW WAY OF CONNECTING THE STICK SHIFT TO THE TRANSMISSION; WITH STURDY METAL RODS INSTEAD OF AN OLD-FASHIONED CABLE. ONLY TROUBLE WAS . . . DR. WAGNER—AND AN UNTOLD NUMBER OF OTHER FORD CUSTOMERS—DID NOT GET THE RODS.

CG/RICK REICHANADTER
HOLLYWOOD FORD

RICK REICHANADTER, HOLLYWOOD FORD, SAYS:
"WERE CUSTOMERS TO YOUR KNOWLEDGE NOTIFIED OF THE FACT THAT SOME OF THE CARS HAD OLD-STYLE SHIFTERS?"
"NO. UH. UH."
"WOULDN'T YOU WANT TO BE TOLD?"
"IF I BOUGHT A CAR?"
"WOULDN'T YOU WANT TO BE TOLD?"
"SURE."

BUT HOLLYWOOD FORD SAYS EVEN DEALERS DIDN'T KNOW. WELL, THE HELP CENTER VOLUNTEERS HELPED GET DR. WAGNER A NEW CAR—WITH RODS. BUT NOW THE STATE ATTORNEY GENERAL'S OFFICE IS ALSO INVESTIGATING.

| CC/MARK BARNETT ASSISTANT STATE ATTORNEY GENERAL | MARK BARNETT, ASSISTANT STATE ATTORNEY GENERAL, SAYS: "WHEN THEY MAKE AN EXPRESS CLAIM THAT A CERTAIN IMPROVEMENT HAS BEEN MADE AND IN FACT IT HASN'T BEEN MADE IN ALL THEIR CARS, THEN THAT'S AN UNFAIR AND DECEPTIVE TRADE PRACTICE. BUT MORE IMPORTANTLY, I THINK AS A GENERAL RULE THERE'S AN IMPLIED STATEMENT MADE THAT WHEN YOU HAVE A 1991 CAR YOU'RE GETTING THE 1991 PARTS." |
|---|---|
| CG/TRACY HOPPE MASTER MECHANIC | BUT THIS A-S-E MASTER MECHANIC TOLD US THAT MANY CAR MANUFACTURERS PUT OUTMODED PARTS IN WHAT ARE SUPPOSED TO BE NEW CARS. TRACY HOPPE, MASTER MECHANIC, SAYS: "UNTIL THEY RUN OUT OF THOSE PARTS, THEY USE THEM UP." "YOU'VE SEEN THIS?" "YES. I'VE SEEN THIS MANY TIMES." |

# Sports Reporting

Many people are attracted to broadcast sports reporting because of their interest in sports and because they think it's more fun than covering city council meetings. The problem is that so many beginners have the same idea that not enough opportunities are available to provide jobs for them all. TV stations that may have six or more general-assignment reporters usually have only one full-time sports reporter-anchor.

Sports reporting also requires some additional skills that general reporting does not. Personality has become important; knowing sports inside out is not enough anymore. Most news managers look for sports people who can attract an audience with their style of delivery.

Good organizational skills also are important. Sports reporters, particularly in small markets, are expected to cover local games and to be able to cut a lot of video quickly from a variety of sports contests that are being recorded throughout the evening. Sports seasons tend to overlap, which means that

**Figure 19.2** Fred Hickman is one of CNN's top sportscasters.
(© 2001 CNN. All rights reserved.)

college and professional football and basketball games are often held at the same times as professional hockey matches, amid a variety of other sports. Many stations also cover high school sports. Collecting all this information and cutting video of all these activities is demanding.

How does a journalism student prepare for a sports reporting job? The best way is probably through an internship. Sports reporters look for sharp college students who know sports and know how to edit videotape. Quick learners may find that they soon cover high school games and even anchor on the weekends. Because most sports anchors, like news anchors, are looking for opportunities in larger markets, frequent turnovers sometimes occur at the sports desk. The weekend sports person who learns the job well sometimes gets the sports anchoring job during the week.

Sports anchors with a lot of talent and personality can demand good salaries in large markets. Like other anchors, however, they often are subject to the ratings and whims of management. Job security is less certain for sports anchors than it is for most beat and general-assignment reporters.

One of the most successful and popular sports anchors on television is ESPN's Dan Patrick, who started out loving sports as a young man playing basketball in high school and college. But he never achieved the kind of success as an athlete that he has as a sports anchor. As the host of ESPN's *Sports Center*, Patrick has, as stated by Mark Lisheron in the *American Journalism Review* (May 1999), "earned a reputation as one of the nation's premier sports broadcasters."

Patrick says he knows it sounds corny, but "I'm still this kid from Mason, Ohio, who got a chance to be on ESPN. I never want to lose sight of that." Patrick

**Figure 19.3**   Dan Patrick of ESPN Radio Network. (Photo by
John Atashian)

says he's at a place where he always dreamed of being; not only to have interviewed the biggest names in sports and to count some of them among his
friends; but also to have achieved such respect in his profession that he can call
star athletes when he needs to and talk to them.

   While attending the University of Dayton, as a broadcast major, Patrick's
success on the basketball court was modest (he didn't make the varsity team),
but his career as a sports reporter was enhanced when the team allowed him
to go courtside for home games, where he would call the play-by-play into a
tape recorder to practice his skills. That practice calling the games helped Patrick
get his first job as weekend anchor at WDTN-TV in Dayton.

   Patrick was unable to get off the weekends at WDTN, so when he graduated from the University of Dayton, he took a job as a morning anchor on that

city's WTUE radio. Not satisfied with his situation, Patrick rented video equipment and taped five minutes of sports news he had memorized and sent the tape to ESPN. Patrick says the network was kind but said he wasn't quite ready for ESPN. Patrick did end up at CNN and, he says, they taught me how to be a journalist. After spending almost six years with CNN, Patrick says he asked for a $10,000-a-year raise. When management offered only $5,000 more, Patrick knocked on ESPN's door again, and this time he was ready.

The man who hired Patrick, managing editor John Walsh, called Patrick the quintessence of what the network was trying to accomplish. Walsh says it was obvious that Patrick was a passionate sports fan—that he was really into his job.

Baseball's Mark Grace says Patrick has earned the respect among top athletes in a way few broadcasters have. Grace says Patrick is very knowledgeable about sports. But he says players also know he can ask tough questions without trashing them—he does what he does with respect.

Patrick's interviewing skills, and attitude, were demonstrated in an interview he did with hockey great Wayne Gretzky. Patrick says he avoided the cliché question about his retirement because he thought it would be presumptuous to suggest he knew when Gretzky should retire. Patrick added: "I want a person I interview to know they are a person, not a sound bite. I want the people I interview to know that I am not going to attack them, that I care about every answer they give me." He said: "You can be hard on an athlete without carrying a hammer."

A broadcast journalism professor at Syracuse University, Hubert Brown, has nothing but praise for Patrick. Syracuse's Newhouse School of Public Communication is often referred to as "Sportscaster U" for having produced Bob Costas and Marv Albert, among many others. Brown says that Patrick's style and thoroughness make him a good model. Brown notes that it's hard to convey to students how people like Patrick make it look so easy. "They think it is stringing together catch phrases," but what you don't see, says Brown, is that Patrick is knowledgeable about a lot of different things—things beyond sports; that he writes and delivers his own material; that his delivery is appropriate to the subject matter; and that he makes subtle shifts in the delivery as the show moves along. Brown concluded: "To put Patrick in a class with Al Michaels and Bob Costas is not a stretch."

Mark Lisheron, who wrote an article about Patrick for the *American Journalism Review*, says that athletes are candid with Patrick because he coaxes rather than cudgels them. Lisheron says Patrick's Q and A feature, "Outtakes," in *ESPN, The Magazine*, rarely fails to produce a provocative exchange with a news-making athlete. Lisheron points out that despite ESPN's location, in Bristol, Connecticut, athletes go out of their way to visit Patrick. Lisheron notes that Michael Jordan, "who needs another interview like he needs another product endorsement, enjoys sitting down with Patrick."

Bob Costas says Patrick is a guy who has a style, not a shtick, that is welcome in this time of trying to impress, to get noticed, to come up with a catch phrase.

Costas adds: "Patrick manages to inject some personality into his delivery without overwhelming the subject matter. He doesn't grab you by the lapels to speak to you."

Patrick obviously has had such success because he learned many of the skills already stressed in this book—good reporting and interviewing techniques and caring and sensitivity. This same point is made by longtime Cleveland sports anchor Jim Donovan. He says that whether a student eventually wants to cover the White House or the White Sox, he or she needs to learn the same reporting skills. Donovan recalls that he has often led newscasts with sports stories, such as the Indians winning the World Series, but he also has found himself at the top of a newscast covering a spring training boating accident that killed two Indian pitchers. Donovan says such a story takes him back to the basics of news reporting. "You're not dealing with your opinion on why this guy should be traded, you're dealing with some really hard facts, and you have to make sure you have it right."

He also has this advice for those who want a future with ESPN. "When you walk into a locker room, interviewing skills are more important than knowledge of sports trivia." Donovan says you'll have to deal with athletes who have won and lost, who want to talk and those who never talk, and if you don't have the reporting skills, I think you'll really fail pretty miserably."

Keith Olbermann, a co-host with Patrick on ESPN before moving over to Fox Sports, says sports reporters need to understand journalistic ethics: "What you can say and what you cannot say, how to develop sources." He adds: "You have to have the same equipment that Dan Rather, Tom Brokaw, and Peter Jennings have. When you have mastered these things," he says, "you can go work on the jokes."

# Weather Reporting

Good weathercasters are also well rewarded. In large markets, weathercasters are often paid almost as much as the news anchors and sometimes even more. In medium-sized markets, weathercasters usually do not earn quite as much as the anchors but often earn more than sportscasters. The competition for jobs is not as keen as it is in sports because most people entering the field consider weather reporting rather dull, which means many opportunities are available for those who pick weather reporting as a career. It's not always as dull as it may seem, however. Most stations expect weathercasters to report from the oceanside when a hurricane is on its way or to be knee-deep in flood-filled streets while predicting when the rain is going to stop.

The weather people most in demand are those with degrees in meteorology. Unfortunately, those delivering the weather in most markets are not trained meteorologists. Some stations still hire people right out of school and expect

**Figure 19.4**  Anchor-reporter Paul Gates of WAFB-TV, Baton
Rouge, Louisiana, works on a script. (Photo by James Terry)

them to deliver professional weather reports. Many viewers do not notice the
difference in the weather person's background, particularly when sophisticated-
looking radar maps and graphics are employed. But students who are serious
about anchoring the weather should study meteorology; the money invested in
earning a degree will certainly pay dividends.

If weather reporting is your goal, you also have to learn about computer and chroma-key (special effects) technology. Jerry Brown, a mete-
orologist for KUTV in Salt Lake City, says: "The [reporter's] discomfort level
in front of the chroma board too often is readily apparent. It's not that the
weathercaster doesn't know what to say. The problem is how to visually integrate a storyline and chroma-key graphics into a cohesive 'show-and-tell' presentation."

Brown says weathercasters must "maintain continuous eye contact with one
of three monitors, ad-lib and synchronize hand and body movement, all the
while pirouetting across the screen. Done right," he says, "it looks effortless."
But it's not easy.

Brown says that when weather interns ask for help setting up a weather-
cast audition tape, he tries his best to help, but he warns, "While a novice news
anchor may on rare occasion master a teleprompter, I have never seen anyone
approach professional level on their first try at chroma-key." Brown adds,
however, that "marked improvement does come with practice." He suggests
seeking a good professional coach. Coach Jeff Puffer, who is with Frank N. Magid

Associates, works with people at the company's offices in Marion, Iowa, but he says he also likes "to work with meteorologists at their own chroma board where they are familiar with the aspect ratio of key wall and graphics." He notes: "You can't be talking about Dallas and looking at Omaha."

Weathercaster Brown makes another important point: "A personable weathercaster is the single most important aspect of a weather presentation." He says, "It constantly dismays me how little attention the average viewer pays to the weather maps I create."

Station managers look for personality along with a knowledge of maps, computers, and chroma-key technology. The auditions for weather anchors are considerably different from auditions for beat reporters. Although the news director looks for good writing and reporting skills, the general manager looks for a great smile and a quick wit.

Sometimes the weather is more than just looking at the day's highs and lows and the five-day forecast. Sometimes the weather is the lead story. Here's an example from reporter Paul Gates of WAFB-TV in Baton Rouge:

SLUG: COLD WEATHER
REPORTER:PAUL GATES
NEWSCAST:SIX P.M.

| | |
|---|---|
| OUTDOOR CONSTRUCTION WORKER WITH BOARDS OVER SHOULDER TALKS TO CAMERA AS HE WALKS AND PUFFS WHITE BREATH. | NAT SOT :03<br><br>"IT'S ICE COLD OUT THERE THIS MORNING, MAN . . . 28 DEGREES THIS MORNING WHEN I CAME OUT, MAN, BUT I GOTTA DO IT THOUGH." |
| VO-CONSTRUCTION GUYS STANDING AROUND FIRE CLAPPING HANDS AND STOMPING FEET. HEATING MAN BOB WALKS UP TO DOOR OF HOME AND DOOR IS OPENED BY HOMEOWNER. | BOB IS LIKE A LOT OF OTHER FOLKS . . . CAUGHT A LITTLE OFF GUARD BY THIS FIRST EARLY FREEZE OF THE SEASON.<br>    BATON ROUGE IS ONE OF FOUR CITIES IN LOUISIANA SETTING A RECORD LOW OF 27 DEGREES. THE OLD RECORD WAS 29 DEGREES, SET BACK IN 1899. HEATING CONTRACTORS WERE DOING A BOOMING BUSINESS TODAY . . . |
| MAN IN DOORWAY TALKING TO BOB—THE | NAT SOT:02<br>"WELL, THE HEATER WON'T COME ON." |

| | |
|---|---|
| HEATING MAN. BOB THEN WALKS INTO HOME OUT OF FRAME | "OK, LET'S HAVE A LOOK AT IT." |
| BOB—THE HEATING MAN SOUND BITE. | SOT :11 "THIS IS THE MOST CALLS I'VE EVER TAKEN IN ONE DAY, EVEN DURING THE SUMMER, SO WE'RE REALLY BUSY AND |
| FONT: BOB LEE SUPERIOR HEAT | WE'RE TRYING TO GET TO EVERYONE AS QUICK AS WE CAN, BUT UNFORTU- NATELY WE'RE GONNA HAVE SOME OF THEM SPILL OVER INTO TOMORROW." |
| VO-TIGHT SHOT OF BOB'S HANDS INSIDE HEATING UNIT . . . WE SEE BOB—IN THE ATTIC WORKING ON UNIT, VARIOUS SHOTS. | BOB SAYS 65 PERCENT OF HIS CALLS ARE TO LIGHT PILOT LIGHTS . . . AND IF YOU DON'T KNOW TOO MUCH ABOUT ALL THAT STUFF IN THE ATTIC, IT'S BEST TO CALL A HEATING EXPERT. |
| BOB—THE HEATING MAN SOUND BITE. | SOT :05 "WHEN WE LIGHT A PILOT LIGHT, WE ALWAYS CHECK AND SERVICE THE FURNACE FOR THE WINTER. IT'S ALWAYS A GOOD IDEA TO HAVE A PROFESSIONAL DO IT." |
| FILE VIDEO AND NAT SOT OF HOUSE BURNING | FLAMES UP . . . NAT SOT HOLD FOR :02 SECONDS |
| VO-CONTINUE FILE VIDEO OF FIRE. | THERE IS DANGER IN THIS COLD WEATHER. TOO MANY PEOPLE MUST RELY ON SPACE HEATERS AND TOO OFTEN THAT CAN BE FATAL |
| SOT OF FIRE DEPARTMENT'S PUBLIC INFORMATION OFFICER. | SOT :11 "YOU'LL HEAR OF A STORY BEFORE THE WINTER'S OUT THAT SOME ELDERLY COUPLE OR SOMEONE HAS |
| FONT: TERRY KENNEDY PUBLIC INFORMATION | PLACED THEIR SPACE HEATER TOO CLOSE TO THE BED WHILE THEY'RE SLEEPING, AND IT STARTS A FIRE AND THEY LOSE THEIR LIFE." |

| | |
|---|---|
| GRAPHICS PRODUCTION. | KEEP SPACE HEATERS CLEAR OF FLAMMABLE OBJECTS. AND GIVE SPACE HEATERS A SOURCE OF OXYGEN. |
| 1. KEEP SPACE HEATERS ...<br>2. GIVE SPACE HEATERS A ... GRAPHICS OVER BACKGROUND OF FLAMES. REPORTER STAND-UP | |
| | GATES BRIDGE STD |
| SOT | |
| | "ONE GOOD THING ABOUT THIS COLD SNAP FOR AREA MERCHANTS ... SLUGGISH WINTER CLOTHING SALES ... WELL, THAT'S REALLY PICKED UP." |
| VO-SHOTS OF CLOTHING SHOPPERS | FOR WEEKS WINTER CLOTHING HAS HUNG LISTLESSLY ON THE RACKS ... BUT NOW, THE WHEELS OF WINTRY COMMERCE ARE TURNING AND THE STUFF IS MOVING OUT |
| TIGHT SHOT OF SHOPPING CART WHEELS ROLLING DOWN AISLE | |
| REPORTER WALKS IN AND CHATS NAT SOT WITH A SMALL CLUSTER OF LADY SHOPPERS. | NAT SOT :03 |
| | "WHAT ARE YOU LADIES SHOPPING FOR? INSULATED THERMAL UNDERWEAR. KINDA GOT CAUGHT BY SURPRISE, UH? YEAH ... UMMMMM, IT'S SO COLD." |
| VO-BOB—THE HEATING MAN WITH A NOTEPAD AND PHONE JAMMED TO EAR RAPIDLY SCRATCHING DOWN NAMES AND NUMBERS | MEANWHILE, BACK WITH BOB OF SUPERIOR HEATING ... |
| CUT TO TIGHT SHOT OF BOB'S NOTEPAD FULL OF NAMES ... | NAT SOT :03 |
| | "YEAH, I GOT A BIG PIECE OF PAPER ... GO WITH THEM." |
| VO-WIDE SHOT OF BOB—THE HEATING MAN TAKING THE INFO OVER THE PHONE. | HE'S STILL MAKING APPOINTMENTS, AND THE ONLY WAY TO GET SERVICE IS TO GET IN LINE.<br>PAUL GATES, WAFB NEWS. |

# Summary

As with just about every other position in this technological era, the better prepared you are, the better chance you have of getting a reporting job. If you have a minor in environmental studies, health studies, economics, or business, for example, you could be more attractive to news directors than people who have only general knowledge. Specialty or beat reporting is one of the most interesting jobs in broadcast news because it provides an opportunity to spend more time developing and working on stories. Many beat reporters also find their work more rewarding because they can develop an expertise that provides an added dimension to their stories; however, one disadvantage is that not as many jobs are available for specialty reporters. There may be 10 general-assignment reporters at a large TV station and only a couple of specialty reporters.

From a practical point of view, however, whatever extra knowledge you have when you apply for work is going to work to your advantage. Even if you do not get a job as, say, an environmental reporter, the news director may be impressed that you took several courses in the subject. If you get a general-assignment job, you will probably find that when an environmental story shows up, you'll be assigned to it. If your work is particularly good, you may wind up with a beat.

# Review Questions

1. Why is there a debate over the use of the term *investigative reporting*?
2. What is the difference between investigative reporting and most other types of reporting?
3. Many radio and TV stations are hiring environmental reporters. What's the best way to prepare for such a career?
4. Why do radio and TV stations devote a lot of time to stories about health and medicine?
5. How can students prepare themselves to be health and medical reporters?
6. One of the most popular specialties is consumer reporting. Why are consumer reporters so popular with audiences?
7. Many people want to be sports reporters, but they face tough competition. Why is that so?
8. Do you believe that there are opportunities in weathercasting? Discuss.

# Exercises

1. Arrange to accompany a radio or TV reporter who is covering an environmental story. Try to understand the issues involved, and check to see if the reporter covered them fairly. Turn in a report.

2.  Ask friends and fellow students if any consumer issues annoy them. Select one that you think has particular merit. After researching it, do some interviews and put together a wraparound or package.

3.  If a radio or TV station in your community assigns a reporter to a health and medicine beat, ask the reporter how she gets most of her story ideas. If there are no medical reporters, ask the news directors how they cover that beat and whether they are happy with the results.

4.  Ask a TV sportscaster if you can spend an afternoon or evening with him to see if you think you would like the job. Later, do the same thing with a weathercaster.

# **20** Ethics and the Law

This chapter and Chapter 21 focus on the important and complex issue of ethics, one of the cornerstones of good journalism. All journalists must be concerned about ethics, and the law is there to remind journalists of their responsibilities, if necessary.

## Gratuities

Reporters are often tempted with gratuities, or gifts. It is impossible for reporters to maintain their credibility if they accept any kind of gift from people or organizations they cover. Many offers come from public-relations people. Some gifts may come at Christmas, whereas others may arrive at the door of a reporter or producer after the broadcast of a story about a product or service. The gifts should be returned.

Some news directors pass out such gifts to non-news staff, but doing so sends the wrong message to the donor. If the gifts are not returned, the senders have no way of knowing that they were not appreciated and might assume that they can expect some favor the next time they're promoting something.

One news director says that when Christmas gifts arrive, he does give them to the people in the mailroom but does not say who sent them. He says he also calls the donor and lets him or her know that he can't accept gifts and has passed them along to the mailroom staff. "That's easier than packing the stuff up and sending it back," he says. "It also lets the PR people know that I can't be bought, and it makes the people in the mailroom a little bit happier."

## Conflict of Interest

Sometimes, the issue of what is an acceptable practice is not so clearly defined. Is it wrong for a theater or film reviewer to receive free tickets from the show's producers? Some newspapers pay for their reviewers' tickets, but most reviewers do accept free tickets, and there is no reason to believe that this practice influences what they write about a film or play.

Some news organizations, however, fear a *conflict of interest*. For example, hotel owners sometimes offer newspeople a free plane ride and accommodations to promote a new hotel. Is it possible for the reporter to maintain objectivity when the host has provided him or her with a thousand dollars or more for travel and entertainment? Some journalists claim it would take more than that to corrupt them. Some of them may even write negative stories about the trip, but the temptation to be favorable toward the host is great. To avoid such potential conflicts of interest, many news directors forbid such trips.

## Accuracy and Responsibility

The need for accuracy in journalism has been stressed throughout this book. Accuracy is also discussed in this chapter because it is an essential part of the discussion of ethics.

Some inaccuracy will always creep into news writing and reporting because people write and report news and people make mistakes. If errors occur, the

**Figure 20.1** An anti-abortion demonstration in Baton Rouge. Reporters must always present both sides of a controversial subject. (Photo by James Terry)

ethical reaction is to correct the mistakes immediately. Accuracy becomes an ethical problem when the facts in a story are wrong not because of carelessness but because of bias, preconceived conclusions, a failure to give all sides of the story, or for any other reason that the information seen and heard by the audience is distorted or untrue.

*NBC News* correspondent Roger O'Neil says, "I'm very concerned about getting the facts straight. I double-check what I say because I know how powerful and frightening my words can be. I can ruin people's lives, and I have. I can ruin businesses, and I have. But fortunately, my facts were right."

Accuracy also means taking the responsibility to write and report the truth in a manner that is as objective and fair as possible. Taking responsibility means the following: (1) looking at *all* the issues, not just the easy or popular ones; (2) examining controversies and producing special reports throughout the year, not just during the sweeps rating periods; (3) covering important stories that don't always offer good pictures; (4) writing and reporting with care, understanding, and compassion; and (5) dealing with people in a professional and civil manner.

# Libel

Although it should not be the motivating factor for insisting on accuracy, there is always the threat of libel facing those journalists who through carelessness, ignorance, or malice make inaccurate statements in their scripts and reports that reflect on the character or reputation of an individual or group. Libel laws differ from state to state, but essentially writers or reporters can be sued for libel if anything they write or report (1) exposes an individual or group to public scorn, hatred, ridicule, or contempt; (2) causes harm to someone in their occupation or profession; or (3) causes someone to be shunned or avoided.

Reporters must also remember that it is not necessary to have actually used a person's name to be sued for libel. If the audience knows to whom a reporter is referring, even without the name, the reporter could be sued for libel if the comments harm the person's reputation.

Although libel traditionally refers to printed material and slander to spoken words, the distinction between the two terms has little meaning for broadcast reporters. Recognizing that broadcast material is usually scripted, many state laws regard any defamatory statements on radio and television as subject to libel laws.

Attorney and former reporter Bruce Sanford says writers and editors should be wary of using certain words. Here is a partial list of what Sanford refers to as "red flag" words:

| | | |
|---|---|---|
| adultery | deadbeat | illegitimate |
| atheist | double-crosser | incompetent |
| bigamist | drunkard | intimate |
| blackmail | ex-convict | liar |
| bribery | fascist | mental disease |
| cheat | fool | perjurer |
| corruption | fraud | shyster |
| coward | gangster | unethical |
| crook | hypocrite | unprofessional |

Remember also that using the word *alleged* before a potentially libelous word does not make it any less libelous.

# Defenses

Courts usually recognize only three defenses against libel: truth, privilege, and fair comment.

The *truth* is the best defense, but in some states the courts have ruled that truth is only a defense if the comments were not malicious.

*Privilege* covers areas such as legislative and judicial hearings and debates and documents that are in the public domain. If a reporter quotes a potentially libelous comment made by a senator during a debate, the reporter could not be sued for libel.

*Fair comment* also is used as a defense against libel. Public officials, performers, sports figures, and others who attract public attention must expect to be criticized and scrutinized more than most people. If a sports commentator, for example, says that college football coach Joe Brown is a "lousy coach and the team would be better off if this inept, incompetent jerk moved on to a high-school coaching job, which he might just possibly be able to handle," he might get a punch in the nose if he ran into the coach, but he would not end up in court for libel.

There are limits, however, to what reporters can say even about public figures—the facts must be true. If the sports commentator had included the comment that "Brown's real problem is that he is smoking too many joints at night," then Brown would have a libel case unless the sports commentator could prove that Coach Brown actually spends his nights smoking marijuana.

# False Light

A complaint similar to libel, called *false light*, involves the improper juxtaposition of video and audio that creates a false impression of someone. This invasion-of-privacy issue has actually caused more suits against TV news organizations than libel has, and it is more difficult to defend.

Karen Frankola, a professor at the University of Missouri, described a case involving a reporter working on a story about genital herpes. The reporter was having difficulty figuring out how to cover the story, so she relied on some walking-down-the-street file video. Frankola said that in the package used on the 6 o'clock news, none of the passersby was identifiable. The story was edited differently for the 11 o'clock news, though, and the audience saw a closeup of a young woman while the anchor was saying, "For the 21 million Americans who have herpes, it's not a cure." The woman in the closeup won damages from the TV station.

Frankola said that false light "may get past a journalist more easily because it's not as obvious that false information is being given." She noted that the reporter in the herpes story did not say "the woman has herpes," which would have been a red flag to the editor. But, Frankola said, "the combination of words and pictures implied that the woman had the disease."

The Reporters' Committee for Freedom of the Press issued a report showing that 47 percent of subpoenas issued to TV stations deal with such invasion-of-privacy actions. The group's executive director, Jane Kirtley, believes the number of suits is growing because "people are developing a much greater sense of privacy, a desire to be let alone."

Most Americans believe that privacy is a cornerstone of their existence. They expect it to be respected. Journalists should invade that privacy with trepidation, particularly at times of grief, as was discussed in the chapters on reporting.

# Boundaries

How far should reporters go to get a story? If reporters have a strong suspicion that someone in government is a crook, don't they have the right to do whatever it takes to report the story to the public? Some journalists say they do. Other newspeople believe that if they bend the rules too much, they become suspect and may be viewed no differently than the people they are investigating. Each reporter must decide the ethical merits involved in certain investigative practices.

## *Controversial Techniques*

Some of the controversial information-gathering techniques employed by investigative reporters include impersonation, misrepresentation, and infiltration. Should journalists use such techniques to get a story? Consider the following scenarios:

- Is it right for a reporter to pretend to be a nurse so that she can get inside a nursing home to investigate charges that residents are being mistreated?
- Is it proper for a journalist to tell a college football coach that he wants to do a story about training when he's really checking on reports of drug abuse and gambling?

- Is it permissible for a reporter to pose as a pregnant woman thinking about having an abortion in order to find out what kind of material a right-to-life organization is providing at its information center?
- Is it ethical for journalists to take jobs in a supermarket and then spy on the operations to try to show improper food handling.

All of these incidents actually occurred, and they represent only a few examples of the controversial methods used on a routine basis. Are they ethical?

Investigative reporter Jim Polk, who moved over to CNN after spending many years with NBC, says he never misrepresents himself, impersonates others, or uses any other techniques that he thinks are unethical. "Our business is the truth," he says, "and I do not think you get the truth by practicing deception."

About the reporter who posed as a nurse to get into a nursing home, Polk admits that there are times when an argument for using such tactics is "honest," but he adds: "All too often the argument is simply an excuse for those who prefer a short cut rather than long-term hard work and drudgery to nail down the facts."

Polk says there is one role that he will play—that of citizen. He says he may go into a courthouse and ask for a document without signing in as a reporter because any citizen is entitled to the same information. "If I am going to put somebody on the air, gather information about an individual, I believe in disclosing who I am."

John Spain, the former general manager of WBRZ-TV in Baton Rouge, who has won many awards for investigative reporting, says that while he has been working in the public's interest, he has "never taken that as a license to break the law or be immoral or do things that are justified under the glorious heading of the First Amendment." Spain says: "I don't think we have any special rights, and I think we have to be very careful when we start thinking we do in terms of being dishonest or breaking the law."

Spain says he has had great success being "upfront with people and telling them who we are and why we've come to talk to them. I don't think I, or anyone on my staff, has ever misrepresented themselves." He adds: "I think we've done some very serious investigations over the years and have been able to practice our craft without misrepresenting ourselves."

*Dateline NBC* correspondent Robert McKeown admits that he has misrepresented himself at times in order to get the "truth." He believes you can't always accomplish your goal if you admit you are a journalist. He recalled that during the Gulf War, he and a camera crew stole some fatigues, flak jackets, and helmets in order to work their way through roadblocks. "I am not sure we would have been successful getting our story—a story that we should have got—unless we misrepresented ourselves."

McKeown says everyone has a "gut feeling about what is right and wrong" when it comes to ethics. He says reporters also have to bring a sense of mission to what they do and, by definition, have to bring "a kind of anti-establishment attitude" to the job. "You have to be prepared to piss people off and realize that in some stories if you don't, the stories are not going to be successful."

## *Hidden Cameras and Microphones*

Reporters sometimes use hidden cameras and microphones when they're doing an investigative story in an effort to record incriminating material. They also use wireless microphones to eavesdrop on conversations. Such devices are routinely used by teams working for *60 Minutes*, *20/20*, and other investigative TV news programs.

There seem to be no laws against using a hidden camera to videotape something that is going on in public. Reporters must know state and federal laws, however, if they plan to use hidden microphones. Federal law forbids their use unless one person involved in the conversation knows of the recording. If a reporter places a hidden microphone in a hotel room to record a conversation between two or more people, that would be a violation of federal law. If a reporter is carrying a hidden microphone, there is no federal violation, but some states do forbid the practice. It's also a violation of some state laws to use so-called wires—microphones that transmit a conversation to another location.

CNN's Jim Polk admits that he has used hidden cameras from the back of a truck with one-way glass, but he says it is really "espionage, spying—a dirty little technique." But, he says, "We have used it on the mob." Polk says that as long as the video that's shot with a hidden camera is of people doing illegal things in public view, he has no problem using the technique. He says, however, that using hidden microphones is "playing with fire. It's a dangerous technique that is easily mishandled, and it should be used with caution and only under certain circumstances."

John Spain agrees, for the most part, but he says he has used hidden cameras on some stories when he thought the video was essential. He recalled using a concealed camera in a story about some alcohol beverage control officers who were getting drunk while they were on duty. "They were supposed to be enforcing the alcohol laws," Spain says, "and we needed the video to show what they actually were doing."

But Spain believes that hidden cameras shouldn't be used unless necessary. He cited the example of back-to-back stories that appeared on the now-defunct *Prime Time Live*. The first story was about a meat-inspection facility. The plant had been exempted from having federal inspectors because it was doing its own inspection. *Prime Time Live* had help from someone at the plant and got a camera inside. What they taped and played on the air was video of carcasses being dragged along the floor and intestines being ruptured on top of meat that had been stamped "U.S. Inspected."

Spain said, "I bought into that story big time, because it was providing a public service. Most people eat meat, and they have a right to know how it is processed. The story also brought about change. The day after it was aired," he said, "the Secretary of Agriculture sent inspectors into the plant."

On the other hand, Spain said he had a lot of trouble with the story done by *Prime Time Live* the following week. Hidden cameras were used again, this time to "expose" a man who had moved to another state to avoid paying child support.

Spain said it bothered him that the network picked on one man out of millions to point out a problem that admittedly is a serious one. "The network crossed the country with the man's wife and daughters and then walked into a place of business and cornered the father with a hidden camera." Spain said that what the man had done was wrong, but that he now had a new wife and children and that, in Spain's opinion, the network was not justified in embarrassing the individual to illustrate the problem.

Spain added that the audience never did hear the man's story because, after the ambush interview, he refused to speak with the reporter. Spain said: "I don't know what the public interest was in the life of a father who didn't pay child support."

## Case Study 1: A Mercy Killing on TV

Dr. Jack Kevorkian, who has played a role in more than 121 deaths since his assisted suicide campaign began in 1990, was finally convicted in a Michigan court and sentenced to 10 to 25 years in jail because of his decision to give *60 Minutes* a videotape of his assisted suicide of 52-year-old Thomas Youk, who had Lou Gehrig's disease. At this writing, Kevorkian is in prison awaiting appeal of his case.

Kevorkian had given *60 Minutes'* producers the videotape of the killing because he wanted to challenge authorities in Michigan to prosecute him for what he claimed was his first case of actual euthanasia, or mercy killing. In all previous cases, Kevorkian assisted his patients in taking their own lives. Although he had been tried in court several times, juries refused to convict him of the assisted suicides. On the *60 Minutes* program, Kevorkian said of Michigan authorities, "either they go or I go. If I'm convicted, I will starve to death in prison or I will go."

The *60 Minutes* decision to broadcast the Kevorkian tape sparked widespread debate and much criticism about the airing of a person dying on primetime television, particularly because it came during a "sweeps" period when ratings are used to set advertising rates. The rating for the program was the highest *60 Minutes* had all season. CBS denied that the "sweeps" had anything to do with its decision to broadcast the material. One source quoted someone with *60 Minutes* as saying that getting

**Case Study 1: continued**

the videotape from Kevorkian was "just too good an opportunity to pass up."

A network spokesman, Kevin Tedesco, said: "We're just letting Dr. Kevorkian tell his story." He added, somewhat defensively, "I really don't think there's a news organization in this country that would pass up this story." That statement was, perhaps, a bit overstated because several CBS affiliates refused to carry the program. The CBS statement said the program performed a public service.

But there was plenty of criticism of the network's decision, not only from journalists but also from those who do not agree with the idea of mercy killing. Even Jerry Lewis, host of a longtime annual Muscular Dystrophy Association telethon, was among those complaining to *60 Minutes*, saying it "amplified the fear" of people who have the disease or who will get a diagnosis of it in the future.

Others criticized the program because they said CBS allowed Kevorkian to "use" the network to present his views. One physician opposed to physician-assisted suicides said that Kevorkian manipulated the legitimate press—that the videotape should not have been shown anywhere except in a court of law. Indeed, what was to prevent CBS from simply turning over the tape to authorities without airing it? In the minds of many, and as acknowledged, in effect, by Tedesco, it was too good a story to ignore.

In a stinging column, the *New York Times* media critic, Caryn James, called the airing of the tape a "stunt death." Marvin Kalb, a former *CBS News* correspondent and director of the Shorenstein Center on the Press, Politics and Public Policy at Harvard University, was especially critical: "To me, it is sad that death has become a form of news-entertainment."

**Case Study 2: Food Lion Sues ABC**

In 1992, two ABC producers for the now-defunct *Prime Time Live* sought undercover jobs as a meat wrapper trainee and a deli clerk in order to investigate allegations of improper food handling by the supermarket chain, Food Lion. It was a misguided idea from the beginning, and it brought ABC and Food Lion into a courtroom battle that lasted seven years.

Although the producers used controversial hidden cameras and microphones and other questionable techniques that were discussed earlier, it was not the techniques themselves that landed the network in court. To obtain the entry-level positions, they concealed their association with the

**Case Study 2: continued**

network by lying about their work experience and references on their employment applications. Although the ruse was unethical, it worked and the two producers were hired. But what they did from then on inside the Food Lion store would be tainted. As most investigative reporters were quoted earlier as saying, they don't break the law to get a story. It obviously did not occur to the producers that there was anything illegal about their actions, or they simply did not care in their quest for "good news."

The hidden-camera exposé by the two producers over a two-week period charged that Food Lion stores knowingly sold rotten meat, fish dipped in bleach, cheese that was nibbled on by rats, and produce removed from fly-infested dumpsters. Although officially, *ABC News* has a policy of using hidden cameras only if less-intrusive methods of reporting are unavailable, the decision was made to use them at the Food Lion store anyway. Could the story have been completed without them?

*Fortune* magazine talked to the key participants in the case and examined thousands of pages of sworn testimony, court documents, and internal memos. It's conclusion: Food Lion may have had a point.

It wondered, like many investigative reporters, if the story could have been done without deceit and hidden cameras. *Fortune* questioned why ABC did not check state or federal health inspection reports to see whether Food Lion had food safety problems. The magazine suggested that producers also could have tested groceries purchased at Food Lion for contamination. ABC did neither. ABC also failed to report that, in general, Food Lion received favorable reports from state and federal health inspectors. ABC also worked closely with union members, whom the network knew had a grudge against the company.

Food Lion charged that it was victimized by ABC's unethical conduct and one-sided reporting. It claimed that ABC producers told lies and induced others to lie and that it ignored evidence that would have undermined its story.

During the week that the *Prime Time Live* story was broadcast about the supermarket chain, the market value of the company's stock fell by 1.3 billion dollars. The chain also said that its profits were clobbered by the program, from $178 million in 1992 to a mere $3.9 million the following year.

Food Lion sued ABC for $2.47 billion dollars. It took four years to get the two sides into court and another three years for the case to end up in the United States Court of Appeals. After millions of dollars in legal fees, the court reversed an earlier court ruling that had found in favor of Food Lion's damage award. The higher court held that Food Lion could not circumvent the First Amendment by seeking to recover defamation-type

## Case Study 2: continued

damages without first proving that the story was intentionally or recklessly untruthful and inaccurate.

Although ABC's damages were limited to its weighty legal expenses, Food Lion could take satisfaction in the court's ruling that ABC was guilty of trespass and breached a duty of loyalty to Food Lion by bringing hidden cameras into nonpublic areas of their employer. The court also said: "We are convinced that the media can do its important job effectively without resorting to the commission of run-of-the mill torts." Nevertheless, all that Food Lion ultimately received for its costly legal effort was $2 in nominal damages on the trespass complaint.

For journalists, the case is more important for ethics than who won or lost money. One of the producers trying to get a job at Food Lion wrote on her application that "I love meat wrapping. I have heard Food Lion is a great company. I would like to make a career with the company." The producers got phony letters of references from some union members who had a grudge against Food Lion.

After getting the jobs and gaining access to the Food Lion store by lying, both producers had microphones in their underwear and tiny cameras hidden in their wigs. Most investigative reporters told us that they believed ABC went too far.

## Case Study 3: ABC Stings the Cops

Another *Prime Time Live* hidden camera story that tried to sting some cops "[raised] as many questions about its own reporting as it did about the police," according to Brill's *Content* (July/August 1999). So-called racial profiling—the practice used by some police authorities of stopping cars when the cars and/or the people driving them meet the profile of suspected criminal activity—has been making headlines lately. Many African-Americans have charged that they have been stopped by police just because of their race and often because of the kind of car they are driving, particularly if it is an expensive one.

Some of these complaints were made about police in New Jersey, so *Prime Time Live* decided to launch a sting operation to see if the complaints were true. Producers hired three African-American men and sent them to Jamesburg, New Jersey, in a new Mercedes with hidden cameras in the rearview mirror, the sunroof, and at the rear of the car.

A description of the sting operation in Brill's *Content* told how the Mercedes and its three ABC undercover black men cruised around Jamesburg hoping that they would be stopped by police. Patrol officers

## Case Study 3: continued

Louis Hornberger and Robert Tonkery obliged them. The car, by the way, had been seen the previous night circling the town. This night, at one of the town's two traffic lights, the Mercedes made an illegal lane change, prompting the two officers to pull the car over.

Brill's *Content* writer Osborne said the traffic stop seemed routine and it might have been handled quickly, but the backseat passenger made the white officers nervous because when they asked for identification, the young man scowled, poked at his heavy leather jacket, and told officers he left his I.D. at home. One of the policemen said later that he became more suspicious when the men in the front of the car identified their companion by two different names.

The officers ordered the men to get out of the car. The officers frisked each of the men and searched the car. They found nothing and told the men they could go. They would say later that they thought they were doing the men a favor because the men did, technically, commit a driving infraction when they made an illegal lane change.

But Brill's *Content* says that when ABC's *Prime Time Live* producers came to Jamesburg three months later and started asking questions, the police officers learned that the three black men in the Mercedes were working for ABC, and that their encounter with the officers was on videotape.

Some carefully edited footage of the sting was included in a *Prime Time Live* segment called "Driving While Black." Jamesburg officials were understandably concerned about the program and demanded an explanation from their police officers. They claimed that the newsmagazine did not tell the whole story. They said that two detectives working undercover with a county-wide drug task force had put them on the lookout for a Mercedes similar to the one used by ABC. The officers also said that ABC had failed to mention several negative and provoking statements made by the backseat passenger, whose conduct had caused them to fear for their safety.

Brill's *Content* said that unedited video of the encounter shows indisputably that the officers were polite and that their decision to order the men out of the car was precipitated by the backseat passenger saying he left his I.D. at home. No law requires that passengers identify themselves to police officers, but the three men apparently were advised by an ABC attorney that refusal to produce I.D. would make the officers suspicious and probably bring about some sort of reaction similar to what the ABC producers were looking for. According to Brill's *Content*, the ABC attorney also advised the ABC undercover men that by having all of their credentials in order and by complying with officers' basic requests, there shouldn't be any reason for them to be ordered out of the car. *Prime Time*

**Case Study 3: continued**

*Live* made no mention on the program of the lawyer's advice, and the men either forgot or ignored it.

The *Prime Time Live* report also failed to mention that their sting Mercedes was driving around the town for two nights before the encounter with the police officers, and the car was not stopped. Another ABC sting car was roaming the streets a month earlier, and the taped conversation showed the men's disappointment when police failed to stop them. A police car had followed the ABC car for several blocks and then suddenly turned away. The tape of that incident showed that one of the men in the car was disappointed: "Oh," the man exclaimed, "he turned, son of a bitch we lost them, damn." The tape then heard the men discussing what they could do differently to make the police officers pull them over. The program that aired made no mention of these unsuccessful attempts to sting police.

Also omitted from the program, for obvious reasons, was the taped conversation in the Mercedes after the encounter with police. The men discussed whether the man in the back should have produced some I.D. "Do you have it with you?" asked one of the men in the front. "Yeah, I got it," the man in the backseat said. "Well, then you should have shown it to them," said the driver. The man in the back then said: "Yeah, but then they wouldn't have forced us out of the car." The driver is then heard saying, "Shh, shh," a reminder that the videotape was still rolling.

In the end, the police officers filed suit against ABC for defamation. The mayor of the town said "there is a law that says police officers can't entrap a suspected criminal. What *Prime Time* did was to make every effort to entrap a police officer." The policemen charge that ABC unfairly branded them as racists.

Brill's *Content* says the unedited tapes do not clearly vindicate the police officers and in some cases even contradict their accounts. As a result, the magazine adds, the hidden camera footage, which in theory could have resolved the dispute, has raised as many questions as it has answered.

As for the officers, they say their run-in with *Prime Time Live* has sapped their enthusiasm for the job. "I'm just worried about making stops," said officer Hornberger. "I see a violation at night, and if I see the driver is black, it's like the blood runs out of me, I want to get out of there. I wonder did they see me on TV? Are they going to start calling me a racist?"

Ironically, the Brill's *Content* report says that the three black men in the Mercedes underwent a transformation of their own. The magazine says the three men who decided to test the police for a nationwide TV audience—and then laughed and bantered on tape after the incident—now claim they suffered an invasion of their privacy, humiliation, embarrassment, and emotional distress.

### Case Study 4: CNN Retracts Its Story

One of the most sensational retractions by any news organization in the 1990s was CNN's admission that its report on the military's alleged use of poison gas was untrue. The CNN "Valley of Death" investigative report was scheduled to launch the network's new magazine show, *News Stand: CNN and Time*. It was a dynamite story about the U.S. military using lethal nerve gas during the Vietnam War. But the story set off a different kind of explosion than was expected in the Atlanta headquarters of CNN. The story wasn't accurate, and several CNN producers lost their jobs in the fallout.

According to the investigative report voiced by one of CNN's top journalists, Peter Arnett, the U.S. conducted a raid into Laos that used nerve gas to kill American defectors. It was a sensational exposé that CNN executives hoped would impress audiences and bring high ratings to its new series that would rival the likes of CBS' *60 Minutes*, NBC's *Dateline*, and ABC's *Prime Time Live*.

The only trouble with the story was that no solid evidence supported that the incident in Laos ever happened. After the program aired, so many questions arose about the story's validity that CNN hired an outside team of investigators to check on its investigators. Less than two weeks later, the team reported: "CNN's conclusion that United States troops used nerve gas during the Vietnamese conflict on a mission in Laos designed to kill American defectors is insupportable."

CNN was forced to retract the story and apologize for a broadcast that had drawn on some of its best talent. In addition to Arnett, the network had involved veteran journalists Jeff Greenfield and Bernard Shaw in the investigative report. The producer of the story, April Oliver, her senior producer Jack Smith, and executive producer Pamela Hill lost their jobs. *Time* magazine, which ran its own version of the story, also had to apologize.

Pulitzer Prize–winning journalist Peter Arnett, who was not fired but no longer reported for CNN, was criticized for insisting he was simply a mouthpiece who bore no responsibility for reporting the story. That statement set off a new debate about just how much involvement celebrity broadcast journalists such as Mike Wallace, Ed Bradley, and Diane Sawyer have in the stories they voice.

Although the public no doubt believes the reporters' involvement is significant, the truth is that producers historically have done most of the work on all investigative reports, developing the storyline, digging for facts, and pre-interviewing those individuals involved in the investigation before they appear on camera with the celebrity reporters. The networks have always been guilty of perpetuating the idea that their stars are much more involved

**Case Study 4: continued**

in the investigative reports than they really are and of downplaying the role of producers who number in the 30s or more on many of the investigative units at the networks. Peter Arnett may have a point.

But how could a story like "Valley of Death" get on CNN and in *Time* magazine when little evidence corroborated the story. Much of the blame seems to rest with editors and top executives who didn't ask enough questions about the story when it was being developed. Too much reliance was placed on the integrity of the staff that was working on the story. Oliver, Hill, and Smith had good track records. They were good journalists and their editors trusted them. In this case that trust—the failure to pay enough attention to the story in its development and final stages—would burn them.

Ted Gup, a former investigative reporter for *Time*, who now teaches journalism at Georgetown University, says the "Valley of Death" fiasco should not be dismissed as an aberration. He says the controversy "represents most ominously of all, with the media at large, a very disturbing trend of senior editors increasingly becoming more gullible, and a tendency for more and more journalists to work in the realm of possibility rather than truth."

## Too Many Investigative Reports on TV?

Referring to some of the cases above and others that raise serious questions about media practices, the *Columbia Journalism Review* (CJR) said the 1990s were a humbling time for journalism, particularly investigative television journalism. CJR noted that an NBC news magazine had to apologize for its fakery in the investigation of General Motors trucks, and ABC and CBS both backed down under pressure from tobacco corporations, with ABC settling out of court a $10 billion libel suit and apologizing on air.

CJR also referred to a misguided investigative report by WCCO-TV about Northwest Airlines, for which the station won an Emmy award. Northwest charged that WCCO had painted a "distorted, untruthful picture" of the carrier's safety practices. The Minnesota News Council, a private watchdog group, upheld the airline's complaint. No monetary damages were involved, but the TV station was badly bruised, according to CJR.

CJR also writes that many journalists mistakenly assume that the First Amendment protects reporters wherever they choose to go, whatever they may do in pursuit of a story. Courts have never supported these assumptions, says CJR. The journal says one way to react to all the court actions resulting from investigative stories in the 1990s may be to ask whether such journalism on television—whether intended to serve the public or lift ratings—is too often brittle, showy, and mean-spirited, besides dancing along the edge of the law.

One such story involved the *Cincinnati Inquirer* and Chiquita Brands International. In 1998, the *Inquirer* published an investigative report about the company, in which it accused Chiquita of bribing foreign officials, mistreating its Central American workers, and using illegal means to circumvent foreign laws forbidding land ownership.

But in less than two months, the newspaper shocked the journalism world with an unusual front-page apology, renouncing the story and announcing that it would pay Chiquita in excess of $10 million.

## Ambush Interviews

The type of interview described by Spain earlier in this chapter regarding the delinquent father who was hounded—an *ambush interview*—is often used by TV reporters, although the technique has received much criticism. As the name implies, reporters who are unable to schedule an interview with an individual often stake out the person's home or office until they are able to ambush the person as he or she comes into or goes out of the building. We have all seen such interviews. The reporter and cameraperson force themselves on the individual, trying to shoot video and ask questions as the person tries to escape. Is this reporting technique appropriate?

*ABC News* correspondent Barry Serafin says an ambush interview is justified only when there's "a genuine public accountability involved. Sometimes you cannot allow a person in public office to refuse to talk to you; you really have to get to the person and make him accountable." Serafin recalled that, during Watergate, journalists "would do an ambush or whatever else it took to get some information."

John Spain says he does not like the ambush interview unless, as Serafin notes, it involves the public interest. "If we have made every effort to interview an individual and have been denied access," says Spain, "we would do an ambush. If you raise your hand and take an oath," he adds, "you have an obligation to answer to the public."

*60 Minutes* co-editor Lesley Stahl recalls that when she was covering the White House during the Watergate scandal, she was assigned to numerous stakeouts, a polite phrase for ambush interviews. Or, as Stahl described it in her book, *Reporting Live* (Simon & Schuster, 1999): "an opportunity for reporters to relinquish their dignity by loitering around someone's office or house waiting to ask a question the target wants to avoid." Stahl said the stakeout became a prime tool of newsgathering once Woodward and Bernstein had guided the Watergate story into the Nixon White House.

Stahl said it was difficult to reach anyone close to Nixon, so CBS decided to intercept the principals at their homes before they left for work in the morning. In her book *Reporting Live*, she writes: "I was one of the instru-ments through which CBS practiced this degrading form of journalism, chosen because I was too new to say no." She said, "I became a *stakeout queen*."

Stahl said it wasn't unusual for her to catch many of the Watergate suspects in their pajamas as they opened their doors to pick up *The Washington Post*. The assignment desk told Stahl to be at the homes before the sun came up. She said it was dirty work, especially when wives came running after you in their bathrobes, hollering, "get off my lawn." Stahl recalled how one day she was sent to stake out Jeb Magruder, deputy director of the Nixon campaign, and she asked his children as they walked to school if their father was still at home. She said Gail Magruder "tore out of the house and chewed my face off." She was right, said Stahl.

On another occasion, Stahl was told to stake out the home of Justice William O. Douglas for a profile that legal correspondent Fred Graham was doing. The desk said they wanted pictures of the justice jogging. When Stahl protested that Douglas was 75 years old and it was hailing out, the assignment editor said con-descendingly, "If you knew more about this town, kid, you'd realize that Douglas is a great outdoorsman and if he doesn't jog, he'll be out there walking his dog, so get there before the sun comes up. Stahl said the crew was just delighted to be sitting in the dark at 5:30 A.M. in front of Douglas's house with hail banging on the car roof. She said the crew blamed her. Nothing happened outside the house until four hours later. "You have to have an iron bladder," she noted, "to be a good staker-outer."

Stahl said Watergate changed journalism forever. She said it introduced an era of reporting through anonymous sources and ushered in a "swarm-around-'em mentality" where reporters and camerapersons hounded people. She called it "undignified and lacking decorum." She added: "It [the practice] reduced our standing with the public."

Stahl said that from Watergate on, nearly every government utterance would be subject to skeptical scrutiny; the assumption was that government offi-cials skirt the truth. Before Watergate, Stahl pointed out that presidents had been protected by newsmen: Franklin D. Roosevelt's wheelchair and John F. Kennedy's women had gone unreported. Hereafter, said Stahl, "presidents would view the press as a squad in a perpetual adversarial crouch, always ready to pounce."

# Reenactments

Considerable debate has been generated over the use of reenactments of events to tell a news story. Most news directors frown on the technique, but some see nothing wrong with them as long as they are clearly designated as such with a supertitle plainly stating "This is a reenactment."

The most important ethical consideration in the use of reenactments is that they should not confuse the audience about what they are looking at. Viewers should be able to determine quickly which scenes are actual and which are reenactments.

Some news directors believe reenactments have no place in news. As one news director puts it, "Let the *Hard Copy* people do the reenactment."

## Crime-Stoppers

The TV program designed to help police catch criminals sometimes uses reenactments of the very worst kind. In two examples aired in Baton Rouge, the TV station provided the TV cameras as actors provided by the police and the local branch of Crime-Stoppers reenacted the actual crimes for the TV audience. As in any major city, some of the crime is carried out by African Americans, including the two crimes depicted in the Crime-Stoppers segments. But the reenactments raised serious ethical issues because the actors who were selected for the videotaping were African American and no effort was made to disguise their race.

In one episode, two African-American males were videotaped jumping over the counter in a bank, where they grabbed money from teller drawers before escaping. As was discussed in this book earlier, the race of people involved in criminal activity should never be disclosed unless police are looking for the suspects and race can help in identifying them; however, showing two black actors jumping over a railing in a bank can hardly help viewers identify the two men who actually committed the crime.

In a second Crime-Stopper reenactment, an African-American couple was engaged to play the roles of two victims of a bedroom shooting. Two additional black people were provided to act as the perpetrators. Although both men wore ski masks, it was obvious they were black. After the shooting, the men were filmed fleeing the room.

When I questioned spokespeople at the TV station and for Crime-Stoppers, they were clear that they had no intention of trying to hide the racial identity of the actors in the reenactments; quite the contrary. "We knew they were African Americans," said the Crime-Stoppers spokesperson—who was not a journalist, by the way—"so why would we keep that secret?" he asked. When I pointed out that just showing two black actors in a reenactment of a crime would be of no use in solving a crime, the spokesman said, "Well, we get results."

The TV news spokesperson said basically the same thing, that Crime-Stoppers reduces crime and the station believes its reenactments are effective. At the same time, the spokesperson acknowledged that his newsroom normally does not identify the race of a suspect in its copy or voiceover stories about a crime, an inconsistency in this writer's opinion.

# Staging

Another serious ethical concern is *staging*, the faking of video or sound or any other aspect of a story. Staging can and should be a cause for dismissal. Ironically, some reporters see little harm in staging if the staging is accurate. "What's wrong," one reporter asks, "if you round up protesters at an abortion clinic who may be out to lunch and get them shouting again? That's what they would be doing after lunch, anyway."

It is not the same, and reporters who think that way pose a serious threat to their news organizations. Many other kinds of staging go on all too often. All of them are unethical. Here are a few examples:

- A reporter misses a news conference, so he asks the newsmaker to repeat a few of the remarks he made and pretends the sound bites actually came from the news conference.
- A news crew goes to a park to film some children playing on swings and seesaws, but there are none there. A cameraperson is sent to find some children.
- A reporter doing a story about drugs on campus needs some video to support the story, so he asks a student he knows to "set up" a group smoking marijuana in a dorm room.
- A documentary unit doing a story on crime asks police officers in a patrol car to make a few passes by the camera with the sirens blasting.

Harmless deceptions? Perhaps. But where does staging end? If reporters are willing to set up a marijuana party, is there anything that they would feel uncomfortable about staging?

Surprisingly, some of our best correspondents sometimes allow themselves to get caught up in such deceptions. *ABC News* correspondent Cokie Roberts did a report showing the capitol dome behind her, but she was not at the capitol, she was in the studio and a picture of the capitol was chroma-keyed behind her. Because she was wearing a winter coat at the time, there is no doubt that she and her executive producer, Rick Kaplan, intended the audience to believe that Roberts was doing her report in front of the capitol.

"So, what's the harm?" one might ask. Filing the report from the studio rather than in front of the capitol had no effect on the story's content. Commenting on the deception, Irv Kass, news director of KNSD-TV in San Diego, says journalists are "in the business of telling the truth. Every time a journalist deceives the public, it hurts our credibility."

Kass notes that both the ABC correspondent and the producer are experienced journalists who will "probably think twice about playing another trick on the viewers." He added that both people should have been given more than just a reprimand, as was the case, for their deception. *ABC News* vice president Richard Ward said the two "made a mistake."

Kass said that what bothers him most about the chroma-key trick is the message ABC sends to young people starting out in the business: "If *World News Tonight* fakes it, maybe we should too."

A more dramatic example of dishonest journalism was *Dateline*'s rigging of a General Motors' pickup truck with small rockets to make the gas tank explode. In that case, a few executives at NBC did lose their jobs, including News President Michael Gartner.

Some news directors insist that staging is never acceptable; others are more flexible. For example, if a reporter arrives to do a feature story about a pizza parlor that claims to make the largest pizzas in the city and discovers no one in the restaurant has ordered the large size, it would be permissible to have a pizza made to show on camera; however, the reporter also should note in the story that while she was in the restaurant, no one actually ordered one of the big pizzas.

Few news directors would object to a reporter asking a clerk in the IRS office to accompany her to the racks displaying various tax forms so that the camera-person would have an appropriate background for the interview. This activity is not really considered staging but setting up a shot, and it is viewed as acceptable. The same would be true, of course, if the crew moved the furniture in the office of someone to be interviewed on camera so that the cameraperson could get a better shot.

# "Unnatural" Sound

Natural sound is one of the most effective tools used by broadcast journalists. No one wants to see children riding down a hill on sleds without hearing their shouts, and video of a marching band would not be interesting without the music. What does a reporter do, however, when the audio recorder or camera does not pick up the sound? Should the reporter add "unnatural sound," that is, sound effects? Sound-effect tapes and records are available to match just about any activity. Certainly, the sound of laughing children is available. The reporter might not be able to match exactly the music the band in the parade was playing, but how many people would know the difference?

The answer to these questions is that such use of sound effects would be unethical. The same goes for dubbing in any natural sound that the recorder might have missed at the scene of a story. If the sound of fire engines was lost at the scene, that's unfortunate; the answer is not to substitute sound effects. It would be better for the reporter or anchor to admit to the audience that there were sound problems on the story.

# Video Deception

Most TV stations maintain a videotape library that includes footage of events going back several years. Most stations pull some of that video, known as *generic footage*, when they need shots of a general nature to cover portions of the script. Some stations routinely superimpose the words *file footage* over such video, but other stations run the video without any such admission unless it's obvious that the video is dated.

Most journalists have no problem using file footage of people walking down the street or shots of cars and trucks rolling down the highway if it works with the script; however, pulling old video from the morgue about disturbances in the Little Haiti section of Miami for a story about a new outbreak of violence in that neighborhood would be deceptive unless the audience knew the difference between the old and new footage they were watching. Instead of the font "file footage," many news directors insist that the file footage have the original date superimposed over the old video.

TV stations usually do not plan to deceive the audience when they use old footage; they are just careless. There have been examples of deliberate deception over the years, however; instances when old war footage was used, for example, to cover new fighting. In some cases, stations have used footage of a completely different war to go along with a story on fighting in another country. Such deception, if discovered (and it often is), could cause the station to lose its license.

# Improper Editing

Video and audio recordings are rarely accepted in court cases because they can easily be doctored. As one audio engineer puts it: "With enough time, I can make people say anything I want." Most of the time, the distortion of people's comments on radio and television is not intentional; the tape is just poorly edited. There have been many cases in which people who have been interviewed by radio and TV reporters complained that the editing changed the meaning of their comments. By clipping or editing a statement, they charged, the editing distorted the point they were trying to make. A reporter or producer intent on showing someone in a certain light can accomplish that goal rather easily. The error of omission is a serious concern. The individual's remarks could certainly be distorted by picking up one part of a person's statement and ignoring an equally important part of it.

When tape must be edited for time purposes (which is almost always the case), the reporter or producer must ensure that the sound bite is representative of what the person said. If it is not, it is essential that in narration following the bite, the reporter accurately sum up the part of the sound bite that was eliminated.

# Avoiding Jump Cuts

Some of the tricks employed in the editing process also raise ethical questions. In order to avoid *jump cuts*—the jerking of the head that occurs when video cuts are juxtaposed—film editors (it started long before the advent of video) came up with cutaways, reversals, and reverse questions.

These techniques are designed to cover up video edits. Editors, producers, and everyone else in the newsroom defend the use of most of these techniques because they make the finished product much smoother to watch. "Who wants to watch a head jumping across the screen?" is the answer editors give for using a cutaway, or a reverse shot. It is hard to argue with that response. Such techniques are not completely honest because the audience usually does not realize what the editors are doing. In an effort to avoid jump cuts, editors also distract the audience's attention from what the editors are doing by inserting other video between the edited material.

In a *cutaway*, it appears that the cameraperson just decided in the middle of an interview or speech to show the TV audience that the room was crowded with spectators and reporters. This cutaway shot may show another cameraperson shooting the scene, or a reporter scribbling in a notepad, or just a row of the audience. That shot makes it possible for the editor to take part of the video comment and marry it to any other video comment made by an individual while he or she was speaking. The first part might have been at the beginning of the speech, while the second comment might have been made 10 or 21 minutes later.

"So what? There's nothing dishonest about that," is the response from many editors. In general there probably isn't anything dishonest about this technique if one accepts that it is not necessary for the audience to know that the tape was edited. The real harm comes when the video is badly edited and does not accurately represent what the individual said during the interview or speech and the audience has no way of knowing this.

Another editing technique used to avoid jump cuts is the *reversal*, also referred to as a *reverse shot* or *listening shot*. After completing an interview, the reporter pretends to be listening to the interviewee while the cameraperson takes some shots of the reporter. The worst examples show the reporters smiling and nodding their heads in agreement. These shots then are sandwiched between two bites of the interview and, again, the audience usually believes that the cameraperson simply decided to take a picture of the reporter at that point in the interview or believes there were two cameras in the room.

One key scene in the Hollywood film *Broadcast News* deals with the unethical use of the reverse shot. In the film, an ethically minded TV news producer breaks off a relationship with an anchor-reporter because he used a reverse shot of himself crying in the middle of an interview when he actually had not cried during the interview itself. A cameraperson took the crying shot later—that was outright deception.

Fortunately, such examples are not typical of the reverse shots that appear in TV news stories. Most objections to the reverse shot are not about deception but about concern over the audience's inability to discern that the video has been edited.

The most dangerous technique, which is not as popular as it once was, is the *reverse question*. A reverse question is one the reporter asks a second time after the interview has been completed. The camera is facing the reporter this time. The technique allows the editor to avoid a jump cut by inserting video and audio of the reporter asking the question. The problem occurs when the reporter does not ask the question exactly the same way the second time.

Newsmakers themselves have sometimes complained about reverse questions when they realized that the questions they heard on their televisions were not exactly the same as those they were asked when they were in front of the camera. If any change at all is made in the second version of the question, it could be a serious ethical issue. Most newsrooms have stopped using reverse questions.

Producers and news directors who routinely allow the use of such techniques sometimes draw the line when the president or some other top official is making an important policy statement. In such cases, many producers allow the jump cut—particularly if it is not jarring—so that the audience knows that the remarks by the chief executive or other official have been edited. Instead of using a jump cut, some producers prefer to use a wipe between bites.

# Inflating the News

Reporters must attempt to keep a news story in perspective. Otherwise, it is easy to give the audience the wrong impression about what is actually happening. As mentioned earlier, a reporter should never stage video by rounding up demonstrators who were on a lunch break; however, let's assume that when the reporter showed up, the protest was in full swing. Did the presence of the camera have an effect on the demonstration? Did the shouting suddenly get louder? If the camera did have an effect on the crowd, which would not be unusual, the audience might get the wrong impression. In such a case, it might be appropriate for the reporter to make a statement such as the following:

> Actually, the turnout for the demonstration was smaller than was predicted . . . and our camera seemed to encourage some in the crowd to whip it up just a bit more than when we first arrived.

It is also important for the cameraperson to show accurately what was going on at the scene. If there were only a half-dozen demonstrators, the audience might, again, get the wrong impression if the camera shot used was a closeup, when a wide shot would have revealed that the group was small.

# Will the Real Reporter Please Stand Up?

There always has been a certain amount of glorification of anchors in broad-casting, and there's a growing tendency to give more credit to anchors and less to those who actually do the work. It's common practice for producers and writers to write copy for anchors. Everyone knows about this practice, and there's no ethical issue involved, even though a portion of the audience proba-bly thinks anchors write their own copy. Many do write part of it; however, some journalists are concerned about the growing practice of using writers and pro-ducers to prepare packages that make use of the anchor's voice; packages that, some would argue, would best be prepared by reporters. Part of the problem, of course, is that some stations are cutting back on their reporting staffs and are compensating for the loss by having writers and producers handle some of the work reporters once did, without leaving the newsroom. Is this deception?

Bill Small, former senior vice president of CBS News, says it's "always improper if you leave the impression that you covered a story when you didn't." Small notes, however, that at CBS and other networks it isn't "uncommon" for producers to do most of the work on some stories. It's routine for producers to conduct an interview in advance of a correspondent's arrival on the scene to "tie it all together."

Small is also concerned about the proliferation of material available to broadcast stations via satellite and the increasing use of the same syndication video by all the networks. "I'm a firm believer that there shouldn't be one story for all the networks," he says. "Each one should do its own." Small is even more annoyed by video news releases, which he calls "handout journalism." He says that if any of this material is picked up, its source should be properly identified.

Professor Robert Mulholland, former president of NBC and now chair of the Medill School of Journalism at Northwestern University, shares some of Small's concerns, particularly on the question of anchors and reporters voicing-over syn-dicated video. Mulholland asks: "How do you know that the video was honestly gathered or edited?" "Things get up on a satellite," he says, "and everybody brings it down. The days when you only broadcast news that your own employ-ees gathered is pretty much gone. . . . The gathering of news has become a pool process, and that disturbs me."

Rob Sunde, former news director of the ABC Information Network, also is concerned about these issues. Regarding the question of writers and producers doing packages that the audience thinks are the product of anchors, Sunde says: "Everyone involved is cheated; those involved in the production and those at home receiving it." He adds: "When we see reporters at the scene, we expect that they covered the story, giving us what they saw, heard, felt, smelled. That's reporting. When someone else takes credit for that or pretends that he or she did the work, that's unethical."

Sunde says one of the worst examples of unethical conduct that he recalls was when a radio reporter for a network used two different names so that he could report for another news group.

# Summary

The title of this chapter, "Ethics and the Law," indicates that the two are sometimes difficult to separate. Accuracy is an ethical journalistic concern, but when information in a story is inaccurate because of bias or carelessness, it can also become a legal issue—libel.

Likewise, the use of certain undercover devices by reporters, such as hidden microphones and cameras, raises ethical questions that must be resolved by each newsperson or news manager. Their use also has legal implications because, in some states, it is forbidden. Certainly, the argument used by many journalists that you "do what you have to do" to catch someone breaking the law or deceiving the public seems reasonable on the surface; however, many reporters believe that they must stay within the law or they are not acting much better than those they are investigating.

Many reporters admit that they "bend" the rules. For example, former *CBS News* correspondent Robert McKeown (now with *Dateline NBC*) misrepresented himself as a soldier in order to get at what he called the "truth" during the Gulf War. A strong argument could be made that the American people had a right to know what was going on during the conflict when the military was less than honest in dealing with the media. Was it wrong for McKeown to circumvent military rules to get his story on the air? Perhaps McKeown expresses it best when he says, "Everyone has a gut feeling about what is right and wrong" when it comes to ethics.

# Review Questions

1. Should reporters ever accept gifts? Discuss this issue.
2. When does accuracy become an ethical issue?
3. What are the defenses against libel? Do they always work?
4. Explain the term *false light*.
5. Name some of the controversial techniques employed by investigative reporters.
6. All ethical journalists are opposed to staging the news. Give some examples of such unethical behavior.
7. For what purpose are reversals used by most TV stations? Is there anything unethical about them?

# Exercises

1. Ask two or more reporters from radio and TV stations to take part in a discussion of controversial techniques used by some investigative reporters. It might be a

good idea to record the session so that it can be played for other classes to get their reactions.

2. Which of the following statements do you think could be considered libelous, and why? Would the defense have any arguments acceptable to the courts? Explain.

The governor drinks so much it's a wonder that he gets any work done.
Part of the governor's problem is that his wife is a drunk.
The governor is a lazy, good-for-nothing fake.
If the governor would stay at home more instead of running around with women, he wouldn't be in such hot water with the voters.

3. Suppose you are a TV reporter assigned to a demonstration. When the assignment editor sent you out, the demonstrators were shouting and waving fists. When you arrived, however, they had stopped for lunch, except for one person who continued to picket. How would you and your cameraperson handle the situation?

# **21** More Ethical Issues

## Cameras in the Courtroom

The use of cameras in courtrooms has raised serious questions about journalistic ethics and the responsibility of the broadcast media, particularly television. The issue of whether to allow camera coverage of trials has been a continuing debate, and it reached its peak with the double-murder trial of O.J. Simpson. TV news representatives generally argue that cameras should be allowed in courtrooms. Those opposed to the idea argue that the cameras compromise the rights and privacy of everyone involved in a trial and could have an impact on the outcome of the trial itself, issues that were clearly defined at the start of the Simpson trial. Even in states where cameras are allowed to record the proceedings, the cameras are operated on a pool basis to minimize the intrusion. The jury is not shown.

There also are a variety of restrictions in most of the states where cameras are allowed. In some states, the judge decides; in others, everyone involved in the case must agree to allow the cameras; in still other states, the decision depends on the nature of the case. And in some states, cameras are permitted only in certain courts. Sound confusing? It is. There is absolutely no consensus on the role of cameras in courtrooms, but those advocating their presence have made significant progress in the past few years.

As just noted, questions about the efficacy of cameras in courtrooms reached a peak during the murder trial of sports hero O.J. Simpson. Superior Court Justice Lance Ito agreed to permit cameras in the Los Angeles courtroom, but even before the jury was selected, he started to have second thoughts about *all* the media coverage. Ito threatened to ban all broadcast coverage of the trial after KNBC-TV reported erroneously that DNA tests showed that Nicole Brown's blood was found on one of Simpson's socks. He said the story was "detrimental to Mr. Simpson's right to a fair trial and it is fundamentally unfair." Judge Ito decided to allow the cameras to remain in the courtroom, but only after threatening to bar them completely.

Few people believed that Judge Ito had the power to terminate media coverage of the trial, which is protected by the First Amendment, but he certainly had the right to forbid cameras in the courtroom. Like the rules in 12 other states, California statutes give judges the power to permit or bar cameras in court.

In South Carolina, the judge in the murder trial of Susan Smith—charged in the drowning deaths of her two children—barred cameras from the court. Judge William Howard said the cameras would have a "chilling effect" on the trial.

## Pros and Cons

What are the advantages and disadvantages of allowing cameras in court? The most obvious reason for cameras, in the opinion of most of the media, is the "public's right to know," which is guaranteed by the First Amendment. Others argued that coverage of the Simpson trial would educate the American people on how the jurisprudence system works.

**Figure 21.1** O.J. Simpson confers with one of his attorneys during his murder trial in Los Angeles. (AP/World Wide Photo)

Cynthia Tucker, writing in the *Cleveland Plain Dealer*, said the only problem with that theory is that "it is not true." She said: "You will learn precious little about the average criminal case from watching the Simpson trial." She added: "You will learn, instead, about the particular justice that is dispensed when a wealthy celebrity is charged with a horrendous crime." Tucker said, "If you want to learn about the average murder trial, you'd be better off spending a month or two in your local county courthouse."

The most important argument against allowing cameras in the courtroom is that the coverage may impact the trial itself and the defendant's right to a fair trial. It is not easy to determine the effects of the live camera in the courtroom, but the acquittal of Simpson of all murder charges made it plain that it did not impact on his right to a fair trial.

## Do Cameras Influence Witnesses?

Elizabeth Semel, a prominent San Diego defense attorney, said she believes cameras change the performances of witnesses. "Who is the audience for the witness?" asked Semel. She said: "*Audience* is a troubling word, but if there is an audience, it should be the jury and not the camera."

That view is shared by Professor Norman Karlin of Southwest Law School. "Lawyers," he said, "tend to 'play' to a camera"; however, a three-year experiment regarding television coverage in selected cities completed by the federal court system showed that cameras had little effect on trial participants, courtroom decorum, or any other aspects of the trials. Regardless of that survey, the federal court system decided to resume its total ban on TV cameras in federal courts. A spokesperson said federal judges remain concerned about the impact that cameras would have on trials. And the circus-like atmosphere brought about by the cameras in the O.J. case will most certainly be a negative factor in their future use in all courts.

Writing in *USA Today*, Tony Mauro said the Simpson case was the "severest test of the right to a fair trial in recent memory." He said the trial became "tangled because of the unprecedented wash of pretrial publicity, the unpredictable effects of Simpson's fame and money, and issues of race and domestic abuse."

No other trial since the advent of television had such a mix of ingredients and was based so strongly on circumstantial evidence. As New Yorker's Jeffrey Toobin observed, the case combined "everything—sex, race, violence, celebrities, sports and the only eyewitness was a dog."

Although many authorities generally favor TV cameras in court, many believe the Simpson trial may have been a special case, warranting different rules. Jay Wright, a communications law professor at Syracuse University, said the difficulties that Judge Ito faced in trying to protect Simpson's fair trial rights were so great that he could not treat it as an ordinary case.

In a column in the *Seattle Times*, Don Williamson referred to the Simpson trial as a "Hollywood re-enactment of a multimedia circus masquerading as

**Figure 21.2**   Police follow the infamous white Bronco in the so-called nonchase of O.J. Simpson in Los Angeles. (AP World Wide Photo)

news coverage." Williamson said the TV coverage, beginning with the "nonchase" involving Simpson and his best friend, Al Cowlings, was a "travesty."

What frightened him most, the columnist said, was that the news coverage never let up. He said the media "was driven to keep pumping out the O.J. stories even when there was no news to report." Williamson said it had nothing to do with "the people's right to know" but instead everyone "trying to out-do the competition." He said he's "angry, embarrassed, and deeply concerned that there is something very wrong with this news business that has been my only job for all of my adult life."

CBS *Evening News* anchor, Dan Rather, said the Simpson story was "overcovered . . . in many instances very well covered, and in some instances, atrociously covered." Rather described the trial as "a great story." He said he was not surprised that people were interested in it and, to a certain degree, "mesmerized."

Jane Pauley of *Dateline* said she doesn't think the media has "the liberty of deciding when we've covered something too much." She added: "You cover it to the degree that people are interested. And we're all a little embarrassed at the interest we take in it." Pauley admitted that, when she could, she followed the trial on her computer in her office, getting the transcripts of the trial virtually in real time, when colleagues and staff thought she was working.

The late *CBS News* correspondent Charles Kuralt said he didn't criticize the news media for overcovering the Simpson story. Kuralt said he couldn't imagine a time when a story like this "wouldn't have excited people's imagination, made them want to know more, made them yearn to know the outcome." He added: "It's not so much about journalism as it says something about human nature."

Although CNN was the only network to carry the trial from beginning to end, all of the networks devoted substantial amounts of time to the story, situating correspondents and cameras at strategic locations outside the courthouse. Writing in *Esquire*, John Tyler said the Simpson trial became a "modern pagan spectacle." He noted that to get an unimpeded view of the courthouse and a sweeping cutaway shot of the glass-towered banking district, every network had to construct a skybox on the parking lot adjacent to the courthouse that was higher than the ones in front. "They were staggered, taller and taller, toward the rear of the lot," observed Tyler, "until those at the very back soared some five stories into the air."

The skyboxes were made of construction scaffolding with white canvas awnings and the "spindly, swaying edifices resembled primitive burial towers," said Tyler. "The correspondents broadcasting live to the morning talk shows seemed like some officiating priestly caste." Tyler said the crowd was drawn to the courthouse "the way a solar eclipse or stunning planetary conjunction could compel ancient tribes to gather at the temple."

Jeff Greenfield, a reporter for ABC News and a syndicated columnist, described the scene outside the Los Angeles courthouse as the "media's Chernobyl." He suggested that if Judge Ito had thrown out the cameras there may have been a "less hysterical approach to the story by the schlock end of our business."

## The Fourth Amendment

In an article in *Playboy*, former Los Angeles Deputy District Attorney Vincent Bugliosi agreed that the Simpson trial had a "faintly festive atmosphere . . . and the TV coverage contributed to this tawdry atmosphere." He said it "cheapens and devalues the whole (trial) process."

Bugliosi said he has "much more substantive reasons why I oppose cameras in the courtroom." He said a trial is a serious and solemn proceeding that determines whether a person's liberty, and sometimes his life, should be taken away from him. "Anything that interferes, or even has the slightest potential of interfering, with the resolution of this determination should be automatically prohibited," said Bugliosi.

As the famed prosecutor who convicted the Charles Manson clan, Bugliosi noted that most people are intensely self-conscious about speaking in public, and with cameras in the courtroom some are not going to be as natural. He said

**Figure 21.3**  Skyboxes used in O.J. Simpson trial.

they are either going to "be more shy and hesitant, or perhaps they will put on an act, not just in their demeanor but, much worse, in the words they use in their testimony." Bugliosi said when that happens, the "fact-finding process and the very purpose of the trial have been compromised."

As for the argument that televising the trial educates people, Bugliosi described that as "transparent sophistry. Their only motivation, though not an improper one, is commercial . . . it's a form of entertainment for them, pure and simple." Bugliosi repeated that "the sole purpose of a criminal trial is to determine whether or not the defendant is guilty of the crime. It is not to educate the public."

*The San Diego Union-Tribune* defended the use of cameras in court. It said the "hype and hysteria" surrounding the murder trial was not caused by the cameras in the courtroom but by "lawyers who want a favorable headline, by reporters who jump to print or broadcast without checking the facts, and by 'friends' with dollar signs in their eyes who are rushing to publish everything they know about the victims and the accused." The newspaper said the "sensationalism that infected media coverage of the trial occurred outside the courtroom—in newsrooms, TV studios, or off-the-record tips over the telephone. The hype comes from the decisions on how to cover the trial made by editors, publishers, producers, and directors."

Many media-watchers agreed that the trouble was not so much the TV inside the courtroom but the TV coverage outside. Judge Burton Roberts, who chaired a New York State panel that looked into the camera-in-court issue, said he believes that "the more public scrutiny there is of a defendant on trial ensures that defendant greater fairness." The judge said the camera also prevents the government "institutions such as the prosecutors and the judiciary from comporting themselves in a fashion which results in a defendant being treated unfairly." The New York State Legislature in 1995 continued the cameras-in-court experiment while rejecting an effort to make the statute permanent.

Los Angeles Municipal Judge Veronica McBeth, who supervises all of the city's criminal cases, agrees with Judge Roberts. McBeth says: "The more people that have information on what goes on in a democracy, the more they can form reasoned opinions."

Conversely, Paul Thaler, author of *The Watchful Eye* (Greenwood Publishing Group, 1994), which deals extensively with media coverage of trials and TV cameras in court, disagrees. He writes: "The media are not just a benign observer. They interfere with the system. And television is driving the other

**Figure 21.4**   A TV cameraman records the proceedings of a court hearing. (AP/World Wide Photos)

media." Thaler, a former reporter and director of journalism and media at Mercy College in New York, also questioned the premise that TV cameras in court are producing objective reality. Is it "reality . . . or the imagination of the producer or editor?" asked Thaler. He stressed that: "At stake . . . is the very linchpin of our democracy: the right to a fair trial, and to equal justice under the law." Thaler added: "Since it is the defendant who stands uniquely to suffer from excessive, intrusive, or skewed publicity, surely it should be the defendant's interests that are uppermost in any consideration of audiovisual coverage." Again, the acquittal of Simpson indicates the cameras were not a factor, at least for the defense.

"The televised trial," he said, "is a trial by entertainment values—the posturing of participants to create images, a world of sound bites and 'spin' in which nearly all are affected by entertainment factors." Thaler also contended that the camera creates more competition, and thus more premature and inaccurate reports.

## Don Hewitt Has Second Thoughts

One of the *giants* of the broadcast news industry, Don Hewitt, the executive producer of *60 Minutes*, says he's no longer sure that cameras in court are a good idea. He noted that "Although for years I favored cameras in courtrooms . . . the issue needs a lot more thought than people in my profession were willing to give it."

The veteran CBS newsman noted that "*Open to the public* doesn't have to mean *open to cameras.*" Hewitt said that broadcast journalists obviously have to be in courtrooms to "observe and report . . . we're reporters and that's what we do. But," he added, "letting cameras in court can turn a courtroom into a movie set."

In his strong criticism of the cameras at the O.J. Simpson trial, Hewitt asked: "Would freedom of the press suffer if there were no cameras? Would TV journalists again be second-class citizens if they had to go back to pad and pencil to cover this trial? No."

Hewitt said: "Even if TV does have the right to go anywhere it pleases . . . it doesn't have to stick its nose into every nook and cranny. An occasional door closed in our face," said Hewitt, "would be good for our souls and might even get some of us off our backsides and back to reporting instead of watching."

Hewitt observed that many reporters "will call me a turncoat," but in discussions with broadcast newspeople and educators during the past two years, I discovered that many of them agree with Hewitt, as does *this* author.

## Cameras Raise Other Issues

Another issue raised during the Simpson trial was the defendant's Fourteenth Amendment right to due process. In 1965, the Supreme Court reversed the conviction of Billy Sol Estes, an associate of the late President Lyndon Johnson, on swindling charges because of the extensive TV coverage of the trial. The court agreed that the televising of his trial had deprived Estes of his Fourteenth Amendment right. At the time, Texas was one of only a few states that had not banned TV cameras in court. Some attorneys believed if Simpson had been convicted that an appeal might have been based on the excessive media coverage of the trial.

The U.S. Supreme Court made broadcast history during the aftermath of Presidential Election 2000. For the first time, it released an audiotape of the legal arguments concerning the presidential election. The tape, recorded by the court, was broadcast to the nation almost immediately after the arguments ended. Although they released an audiotape, the justices turned down a request to permit live television and radio coverage of the proceeding.

Radio and Television News Directors' Association (RTNDA) President Barbara Cochran, who made the request on behalf of the broadcast media, called the release of the audiotape, "a great first step for electronic journalism, and, most important, for the public."

Arguments before the Florida Supreme Court, concerning Election 2000, were broadcast live on television and radio.

## Checkbook Journalism

Critics of the media coverage of the Simpson trial also strongly criticized checkbook journalism—the purchase of witnesses' statements. Admittedly, most purchases were made by the tabloid papers *and* TV programs that pose as news broadcasts—*The Enquirer*, *Current Affair*, and *Hard Copy*. Did these tabloids have any impact on the trial? Did they influence the jury decision in any way? Did it taint the witnesses in the trial?

*New Yorker* writer Jeffrey Toobin condemned the practice as a "disgrace to law." He said there was no good purpose to the tabloids' purchase of witness statements and "it does seriously damage cases . . . taints witnesses . . . and really makes their testimony less credible."

During a televised debate on the subject on *The Charlie Rose Show* (WNET—Educational Broadcasting Company), former prosecutor Toobin said that paying witnesses to publish their stories "undermines what prosecutors are able to do in court." Toobin says that repeated questioning of witnesses by the prosecution and defense is going to "generate inconsistencies," but paying for witnesses' statements is going to make the situation "infinitely worse because jurors aren't stupid. They know what *A Current Affair* . . . *Hard Copy*, and *The Enquirer* want out of people. They want scandal . . . sensation . . . and they'll jazz up a story to get that."

Attorney Raoul Felder, who also took part in the WNET debate, said he was not sure that media payments were always bad. He cited the incident in which people who worked in a store selling knives were paid to tell how they sold a knife to Simpson. The owner was paid $3,000 for his story and it was corroborated by three other people, who also got paid. But Felder said he didn't think "anybody thought he was not telling the truth."

Felder admitted that there seemed to be a question about whether another witness, Rosa Lopez, was telling the truth when she sold a story to a tabloid claiming that she saw Simpson's white Bronco parked on the street outside his home at the time of the murders. Toobin's argument was that a witness might tell a story one way and then change it after realizing that the tabloids would only pay for a story if it was told in a way that appealed to the public.

There was a lot of criticism about the media, particularly the tabloids, for paying for information in the JonBenét Ramsey murder case.

## Responsible Reporting

NPR correspondent Susan Stamberg says cable television has had such an impact on news, particularly at the network level, that "everyone is desperate. They're scrambling and as a result the level of public debate and decency is utterly debased. Life and death issues have become spectator sports, undermining the role of journalism. Tragedy, life, reality becomes an entertaining thing to turn on when you are eating dinner. That's where these electronic possibilities have brought us." Stamberg added: "It's almost that all we talk about is sex because it grabs the public's attention."

The late NBC correspondent Pauline Frederick was concerned about these things two decades ago when she told an RNTDA awards banquet that it seemed to her that "the standard for broadcasting should be what Walter Lippmann prescribed for statesmanship. Lippmann said, 'Statesmanship consists in giving the people not what they want but what they will learn to want.'"

Frederick asked if broadcasting was "exercising such statesmanship by offering details of rape, pillage, destruction, drugs, incest, life beyond the pill, teenage suicide, child molesting, battered parents, the degradation of people in pieces, and how to beat the system." Frederick said these subjects "sound like some of the titles for X-rated movies."

# Tabloid Journalism

Most critics place much of the responsibility for changing standards on the popularity of tabloid programs such as *Hard Copy*, *A Current Affair*, and *Inside Story*. The fact that these programs regularly follow local and network newscasts in many markets has blurred the real meaning of news for many viewers.

Former *CBS News* correspondent Betsy Aaron takes the analogy a step further. She says some of the things on network news are "worse than 'Hard Copy.' We're pretending we're 'Hard Copy' people, but we want to keep our clothes on, so we're born-again virgins every night." She says the theory is "We'll do the *Hard Copy* stories but we'll do them the right way."

In *Reporting Live* (Simon & Schuster, 1999), *60 Minutes* co-editor Lesley Stahl referred to the syndicated shows *Hard Copy*, *Inside Edition*, and *A Current Affair* as tabloid shows whose formats and style look like a network news broadcast. "The lines between these shows and us are blurring and it isn't just how we look. More and more we are covering their subject, the world of personality, the private lives of famous people are becoming our territory too, as the competition for ratings heated up."

*ABC News* correspondent Judy Muller notes in *Now This* (Putnam, 2000) that while the tabloid press covers what might be called "backyard fence journalism," that is the stuff "everybody's talking about and the mainstream press wanders into that backyard not only because of ratings but because editors and reporters are human and like a good story as much as anybody. At the same time," she adds, "hanging around the back fence for too long can warp our perspective."

Muller regretfully pointed out that the standard format for local news is usually a program chock full of crime, occasional high-speed chases, and many, many maudlin moments in which the anchors ad-lib, ad nauseum.

But Muller said not only local news is at fault. She said network news certainly has its own share of maudlin moments, like the deaths of JFK, Jr. and his wife, Carolyn Bessette, and her sister. She said that while the networks started out tastefully enough, the coverage degenerated into a weeklong wailing and gnashing of newsteeth, punctuated by the reporting of each successive sign (a floating suitcase, a medicine vial) confirming the obvious—that they were dead.

News Director Will Wright of WWOR-TV says there is an "appetite" for tabloid TV. "As stations try to survive the ratings war, they will try anything—they will tinker with formats and try new ideas to grab attention. There is an overwhelming pressure to make sure their jobs are secure. Ultimately," Wright says, "we do have to stay the course and do journalism the way it was meant to be done, with honesty, integrity, veracity and a sense of fairness."

John Spain agrees. He says that when a station is trying to find itself it looks at all sorts of opinions and may go for a "quick flash." He says, however, that the audience will ultimately reject that approach because it knows better.

# Taboo Subjects?

In the 1940s and 1950s, the word *rape* was not used on the air. The euphemism "criminal assault" was commonly used instead. Now, of course, rape is a frequent subject of discussion on talk shows and newscasts. In the earlier days of broadcasting, it would have been equally repugnant to refer to condoms on the air. Now, however, the broadcast debate on whether condoms should be distributed in schools is commonplace.

Even as late as the early 1960s, a radio talk-show host broke off an interview with an advocate of euthanasia because he was getting threats from listeners who warned that they were going to complain to the Federal Communications Commission (FCC) if he continued the discussion.

It is difficult to think of a subject that might be considered taboo for broadcast in the new millennium. The decisions on good taste normally reflect the policies of station management. Some stations are more conservative than others. If management thinks that certain language or subjects are not acceptable for broadcast, those feelings normally work their way down to the news department.

# The Fairness Doctrine

Like many of the issues discussed in this chapter and Chapter 20, fairness is both a legal and an ethical consideration. Until now we have concentrated on the ethical importance of fairness. Now let's consider the legal aspects. Do broadcast stations have a legal responsibility to be fair? Broadcast managers, the FCC, Congress, and numerous special interest groups have been fighting over that issue for decades.

In 1949, the FCC established the Fairness Doctrine, which said, in part, that broadcasters had an obligation to serve the public interest by "not refusing to broadcast opposing views where a demand is made of the station for broadcast time." It also said that licensees have a duty "to encourage and implement the broadcast of all sides of controversial issues."

Over the following years, the broadcast industry and the RTNDA applied extreme pressure on the FCC to eliminate the doctrine, arguing that because newspapers are not forced to present all sides of an issue, broadcasters should not be required to do so either. According to supporters of the Fairness Doctrine, the major distinction between newspapers and broadcasters is that the government, in selecting only one licensee for a frequency, is in effect limiting access to the airwaves, which have traditionally been considered the property of the public.

The Fairness Doctrine was challenged on occasion but was upheld in the courts. In 1964, in a landmark case known as *Red Lion* (which is described in detail in the next section), the Supreme Court upheld the doctrine. Over the intervening years, however, even the FCC itself questioned the Fairness Doctrine.

In 1984, twenty years after the Supreme Court ruling, the FCC, while finding that a TV station in Syracuse, New York, had violated the Fairness Doctrine, also acknowledged that the doctrine was not serving the public and was probably unconstitutional. The TV station, WTVH, and its owner, Meredith Broadcasting, used the FCC statement to challenge the Fairness Doctrine in the U.S. Court of Appeals. The court refused to decide the case, saying that the FCC had the power to eliminate the doctrine if it didn't like it. That's exactly what the FCC did; however, that did not end the issue. Strong support has always existed in Congress for the doctrine. In fact, Congress passed a bill in 1987 making the Fairness Doctrine law. The bill was vetoed by President Reagan.

The Fairness Doctrine got a new look in Congress and elsewhere, in 1995, because of the bombing of the federal building in Oklahoma City. President Clinton started a controversy when he accused certain broadcasters (not by name) of spreading hate on the airwaves. He appeared to be speaking of Oliver North, G. Gordon Liddy, Rush Limbaugh, and other right-wing commentators and talk-show hosts who criticize the government, often suggesting that strong action by President Clinton could increase antigovernment violence and spread hate that divides Americans.

Should these commentators go unchallenged? Should they be allowed to use the airwaves, which supposedly belong to all Americans, to urge radical and often violent behavior? The ultra-conservative broadcasters claim their First Amendment rights, and they have a legitimate point. But some people ask: Shouldn't those who oppose such views have a right to use the airwaves to express their opinions as well?

Pollsters tell us that about 20 percent of Americans strongly oppose any sort of government. How many of those people are capable of violence is, of course, unknown. But should those who feed that hatred of the government be allowed to espouse their views on radio and TV without allowing equal time for opposing views? The constitution and the First Amendment do *not* refer to fairness in speech, just to its protection.

Many people believe the Fairness Doctrine, when it was in force, was unconstitutional, and it may very well have been; however, one cannot help but wonder if our founding fathers were sitting around the table in Philadelphia today, would they add a line or two to the First Amendment after watching the coverage of the bomb attack on the federal building in Oklahoma City, and listening to convicted criminal G. Gordon Liddy speaking about "shooting federal agents in the head or groin," if they invaded one's domain.

Some radio and TV managers claim they carry liberal talk-show hosts to counter Rush Limbaugh, but, if they are, few Americans are familiar with these people.

When I speak with colleagues around the country—reporters, writers, former broadcast executives who are no longer in management—I do not hear the kind of opposition to the Fairness Doctrine that the RTNDA has been editorializing about for the past decade. The RTNDA described the failure of Congress, so far, to act on renewal of the Fairness Doctrine as a "big win for electronic journalists." Wrong—it was a big win for broadcast owners, who do not wish to deal with the expense and annoyance of offering equal time. Fairness *should* be a journalistic concept, but it has become a *political* and *financial* issue. The Fairness Doctrine, if made law again, would greatly complicate matters for management, particularly in radio, which has discovered a gold mine in people like Limbaugh and other ultra-conservatives.

# The *Red Lion* Decision

The constitutionality of the Fairness Doctrine was tested in 1964 in the land-mark *Red Lion* case involving a New York writer, Fred Cook, and the Red Lion Broadcasting Company, which owned radio station WGGB in Red Lion, Pennsylvania.

In a broadcast aired by WGGB, the Reverend Billy James Hargis accused Cook of writing for a magazine that championed communist causes and of writing a book that was intended to destroy Senator Barry Goldwater. Cook demanded that the radio station give him airtime to reply. When the station refused, Cook asked the FCC to intervene. It did, ordering the station to give Cook free time. When WGGB management still refused to grant the time to Cook, the case ended up in the courts. It eventually reached the U.S. Supreme Court, which ruled that Cook had a right to the free time. The Court said that if anyone's "honesty, character, or integrity . . . is challenged on the air, the station must notify those attacked . . . and offer air time for reply." The Court ruling said the station must notify the individual or organization that was attacked even if the subject of the attack was unaware of it. The ruling requires stations to send a script or tape of what was said about the individual or group within seven days of the broadcast and to provide airtime for a reply.

# Invasion of Privacy

Privacy is defined generally as "the right to be let alone," and that concept has become increasingly more difficult with the *explosion* of the Information Age. The explosion was mainly the result of the development of a variety of electronic devices, particularly the computer. For broadcast journalists, microphones, tape recorders, cameras, and telephoto lenses have been wonderful additions to the practice of collecting news. But they also have caused their share of troubles when it comes to privacy.

The Constitution does not say anything about the right of privacy, at least by name; however, several amendments to the Constitution and the Declaration of Independence's demand for the right to "life, liberty, and the pursuit of hap-piness" make it clear that the founding fathers were concerned with privacy. Also, the Supreme Court for more than 40 years has recognized privacy as a constitutional right.

From a media perspective, the right to privacy often conflicts (as was pointed out in other parts of the book) with the First Amendment, freedom of the press, or the people's right to know. For example, the courts have found that it is not an invasion of privacy in most cases to take photographs or to use film and video cameras in a public place; however, the use of these same devices to get pic-tures in private places can, and often does, get broadcast journalists in trouble.

CBS was among those charged with such violations when a reporter and camera crew for the now-defunct *Street Stories* accompanied the Secret Service on a raid on a Brooklyn, New York, apartment, which was supposed to be the site for a credit card scheme. The Secret Service, apparently anxious to get a little publicity for its activities, invited the camera crew and reporter to follow agents as they crashed into the home of Babutunde Ayeni. He was not at home at the time, but his wife and four-year-old son were.

The agents had a search warrant, but Mrs. Ayeni was puzzled about the camera crew. She thought, quite naturally, that the camerapeople also were agents. She wanted to know why the raid was being taped. As it turned out, the agents found no evidence of any credit card scheme and said so on camera.

Writing about the incident, Cessna Catherine Winslow, a freelance writer, said that CBS News argued that because the reporter and crew had permission of federal agents to accompany them on the raid, they should be entitled to qualified immunity enjoyed by government officials. After that argument was dismissed, CBS settled out of court with the Ayeni family, who claimed that their rights were violated during the raid.

In explaining his refusal to dismiss the case, Federal District Court Judge Jack B. Weinstein chastised CBS and the federal agents, saying that "CBS had no greater right than that of a thief to be in the (Ayeni) home." The Judge further said: "The images, though created by the camera, are part of the household . . . and cannot be removed without permission or official right." He added: "The television tape was a seizure of information for non-governmental purposes," and "the case raises grave issues of the right to privacy in the home from the intruding eye and ear of a private broadcaster's camera."

One lawyer for the Ayeni family, Harry Batchelder, Jr., criticized programs in which TV crews "just blow in with agents and take everybody's photographs and say they have consent." The attorney for RTNDA agreed. Larry Scharff said the incident "calls into question many assumptions newspeople have about their legal right to accompany police and public officials onto private property." He warned journalists to be more sensitive about shooting stories on private property.

Videotaping in a public place also can be a problem for broadcast journalists. A CBS-owned station, WCBS-TV in New York, was sued after a camera crew and reporter entered a famous restaurant, Le Mistral, unannounced and began filming the interior of the restaurant and its customers. The film was for a series the reporter was doing on restaurant health code violations. The restaurant won its suit against CBS for invasion of privacy and trespass.

In summary, Broadcast journalists can photograph in public places, but if their behavior becomes overly intrusive, they also can find themselves in court.

# Elián Gonzalez

At age five, Elián Gonzalez made television news history. He is the Cuban boy who was rescued from the Atlantic ocean off the coast of Florida on Thanksgiving Day, floating in an inner tube. His mother and 10 others, who escaped Cuba with him, drowned when their boat sank. Thus began a saga that continued for seven months in which this child, during most of that time, starred on network and local television and other media.

He became "probably the most famous child on the face of the earth," Eason Jordan, the president of news gathering for CNN, told the *New York Times*. Was the coverage excessive? The *New York Times* Jim Rutenberg wrote: "It seems the television news divisions just couldn't get enough of Elián. But, then again, neither could the public."

Nary a day went by during a five-month period that the story was not covered on network television from the day Elián was rescued until the night armed federal agents spirited him away from his great-uncle's house in Miami so he could be reunited with his father. Rutenberg reported that on that day, the three major 24-hour news channels were in all-Elián-all-the-time mode. They were watched by household audiences three times as large as their average daily audiences the previous month. He cited Nielsen Media Research data for the basis of this statement.

On that day, Fox News Channel had the second largest rating in its three-year history, according to Nielsen data. News executives, defending the constant and unrelenting coverage, told the *Times* that the Elián saga had every element that drives people to watch TV news. They compared it to a storyline worthy of a soap opera. The networks devoted more time to the story than to either presidential candidate. "This is a drama, and it's a drama that is true," John Moody, vice president of news at the Fox TV Channel, told the *Times*.

Elián's survival story was amazing, beginning when he was rescued Thanksgiving Day, later telling how porpoises kept him afloat as he clung to the inner tube. In addition to the unusual human interest elements, the story involved President Clinton, Vice President Gore, Congress, Attorney General Janet Reno, Fidél Castro, the Supreme Court, Cuban-American relations, a political fight with implications in the presidential campaign, demonstrations in Miami and Havana, family relations, and a custody battle.

The battle pitted Elián's great-uncle in Miami against Elián's father, who lived in Cuba. His uncle had refused to turn over Elián to his father because he didn't want him to grow up in communist Cuba, despite a Justice Department order directing the uncle to release the boy. The Miami relatives fought that order all the way up to the Supreme Court, which refused to hear an appeal. Thus, after 217 days, the saga was over and Elián flew back to Cuba with his father.

The *New York Times* reported that Elián's departure for Cuba received live coverage from every news organization, with the all-news cable channels covering the story for most of a five-hour period and ABC, CBS, and NBC interrupting programming for about an hour during the departure. Steve Capus, executive producer of special coverage for MSNBC, told the *Times*: "In the cable news business, a day like this is what we live for." Of course, the coverage continued from Cuba.

The news coverage posed ethical issues. Reporter Edna Buchanan, in an essay for the *New York Times*, says television was used by Elián's Miami family. She describes this scene outside the house where Elián was kept:

> Close to 100 cameras dominate the neighborhood, lenses trained like weapons on the house 24 hours a day. But the scene is strangely quiet . . . Hours later, it's time for the television news. Protestors descend, charging the scene with tension. Elián appears outside the house, and the crowd cheers on cue. Upset by something, maddened supporters charge the barricades, and the police force them back. When the live TV shots are over, the protestors depart until the next newscast. Relatives rush across the street to the press encampment, interrupting shows in progress, announcing, "I want to go live," and would be accommodated.

Buchanan also maintains that after Elián was taken from the house by federal agents, "violence surged when cameras rolled." And she concluded: "The entire spectacle was a media event."

The Miami family fully expected the boy to be taken from them, but they wanted it to be televised live, writes *New York Times* Caryn James, in "Critics Corner." But it was not to be. Ironically, she said, a still photo became the "instant icon" of the television drama.

Where were the TV cameras? An NBC cameraperson, Tony Zombado, and a soundperson, providing pool coverage for the networks and cable channels, raced the agents to the door. But Zombado said he was roughed up by the agents and by the time he recovered, the three-minute raid was over. At one point, he said, a family member was pulling him into the house, while a federal agent was pulling him out.

The still photo seen around the world showed a federal agent in riot gear inside the house with a gun pointed in the direction of Elián in the arms of the man who had rescued him from the sea. It was shown over and over again all day, but rarely without the words "searing" and "chilling" attached, James said. Look at the picture. Is the gun pointed at Elián? Is the finger on the trigger? Both allegations were made that day.

Attorney General Janet Reno said the gun was not pointed at the child and the agent's finger was not on the trigger. Just the opposite view was presented in a televised tour of the house, featuring the man who was holding the boy.

Critic James praised Dan Rather of CBS for providing the "most cogent analysis, and reminding viewers that the circumstances behind the volatile picture had to be seen from two sides." On the other hand, she criticized NBC's Brian Williams, who said: "It's feared that this photograph will have an incendiary effect" and that the "excuse given by the federal government for the armaments" was that they had information that guns may have been in the house. James said: "The word 'excuse' may have been careless rather than deliberate, but it was characteristic of the tone that undercut any appearance of balance."

Pictures never lie. Or do they? James reports that CNN briefly showed a version of the photo that zoomed in to eliminate the man holding the boy, making the gun appear aimed at Elián, when in reality is wasn't. One wonders

**Figure 21.5**   The world's press corps focus their lenses on Cuban shipwreck victim 6-year-old Elián Gonzalez across the street from Elián's relatives' house. (Courtesy of Reuters/Rick Wilking/Archive Photos)

how much coverage would have been devoted to the story had little Elián not been so cute.

## Civic Journalism

In various parts of the book, including the two chapters on ethics and the following chapter on tabloid journalism, we indicate that journalism is in trouble. The American people do not have the same high regard for the media that they once did. The line between news and entertainment has narrowed. There has been an alarming increase in tabloid journalism and irresponsible reporting. In the minds of many serious newspeople, journalism is *broke* and needs some fixing. Many people believe that the media is no longer adequately serving the needs of the people.

One of those people who share this view is Ed Fouhy, a former network news executive who now is Executive Director of the Pew Center for Civic Journalism. Fouhy says one way to serve viewers is to provide what some people refer to as "civic journalism" or "public journalism." Fouhy says many stations are attempting to secure their future by getting more involved with their audiences, or what he calls "digging roots into the community, deeper than ever before." Fouhy said: "It's time for a fundamental change in the way we do our business, including how we define what news is and how we serve our viewers."

The former network executive cited as a positive example of change the news operation at WISC-TV in Madison, Wisconsin. He said one of the ways news director Tom Bier has dug roots into the community is by getting involved in the "we the people" project. Fouhy says the project is a "model of civic journalism."

Bier is a member of a journalistic roundtable that meets and picks an issue facing the state, such as financing the public schools or the choices in health care. The topic is then discussed at a televised town meeting on WISC-TV and the public radio and TV stations. Bier sees a need to get more involved in the community. "We live here," he says. "We send our kids to the public schools. We have a stake in the community."

Similar experiments have been going on in various parts of the nation: At WSOC-TV in Charlotte, North Carolina; WCTV in Tallahassee, Florida; WHAS-TV in Louisville, Kentucky; and KRON-TV in San Francisco. KRON shared the 1999 James K. Batten Award for Excellence in Civic Journalism for innovative efforts that produced in-depth journalism and paved the way for news organizations to play new roles in their communities.

"Each of the winners courageously and thoroughly explored a sensitive subject in ways that encouraged unprecedented levels of reader and viewer response," said Jan Schaffer, executive director of the Pew Center, which sponsored the awards.

In San Francisco, thousands of people engaged in an online conversation about race relations. "As a result," Schaffer said, "the one-way conversation of traditional journalism became an active dialogue that continued long after the journalism wound down."

KRON-TV launched "About Race," its year-long exploration of how race and ethnicity shape the Bay Area, with an unprecedented five-part series on the 6 P.M. newscast during a sweeps period. Coverage explored the genetics of race, diversity in the workplace and in schools, talking about race, and a look at efforts to bridge the racial divide. The TV station scheduled 18 other stories over the year, including a one-hour special. Collaborating with KRON-TV were the *San Francisco Chronicle*, KQED-FM public radio, and the Bay-TV cable affiliate.

Ed Fouhy stressed that this sort of alliance among TV and radio stations and newspapers in the market is essential because the "alienation of citizens is so deep that early efforts to re-engage them through the media are dismissed as just more cynical attempts to manipulate viewers or readers—to build circulation or ratings."

But, Fouhy said, when all the media cooperates—and is seen to be doing so—"there is a mutual validation effect." He said that when the community understands that if the traditional rivals for advertising dollars are cooperating, then the topic they are organizing around is important.

Fouhy says that this kind of cooperative effort shows a respect for the wisdom and intelligence of ordinary people. "What you won't find," he says, "is the journalistic model that encourages what one critic calls 'learned helplessness.'" Fouhy said the traditional way of telling a story that spotlights a problem encourages the feeling that it is so big and complicated that the viewer or reader is left with a sense that solving it is beyond the capacity of ordinary men and women.

"Does this mean that civic journalists pander to the desire for neat and simple solutions to complex policy questions?" asks Fouhy. "Of course not," he says. "The people who are practicing civic journalism are thoughtful men and women with a deep devotion to enduring journalistic values."

So, if Fouhy is right and civic journalism is a solution to the often-voiced criticism that journalism is not the force it used to be, why aren't more news organizations getting involved in civic journalism? Probably because many news managers still think that journalists must keep themselves separate from the rest of society and shouldn't be joining forces with any other constituencies or it will conflict with their traditional position of maintaining complete objectivity.

A newspaper executive from Colorado tried to defuse some of these concerns during a symposium honoring media organizations for their accomplishments in civic journalism. Steve Smith, editor of the *Colorado Springs Gazette*, says part of the misunderstanding about civic journalism is that some news managers think in terms of it being different from the traditional practices of journalism.

He said one of the reasons some journalists react negatively to civic journalism is that they believe that the values that brought them into journalism are in conflict with the civic journalism concept of serving the whole community. But Smith stressed that civic journalism is not meant to replace traditional journalism practices, routines, and reflexes—but is "the combination of a set of overarching values, a combination with our best practices, values, and ethics, that I think constitutes civic journalism." He said this is a powerful combination and is what begins to separate civic journalism from traditional practice.

Smith said the core values of journalists are pursuit of truth, fairness, and balance. He said these values drive our "Fourth Estate" watchdog responsibility. But he asked: "What about the value we share with citizens—that we want our communities to be good places in which to live? I would argue that 'community' is a core value." He said that we should not think of communities in terms of their segments or their separate elements, but as a whole, an aggregation of citizens who have a collective responsibility to their community. He said community value is the core civic value behind the experiments in civic journalism.

# Summary

This chapter discusses the responsibilities that accompany the new technology available to broadcast journalists. Radio and television stations, for example, are broadcasting trials from all but a few states. Some of these states have restrictions. Judges seem divided on the propriety of having cameras in the courtroom, particularly when they are used to report on so-called sensitive issues. Judge Lance Ito reluctantly permitted a camera in his courtroom during the O.J. Simpson trial and probably will ban them in future cases he handles.

Almost all broadcasters support cameras in the courtroom, maintaining that they have a First Amendment right to bring their gear into court because it is just a much heavier version of a print journalist's pen and pencil. A slight exaggeration, perhaps, because pens and pencils have no "live" capability.

Even if you accept that cameras have a right to feed trials, regardless of their nature, into living rooms, the question of responsibility remains, and that is an ethical issue in the minds of many newspeople. Does a network have a responsibility to feed out "everything" from a courtroom, as did CNN during the Simpson trial? If they do not broadcast everything, some executives claim, they would be censoring the news. Others argue that journalists always have censored news because of time and space constraints and to eliminate bad taste.

This chapter also discusses tabloid journalism. There seems to be a unanimous opinion that local stations, and networks to a lesser degree, are moving more and more toward tabloid journalism, where sensational stories are the norm. This trend is blamed mainly on money and ratings. As one journalist says, "When you are hurting in the ratings and the advertising revenue keeps dropping, you will try anything." One can only hope that this is a short-lived phenomenon.

## Review Questions

1. How many states still ban cameras in courtrooms?
2. What types of restrictions do some states have on cameras?
3. What is the media's argument for using cameras in courtrooms?
4. Did the camera in the Simpson courtroom impact on the fairness of his trial?
5. What was the Fairness Doctrine? How do you feel about the issues?
6. What was the *Red Lion* decision?

## Exercises

1. If cameras are allowed in courtrooms in your state, attend a trial where cameras are being used, and discuss whether you believe they were beneficial for the public or detrimental to those involved in the trial. If cameras are still forbidden in your state, interview a judge about the issue.
2. Assemble a group of journalists, lawyers, professors, and other appropriate people to discuss all aspects of journalistic ethics, including the media coverage of the Simpson murder trial, the Smith drowning trial, and checkbook journalism. Record the panel discussion for use in other classes.
3. Host a similar debate with news directors on the issue of tabloid journalism.
4. Watch each of the TV stations in your market, and report on their selection of stories and how they presented those stories.

# $\mathbf{22}$ Tabloid Journalism

As alluded to in Chapter 21, one of the most serious concerns of the 1990s for journalists was the increase of tabloid journalism. The explosion of the Internet and the emergence of a host of new magazine and talk shows on cable and the traditional networks brought about a new wave of sleaze journalism. But even more alarming than the expansion of such so-called news was the narrowing of the line between tabloid practices and those appearing in the so-called mainstream media. In the past decade, it has become increasingly more difficult to distinguish between the two.

We will look at two such examples, the sex scandal involving President Clinton and Monica Lewinsky and the murder of JonBenét Ramsey in Boulder, Colorado. Both stories were marked by irresponsible reporting. Although in many cases, the tabloids were out front in such reporting, the mainstream media often picked up the stories and ran with them and even developed sleaze of their own. Sometimes the so-called legitimate media even outdid the tabloids. Both the print and broadcast media were guilty of exploiting the subjects, resorting to rumor, and using unidentified and informed sources and unsubstantiated leaks.

The coverage concerned serious journalists who feared that the spread of tabloid news and practices would further alienate a public that has become increasingly more suspicious and untrusting of the media.

## The Clinton-Lewinsky Scandal

The reputation of President Bill Clinton was not the only thing to suffer in his affair at the White House with intern Monica Lewinsky. The news media also lost prestige through its coverage of the sexual encounter. As the *Columbia Journalism Review* put it, the American news media's reputation as truth-teller to the country was besmirched by perceptions, in and out of the news business, about how the story was reported.

Although many news outlets acted with considerable responsibility, especially after the first few frantic days of the scandal, the *Review* said the story also triggered "a piranha-like frenzy in pursuit of the relatively few tidbits tossed into the journalistic waters."

The writer of the *Journalism Review* story, Jules Witcover, said that "while it was evident there were wholesale leaks from lawyers and investigators, either legal restraints or reportorial pledges of anonymity kept the public from knowing with any certainty the sources of key elements in the saga."

The veteran journalist, now with the *Baltimore Sun*, said that into the vacuum created by a scarcity of clear and credible attribution, "raced all manner of rumor, gossip, and especially, hollow sourcing, making the reports of some mainstream outlets scarcely distinguishable from supermarket tabloids." He added that the rush to be first or to be more sensational created a picture of irresponsibility seldom seen in the reporting of presidential affairs.

**Figure 22.1**   Former White House intern Monica Lewinsky hugs President Clinton at the White House on November 6, 1996, during a ceremony gathering the White House interns. (Reuters/NBC TV/Archive Photos)

Among the speculative reports was *ABC News*'s White House correspondent Sam Donaldson's claim shortly after the scandal broke that Clinton could resign before the next week was out. "If he's not telling the truth," Donaldson said, "I think his presidency is numbered in days. This isn't going to drag out." Really?

Almost from the beginning, and throughout the scandal, the president had most of the American people's support, and much of the president's troubles were rubbing off on the press. A *Washington Post* poll taken 10 days after the story broke found that 56 percent of those surveyed believed that the news media were treating Clinton unfairly, and 74 percent said the media were giving the story too much attention.

The combination of all-news TV channels, the Internet, and the traditional networks assured nonstop coverage. But that coverage came under fire almost immediately for its rumor-mongering, unattributed sources, and speculation. Commenting on the lack of credible sources, Witcover said, "As leaks flew wildly from these unspecified sources, the American public was left as seldom before in a major news event to guess where stories came from and why."

Witcover noted that it was sadly appropriate that the first hint of the Paula Jones story, in which she accused Clinton of making sexual advances to her when he was governor of Arkansas, really broke not in the mainstream media but in the "wildly irresponsible Internet site of Matt Drudge, a reckless trader in rumor and gossip who makes no pretense of checking on the accuracy of what he reports."

After *Newsweek* magazine, which had been cautiously holding the same story, published it, the scandal spread quickly. A few days later, the *New York Times* reported that President Clinton had denied accusations of having had a sexual affair with a 21-year-old White House intern. After that, the media jumped on the story and ran with it, quoting questionable sources in an effort to beat the competition.

The usually responsible *Washington Post* cited "sources familiar with the investigation" as saying that the FBI had secretly taped Lewinsky by placing a wire on Linda Tripp, a friend of Lewinsky's, and had gotten information that helped persuade Attorney General Janet Reno to get authorization from a three-judge panel overseeing the independent counsel to expand the Clinton investigation.

The next day, Witcover said, "taste went out the window" when ABC correspondent Jackie Judd reported that a source with direct knowledge of Lewinsky's allegations said she admitted going to the White House for sex with Clinton in the early evening or early mornings on the weekends when certain aides, who would have been alarmed by her visits, were not in the office. Judd said that according to the source, which was not identified, Lewinsky said she saved a dress with the president's semen stain on it. Judd said, "if true," this information could provide physical evidence of what really happened between Clinton and Lewinsky. Witcover said this use of the phrase "if true" became a gate-opener for any rumor to make its way into the mainstream.

## Unconfirmed Reports Abound

The story of the stained dress spread through the media like a brushfire, with all sorts of additional unconfirmed elaborations about searches for the dress and DNA tests on it. All of these reports were printed and broadcast despite disavowals from Lewinsky's attorney.

*The New York Post* added its own twist to the story, saying that Monica kept the dress as a souvenir and didn't send it to the cleaners. *The Village Voice*, in a strong attack on the Judd story, called it hearsay and noted that it was picked up by other news organizations as though the dress really existed. Shortly after the ABC story ran, *CBS News* reported that no DNA evidence or stains had been found on a dress that belongs to Lewinsky and that was tested by the FBI.

Witcover said a close competitor for the sleaziest report award was the one regarding the president's alleged sexual preference. The Scripts Howard News Service reported that one person who had listened to the Lewinsky-Tripp tapes said Lewinsky described how Clinton allegedly first urged her to have oral sex, telling her that such acts were not technically adultery.

## Many Ways of Saying the Source Is Unreliable

Here are some other phrases used by the media to attribute information when they had no real sources on the sex scandal:

*The Los Angeles Times*: "People familiar with the investigation" say . . .

*The Washington Post*: "Sources familiar with the probe" say . . .

*The Wall Street Journal*: "A law enforcement official and unsubstantiated reports" say . . .

*The Chicago Tribune* quoted ABC news on the dress story, and even used the same ABC disclaimer, "if true."

*The Dallas Morning News* quoted "sources" for its story, saying that a secret service agent was prepared to testify that he saw President Clinton and Monica Lewinsky in a compromising situation at the White House.

Of course, every time these "mainstream" publications and broadcasts carried such stories, the late-night tabloid talk shows had a feast and moved the already unconfirmed reports to a new level of speculation.

For example, Larry King referred to a *New York Times* story about a message allegedly left on Lewinsky's answering machine when there was, in fact, no such story. Before the broadcast was over, King had to apologize, admitting the *Times* was not actually going to print such a story. The use of terms like *unconfirmed* and *usually reliable* sources snowballed so much that it was impossible to determine whose unconfirmed or usually reliable source belonged to which newspaper or broadcast.

CNBC gave much of its broadcast time to reckless talk and speculation, and one of the worst was a comment by conservative columnist Arianna

Huffington, offering a report on "Equal Time" that Clinton had an affair with Sheila Lawrence, the widow of the late ambassador whose body was exhumed from Arlington National Cemetery after it was revealed he had lied about his military record. Huffington tried to cover her tracks a bit when she confessed "we're not there yet in terms of proving it."

## *White House Scolds* The Wall Street Journal

*The Wall Street Journal*'s recklessness in reporting this case shocked many of its most loyal supporters. Not wishing to wait for its paper to come out the next morning, the *Journal* put on its Website and wire service that a White House steward had told a grand jury that he had seen Clinton and Lewinsky alone in a study next to the Oval Office. The *Journal* was in such a rush it didn't bother to check the story out with the White House, which brought a response from White House deputy press secretary Joe Lockhart that the "normal rules of checking and getting a response to a story seem to have given way to the technology of the Internet and the competitive pressure of getting it first."

The *Journal* story, by the way, used as its source "two individuals familiar with" the steward's testimony. The steward's attorney denied the story, but it did not stop a rash of other media outlets from giving the public the same story, sometimes with a different set of sources.

White House press secretary Michael McCurry called the *Journal*'s performance "one of the sorriest episodes of journalism I have ever witnessed." The *Journal*, by the way, apologized for the story a few days later, saying it was not true.

## *Gary Hart Scandal Sets Stage for Clinton Coverage*

In his story in the *Columbia Journalism Review*, Jules Witcover recalled how in 1984, nothing was written in the media about presidential candidate Gary Hart's alleged marital infidelity because there was no proof and no one was willing to talk. But Witcover pointed out that three years later *Newsweek* reported that Hart's marriage had been rocky and he had been haunted by rumors of womanizing.

After that report, the *Miami Herald* got a tip that triggered a stakeout of Hart's Washington townhouse, from which he was seen leaving with Donna Rice. Following that, the *National Enquirer* published photos of the couple on the island of Bimini, and Hart's run for the White House was over. "Clearly," wrote Witcover, "the old rule that questions about a public figure's private life were taboo no longer applied."

A nationally syndicated political columnist, E. J. Dionne of the *Washington Post*, agrees. Addressing a group of ombudsmen at a conference in Chicago, Dionne said he believes that beginning with the Gary Hart story, journalists started having a problem making distinctions. Before that, he said, "journalists had always drawn a very thick line between the public and the private, were very reluctant to cross it, and after the Hart episode, the line became very, very blurred indeed." Dionne said: "We fret as much today about a politician's sexual life as we do about his foreign policy."

He added that the boxes journalists are in right now were created because "we are stuck in the middle in that contest over boundaries between the public and the private." Dionne said: "I think it's clear that if we obliterate all distinctions between the public and private we will go down a road that involves threats to liberty and also a debasement of democratic politics."

Picking up on the analogy between Hart and Clinton, Jules Witcover noted that by the time it was Bill Clinton's turn, the mainstream press was "dragged into hot pursuit of the gossip tabloids that not too many years earlier had been treated like a pack of dogs by the supposedly ethical betters."

The veteran journalist concluded that since the media picked up the Clinton scandal scent, "the once-firm line between rumor and truth, between gossip and verification, has been crumbling." The assault, he added, "has been led by the trashy tabloids but increasingly accompanied by major newspapers and television, with copy-cat tabloid radio and TV talk shows piling on."

Even the usually responsible *60 Minutes* got caught up in the trash, opting to give airtime to Kathleen Willey, a former White House volunteer, who had claimed that when she was visiting the president at the White House, he took her hand and placed it on his genitals. Her claim received a wave of media attention, as might be expected, but no one had actually interviewed Willey on television before she sat opposite Ed Bradley.

During the interview, Bradley asked the woman if the President had been "aroused" when he allegedly placed her hand on his genitals. Many journalists believe the question was in bad taste and should not have been asked. There also was some criticism of *60 Minutes* for scheduling the interview in the first place because of Ms. Willey's questionable credibility. Shortly after her appearance on the program, the White House released several letters of a friendly nature that Ms. Willey sent to the President after she allegedly was groped by Clinton. When Bradley was asked if the question about Clinton being "aroused" was his idea or a producer's, he refused comment.

When questioned about why he decided to put Willey on *60 Minutes*, executive producer Don Hewitt was defensive. He said he did so because he was convinced that there was a lot more to the Clinton scandal than just sex and that the American people were entitled to know about the other issues. Just how Willey's fondling claim against the President on national TV could play a role in uncovering such evidence of other wrongdoings was not made plain by the producer.

According to *60 Minutes*, at the time Willey was scheduled to appear on the program, producers did not know that she had written those friendly letters to the President *after* the alleged sexual encounter with him. Whether that information might have influenced the producers' decision to have her on the program is not known. As of this writing, there still is no evidence that Willey's accusations are true.

Commenting on the Lewinsky-Clinton-Starr coverage, the veteran journalist and best-selling author, David Halberstam, said the year of the scandal was "the worst year for American journalism since I entered the profession forty-four years ago." He added: "What is disturbing about the bad odor of journalism today is that, I think, many of the critics are right, and the people who have been performing as journalists have in fact seriously trivialized the profession, often doing what is fashionable than what is right."

# Are News Standards Dwindling?

Are respectable news organizations lowering standards and is the public turning against "trash TV" or is TV giving the public what it wants to know? Both questions were asked at a DuPont Forum at Columbia University. Joan Konner, the dean of the Columbia University Graduate School of Journalism, set the tone for the forum, saying that the "very definition of news seems to have changed radically in the last decade. Sleaze and titillation from all news sources mirror the content of the sensational supermarket tabloids," Konner said.

The keynote speaker, Hedrick Smith, a Former *New York Times* correspondent and PBS documentary producer, shared Konner's disappointment in the media, complaining that TV offers so much opportunity "for mischief and slanting the news."

*NBC News* President Andrew Lack noted that news is a business and social mayhem has never been more marketable. He said: "We can pretend that each and every scandal has real news value, and they do because they are serious subjects after all, but," Lack added, "that's not why they top the news morning, noon, and night. My guess," he said, "is that the audience laps them up because in some ways they are pure entertainment." In other words, the public wants entertainment more than it wants news, and that is what the media is giving it. A frightening but rational explanation for what, in the minds of many journalists, is seriously handicapping the news industry.

In their excellent book on the media coverage of the Clinton-Lewinsky scandal, *Warp Speed*, Bill Kovach and Tom Rosenstiel say that the ordeal with Kenneth Starr and the impeachment trial that the ordeal precipitated "were part of a kind of cultural civil war in America in which the press plays a peculiarly important role."

The authors say that the Clinton scandal represented for the press the moment when the new *post-O.J. media culture* turned its camera lens to a major political event for the first time. They describe the *post-O.J. media culture* as a "newly diversified mass media in which the culture of entertainment, infotainment, argument, analysis, tabloid, and mainstream press not only work side by side but intermingle and merge." It is a culture, they add, "in which Matt Drudge sits alongside William Safire on *Meet the Press*, and Ted Koppel talks about the nuances of oral sex, in which *Hard Copy* and *CBS News* jostle for camera position outside the federal grand jury to hear from a special prosecutor."

Kovach and Rosenstiel say that many of the new media outlets are engaged in commenting on information rather than gathering it. They say the rise of 24-hour news stations and Internet news and information sites has placed demands on the press to have something to fill the time. "Whole new news organizations such as MSNBC are being built around such chatter," the authors say, "creating a new medium of talk radio TV."

There was little in the way of news or entertainment in the next case study of tabloid journalism, but the media gave the public much more than it really needed to know about the murder of a young child in Colorado.

# The JonBenét Ramsey Murder Case

When six-year-old JonBenét Ramsey was found murdered in her home in Boulder, Colorado, it launched a media frenzy that had not been equaled since the O. J. Simpson murder case and the Clinton-Lewinsky sex scandal.

Like the O.J. case, Boulder police bungled the case from the start. They did not secure the crime scene or protect forensic evidence. Police also had a running battle with the DA's office on how to handle the investigation and leaked information to the press on a regular basis.

At first, the story looked like a routine kidnapping. On Christmas Eve 1992, Mrs. Ramsey discovered a ransom note allegedly written by someone representing a foreign power. The note threatened that JonBenét would be beheaded if the family called police. But they did. Later, during a routine search of the house by a detective and Mr. Ramsey, the father discovered the body of the child in a room in the cellar of the home. Her skull had been fractured and she was strangled.

The police quickly centered on the parents as the perpetrators of the crime, and the media fully embraced that conclusion, although there never was any hard evidence that John and Patsy Ramsey were guilty. After a year-long investigation, a grand jury refused to indict them or anyone else.

Approximately 800 children ages 12 and under were murdered in the United States in the year JonBenét was killed, and the murder should have been no more than a Denver-area story, but according to Brill's *Content* magazine, the media was hungry for a sensational story to follow the void left by the end of the Clinton-Lewinsky affair. The magazine said the fact that the child beauty queen was murdered during the slowest news week of the year—between Christmas and the new year—also contributed to the extraordinary media interest in the story. Several hundred representatives from the tabloids and the mainstream media would flood Boulder shortly after the murder. The strong interest in the little girl was fueled by the widely publicized videos and photographs of JonBenét performing at various child beauty pageants.

Brill's *Content* said the murder case had nothing to it except the alluring pictures and video of a little girl dolled up for a beauty contest. The magazine said there never was any real news in the story, but that didn't stop the media. In the two years between the time the story broke and the failure of the grand jury to indict the Ramseys, the tabloids and mainstream media printed and broadcast almost 1,000 stories about the murder case.

Among other TV shows, *20/20*, *48 Hours*, *Hard Copy*, *American Journal*, *Dateline NBC*, and *Entertainment Tonight* aired more than 400 segments about the case. The scandal-loving Geraldo Rivera did 195 shows on the Ramseys on both CNBC's *Rivera Live* and the now-defunct *Geraldo Rivera Show*. CNN's Larry King had at least 44 segments about JonBenét. Even the usually more conservative print magazines *Newsweek* and *Time* carried 55 stories on the murder case and, of course, the tabloids feasted on it. The *Globe*, the *National Enquirer*, the *National Examiner*, and the *Star* published more than 500 stories on the subject.

*NBC News*'s legal correspondent, Dan Abrams, defended the media's coverage of the story, saying that unsolved murders always fascinate the public and that this case had much more, including a mishandled police investigation. But Patricia Calhoun, the editor of Denver's weekly alternative paper, *The Westword*, disagrees. She noted that the murder case was a national springboard for a lot of people. It was a career-builder for many journalists, all of whom had a strong motive for keeping the story alive.

Brill's *Content* said "a cadre of journalists who made it their business to keep the business of JonBenét alive relied on sensationalism, untraditional tactics, and rule-bending to keep this nonstory in the headlines." In the process, the magazine added, they and their nonstory became "the quintessential symbol of a new age in which journalists, faced with the job of finding the next Big Story to feed the insatiable news machine, will reach down for material that by any standard is not news and rely on the work of bottom feeders to fill their pages and airwaves."

One of those bottom feeders was Jeff Shapiro, who worked as a stringer for the *Globe*. He said that there wasn't anything he would not do to get a story except break the law and pay sources. He quit after a year when he said he began to question the *Globe*'s fairness, particularly their interest only in stories that "fingered the Ramseys as the killers."

Shapiro, who would later string for *Time* magazine, cited one example of the *Globe*'s duplicity when an editor called Shapiro and claimed he had a new lead for him. The so-called new lead was that a *Globe* source had discovered that John Ramsey had given his pilot a box of evidence to hide for him. The *Globe* editor said the box contained the rope used to kill JonBenét and the duct tape used to cover her mouth.

Shapiro then told police about the *Globe* "scoop," and when the cops arrived at the pilot's house to talk to him, Shapiro was there to observe the incident and report it back to the *Globe*. The *Globe* had gone full circle with the story, making it up, suckering the cops into it, and then reporting that the cops were investigating the pilot.

This tabloid determination to "get the Ramseys" and the mainstream media's often willingness to go along brought about a special *Investigative Reports* program on the Arts and Entertainment (A&E) network. It was titled "The story of JonBenét Ramsey—the Ramseys vs. the Media."

Veteran journalist Bill Curtis anchored the program and set the tone by declaring that "almost all Americans now believe that the Ramseys committed the murder of their child because that has been the verdict of the American media." Curtis said that from the very beginning, police were leaking stories to the media indicating they were suspicious of John and Patsy Ramsey and that only the parents could have killed the child. The police leaks to the media also said that only someone who knew the Ramsey home could have killed the child.

Even the Boulder City police chief Tom Koby became concerned with the leaks and the media reporting of them. Koby said that in his 28 years in the business he had never seen such media focus on an event and that it was making it more difficult for him to do his job. Curtis said the media-fed leaks reported one alleged fact after another, which taken together could only implicate the Ramseys.

Two of those leaks dealt with police concerns about finding no footprints outside the house and no signs of a break-in. Actually, there were a broken window and even some open windows in the house, a fact that police didn't tell the media for a year. It also was confirmed by experts not working for police that there was not enough snow on the ground around the Ramsey house on Christmas for there to be any footprints, if there had been an intruder. This finding was virtually ignored by the media.

Curtis noted that just four days after the murder, the media were reporting another leak, that police were suspicious of the Ramseys because of their behavior—that they thought the couple were faking their grief. *Vanity Fair* had reported that a policeman told them that he observed Mrs. Ramsey supposedly weeping, but instead she was really peering at him through her fingers.

Another erroneous story carried by the media was that John Ramsey was not so grief-stricken by the tragedy to fly his family in his own plane from Boulder to Atlanta. The truth is that the Lockheed-Martin corporation, which had purchased Ramsey's company, supplied the plane that took the family to Atlanta.

Another false leak published by *Vanity Fair* that was not corrected by police was that they, the police, were concerned because John Ramsey had allegedly left the house for an hour, supposedly to get mail, shortly after JonBenét's body was found. The *Vanity Fair* article said police did not know where Ramsey had gone. Police later confirmed that this story was false.

The media also reported, incorrectly, that a day after JonBenét's funeral the Ramseys had hired some top criminal attorneys to defend themselves. Actually, a close friend of the Ramseys decided to do this because, as he would explain later, "it's foolish to blindly throw oneself into the justice system and trust the results." He added that one must be "thoughtful about how one acts, especially in a case when the media attention reaches the point of near hysteria, and which from the outset portrays certain people as being guilty."

Curtis noted that another false story reported by the media said the Ramseys had hired publicists—an indication that they were using their wealth to escape justice. In truth, the Ramseys did not hire publicists. The family lawyer, Bryan Morgan, hired some people to handle the hundreds of phone calls and letters that were coming into the office each day about the case.

The Ramseys' decision to go on CNN to tell their side of the story turned out to be a media mistake. It set off another round of negative stories in the media saying, in effect, that the Ramseys were play-acting, talking to TV rather than the police.

When they returned to Boulder from Atlanta, the Ramseys were besieged by media who, according to Curtis, were building a new element in the case against them: alleged police leaks that the Ramseys had sexually abused Jon-Benét. There was absolutely no evidence of sexual molestation during the investigation, but the leak caused a media firestorm.

Even when the Ramseys tried to cooperate with the media, their efforts backfired. The couple agreed to allow the media to take pictures of them leaving a church service as they walked to a nearby community center. But the congregation, as a sign of support, lined the pavement as the Ramseys were walking from the church, and the media said the demonstration was a cynical attempt to manipulate public opinion. Actually, the minister of the church orchestrated the congregation's show of support, but this fact was never revealed to the public.

The media also reported that the Ramseys were not cooperating with the police investigation, but Curtis pointed out that they had given police samples of their blood and hair and their fingerprints and writing samples.

The nation also saw District Attorney Alex Hunter's news conference, in which he claimed that the list of suspects in the JonBenét case was narrowing. He said the killer or killers of the child should know that the list will soon have just one name on it. This was generally interpreted to be a reference to the Ramseys.

Some media reported that the police had sought a search warrant to look for pornography in the Ramsey house, which also was not true. The *Star* tabloid carried a headline: DAD LINKED TO KIDDIE PORN SCANDAL. Another head read: DADDY CHOKED BEAUTY WITH BARE HANDS. There also were media stories that John Ramsey had visited a porn store in Denver, a claim that was never substantiated. Even the *Sunday Times* in London carried a headline about "KIDDIE PORN" being involved in the child's death.

The media also tried to make something out of the fact that Mrs. Ramsey had taken JonBenét to a pediatrician 27 times in the four years before her death.

**Figure 22.2**   Boulder District Attorney Alex Hunter arriving with prosecutors to
make a statement to the press about the JonBenét Ramsey murder case,
Colorado, October 13, 1999. Hunter said that the grand jury had finished its
work without finding enough evidence to warrant an indictment. (Courtesy
Reuters/NBC TV/Archive Photos)

The child's physician was interviewed on *Investigative Reports* and said there
was nothing unusual about such visits, that there were absolutely no signs of
abuse, and that many of the visits—some 21 of them—were for colds, hay fever,
and routine medical examinations.

The Boulder Police Chief, Tom Koby, held a news conference to express his
concern about the media coverage. Koby said one journalist, a "major media
person," told him: "Tom, why are you so mad at us, don't you understand that
we know the Ramseys did it and we are going to help you get them." Koby
replied, "Do you hear what you just said, how wrong that is, how scary it is?
How in violation that is to everything that you are supposed to believe? I'm not
mad at you," the Police Chief added, "I'm disappointed in you."

The media even took away the Ramseys' right to grieve. The couple did not
visit JonBenét's gravesite because of the ever-present and intrusive media.
Reporters and cameras, some of them hidden in bushes, surrounded the
gravesite. John Ramsey said he was not comfortable going to the grave.

*Vanity Fair*'s irresponsible coverage of the story included a report that the
Boulder Police were so sure of the Ramseys' guilt that they had been holding a
murder warrant for them since May following the murder. The magazine also

carried a story saying that police were investigating whether JonBenét's nine-year-old brother could have killed his sister. No evidence of this nature was ever produced.

"Fox in Depth" featured on one of its programs an interview with Kim Ballard, a woman who alleged that she had been Ramsey's mistress. Ballard said she didn't know whether Ramsey had killed the child, but that she thought he was involved in some way. There has been no evidence that Ramsey even knows Ballard.

The tabloid and so-called mainstream TV programs—the difference between the two often seems difficult to distinguish—have continued, without letting up, their discussions about the murder, and, in most cases, they condemn the Ramseys.

Geraldo Rivera even held a mock trial for the Ramseys on one of his shows. There was a make-believe judge and jury, and when the verdicts convicting both Mr. and Mrs. Ramsey of the wrongful death of their child were read, the studio audience broke out into wild cheers. It's difficult to remember that Rivera was a legitimate journalist many years ago until he realized he could make a lot more money in tabloid journalism.

On another Rivera show, author Cyril Wecht told the audience that Boulder police "just need to do what they should do—arrest the people," an obvious reference to the Ramseys. The audience cheered wildly.

The *Globe* tabloid touched off another wave of irresponsible talk show discussion when it reported that JonBenét, after wetting her own bed, went to her mother's bed and Mrs. Ramsey allegedly lost it and battered the child. The tabloid headline read: JONBENÉT DIES IN MOTHER'S BED. There was never any evidence that such an incident ever occurred, but that didn't stop *Hard Copy* from also discussing it.

When questioned on the A&E special report about the media's coverage of the tragedy, John Ramsey's brother Jeff said the media essentially fueled the fire against the family. He said that what the media has done to the entire family is horrible. Ramsey added: "The media has become a profit-making business machine, not interested in news anymore, it's entertainment."

When Lucinda Ramsey, the former wife of John Ramsey, was asked why she thought the media treated the Ramseys the way they have, she said, "Maybe they forgot the basic constitutional right of presumption of innocence, relied too much on gossip, chased the dollar, and wanted to get the story first. Certainly," she added, "the media ruined lives."

When questioned about the mainstream media's behavior, Barrie Hartman, the editor of Boulder's largest paper, the *Daily Camera*, said that when the tabloids print a story the rest of the media think they have to report it too. What happens then, he said, "is that a lot of those tabloid stories become fact when the legitimate media picks them up."

A Denver TV reporter, Julie Hayden of Channel 7, said she felt guilty carrying some stories that she felt were not fair, but, she added, the competitive pressure was intense and if someone else has a story and we don't, "my boss wants to know why. If people stop watching me," she said, "we go hungry."

Bill Curtis summed up the media coverage of the JonBenét killing this way: "Journalists are worried about a profession driven by intense competition, a lack of regulation, and corporate ownership that increasingly views news as a profit-making rather than a journalistic activity. The result," concluded Curtis, " is that news has become entertainment and tragedy, public spectacle."

Earlier in the chapter we quoted E. J. Dionne, a nationally syndicated columnist for the *Washington Post* criticizing the media about what he described as the confusion between fact and opinion not only in commentary but also what increasingly passes for journalism. Dionne stated that the "journalistic tradition most of us aspire to uphold involves doing the hard work of verifying facts, especially if those facts involve charges against somebody else."

Dionne recalled the words of another journalist, *New York Times* writer Michiko Kakutani, who wrote that throughout our culture, the old notions of truth and knowledge are being replaced by the new ones of opinion, perception, and credibility. She added: "What we're creating is a world in which truths are replaced by opinions."

# 23 Producing

## The Producers

"It's a bear out there anymore," says Julie Frisoni, executive producer of KPNX-TV, Phoenix. "Gone are the days when there were only three stations doing news." There are now six stations in the Phoenix area to compete with—seven, when you consider Telemundo, the Spanish-language station. The battle for viewers is intense. Because of the strong competition in Phoenix, it's a great city to look for changes, trends, and innovation in news, particularly as it applies to producing.

Frisoni describes her station, which is the most watched in Phoenix, as *producer-driven*. Although the assignment editor hands out assignments, the producer often tells the assignment editor which stories to cover.

The success of television news programs—regardless of whether they are at the network or local level—depends on the news gatherers, reporters, and camerapersons. But the ability of the producers, the executive producer, and the line producer are equally important. The producers determine what goes into the nightly news, how much time is devoted to each story, and in what order the stories will appear. The producers determine how many packages and how many voiceovers and readers will be used. In other words, they shape the news broadcast.

No two producers would create exactly the same newscast, as no two writers or reporters would write or report a story the same way. As in all three cases, however, there are certain rules and philosophies about approaching the writing and reporting of a story and the production of a newscast. You have read about the differences and similarities in style and philosophy in various parts of this book. This chapter discusses the thinking of producers on news and how they put their newscasts together; and we also illustrate how producers are used differently in various markets.

### The Executive Producer

The executive producer is in charge of show producers and is responsible for the long-term look of the newscasts. He or she determines the set, the style of the opening and close, the choice of anchors, the philosophy, and other details, in consultation with the news director and the station's general manager. The executive producer reports directly to the news director. If there are problems with the newscast, the executive producer will have to do some explaining after the show. Of course, the executive producer will go over the problem, whatever it might be, with the line producer before the news director calls.

If the ratings slip, the executive producer must explain why and try to fix the problem. Otherwise, he or she may be looking for another job. If that happens, a line producer sometimes inherits the job or someone new may be hired from outside. Because ratings are a serious concern for all producers, they constantly *work on the edge*.

## *The Line Producer (Show Producer)*

On a day-to-day basis, the line (or show) producer is mostly responsible for deciding what goes into the news broadcast and makes sure it's ready to go on the air. The executive producer and news director will be watching in the wings, but most of the responsibility for preparing the newscasts is given to the line producer. He or she prepares the *rundown (lineup)*, which outlines which packages, voiceovers, and readers will appear in the show, in what order, and how much time will be devoted to each story.

If there is any doubt about which story should lead the newscast, the line producer consults with the executive producer and often includes the news director in that conversation. That also applies, of course, to any problem that may arise concerning the newscast that cannot be resolved simply.

The line producer works closely with the assignment editor and reporters. They talk about the rundown, reporter assignments, the angle the producer wishes the stories to take, story times, and whether the story is used as a package or a voiceover. As the day progresses, the line producer usually updates the rundown to reflect any breaking stories. If the producer has a special liking for a story, he or she tells the assignment editor and a reporter is assigned to the story. Sometimes the producer, in consultation with the assignment editor, decides which reporter covers a particular story. But a good producer doesn't micromanage and allows the assignment editor to determine most staffing decisions. As you can see, it takes a lot of people, working as a team, to put a newscast on the air. They're like links in a chain.

## *Associate Producers*

In large city and network newsrooms, the line producer sometimes has assistants to help carry the load. These assistant or associate producers help reporters put together packages when they are in a rush or have been assigned to a second story. They cut sound bites and pick video for the packages. When a package is reduced to a voiceover, the associate producer usually handles all the details, including writing the script.

The associate producer also takes in the microwave or satellite feed from reporters in the field. They work closely with the line producer, informing him or her if the feed has any problems. The associate producer often cuts parts of the feed to be used as voiceovers. Again, depending on the size of the news operation, there may not be any associate producers—writers are assigned the same duties. In many smaller markets, reporters are always responsible for cutting their own tape and putting the package together—with little or no help.

Not all stations in large markets use associate producers. "We don't use them anymore," says KPNX-TV Phoenix executive producer Julie Frisoni. "Instead, we hire more show producers. It's more expensive since producers are paid more than associate producers. But since they have more experience, it gives us more flexibility." If a show producer calls in sick, she adds, any of the other producers can step into her shoes. Whereas associate producers aren't qualified to handle newscasts, says Frisoni.

### Field Producers

Usually found in larger markets and at the networks, field producers help reporters with research, plus the detail work, setting up interviews, locating people at the scene of the story (often in advance), directing the cameraperson, and making travel arrangements. The field producer is often described as the "advance" person—the "facilitator." He or she often speaks with the newsmakers in advance of the reporter's arrival, briefs the reporter on what the interviewees know about the story, and suggests questions to ask in interviews.

## The Staff Meetings

The producers can be found in various parts of the newsroom, speaking to each other, with reporters, the assignment editor, and the news director. Most of them hold staff meetings as many as three times a day—in the morning, the late afternoon, and after the early evening newscast—to discuss that day's news coverage. That's where initial newscast decisions are made: What will the lead story be? Which stories will be covered? and Which reporter and cameraperson will cover them? Keep in mind these decisions are subject to change, depending on the day's events. The last meeting of the day is a debriefing to discuss what went right and wrong with the early evening newscasts and to plan coverage for the late evening news.

The meeting is a place to discuss story ideas—it's not unlike a *war room* where the battle plan is set for that day's action. All staff members are expected to contribute and share information. A good producer is a good listener who realizes that ideas are not limited to the assignment editor.

At KPNX-TV, there are six war rooms in the Phoenix area to compete with, and seven, when you consider Telemundo, the Spanish-language station. The battle for viewers is intense. Because of the strong competitiveness in Phoenix, we decided it would be a great city to look for changes, trends, and innovation in news, particularly as it applies to producing.

Earlier in the chapter, we gave an overview of how producers earn their salaries. As you will learn after reading about what is happening in Phoenix, the job descriptions do not always indicate what people actually do.

During the meeting, the staff goes over each story available for the day's newscasts. Decisions are made, and the line (show) producers of the early evening newscasts create a rundown (lineup), which is a list of stories planned for those newscasts. Reporters and *photo-journalists* (videographers) are then assigned to stories. KPNX-TV calls their photographers *photo-journalists* because they are qualified to report in addition to taking pictures. However, most of the reporting is done by reporters.

As stated above, the early rundown is subject to change as the day's news events unfold. Sometimes the pre- and final rundown look alike. On other days, there are so many new developments and breaking news stories that the final rundown lineup barely resembles the pre-rundown.

KPNX-TV in Phoenix, has three meetings a day:

9:00 A.M.—The first meeting, called the *editorial meeting*. The news staff is briefed on which stories are being covered, which ones are assigned for the rest of the day, and which reporters and videographers are assigned to them. Note that the assignments are not set in stone, and it's not unusual for assignments to change at the meeting.

1:45 P.M.—Producers of the 5:00 P.M. and 6:00 P.M. newscasts are updated on which stories will be available for their broadcasts. The 10 P.M. news staff gets its first orientation and begins assigning stories for its newscast.

6:30 P.M.—This meeting follows the early evening newscasts. It consists of a *debriefing* in which the staff talks about what went right and wrong on the 5:00 P.M. and 6:00 P.M. newscasts. The news director critiques the broadcasts and others chime in. They also discuss the upcoming 10:00 P.M. newscast and make additional assignments for it.

# Who's the Real Boss?

Sometimes, it's not easy to spot who is in charge. For example, at KTVK-TV in Phoenix, the executive producer is "the real hands-on, day-to-day manager of the news room." According to news director Dennis O'Neill, the executive producer oversees all content and has the final word on what goes into the shows. O'Neill said, "the executive producer supervises all reporters and producers, making sure the style is consistent from day-to-day."

"Executive producers are more like what news directors used to be," said O'Neill. She makes sure all detail work is performed daily. "She's responsible for both coverage and content," O'Neill added, "and if there's a breakdown in coverage, or a problem with the broadcast, we go to the executive producer." The executive producer works closely with and supervises show producers, who are responsible for individual shows. O'Neill said the assignment editor used to decide what stories to cover, but now the executive producer makes those decisions. The assignment editor makes the logistical decisions, by assigning reporters and photographers to stories.

The individual show producers (line producers) put together the rundowns and determine the form of the stories—whether they should be packages or V/Os, and so forth. The show producers also write part of the script. KTVK-TV broadcasts 6.5 hours of news daily and has a staff of 125. It's an independent station, which means that it often covers national stories in addition to state and local news.

Executive producer Frisoni says in addition to overseeing the other producers, she checks all scripts before they get on the air for accuracy and libel and makes certain that quotes are properly attributed. She said, "I'm the backstop."

## The Golden People

O'Neill says that "good producers are worth their weight in gold. We have 11 producers," he said, "and they're hard to keep." Producers are in such demand, according to O'Neill, that Don Fitzpatrick Associates—a broadcast news headhunter—has one person assigned full-time to searching for show and executive producers.

Frisoni advises those considering a broadcast journalism career to give serious consideration to becoming a producer. "The future is unbelievable. I have an opening right now that I am unable to fill," she said. It used to take five years to get a producing job in Phoenix, the 17th largest market. Now it takes only three years," she said. "KPNX-TV gets four or five reporter resume tapes a day. By contrast, I may get one good tape a month from a producer," Frisoni said.

O'Neill also discussed a growing trend in the industry—the use of field producers who don't get on TV. KTVK-TV has four or five such producers who do most of the research and legwork for the reporters. They are paid a lot less than the reporters.

## Philosophy

One important change is that producers seem to be getting away from some of the small talk on the set of KNXV-TV. Their slogan is "We Won't Waste Your

Time." One thing is certain: Phoenix viewers have an incredible amount of choices, as was mentioned earlier, with seven TV stations doing early evening newscasts—six of them in English and one in Spanish. The market has a large Spanish population.

O'Neill says you will not see a lot of Washington stuff on his station, although the station does cover national news now that it's independent and no longer gets any help from a network. The station's philosophy: Tune into the show any time and get caught up on all the news. He said, "We review the top stories about every 10 minutes" to accommodate viewers who are coming home from work at different times. "Because we are now independent," O'Neill said, "we can cover breaking news with ease."

One major concern at KPNX-TV is ethics. Julie Frisoni says the news department is very serious about the issue—and has seminars on ethics for the whole staff. Frisoni says the news department did a lot of soul searching after three members of the staff "became the news." She said the staff began to notice how callous some journalists act and decided to change their ways, to "put ourselves in the shoes of the newsmaker."

The events that resulted in the attitude change at the station were when a KPNX-TV sports reporter was killed in an auto accident in Washington, D.C., and became a front-page story, as did a photographer who lost part of his leg, and an anchor who suffered a heart attack. "For the first time we realized what it was like to be on the other side of the camera," Frisoni said, "and we didn't like what we saw." She added: "We had forgotten why we got into this business in the first place." The producer said, "We've changed." They have discovered that "we can be successful without being flashy."

Everyone involved in news coverage should learn what it's like to be on the other side of the camera as the subject of a news story. And they should periodically take a refresher course.

# The Rundown (Lineup)

The rundown, or lineup, is what comes out of the staff meetings. The decisions reached at the morning meeting determine what goes into the rundown for the evening news, and the discussions at the afternoon meeting establish what the late-night news looks like. But all this is subject to change depending on breaking news stories, as the lineup is a living document. At times, the pre-lineup looks exactly like the newscast, but at other times it looks nothing like it because of unpredictable developments.

An example is the 2001 earthquake in Seattle that occurred on the morning of February 28. Typically, when a major story like that occurs, the station's entire effort is devoted to that story and the planned coverage is shoved aside. The day of the earthquake, Seattle's major stations were continuously on the air live. CNN and other stations around the nation were picking up the Seattle station's coverage. Of course, the final lineup was nothing like the original. The uncertainty of television news can make life difficult, but at the same time it makes it interesting and sometimes exciting.

Some nights, producers wish they could just toss everything in the air and put it in the show the way it falls down. Unfortunately, it doesn't work that way. A lot of thought must go into the arrangement of stories in the newscast to make it clear and interesting.

As mentioned earlier, no two producers are likely to agree on the exact order of the stories in a newscast. If you examined the newscasts produced at stations in the same market on the same night, even the lead stories are often different unless some story completely dominates the news.

So, the news judgment of each producer comes into play, along with individual biases and the ability of assignment editors, reporters, and others to come up with good material. The result is the rundown: The list of stories in the order they'll appear on the air, including the time allotted to each story and visuals such as videotape.

# Peaks and Valleys

One popular approach to producing a newscast is known as the *peak-and-valley* format. Although the phrase has been around for decades, many producers use the format without using that name. This format treats every segment, or block, in the newscast as a sort of mini-newscast that can stand on its own. That doesn't mean that each section has weather, sports, and financial news; but there is a good, strong story at the top of each segment, along with some less important stories and, in some segments, perhaps a feature or special report. Each segment ends with a strong story before the commercial.

The concept behind peaks and valleys is that if you sprinkle your most interesting and important stories throughout the newscast, you'll hold your audience. If you place all your top stories in the early part of the newscast, you'll lose the audience because the newscast—and your audience—will fizz out by the middle. Worse yet, the audience will switch to your competition. Instead, you should sprinkle your most interesting and important stories throughout the newscast. Some stations lead with their top story, bar none. Others mention the top story in the lead as a tease, and then run the story later in the newscast.

Interestingly enough, Julie Frisoni says KPNX-TV doesn't subscribe to the peaks and valleys philosophy. "We can be pretty selective. We have very few valleys because our news hole is so small anymore." She says peaks and valleys are not as important as the ratings. "Ratings is the most important consideration," she says. In this competitive market, producers must learn how to "manage the meters."

She is referring to the meters that AC Nielsen, the audience research firm, places in homes to measure viewing habits. Each day, they receive "overnights" from Nielsen. It tells us what the audience thought of the previous day's newscasts. It tells us how many people are watching in 15-minute increments. You can tell when you're gaining viewers and when you're losing viewers from the Nielsen data.

"Nielsen is the only game in town. We have to figure out how to play it to win," she added. "We look at the ratings book every day." What does it tell us? For example, she said, "it told us amateur video, shot by a neighbor, of an unattended baby lying in a driveway for 40 minutes outside a babysitter's house, was a hot button issue." "The numbers on that story were phenomenal," Frisoni said. "We used the story on both 5 and 6 on Tuesday, brought it back on Wednesday with an updated version, and did another update on Thursday."

What else do we learn from Nielsen ratings? "You must learn when you can and cannot be in a commercial break. We used to place the first commercial wherever. We didn't think it mattered," she added. "The meters taught us it did matter big time. Now, the first commercial shall never air before seven minutes into the newscast. Otherwise," she said, "you lose the audience. That's a rule. The meters also taught us to do at least seven minutes of news before the commercial break in the first and second quarter-hours of the newscast."

Why do the meters determine what we do? Frisoni explains that if you don't follow them, your ratings drop and so does your audience. Frisoni cites this illustration of how to program news:

| | |
|---|---|
| 6:00–6:08 | uninterrupted news (at least 7 minutes) |
| 6:08–10 | commercials |
| 6:10–13 | second news segment |
| 6:13–15 | commercial |
| 6:15–22 | uninterrupted news (at least 7 minutes) |
| 6:22–24 | commercials |

Frisoni also notes that ratings indicate that "weather is the most promotable element in our newscast. Most people tell us weather is the reason they watch local news," she adds. And that's why weather is teased throughout the newscast.

It is extremely important before going to a commercial to tease a strong story, along with one or two other stories that have special appeal. The idea is that if you do not hook listeners on the first tease, you may get them on the second or third. If you do, it will help keep the audience around through the commercial, which is the valley of the newscast. After the commercial, the audience expects another good story at the top of the next segment, and the process begins all over again. A peak and then a valley and another peak and another valley, throughout each section of the newscast.

This theory of producing is different from the traditional approach (which started in radio), which gives the audience the best stories at the top of the newscast and follows them with stories of less and less interest until it's time to say goodbye. This format made sense for radio and for the early TV newscasts, which did not run more than 15 minutes. The same so-called *inverted pyramid* system also was used by many TV producers even when newscasts expanded to 30 minutes. (Actually they only had about 20 minutes of news to offer because of commercials and opens and closes.)

The inverted pyramid approach continues in many small markets because it often was difficult to find just one strong story each night. The producers of these shows, particularly the less creative ones, try to hold an audience by teasing sports and weather. In many communities, of course, sports and the weather are important news, as are college and high school sports scores. In farming communities, the weather may be the best story of the day, night, and week; however, creative producers, even in small markets, should try to use the peak-and-valley theory. This approach has become practically essential for any TV station that has an hour newscast. Some stations are now running news for 90 minutes, and some even for two hours.

# Rhythm and Flow

Commenting on the peak-and-valley theory, former CNN executive vice president Ted Kavanau said packages, voiceovers, and copy stories (anchor readers) should be used to create a rhythm and flow in each section. He suggested using a good tape story at the top of the segment, then some anchor copy and maybe a voiceover, and some more copy until "you build to a package," a story with some emotion in it. If you have more time in the segment, Kavanau says, start the process again: good tape-copy-tape-copy-package-copy-tape-copy-package-copy.

Although packages appeal most to the audience, producers shouldn't play one off another. You should place them effectively throughout the newscast, limiting one to each section. The package also serves another important purpose: It gives the anchors a breather and a chance for them, the producers, and the director to get organized for the rest of the show.

The line producer, who sits near the director in the control room, often needs time to reshuffle parts of the rundown and script because of late-breaking news and because packages often are not ready on time to be aired. Problems also develop when videotapes, or the decks that play them, malfunction.

# A Difference of Opinion

As we stated earlier, no two producers are likely to decide the exact same order of the stories in a newscast. If you examine the newscasts at different stations in the same market on the same night, you'd see that even the lead stories are often different unless some story completely dominates the news.

"We always consider the who-cares and so-what factors," says Denise Clod-jeaux, a former producer and now news director of KEZI-TV, Eugene, Oregon. "If your reaction to a story is who cares or so what, then it doesn't belong in a newscast," she said.

At KTVK-TV, executive producer Lisa Hudson led a newscast with an interview with the mother of a Phoenix man who committed suicide with the help of Dr. Kevorkian. She admitted that the mother had already been interviewed by a Phoenix newspaper but said "It's different on TV. You see and hear the mother. The emotion and facial expressions that don't come through in a newspaper story, come through on TV."

Hudson also noted that her news runs 90 minutes and that her audience changes. When the show starts at 5 P.M., the audience is older. As the newscast continues, the makeup of the audience becomes younger. She said she treats each block like a different newscast, designing it for the changing audience.

The producer also said that at 5:30 P.M. she goes head-to-head with the network newscasts, so she packs that segment with a lot of national stories, leading with the big national story of the day. Again, KTVK-TV is an independent station, which broadcasts national and international as well as local news.

TV news consultant and former producer Mary Cox provides her "baker's dozen" suggestions for news producers:

1. Ask: What's the viewers' benefit?
2. Win the lead.
3. Put news in every section.
4. Make the show video-driven—go from video to video to video. (Most producers disagree on this one.)
5. Write tight, to the point.
6. Look for live opportunities without going live for the sake of going live.
7. Give stories the time they need.
8. Don't "force" a package, even if a reporter worked all day on it. If it doesn't work, dump it.
9. Tease news at the end of every section.
10. Include some of the newscast's best writing and video in the teases.
11. Go out strong, with a big finish (generally a package) to keep the audience with you.
12. Create a "magic moment" consisting of something memorable, such as great photography.
13. Avoid getting locked into local, local, local, national, national, national. People don't think that way and they don't tell stories that way.

The rundown, shown in Figure 23.1 beginning on the next page, was prepared by the executive producer at WHAS-TV in Louisville, Kentucky. This particular rundown was for the evening news on the day after the Oklahoma bomb blast, so it was top heavy with news of the bombing. WHAS-TV dumped the regular newscast and went live with the network feed from the scene.

| PAGE | ANC | SLUG | FORM | PB | TAPE# | WTR | ? | TTIME | TRT | BKTIME |
|------|-----|------|------|----|----|-----|---|-------|-----|--------|
| S-3B | GARY | VA BOMB SCARE | ENG# VO OS | -- | ------ | --- | R | :30 | 0:51 | JE- | 1:58 |
| ***** | **** | 8:00PM*********** | ************* | ** | ****** | *** | R | 0:00 | 0:00 | - | 1:07 |
| ***** | **** | DATE: 04/20/95 | P: BUNTON | | | | R | | 0:00 | - | 1:07 |
| | | HEADLINES | | | | | R | | 0:00 | DB- | 1:07 |
| | | §§ ↑↑ | | | | | R | | 0:00 | - | 1:07 |
| | | §§ ↑↑ | | | | | R | | 0:00 | - | 1:07 |
| | | §§ ↑↑ | | | | | R | | 0:00 | - | 1:07 |
| | | | | | | | R | | 0:00 | - | 1:07 |
| 00000 | ---- | | OPEN CART | | | | R | :20 | 0:20 | - | 1:07 |
| S-1 | G/S | VIDEO OPEN | ENG# SOT | | | X | R | 00:05 | 0:25 | DB- | 0:47 |
| | | | W/BANNER | B2 | ------ | --- | R | | 0:00 | - | 0:22 |
| | | | 2SHOT | | | | R | | 0:00 | - | 0:22 |
| S-1A | SGC | WEATHER UPDATE | WX STUFF | | | X | R | 0:30 | 0:39 | DB- | 0:22 |
| | | | | | | | R | | 0:00 | | 0:17 |
| | | | | | | | R | | 0:00 | | 0:17 |
| S-2 | S/G | OKC TODAY | INTRO/ESS/OS | | | X | R | 0:00 | 0:35 | DB | 0:17 |
| 00 | ---- | ROEDEMEIER CART | ENG# PKG | B3 | 95-54 | --- | R | 0:31 | 1:11 | KD | 0:52 |
| | | | ESS BANNER | | | | R | | 0:00 | | 2:03 |
| NEW2A | GARY | OKC TAG | COPY | | | X | R | 0:00 | 0:13 | KD | 2:03 |
| | | | | | | | R | | 0:00 | | 2:16 |
| S-3 | SWAN | GENERAL SECURITY | ENG# VO OS | B4 | ------ | X-- | R | 0:00 | 0:25 | SC | 2:16 |
| | | | WIPE TO | | | | R | | 0:00 | | 2:41 |
| S-3A | SWAN | SECURITY SOUND | ENG# SOT/VO | B2 | ------ | X-- | R | 0:11 | 0:17 | SC | 2:41 |
| | | | | | | | R | | 0:00 | | 2:58 |
| S-3B | GARY | MISSING WOMAN | ENG# VO | B3 | ------ | X-- | R | 0:00 | 0:26 | AJ | 2:58 |
| | | | | | | | R | | 0:00 | | 3:24 |
| S-4 | SWAN | TOSS TO JTURNER | IN/OS/DBLBOX | | | X | R | 0:00 | 0:21 | JE | 3:24 |
| S-5 | JTUR | BOMB FACTS | CAM 7 | | | X | R | 0:00 | 0:15 | JE | 3:45 |
| 00 | ---- | JTURNER CART | ENG# PKG | B4 | ------ | --- | R | 0:48 | 1:30 | JE | 4:00 |
| | | | ESS BANNER | | | | R | | 0:00 | | 5:30 |
| S-5A | S/J | BOMB TAG | DOUBLE BOX | | | X | R | 0:00 | 0:17 | JE | 5:30 |
| | | | | | | | R | | 0:00 | | 5:47 |
| S-6 | GARY | PEOPLE REACTION | INTRO/OS | | | X | R | 0:00 | 0:17 | PC | 5:47 |
| 00 | ---- | CTURNER CART | ENG# PKG | B2 | ------ | --- | R | 1:15 | 1:38 | PC | 5:55 |
| | | | ESS BANNER | | | | R | | 0:00 | | 7:33 |
| S-7 | SWAN | CHURCH SERVICE | ENG# VO | B3 | ------ | X-- | R | :05 | 0:21 | DB | 7:33 |
| | | | | | | | R | | 0:00 | | 7:54 |
| S-9 | G/S | TEASE#1 (CRIME | ENG# | B4 | _____ | X | R | 0:08 | 0:22 | AD | 7:54 |
| | | WEATHER RADAR) | | | | | R | | 0:00 | | 8:16 |
| ***** | **** | ===== BREAK #1 *** | ************* | ** | ****** | *** | R | 02:20 | 2:20 | | 8:16 |
| S-10 | SWAN | THUNDER PREPS | INTRO/OS | | | X | R | 0:00 | 0:13 | LS | 10:36 |
| 00 | ---- | LASMITH CART | ENG# PKG | B2 | ------ | --- | R | 0:32 | 1:30 | | 10:49 |
| S-10A | SWAN | THUNDER TAG | COPY | | | X | R | 0:00 | 0:12 | LS | 12:19 |
| | | | | | | | R | | 0:00 | | 12:31 |
| | | | | | | | R | 0:00 | 0:00 | | 12:31 |
| S-12 | GARY | TOSS TO DOYLE | INTRO | | | X | R | 0:00 | 0:13 | AD | 12:31 |
| S-13 | DOYL | KIDS & CRIME | INTRO/OSONSET | | | X | R | 0:00 | 0:13 | AD | 12:44 |
| 00 | ---- | DOYLE CART | ENG# PKG | B3 | ------ | --- | R | 0:49 | 1:28 | AD | 12:57 |
| S-13A | DOYL | CRIME TAG | ESS | | | X | R | 0:00 | 0:24 | AD | 14:25 |
| | GSD | WRAP UP | THREE SHOT | | | | R | | 0:00 | | 14:49 |
| | | | | | | | R | | 0:00 | | 14:49 |
| S-14 | S/G | TEASE#2 (WEATHER) S | RADAR | | | X | R | 0:00 | 0:15 | DB | 14:49 |
| ***** | **** | ===== BREAK #2 *** | ************* | ** | ****** | *** | R | 02:10 | 2:10 | | 15:04 |
| | | WX OPEN/TAYLOR | | | | | R | 00:10 | 0:10 | | 17:14 |
| S-15 | TAYL | WEATHER | ENG# VO&KEY | B4 | _____ | X | R | 02:15 | 2:15 | KD | 17:24 |
| | | | | | | | R | | 0:00 | | 19:39 |
| S-16 | | WXR WRAP | ZSHOT | | | X | R | :10 | 0:10 | KD | 19:39 |
| | | | | | | | R | 2 | 0:00 | | 19:49 |
| S-17 | S/G | TEASE#3 (SPORTS) | COPY | | | X | R | 0:00 | 0:15 | DB | 19:49 |

**Figure 23.1**

```
DEARING                     THU APR 20 17:37  PAGE  2
                RADAR              RADAR                                     R   0:00  0:00        20:04
*****  ****  ===== BREAK #3  ***  *************  **  ******  ***  R   02:10  2:10        20:04
                SPORTSOPEN/GUPTON                                            R   00:10  0:10        22:14
S-18           1ST SPORTS         ENG #      /VO  B3  _____             R   00:03  0:05        22:24
                                                                            R           0:00        22:29
SP-1   GUPR   ROYAL DONATION      ENG #      /VO  B4  _____             R   0:00   0:21  DB   22:29
                                   WIPE  TO                                  R           0:00        22:50
SP-2   GUPR   ROYAL BITE          ENG#   SOT   B2  _____             R           0:10        22:50
SP-5   GUPR   ELTISH              COPY                                       R           0:15        23:00
SP-6   GUPR   HUBBARD LEWIS       ENG#   VO    B2  _____             R           0:20        23:15
                                   WIPE   TO                                 R           0:00        23:35
SP-7   GUPR   RYDER REAX          ENG#   SOT   B3  _____             R           0:15        23:35
SP-8   GUPR   HOLE IN ONE         ENG    VO          S-___             R           0:00        23:50
                                                                            R           0:00        23:50
S-19   GSD    SPORTS WRAP         3SHOT                        X      R   :10    0:10  KD   23:50
                                                                            R           0:00        24:00
S-20   G/S    TEASE #4 (BOMB  )   ESS  FULL     _   _____   X      R   0:00   0:15  DB   24:00
*****  ****  ===== BREAK #4 ***  *************  **  ******  ***  R   02:55  2:55        24:15
S-21   SWAN   NIGHTTEAM TEASE     ENG#   VO  OS  B4  _____   ___  R   00:20  0:20        27:10
                                                                            R   0:00   0:00        27:30
S-22   GSC    WXR WRAP            3SHOT/GRAPHX             X      R   :20    0:20  KD   27:30
                                                                            R           0:00        27:50
S-23   G/S    BOMB ESSAY          INTRO                   X      R   0:00   0:22  DB   27:50
00     ----   SAMLER CART         ENG#   PKG   B2  ------   ---  R   1:46   1:46        28:12
                                                                            R           0:00        29:58
                                   AUDIO  CART                               R   :02    0:02        29:58
*****  ****  **** END BREAK ***  *************  **  ******  ***  R   0:00   0:00        30:00
```

**Figure 23.1**  continued

It's a good idea to avoid leaving viewers with a sense that "there's nothing good in the news tonight" by working some "uplifting" stories into the show.

# Bright Future

There seems little doubt that the future is bright for those who decide to go into producing. The expansion of local news and the spread of all-news channels to more cities have created a need for producers of all kinds.

There is a high demand for producers because so many young people want to be on the air. What they do not understand is that producer jobs also require lots of talent. Terry Likes and Barry Gresham of Western Kentucky University say "the general perception is that, until recently, the producer was the unseen, underpaid, unheralded coordinator of the newsroom ... that captures little limelight compared to on-air talent." But the authors of an article in the *RTNDA Communicator* say that, to the news director, "the producer position requires loads of talent." The authors quote a variety of news managers on the subject:

- Michael Castengera, TV news consultant and former news director, notes that good producers need a lot of skills not required in the past, such as knowledge of ESS, microwave, satellite, and computer technologies. He says that, at his former station, producers were on a faster career track and were paid more than reporters. He adds that the lack of good producers has reached a crisis point.

- Producers also have to be good writers and reporters. Former WSMV-TV news director Allan Griggs reminds us that producing is a "tough, demanding, physically and emotionally draining job." He adds that good producers are "unique" because they are not bothered "by long hours and the tough demands of the job."

Authors Likes and Gresham say the good news for those who decide on a future in producing is that salaries are probably going to keep climbing as the demand for good producers increases. It's also important to remember that producers have a much better chance of getting into management than anchors.

Al Tompkins, who has 24 years of professional experience in major markets, says good producers manage things and lead people; they learn the skills of communication; they remember to use active listening. Tompkins—now with the Poynter Institute in St. Petersburg—says successful producers come to work with "first-day enthusiasm." Tompkins offers the following list of things that news directors want from producers:

- *Be an adviser to your boss.* Be strong enough to give him or her the good news as well as the bad. Help your boss know what is really happening out in the trenches.
- *Value the judgments and contributions of others.* Listen to reporters, directors, and photojournalists; respect their ideas and expertise; allow them to help you discover that there is not one truth, but many truths.
- *Discover all you can about your audience and seek to serve them.* Draw from personal experience, research, a wide network of diverse contacts; recognize that viewers are usually not all like journalists in the way they live, think, or view the content and execution of newscasts.
- *Be a writing example.* Teach, delegate, coach, and resist the tendency "to do it all yourself." Help to develop associate producers. Ask open-ended questions. Listen more than you speak.
- *Anticipate major events.* Tompkins says effective producers know what graphics are needed to cover the big story and what special decisions about spending or staffing or equipment need to be made in advance.
- *Recognize that lead-in programming is important.* Tompkins advises producers to know their lead-in programming because it will help them to step back from the show, consider the lead-in, and write preshow teases to the ear of the audience. He says the best place to capture the viewers is the show before your own program.
- *Step back from the show.* Tompkins says producers should take a good look at the broadcast they are about to present and ask if it truly reflects what happened in the community that day. Does it portray the community as it really is, or as the producer narrowly defined it?
- *Producing is the glue that holds the newsroom together.* Producers set the tone; they regulate style; they shape content. Effective producers nurture, value, and

defend the principle of an individual's right to express ideas even if they are unpopular.

# Energy

Another veteran producer, Ted Kavanau, now president of Television Innovations, says energy is the key to success for a TV producer. He says a casual person rarely makes a good producer. "An energetic producer always does a more exciting program . . . a fast-moving and interesting-looking newscast," said Kavanau. He also stressed that flow is important. Kavanau added that producers should find the most important reason a story should follow the previous one. Here is some other advice from Kavanau:

- Bridge your stories by using those that help bring you from one category to another.
- Write short leads to tape. Don't punish people with talk when you have good video.
- If you have good pictures, make them last by writing enough copy.
- End segments with strength. Never use a weak story at the top of a segment.
- Like packages, never put features back-to-back.

# Still Pictures

Many producers tend to avoid still pictures, but when used correctly, especially in a sequence, they can be effective—almost as much as video.

Maps and other graphics also should be used to support copy. If a plane has crashed in some relatively unknown area, it helps the viewer if you show a map and indicate with a star where the plane went down. The map should include at least one town familiar to your audience.

# Live Shots

Ever since the technology allowed TV stations to go live from the scene on a daily basis, there has been a debate about whether the technique is being overused—such as going live for live's sake.

If there is a major traffic snarl in New York City because of road construction during the rush hour, does it make any sense to send a reporter back to the scene for the 11 P.M. news—as one station did—when the highway is virtually abandoned? Even the reporter at the scene was annoyed by this decision, because it was cold and she was shivering. "What the hell am I doing here?" she asked on the two-way radio, before the anchor tossed the broadcast to her.

The need to use the live shot as much as possible seems to have diminished somewhat as the novelty wore off and station managers have complained less to news directors, "We paid a bunch for this stuff . . . make it pay for itself." But Alice Scott, a former reporter at KCRA-TV in Sacramento, says she did at least three live shots a week and many of them were "live for live's sake." She says she used to argue the point until she realized that "marketing is important to the station."

Marcia Crawley of WFLA-TV in Tampa-St. Petersburg says most reporters have no idea why they do so many live shots, and it's frustrating to have to do them when there is no apparent reason.

Most stations in the Phoenix market are heavy "live" stations. Why live? KPNX-TV's Julie Frisoni says it demonstrates to the audience that "you're out there, in their community, covering a story important to them. Our research shows that the viewer's perception of a reporter, who appears live, has more facts than the reporter doing a story from the station even though both use the same facts," says Frisoni.

In addition, Frisoni believes that a reporter at the scene tends to be more on top of a story than a reporter getting his or her information over the phone. Finally, she says, newsmakers are more likely to talk to a reporter in person than on the phone. She says, "it's easy to say no to a strange voice on the phone, but it's difficult to say no to a reporter while looking him in the eye."

# Back Timing

One major task for the line producer is to ensure that the newscast gets off the air on time. This is particularly important when computers are in charge of establishing when programs and commercials start and end. We all have witnessed situations when one program is cut off abruptly by a new program. That situation happens because a computer has established the time when the new program or commercial is supposed to start, and start it will, on time.

The timing is particularly critical when local news is followed by a network program. The network computer will take over regardless. If the local news anchors are still saying goodbye, or the station's final commercial or logo is still playing, something is going to get cut off if the newscast timing is not accurate. If your commercial is cut, that revenue goes down the drain.

To defend against such problems, the show producer must always know whether the newscast is "running on time." It is virtually impossible for the producer to keep the newscast flowing exactly on time for 30 minutes or an hour because sometimes anchors stumble on some lines or make an unscheduled remark coming out of a tape, or a package sticks in the tape deck and has to be re-cued. That's why producing is so difficult; the unexpected often happens.

The producer must always know if the newscast is ahead or behind schedule. If the newscast is short, because a tape gets caught in the playback, the producer must find something else to take its place. The same is true if the show is running long—something must be cut. So, producers use a technique called *back timing* to make sure the program ends on time. In most newsrooms, the computer system back times a show for you, but a producer always needs to be able to do the math on her own.

The computer automatically tells you where you stand on time at each point in the newscast. A "minus" sign means the show is running long. Figuring the time works like this: Take the total amount of time for the show (i.e., 30 minutes). Subtract time for commercials (usually 8:00), time for weather (usually 2:30), and time for sports (usually 3:00). The number left is your news hole—the time you have for news. In most cases, it's between 10 and 13 minutes. Add up the time each story takes—from the anchor introduction, the tape time, and the anchor time, then see how it works!

Throughout the show, the producer must keep track of the time—whether the show is "short" or "long." "At times, you make split-second decisions to drop a story if the show is running long. If the show is running short, you may ask your anchors to chat a little more or read pad copy (extra news stories that the anchor can read if the show is running short). Sports and weather often lose time if there's a lot of news happening. With experience, a producer can often sense if the show is running on time.

The bottom line—whether you use a computer or your own math—is to get off on time. Network news waits for no one, especially a producer who mis-times a show.

# Summary

The best opportunities for young people entering broadcast news are in producing. The expansion of local news and the spread of all-news channels to more cities should create a need for producers of all kinds. There is a high demand for producers because so many young people want to go on the air because of the perceived "glamour" and higher salaries usually associated with such jobs; however, the competition for anchor and reporter positions is much greater.

There also are substantial rewards in producing news programs. Certainly, salaries are going to continue to improve as the demand increases for people to produce news. Although producers work behind the scenes, their jobs are exciting and occasionally also glamorous. The excitement comes in the realization that as a producer you are "in control." What you do in the newsroom determines what goes on the air. You are limited only by your own imagination and creativity. As was pointed out, in many newsrooms, the producers are in complete charge of the news.

Along with that power, however, comes a lot of responsibility and risk. You will need good news judgment and other skills in many areas. Good writing is essential. Some experience in reporting is also desirable. You will also need to have an excellent knowledge of production techniques—microwave and satellite feeds, computer technologies, video editing, electronic still storage, and several emerging technologies.

Another important consideration is stress. It's a tough, emotionally and physically draining position with long hours. But the potential rewards are great if you have any interest in management. Producers are on the best track to the management offices. You must learn how to do just about everything in the newsroom, and how to work with and manage a variety of co-workers. Who could be better qualified for the "boss's" job?

# Review Questions

1. List the various duties of the executive producer.
2. What are the responsibilities of the line producer?
3. Describe what the field producer does.
4. What is a rundown and why is it so important?
5. Explain the "peak-and-valley" theory of producing.
6. What is the meaning of the term *inverted pyramid* in producing?
7. What is a live shot and when should it be used?
8. What's the purpose of the staff meetings?
9. Explain the term *back times*. Why is it so important?
10. Why are the meters so important?

# Exercises

1. Try to arrange with one of your local TV stations to "hang out" with a producer. Weekends are the best time because the pace is usually slower.
2. Arrange to accompany a field producer on a photo shoot. If there are none in your market, go along with the reporter who, in this case, is the field producer.
3. Take notes as you watch a local newscast, and try to determine what kind of a format the producer is using. See if you can spot "peaks and valleys."

# **24** Using the Hardware

Although we emphasize the need for journalists to develop writing and reporting skills, students also need to acquire some basic technical and production skills, such as how to use video cameras, tape recorders, and editing machines. These skills are necessary in the increasingly competitive world of broadcast journalism.

Some stations have always required reporters to shoot their own stories, interviews, and even standup reports and then bring that material back to the station, where they edit it for that evening's newscast. At some of these stations, the reporters sometimes even anchor the news and introduce the packages they have shot and edited. The advantage of working at small stations is that you get to do everything and, therefore, have an opportunity to learn *how* to do everything.

This chapter introduces some of the technological tools used in broadcast news and the skills necessary to operate them.

## Checking the Equipment

Camera equipment keeps getting better and easier to operate. Most people with even minimal technical skills can learn how to work a camera with a few lessons. This chapter does not attempt to provide those lessons, but it does offer some advice on how to shoot the kind of video necessary to put together a good package. Before discussing shooting techniques, let's look at some basic procedures that reporters must follow when using video equipment.

Make sure all the equipment is operating properly before leaving to do a story. Shoot some video and play it back to be sure that the camera and recorder are functioning. Also test the microphone and the lights. Don't wait until you arrive at the scene to discover that something is not working.

### *Batteries and a Power Cord*

Be sure to have plenty of battery power, and carry an extension cord and an AC adaptor. Some new batteries will power equipment for up to four hours. One

**Figure 24.1** Microwave dishes outside CNN headquarters in Atlanta.
(© 1992. All rights reserved.)

good battery and a backup should be all you need to complete your story, but if you have access to more, take them along. Batteries are often the weak link in your equipment chain. It's hard to tell exactly how long batteries will last, especially under different temperature conditions.

There are new batteries out now that perform well and, in some cases, last a lot longer than the old nickel cadmium or "nicad" batteries. These batteries are lithium ion and nickel metal hydride, as well as some other exotic formulations—a fuel cell has even been developed to power a camcorder.

A word of caution: Keep all types of batteries away from extreme temperatures. Always keep them as close to room temperature as possible. Even when fully charged, nickel batteries quickly lose their power in below-freezing temperature. Many photographers keep their batteries in inside jacket pockets in winter. Never leave batteries in the trunk of a car or in direct sunlight when it's hot outside.

If you are working indoors and doing interviews, using an AC power source helps conserve your batteries for shooting outdoors. It's also a good idea to carry a three-to-two prong adaptor because many older buildings do not have three-prong outlets. A four- or six-outlet power strip also comes in handy. If a backup microphone and light are available, bring them along in case a problem develops.

## Tripods

Most camerapeople who have been in the business for a while have little trouble shooting video with the camera on their shoulders. But even the pros use a tripod for an interview if they have the time to set it up. For beginners, it is best to use a tripod as much as possible, particularly for interviews, because weaving and bobbing heads are not acceptable in professional newscasts. Try shooting some of your cover footage (discussed later in this chapter) without a tripod when the video is not critical, so that you can start to feel comfortable with the camera on your shoulder. Unfortunately, many of the cameras used in colleges are difficult to use on the shoulder because they are lightweight models. It is easier to shoot from the shoulder with the heavier, more expensive professional cameras because the weight adds stability.

## Earphones

A common problem for young people just starting to work with equipment is recording good sound. A particular problem is the set of switches on the camcorder that directs the signal from the two microphone inputs to the two (or four) audio channels on the tape. A set of earphones is critical in ensuring that you are getting the signal from the handheld microphone to the tape. If you aren't listening, you could end up with both audio tracks containing a signal from the shotgun microphone mounted on the camera. If you are responsible for recording good sound, wear earphones during the interview. You cannot depend on the camera's sound-meter reading because it just tells you that sound is being picked up. It does not guarantee that the sound is being recorded or that the quality is good. The only way to pick up static or other disturbances is to listen to the sound through earphones.

## Filters

Every camera has a built-in filter system to accommodate different lighting situations. If you are shooting indoors with artificial light, you should use a different filter than you would outdoors in natural light. If you use the wrong filters, the colors on the tape will be badly distorted. News photographer Lennie Tierney says there are two essential numbers to remember when thinking about filters: 3,200 degrees K (Kelvin) and 5,600 degrees K.

Indoor light or artificial light is 3,200 K light, and outdoor or sunlight is 5,600 K light. Cameras may also have additional filters for shooting outdoors in bright situations, such as after a snowfall or on the beach. The initials ND that appear on some 5,600 K filters stand for "neutral density." These filters produce the same colored video as the 5,600 K filter but reduce the amount of light entering the camera.

## White Balancing

Along with filters, a white balancing system is also built into video cameras to provide accurate color. Tierney explains how the system works: Anyone who has ever looked at a sunset knows that sunlight varies quite a bit in color. Indoor lighting also varies, but our eyes naturally adjust to different lights to make things look normal. To a video camera, fluorescent lights look green, incandescent lights look red, and sunlight looks blue. If you don't use the right filter and white balance your camera, the video will be off color.

To white balance the camera, you must aim it at something white—such as a white wall or piece of white paper—while you push the white balance switch or button on the camera. You must repeat this process each time you shoot at a different location.

All modern ENG video cameras have preset and automatic white balance settings. In the preset mode, the video will look good if the color temperature of the light in which you're shooting is near 3,200 K indoors or 5,600 K outdoors. Many photographers use the preset white balance for most of their shooting.

The automatic white balance setting is for use when the light in which you're shooting is not near 3,200 K or 5,600 K. Fluorescent lights, for example, are not close to 3,200 K, so to make the video look right, flip the white balance selector to automatic, fill the screen of your viewfinder with a white object, and then hit the white balance switch on the camera. This process prevents the video from having a sickly green fluorescent look.

## Mixed Light

Any light entering a room through a window can cause problems for news photographers. The best practice is to avoid shooting near windows. Even a window

**Figure 24.2**
A WAFB-TV microwave truck prepares to send a live signal to the station's tower, seen in the distance.
(Photo by James Terry)

with the blinds closed can create a distracting blue highlight if it is in the background of an interview shot. For a beginner, it is best to shoot the interview either with all artificial light or outside with natural light. If there is enough light coming through a window, the interview can be shot nicely with the natural sunlight if the outdoor camera filter (3,200 K) is used. As you gain experience, you'll learn the various filter and white balancing combinations to use in mixed lighting.

Most professional news photographers use what are called *dichroic* or "dicro" filters that clip on the front of their lights. Dicro filters simulate sunlight and allow you to use your artificial light during the day to augment the natural sunlight already present. Dicro filters on a light can be used to illuminate a head when shooting in a room already filled with natural sunlight from windows. Dicro filters also are commonly used during the day to brighten the face of your subject when you have a bright background to light a reporter doing a daytime shot or to brighten a head when shooting during the day in deep shade.

Meanwhile, Lennie Tierney provides these tips to help you avoid mistakes:

1. Always check your filter first. It must be on 3,200 K for artificial light or 5,600 K for sunlight.
2. When in doubt about lighting color (temperature), check that you are using the appropriate filter, then switch to automatic setting and white balance your camera on a white object.
3. When in a hurry, use the preset setting and the appropriate filter.

## Focusing

Poor focus can destroy a story. Tierney advises beginning photographers to focus every shot. "I zoom in to every subject, focus on it, and then pull out to set the composition I want. When shooting a large subject, such as a stadium," Tierney says, "I'd zoom in to the farthest part of the subject, like the backfield fence, focus on it, and then pull out to reveal the entire subject."

Tierney says shooting moving subjects is more difficult, especially in low-light situations such as at a basketball game. "It is second nature to an experienced photographer to roll the focus barrel on the camera lens in the right direction in order to keep the subject in focus as it gets closer or farther away," says Tierney. He suggests that beginning photographers practice this technique by shooting people as they walk around the newsroom. When you are shooting a head, zoom in and focus on the eye or nose—the same way you would if you were using a 35 mm camera.

Most lenses have a "macro" function that allows you to shoot small things very close to the lens. If your lens is in "macro" function when you are trying to shoot normally, everything will be out of focus no matter if zoomed in or out. In most cases, the macro function is a ring on the barrel of the lens near the aperture (iris) ring. You can feel it click into place when it is secured in the disabled mode.

### *Time Coding*

Most video recorders purchased today record not only pictures and sound but also a numbered index called a *time code*. This time code can be set for running time or time of day. When the running-time code is set, the time code on the tape advances by hours, minutes, seconds, and frames. For the time-of-day code, the recorder is set to the correct time of day, and whenever the tape records, the correct time of day appears on the tape. This setting is often used when shooting sports highlights. The photographer is often on the sidelines shooting with the time-of-day code while the reporter is in the press box. When some exciting play is made, the reporter simply notes the time. During the editing process, the editor then finds the time of day given to him or her by the reporter, and the exciting play is easily isolated because broadcast cameras generally have Record Run, Free Run, and Date/Time code functions. Tierney recommends Record Run (r-run). He says he's never found a practical use for Free Run in the news environment. If the camera is in Free Run, editing will be a "nightmare," he says.

## Shooting Techniques

Let's look now at a few fundamental shooting techniques that beginners should learn immediately. First, avoid zooms and pans. Unless there is some important reason to zoom in or pan on something, avoid those movements. It is better to cut from one shot to another.

Consider composition carefully. Shoot heads slightly off center, not right in the middle. Shoot the head over the reporter's shoulder or at a slight angle. Profiles do not work well because they lose the viewer's attention. The head should be looking at the reporter and, as a result, at the audience at home if the camera is positioned correctly, just behind or slightly to the side of the reporter. It is sometimes effective to shoot the head tightly at a slight angle. The head should be in the corner with little or no open space. These shots are common on *Sunday Morning*, *60 Minutes*, and other investigative and magazine programs. Some of the best photographers in the business are assigned to these programs, so students should routinely watch these shows for both their editorial content and their camera work.

Keep in mind, however, that these programs normally do not font heads. Camerapeople working for a regular newscast must get some medium shots that will leave enough room for fonts. Some news directors discourage tight head shots because most sound bites are short, and it is difficult to font them. Tight shots are sometimes effective, however, if the interview is dramatic or emotional or the head is interesting because of age, beauty, or some other reason.

Some camerapeople like to get a variety of headshots, but it is important to remember not to change shots while someone is speaking unless there is a good reason. If, for example, the person on camera begins to cry, you would probably want to zoom in for a closeup; however, that movement should be done slowly.

Remember that the reporter will not appear on camera most of the time, so all of the shots should concentrate on the head. The reporter is brought into the picture after the interview is completed, when the cameraperson shoots the cutaways and reversals that are used as a part of the editing process to avoid jump cuts. As discussed earlier, editing interviews presents a problem because sound bites cannot be juxtaposed without creating a jump cut. Without something in between the two sound bites, the head appears to jerk when the sound bites are edited together.

Although Chapter 20, "Ethics and the Law," details the ethical aspects of using reversals, we have included examples of how to shoot this popular method of avoiding the jump cut because reporters and camerapeople are routinely expected to shoot them.

In Figure 24.3, the cameraperson is shooting the newsmaker. In Figure 24.4, the camera is reversed, and the reporter is being photographed as though she were listening to the newsmaker. The reverse shot works best when part of the interviewee's shoulder and cheek is in the picture. It is important, however, to remember that the camera must shoot over the correct shoulder. One way is to imagine that a line is running between the reporter and the newsmaker. The cameraperson should not cross that line when shooting the reversal or the reporter will appear to be looking in the wrong direction.

**Figure 24.3**  Cameraman John Connelly shoots an interview over the shoulder of Reporter Cynthia Nickerson of WBRZ-TV, Baton Rouge, Louisiana. (Photo by James Terry)

**Figure 24.4**   Cameraman Connelly gets reversal shots for use in editing the Nickerson interview. (Photo by James Terry)

## Cover Footage

The best way to avoid jump cuts is to use appropriate *cover footage*—video illustrating what the newsmaker is discussing. Good pictures usually are more interesting than heads, anyway, and cover footage allows editors to connect as many sound bites as they like without jump cuts.

## Establishing Shots

Some of the first pictures a cameraperson takes at the scene are establishing shots. These are wide shots of the activity at the scene of a fire or an accident, of floodwaters pounding against seawalls, or of baseball fans lined up outside the stadium before a World Series game. Establishing shots set the stage for what is to follow, and they often provide the opening video for the story.

## Sequential Shooting

Good videographers shoot their cover footage in a sequential manner to make the story visually interesting and to greatly reduce editing time. Sequential shooting is a way to tell a story with pictures and lead the audience along. Here's an example of a feature story on a police cadet at a practice range shooting a pistol at targets:

Shot 1: Tight on the trunk lock as the key is inserted. Pull out as trunk lid opens to reveal gun case.

Shot 2: Tight shot looking up at cadet's face as he works in trunk.

Shot 3: Over the shoulder of cadet's hands lifting gun from case.

Shot 4: Tight shot of box of bullets in case as cadet's hand grabs them and moves them out of the shot.

Shot 5: Shot from behind as the cadet walks with gun toward range.

Shot 6: Medium shot of table at range. Cadet's hands place gun and bullets in shot.

Shot 7: Tight face shot.

Shot 8: Over-the-shoulder shot of bullets being loaded in gun.

Shot 9: Empty shot with out-of-focus background, then gun is raised into shot creating closeup of gun filling screen. Bang, Bang.

Shot 10: Closeup down range of holes being made in target.

When things are shot in this manner, there is no question about what shot comes next when you get in the editing booth to cut your story. Of course, discretion must be used. This type of shooting requires you to direct your subjects a bit—something that can be inappropriate and even unethical in some circumstances. As you get better at using this technique, however, you'll find ways to shoot sequentially on most assignments.

## Shooting Enough Footage

Reporters, especially inexperienced ones, often wonder whether they've asked enough questions. Camerapeople often feel the same way. With experience, they

**Figure 24.5** The control room at WBRZ-TV, Baton Rouge, Louisiana. (Photo by James Terry)

learn when they've shot enough pictures, but initially they all tend to overshoot, fearing, like reporters, that they might miss something. Eventually, a camera-person and a reporter who work together come to know when they have enough video. Until that time, shooting too much video is better than returning to the newsroom with too little.

# Recording Natural Sound

The importance of natural sound was discussed earlier; however, we will end this chapter with a reminder. Good pictures are essential for good television, but pictures are not nearly as effective without their natural sound. As for radio, natural sound is crucial because the sound provides many of the "pictures" for the radio audience.

# 25 The Job Search in a Changing Industry

It is difficult to predict where broadcast news is heading, but the so-called Information Superhighway already has had a major impact on news and all other programming. The Internet and broadcasters' use of Websites, which allow viewers to punch up news and ask for more details about certain stories that they are interested in, has been a major factor. The growing use of data-bases and the ability of people throughout the world to communicate with each other through their computers on the Internet also have presented a major distraction from TV.

Think of it this way: All those who loved shortwave radio over the decades have a new way to talk to one another instantly. Following the Oklahoma City bombing, thousands of Europeans, Asians, and others worldwide discussed the crime and tragedy and offered condolences to Americans, via their computers.

The communications explosion has meant new jobs for young people and new opportunities for those already in communications, as many workers leave traditional jobs in news to accept employment in allied areas, like the Internet. Some broadcast managers report losing workers to the new opportunities on the Internet.

So these are exciting times for young people going into communications. There are lots of new opportunities, but many of them may be different from the traditional ones. For example, "news-on-demand" is requiring a lot of people to gather additional information on stories and to work on the "outtakes" of stories that are normally gathered for the traditional two-minute packages. The only thing certain about the new technologies is that they are moving fast—almost too fast to keep up with. By the time you read this book, many of the things we say are likely to happen may well have already come about.

Another trend is that some television newspeople are now required to file their television stories, not only over the air, but also on the Internet and other media owned by their employer. This process is called *convergence*. Additionally, increasingly more television reporters are expected to be a "one-person band," doing their own camera work and editing in addition to reporting. Even

CNN is considering at least a modified form of both concepts (see "One-Person Band" and "Convergence" in Chapter 11).

By the year 2001, as the economy began to slow, the exodus of traditional broadcasters to the Internet had slowed, and CBS, NBC, News Corp, *The New York Times*, and Knight Ridder had cut back their online staffs from 16 to 50 percent. Is this situation a temporary aberration reflecting a soft economy? Perhaps.

# The Future of Broadcast News

The debate about the future of the traditional news networks has been going on for several years. There continues to be a serious question about whether the networks will continue to provide the kind of news that we have come to expect.

The all-news cable networks and even some local stations doing all news have taken away much of the clout that ABC, CBS, and NBC once had. CNN, Fox, and MSNBC have virtually taken over breaking news at all times from the networks, which have found it difficult to compete with news operations that *never sleep.*

The days when Americans turned to CBS and the other networks for breaking news have disappeared for all but those who do not have cable, and that number has dwindled greatly. Even the number of households that have the Internet is growing at an explosive rate.

This lack of tuning into the major networks is especially true for breaking news stories, such as Election 2000 when it took five weeks to determine who was elected president. CNN had great ratings for almost all of the entire period. The challenge of CNN and the rest of the cable news networks and stations has caused serious financial problems for the networks and, as more and more cable stations come into homes, those financial problems continue to exacerbate.

The traditional networks have cut back their news staffs drastically. The days when CBS, ABC, and NBC had almost unlimited funds for covering the news have long disappeared because of shrinking advertising dollars and a shrinking audience. Advertisers now have more places to spend their money, and they are spending much of it on cable channels that allow them to target specific audiences. The catch-all approach to reaching consumers—which is what the networks offer—has become much less attractive.

Does this mean that anchors of network evening newscasts will disappear? That suggestion has been around for some time now, and the trio is still on the air. But there is still reason to believe that what they will be anchoring may be different in the coming years. The financial resources the networks have to work with for news will no doubt continue to be limited. The networks already have closed down some of their national and international bureaus, and the extensive cutbacks in news personnel that have been going on for several years probably aren't over.

*ABC News* correspondent Ted Koppel predicted in *Modern Maturity* mag-azine that one network evening newscast will eventually disappear, one will take the high road, and one will take the low road. And as this book went to press, CNN announced a 10 percent cutback and stated that it is placing a greater emphasis on news personalities.

In March 2001, the three network news anchors discussed the state of their newscasts. They appeared on PBS's *News Hour with Jim Lehrer* in a segment hosted by media correspondent Terence Smith. Here are some excerpts:

**TERENCE SMITH:** The network evening news broadcasts of today are a far cry from what they once were . . . Collectively, their share of television sets in use at that hour, a key industry barometer, has declined precipitously from an average of 75 percent 30 years ago, to 44 percent today . . . Where has the audience gone?

**PETER JENNINGS:** Everywhere. Absolutely everywhere. It's gone to the cable channels, which deliver news, it's gone to all of the 75 or 275 channels that you can get on an average home set today.

**TOM BROKAW:** In 1970, when it got dark in America, there were only two planets in the universe: CBS and NBC. ABC wasn't even a player then. Now when it gets dark in the television universe, it's filled with planets out there and people have that many more choices.

**DAN RATHER:** I think it's inevitable that our audience share will go even lower . . .

**SMITH:** Many Americans get their news from all-news radio, the Internet, local news, and cable news—long before network anchors say "good evening." Critics sometimes assail the evening broadcasts as "news you already know."

**JENNINGS:** We have tried to change and give . . . a dimension of added value to the major stories of the day. So in some respects the big story of the day, the president does "x," is not as important to us as the second story, which is the president did "x" *because*.

**SMITH:** Is the impact of the three nightly news [broadcasts] less or different today than it was before?

**JENNINGS:** I suspect it may be diffused. I think that we have to work harder at finding those stories that have a major impact on the audience . . . the greatest single impact that I can remember had to do with the famine in Ethiopia and Sudan . . . But there are fewer and fewer opportunities.

| | |
|---|---|
| SMITH: | Three white male anchors still deliver the half-hour broadcast at essentially the same time and in the same format since Cronkite began the tradition. |
| JENNINGS: | It has stayed the same essentially in its form. Automobiles still have four tires and a central engine that transports them, but they have a different look about them, different styling, and we have different expectations of them as well. An audience's changing needs . . . |
| RATHER: | I think it's valid criticism to say that we haven't been thoughtful enough, nor have we acted quickly enough . . . to the changing needs of the audience and new ways of coverage and new ways of broadcasting. |
| SMITH: | And the news itself may also seem less urgent these days. |
| ED FOUHY [who worked for all three networks]: | All through those years of the Cold War, one reason we turned it on was to see whether or not something really awful had happened in the world. |
| SMITH: | While the structure hasn't fundamentally changed, the content of the news broadcast is different. Once, they sought to match the stories above the fold on the front page of the *Washington Post* and the *New York Times* . . . Now, traditional hard news is generally presented in the first block and, in some cases, only in the first segment . . . Before the broadcast typically turns to softer, lifestyle trend issues, the so-called news you can use. Has the emphasis on soft news attracted new viewers or turned people off? |
| RATHER: | I'm of the school that says it may have turned some off. I'm in the minority. It's fair to say that majority thinking in television newsrooms these days is that you can't win with hard news and only hard news all the time . . . |
| SMITH: | At NBC, Tom Brokaw welcomes the changes in content. |
| BROKAW: | We have reduced the number of stories, we've spent more time on them, and what we try to do is say we think these are the biggest stories and the most important stories in your life. And by the way, here are some stories as well that are not in the day's news that are going to affect your lives as well in a variety of ways, about finance, health, changing the |

shape of the American family. That is all now part of what I believe is our agenda.

SMITH:  A recent study from Harvard's Shorenstein Center for the Press, Politics and Public Policy shows soft news is hastening the decline in news audiences nationally. Av Westin agrees.

AV WESTIN [a veteran network television producer]:  We in the television news business . . . have video-educated the American public to expect . . . more entertainment or more news you can use. And that used to be a pejorative phrase . . .

SMITH:  Nancy Maynard, a media analyst, says each of the broadcasts is seeking a certain slice of the audience . . .

NANCY MAYNARD [a media analyst]:  NBC's approach is much more lifestyle oriented. And it really does try to pull the women into the broadcast with issues that it feels are important trend issues . . . very different from the policy-oriented approach that CBS continues to use . . . And ABC has a very conversational approach. It's kind of a mix of the two, somewhat hard and somewhat soft.

SMITH:  Reports of the death of these broadcasts are premature. Taken together, the big three . . . command a huge audience, some 30 million viewers a night. No other news media—print, broadcast, or Internet—approaches that collective reach. But the network evening news broadcasts have lost the primacy they once had within their news divisions to the more profitable primetime magazine shows.

And while the overall viewing numbers remain large, the evening news audiences have shrunk to the point that the top-rated morning news show, *The Today Show*, has a rating that occasionally approaches that of the third-place *CBS Evening News*.

Worse yet, although the network news audience has always had a large number of older viewers, the collective audience is even older than it used to be. And there is the unknown variable of the Internet, especially among younger viewers.

MAYNARD:  We now have refrigeration for information. It's called digital information technology. You can store it, you can retrieve it at will.

SMITH:  Despite staff layoffs, foreign and domestic bureau closings, and resource cutbacks, the evening news broadcasts still do make money—a lot of it. The ratings leader, *NBC's Nightly News*, for example, reportedly generates $200 million a year in revenue and tens of millions in profits. That's why ratings, such as these minute-to-minute snapshots of all the content plays, remain crucial to the broadcast. Will the evening news broadcast continue in their current time slots?

JENNINGS: The hardest thing in the world to change is an audience's news habit.

RATHER: I dream of having a newscast 10 o'clock at night in the Eastern Time zone. Ten o'clock to eleven o'clock—what I'll call primetime.

BROKAW: What may change is that the cost of entertainment [programs] becomes so great that the network may decide that it needs a 10 o'clock newscast for an hour with some inserts for local news, much like the *Today* program has now. That's a model that I would encourage . . . maybe in the place of the nightly news, although I think there will always be a place for something at the end of the day for half an hour.

The networks themselves appear to be accepting their limitations in news, as indicated by some networks' decisions to ignore live coverage of some events that would have been routine in the past.

Also disappearing are some of the one-hour news specials that were once so popular. The networks' philosophy seems to be: Those who want such mate-

**Figure 25.1**
*NBC News* anchor Tom Brokaw.
(Courtesy NBC News)

rial can find it on CNN and the other all-news outlets and public broadcasting—why lose revenue from the "soaps" and other programming for special reports?

It also seems clear that the increasing influence in broadcasting of profit-minded corporations, such as General Electric (which owns NBC and WNBC), means that network news will be expected to do more to pay its own way than it has in the past.

The mergers of Disney and ABC and CNN and Time Warner also caused concern for news analysts, but those marriages have apparently not had any great impact on news operations. But the merger of CNN Time Warner into America Online has begun to raise some questions. CNN reporters are being required to operate cameras and editing equipment and to file reports for radio and the Internet.

Correspondent Ed Bradley and former CBS *Evening News* anchor Walter Cronkite both criticized the personnel cuts at the traditional networks. Cronkite acknowledges that the networks have economic problems, but claims that they have "cut more than the fat of the [news] budget, they've cut right down to the bone, to the point of amputation."

Bradley uses a similar analogy, saying the personnel cuts took not only the fat but "the muscle, bone, and the sinew of the news organizations. . . . We lost a lot of good people." (Many of those people moved to CNN.) Bradley adds: "There's more concern about news being profitable . . . and justifying expenditures, and I think it's going to dictate the kind of news we see on the air."

Bradley says, "The 'Evening News' is an expensive operation to tell people in 22 minutes what happened in their world today, but it's important for our network to fund it." Cronkite notes that because of all the news on satellites and on CNN, "somebody is always taking the bloom off the [networks'] breaking news story." As a result, he says, the networks probably have to consider "more interpretative type stories. I just hope," he says, "they stick with serious interpretative stories and don't go too soft."

Peter Herford, a veteran journalist and former *CBS News* vice president, said the three New York–based networks "are trying to maintain an image of national and international coverage while simultaneously making the transition to a different kind of network evening news."

He says stories that report on lifestyles and trends and background reports on the news are "becoming a staple of the network diet . . . because it is easier to control the costs of stories planned in advance than for the kind of crash-and-burn coverage which characterized network news in the past."

There are some bright spots. ABC's *Nightline* takes the high road, covering the major story of the day, in depth, without talking down to its audience. It does it five nights a week during a half-hour program that sometimes runs longer. Also taking the high road weekdays is PBS's *News Hour* with Jim Lehrer, the best and only one-hour commercial-free news program on television. And one might say that CNN, in its totality, has become what ABC, NBC, and CBS were like before their drastic cutbacks. Many of the CNN correspondents formerly worked for the traditional networks. But major changes were announced at CNN after the merger with AOL. Time will tell how they play out. While the traditional networks have cut back on their worldwide coverage, the network news magazine shows, such as *60 Minutes II, 20/20,* and *Dateline* have proliferated.

# The New Players

Although many jobs are disappearing along with the networks' viewers, Herford is optimistic. "From the standpoint of broadcast journalism as a craft," he says, "there is a great deal of hope." He said that instead of only three broadcast networks, there are now several nationally distributed sources of information.

What impact does the reduction of jobs at the networks have on the future of people who hope for careers in broadcasting? Actually, it's not too much because the entry-level jobs available to college graduates are rarely found at the networks, with the exception of CNN.

Because of its nonunion status, CNN still offers opportunities for newcomers, although not as many as it did in the 1980s when the network was just getting started. Many of the people who began with CNN in Atlanta started in entry-level video journalist (VJ) jobs and have moved on to become anchors, writers, reporters, editors, and producers. There should continue to be good opportunities for achievers as more local all-news operations expand, but by far most of the positions for people entering the field are still likely to be at local stations, which have shown good profits for years. Many of those stations are expanding their news programs, which means more jobs for you.

# Getting Started

Before you send out résumés and audition tapes, ask yourself some questions: Do I want to stay in my hometown? If I'm willing to move, do I want to head for a big city, a small town, or anyplace where there's an opening?

The best answer to all of your questions should probably be "I'll go anyplace I can find a job and I'll do whatever they want me to as long as it's in broadcasting." If that is your answer, you have the best shot at finding work. A lot of people will not go to Alaska, for example, so finding work there is much easier than in California, New York, or Florida.

The best approach is to complete an internship while you are still in college. Try to get one at a local station in the town where you wish to work. If the news director gets to know you and likes your work, there may be a job waiting for you when you graduate. News directors like to hire people who want to stay around for a while because there is usually a high turnover at local stations. So if you let the boss know you plan to stay in the area, it could work to your benefit.

**Figure 25.2**
Professor Mike Kabel works with broadcast students at Southern University in Baton Rouge, Louisiana. (Photo by James Terry)

All things being equal, an intern has an advantage on others in the job market because when a job becomes available, that person is a known quantity. The news director knows his or her work. For those who want to go to large-market stations right away, it usually means starting as a researcher or desk assistant.

Large metropolitan-area radio and TV stations do hire college graduates without experience for entry-level positions that sometimes lead to writer, reporter, and producer jobs; but there is no guarantee they will, and it sometimes takes a year or more to climb out of those entry-level situations.

Which is the best approach—the large or small market? Most professionals would probably say the small market because it gives you an opportunity to learn how to do everything. Former network correspondent Betsy Aaron says the small stations are the best route to go because "you get a chance to do things, to make mistakes. Starting at the networks leaves a big hole in your education and experience." Aaron started out as a secretary-researcher for network radio commentator Edward P. Morgan in 1959. "In those days," she says, "very few women were being hired as reporters."

Aaron recalls that while she was working in Washington for Morgan, she got a call from ABC. "It had a fancy job title," she says, "but it was basically another secretary job." She stayed at that job for two years and finally decided to send out a résumé tape to approximately 80 stations.

She was hired by a Philadelphia station, "but I was hired as a token," she acknowledges, "but I ended up being the first woman to cover city hall after I warned them that I would not do very well on the cooking and social beat. I'm sure that's what they hired me for." But she quickly adds that it was a great place to learn because "they let you do everything, even edit your own film."

# Women's Progress: Slow but Improving

Aaron says that when she started with CBS in 1976 the only women she can recall being in TV news at the time were Lisa Howard at ABC and Pauline Frederick at NBC. Aaron says, somewhat bitterly, "For a time, I thought I was 'one of the boys' and was being treated equally. It wasn't until much later that I realized that I had never been treated equally."

Aaron says that what saddens her the most is that "the young men who are making the decisions about which women go on the air today are making those decisions the same way the older men used to make them. Women in their fifties don't fit anyplace."

Lesley Stahl, co-editor of *60 Minutes*, is among the top women to have achieved success in television news, but she admits the road was not always easy. In her memoir *Reporting Live* (Simon & Schuster, 1999), she writes: "I knew my colleagues saw me as a lightweight unqualified to join the Super Bowl champs of TV news." She added: "I had to find ways to convey my seriousness, to send out signals that I was resolute and earnest, not what the wrapping said I was." She said to improve her image she wore glasses and worked around the clock." Stahl said she kept telling herself that if she worked hard and was good, they'd have to use her.

Stahl says that by the time she was 30, she knew that "I wanted to be a journalist, which would mean, in the environment of the early 1970s, surmounting my femaleness and my blondness."

Stahl started her career in broadcasting in 1972 as an on-air reporter at Channel 5 in Boston. During that same year, the Equal Employment Opportunity Act had just passed and the FCC had recently included women in its affirmative action program for television broadcasting.

Because of the Act, the networks were scouring the country for women, and a friend of Stahl's in New York called her to say that CBS had issued a memo mandating that the next reporter hired had to be a woman. Stahl said she applied to all three networks and got the attention of the CBS news bureau chief in Washington. He gave her two days to get rid of her apartment in Boston and be at work in Washington, and she did it.

After several weeks of doing reports for CBS Radio, she started doing stories for *The CBS Evening News* with Walter Cronkite. Stahl continued as a reporter for CBS News for more than 25 years, including assignments as White House correspondent during three administrations. She has been with *60 Minutes* since 1991.

Although Stahl admits that her career has been all she could have asked for, she said it was far from easy and she was often insecure. One reason was that her very presence at CBS, in her early years especially, seemed to inspire resentment among several of the camera crews. Most of the CBS cameramen were veterans in their 50s and 60s, she said, and their attitude toward the new hires was not exactly welcoming. "They acted as though we had cut in line," Stahl said, "like we hadn't paid our dues, didn't belong in the precious orbit of the CBS Washington Bureau."

Stahl recalled that on one occasion when she was covering a political rally, she asked a cameraman to shoot some video of the buses that had carried the people to the scene and the cameraman yelled at her, "What kind of stupid idea is that?" Stahl said the urge to weep became a recurring problem, but she would hold it until she got to a stall in a ladies' room, where she would sob out of sight of her crew. Stahl said that often in the crew cars she would be locked up "with her tormentors" for hours. She recalled one time when one of the cameramen argued into his walkie-talkie, "Do I have to work with her," making sure that she heard the comment.

In *Now This: Radio, Television . . . and the Real World* (Putnam, 2000), *ABC News* correspondent Judy Muller recalls how she began in broadcasting. Her career started after she quit teaching in New Jersey to be home with her two baby daughters. Muller had been writing for a weekly newspaper, which she said had its limitations—namely, no money and no hope of any to come, so she decided to try her hand, and voice, at radio news. She applied for a job at a little station, WHTG in Eatontown, New Jersey, which was so little, she said, that you were expected to unlock the door in the morning, read all the dials and gauges, and note them in a log that got that station actually operational. After that, she says, you literally sat down, switched on the microphone, and started talking.

Although Muller learned what she was supposed to do, she never got to do it. Two days before she was to start, the news director (who also was program manager, general manager, and sales manager) called her to say that the owners had changed their minds because they thought a woman with two small children might be unreliable. "Today," Muller said, "such comments would be fighting words—litigious, even. For me," continued Muller, "WHTG was the first ambush along the trail, the first pounce of the cougar, albeit a minor skirmish."

Muller had better luck at WHWH in Princeton. She said she wandered into the station at a time when broadcasters were under growing pressure to add women to the mix. So, despite never having worked at a radio station before, Muller said the fact that she could write coherently and speak clearly pretty much guaranteed her the job, particularly because her voice sounded like a guy's.

Muller says that initial job in broadcasting slanted her thinking on affirmative action ever since, noting that she probably would never have had an opportunity to demonstrate her own abilities had those men in the radio station not felt the pressure to add "diversity" long before that term became a buzzword.

Muller notes that the training she got as a reporter was terrific because "you learn to ask good questions and to write fast and succinctly, and it teaches you to ad-lib."

**Figure 25.3** Judy Muller in Westmannaeyjar, Iceland, covering the story of the return of Keiko the Whale for ABC's *World News Tonight*, September 1998.

When Muller's husband was transferred to Denver, she made the rounds of top radio stations there and landed a job at KHOW as a morning news anchor. She says that station also was a great place to hone her skills. She also learned how to stand up for her rights.

When she learned that the news director had hired a man from another station and was paying him more money, she stormed into the boss's office to demand to know why. She said he told her because the man had a family to support and that she, Muller, had a husband who was making a good living. Muller said she threatened to get a lawyer and the news director recanted, bringing her salary up to the level of the man's almost immediately.

Muller said she was anxious to move up and applied to WCBS Radio in New York. The station did not need a reporter but sent Muller's résumé and audition tape to the network and, to her surprise, she was hired.

After several years with the CBS Radio network as a reporter and commentator, ABC offered her a TV reporting job. Muller said the offer was flattering but a little frightening. "I had never expected to start a new career at the age of 43 in a whole new medium, especially one that so clearly favored youth and beauty. But Muller sold her house and moved with her children to Los Angeles to begin a new world in TV news.

Countless other women struggled throughout their careers to break the "glass ceiling." Speaking at the Radio and Television News Directors Association

(RTNDA) annual banquet in 1980, when she received the Paul White Award, Pauline Frederick said she never knew Paul White, but "it probably was just as well because he probably would not have hired me." Frederick said she had what was considered taboo at the time—a woman's voice. Nan Siemer, a former editor for WTOP-Radio in Washington, D.C., says that when she started out in the 1970s, she probably got her first job because she had a deep voice.

In the year 2000, minorities and women were having their best year ever in the television news job market. Minorities filled 21 percent of the jobs, compared to 19 percent the year before, according to the 2000 RTNDA/Ball State University survey. The percentage of all minority groups increased, except for Native Americans, which remained about the same. African Americans accounted for most of the increase.

According to the survey, African Americans made up 11 percent of the TV news workforce in 2000, Hispanics 7 percent, Asian Americans 3 percent, and Native Americans approximately 1 percent. The presence of minority TV news directors was at an all-time high. It increased to a record 14 percent, up from 8 percent the year before and 10 percent in 1998. Nine percent of the news directors were Hispanic.

While the elimination of the FCC's tough equal employment rules obviously had no effect in television, it's not clear if the change affected the radio news job market, where minority representation decreased by 1 percent to 10 percent. Asian Americans accounted for the drop.

In the same study, women constituted 40 percent of the television news workforce, an all-time high and a record for the second year in a row. The number of female TV news directors also hit a record 24 percent.

RTNDA president Barbara Cochran said she was encouraged by the growth in employment for minorities and women, especially coming two years after the equal employment guidelines were nullified. The RTNDA has been promoting diversity in the newsroom, and Cochran pledged to "pursue, develop, and promote" hiring goals that reflect the changing face of America. Cochran applauded NBC and CBS for appointing new vice presidents for diversity. And Cochran asks: "How will news organizations reach new audiences if the workforce does not reflect the changing population?"

But she said, while minority employees were having their best year ever, broadcasters were having a great deal of difficulty attracting and keeping them, amid fierce competition for talent. Some of the competition came from newspapers, which have launched a multimillion-dollar campaign to recruit minorities. She pointed out that minority representation on newspapers is a little more than half that of broadcast news.

A panel discussing two surveys by the Freedom Forum of minority journalists has concluded that retaining minority journalists in television and newspapers has become a stern challenge to the industry.

According to census projections, in the year 2000, minorities made up 28 percent of the U.S. population, consisting of 12 percent African American, 11 percent Hispanic,[1] 4 percent Asian,[2] and 1 percent Native Americans.[3] Whites made up the remaining 72 percent.

# "The Corn Fields"

Like Betsy Aaron, Siemer thinks people entering the broadcast field should start in small markets or, as Siemer puts it, "the corn fields." She began at a radio station in Danville, Illinois, after graduating from Lindenwood College, a small school in St. Louis. She worked for several other small stations over a seven-year period, getting fired a couple of times when new owners took over the stations. She took some time off to complete her master's degree. Then she returned to work but lost that job in another ownership change. At that point, she says, "I decided to set my sights on Washington, D.C. I spent six months interviewing with every station in the city."

When she was about to give up, Siemer heard of an opening at WTOP-Radio. "Because I had made some good contacts at RTNDA meetings," she says, "I got the job." She admits, "Sometimes it's not what you know but who you know." Her advice to college students: "Get involved in RTNDA as soon as you can."

Rob Sunde, former news director of the ABC Information Network and past chairperson of RTNDA, agrees that the place to start a career is at smaller stations. "Work long hours, do as much as you can, and perfect your skills as much as possible," is Sunde's advice to those starting out in broadcast journalism.

Sunde started out in the 1950s at age 15, working weekends for a station in his hometown in Connecticut. He worked at five different radio stations over a three-year period, and, after a break for military service, he spent another six years with local stations before ending up at CBS and later at ABC. Was it a good way to get started? "It was at the time," Sunde said, "but times have changed."

# Education Is Essential

Sunde says that today the most important thing for young people is a college education. He dropped out of Brown University when he found that juggling his studies and full-time employment at radio stations was too much to handle. "In those days," he says, "things were still experimental, and there was a lot of 'flying by the seat of your pants,' but things are different now and young people must be better educated."

Walter Cronkite, who also did not finish his college education, agrees that people didn't need a degree to break into journalism in those days. Now, he

---

[1] Information of persons of Hispanic origin in this report was collected in the 50 states and the District of Columbia, but not Puerto Rico.

[2] Asian represents Asians and Pacific Islanders.

[3] Native American represents American Indians, Eskimos, and Aleuts.

notes, a college degree is necessary to get a good newspaper or broadcast news job, and many successful people in journalism have advanced degrees in specialty areas, such as economics.

# The Job Search

You should start your job search by reading the help-wanted advertisements in *Broadcasting Cable* magazine and in flyers available from the RTNDA and other broadcast and professional associations, such as the Society of Professional Journalists (SPJ).

As you look for such leads, prepare a good résumé and résumé tape so they will be ready to send if you find any interesting openings. Undoubtedly, the most important factor in getting a reporting job is a résumé tape.

If you want a job in television, the tape should include an assortment of your very best packages and, if possible, a sample of some anchoring. If you want to work in radio, put together a sample of some good wraparounds and any anchoring you may have done.

The most important thing to remember in preparing a résumé tape is that you will not have much time to sell yourself. News directors get numerous tapes every week; they do not have the time or the desire to look at tapes unless they are hooked immediately. Most news directors admit that they rarely watch or listen to a tape for more than 20 seconds unless they hear or see something that impresses them. If something does, you have a good chance that they will continue to watch or listen to the rest of the tape. So, put your best package or wraparound up front; use strong video and sound at the top; and make sure the story itself is a grabber.

Don't make compromises. News directors may take into consideration that you are not using top-of-the-line equipment in your college journalism courses, but don't count on it. You will be competing with students who do have access to professional equipment. If your video is poorly shot and out of focus, you will be at a great disadvantage, even if your story is a good one. The same applies to sound. If it is distorted or hard to understand, news directors will be turned off, so use high-quality video and sound.

Should you use gimmicks on your videotape? Some news directors say they don't mind these techniques, provided they are done well. If you have a strong on-camera presence, a standup open on your tape may be effective. A montage of such standups, if kept to 5 or 10 seconds each, might also impress news directors. If you do not have a strong personality, you are better off starting your tape with strong video and sound. Most news directors will be evaluating your ability to package or wrap a story in a professional manner. If they are looking for a combination reporter-weekend anchor, they will be looking for samples of anchoring as well.

**Figure 25.4** Broadcasting students at Southern Illinois University. (Courtesy of Marilyn Lingle/Southern Illinois University)

Also remember that most news managers will not return your tapes unless you include an envelope with postage. Sometimes it's possible to find short tapes that are being discarded by advertising agencies and TV stations to use for your audition tapes. Otherwise, the cost of buying tapes can be high, so you may wish to send along envelopes and postage in the hope that you will get your tapes back.

## The Résumé

Although the audition tape is the most important job-search material you send to radio and TV stations, you also should include a printed résumé. Make it brief. If you are applying for your first job, news directors will know that you do not have much experience, so don't try to embellish your résumé. If your only experience is working with the university radio or TV station, list it first. If you have completed an internship with a commercial station, you certainly should list it first, with details about what you did. Do not start off the résumé, as so many students do, with your career goals. News directors want to know what you have done, not what you want to do.

List your education after your experience. If you have taken a minor in business, political science, economics, or some other area that might make you more attractive to news directors, you should include that information as well. Be sure to list any foreign languages that you can speak fluently.

If you have won any awards from RTNDA, SPJ, or any other organization for your broadcast work, you should mention those citations. Also list any involvement that you might have with student chapters of RTNDA or SPJ, particularly if you headed up one of those chapters or served on any committees that might have taken part in regional or national conferences. Attendance at those conferences, by the way, is a valuable experience and a great way to make contacts with working broadcast journalists and news directors.

If you have computer skills, say so. Also list any cameras, editing systems, or other radio or TV control room equipment that you know how to use.

# References

If you have developed relationships with people in the field who are willing to give references, such as the general manager or news director of a radio or TV station where you did an internship, you should list these people. Ask references if it's okay to use their names before listing them, however.

Most news directors are not likely to call your journalism professor to ask about you unless they are really impressed with your résumé tape. But sometimes your professor can be helpful. He or she may be active in RTNDA or SPJ and may have served on panels with news directors at national or regional meetings. The news director you're contacting may even be a graduate of your university.

Unless your hobbies have some practical application, such as flying or photography, don't list them. News directors are not likely to be interested in your stamp or coin collections.

Put some effort into the way you lay out and design your résumé. If it shows creativity, the news director is likely to think that you are creative. Consider a professional résumé preparation service, but only one with a good reputation. Some less professional services have been known to make grammatical errors.

Be sure to list your name, address, and telephone number at the top of your résumé. Figure 25.5 shows how a student who did an internship at a local TV station might organize her résumé.

# Cover Letters

A brief cover letter addressed personally to each news director you contact should be included along with your résumé tape and printed résumé. Be sure to use the news director's name—never write "Dear News Director." And spell the news director's name correctly; also be certain there are no misspellings or grammatical errors in the letter. If there are, the news director will never get to

KAREN DRAKE
110 E. Main St.
Baton Rouge, LA 70810
(504) 555-1234

WORK EXPERIENCE

Summer 1992—Summer intern as assistant at assignment desk, WBRZ-TV, Baton Rouge, LA. Monitored and logged satellite feeds, prepared read stories for anchors and helped sports anchor select game footage for broadcast. Accompanied reporters on shoots and worked Teleprompter.

1993–95 Reporter and producer, "Impact," the Southern University weekly TV news and features program on Channel 22 in Baton Rouge. Responsibilities included reporting and producing a package each week, anchoring the program twice a month, working the studio camera and shooting ENG.

EDUCATION

1996 B.S., Mass Communications, Southern University
Major: Broadcast News sequence
Minor: Political Science
GPA. 3.4/4.0 On dean's list five of eight semesters

SPECIAL SKILLS

Proficient with Macwrite, Macintosh computer system.
Experience with Panasonic ENG cameras F-250 and AG460, Panasonic 300CLE and WV-F300 studio cameras and panasonic AG-7750 and AG-7700 editing systems.

MEMBERSHIPS

National Association of Black Journalists

REFERENCES

John Spain, Station Manager
WBRZ-TV
Baton Rouge, LA 70832
(504) 555-5678

Professor Ted White
Chair, Department of Mass Communications
Southern University
Baton Rouge, LA 70821
(504) 555-9112

Professor Mike Kabel
Executive Producer, "Impact"
Southern University
Baton Rouge, LA 70821
(504) 555-3456

**Figure 25.5** A sample résumé.

your résumé or your videotape. As stressed throughout this book, accuracy is the most important aspect of journalism, and if you cannot be accurate in your job-search materials, you are not likely to find a job.

Your letter should be straightforward and honest. If you do not have much experience, say so, but stress the skills you do have. Make it clear that you are eager to learn and are prepared to work hard. Figure 25.6 is an example of a cover letter.

The cover letter accomplishes several things. It introduces you to the news director and lets him or her know where you heard about the job opening. It also tells the news director a little about you before he or she looks at the résumé, but it does not summarize the résumé. In this case, Karen Drake indicates what skills she would bring to the job and makes clear that she is enthusiastic and expects to work hard. The tone of her letter shows a modest confidence. The letter also mentions the name of her strongest reference, a TV station general manager with a national reputation. Note that the letter also expresses Drake's desire to hear from the news director. The letter is only four paragraphs, which is as much as any news director will probably read from someone applying for a job.

# Writing Tests

Some news organizations, such as CNN in Atlanta, which encourages graduating students to apply for entry-level positions, require applicants to take writing tests. The best way to prepare for a writing test is to practice rewriting newspaper wire copy into broadcast style. Do several such rewrites before you take the test, and ask one of your professors or someone you are working with at a radio or TV station to review the copy.

# The Job Interview

If he or she is impressed with your videotape, the news director may contact your references. If he or she gets a positive response, you will be asked to visit the station for a personal interview. The materials you sent got you an interview; now the interview will decide whether you get the job.

As soon as you hear about the interview, talk to your professors about the station that has invited you. They may know someone at the station or something about the station's reputation for news. Check out the station's Website. This enables you to find out about the station and look at a newscast. Another important way to prepare for the interview is to learn as much as possible about the city or town in which the station is located. Find out the name of the major newspaper in the city, and if you have time, have a Sunday edition sent to you. If there isn't enough time to do that, try to arrive in the city as early as possible

```
                                110 E. Main Street
                                Baton Rouge, LA 70810
                                June 27, 1993

Mr. Frank Walsh
News Director
KTHU-TV
Centerville, CT 06880

Dear Mr. Walsh:

I would like to be considered for the opening you
listed in Broadcast magazine. I recently received
my degree in mass communications from Southern Uni-
versity, where I reported, produced and anchored
many stories for "Impact," the university's weekly
television program on Channel 22 in Baton Rouge,
Louisiana. The enclosed videotape displays some of
my "Impact" stories.

As the enclosed résumé describes in detail, last
summer I worked as an intern at WBRZ-TV in Baton
Rouge, where I performed various tasks at the as-
signment desk. I am sure that Station Manager John
Spain would tell you that I carried out my duties
with enthusiasm and diligence.

I believe that my experience with "Impact" and at
WBRZ-TV makes me an ideal candidate for the position
at WZZZ-TV.

I hope for a chance to meet with you after you view
my videotape. I can be reached at (504) 555-1234.

                                Sincerely,

                                Karen Drake
```

**Figure 25.6**  Sample cover letter.

before the interview and read through the papers. The chamber of commerce is also a good source of information.

If you can, arrive a day early. If you are interviewing for a radio job, listen to the station in your motel room; if you are interviewing for a TV station job, watch as many of the station's newscasts as possible. Appearing knowledgeable about the station and the city during the interview will let the news director know that you are interested enough in the job to have done your homework. For example, tell the news director that you arrived in town the night before and that you were impressed with the station's coverage of a breaking story. But be honest. If the story really was good, then the news director will be impressed that you knew it; however, if the story was not that well done, you will lose points by saying that you thought it was. The news director will know better.

Once the interview shifts to what you can do for the station, the pressure will build. This is when you must be at your best. During the interview, don't stress your feelings about pay, benefits, work shifts, and vacations. You will impress the news director if you ask intelligent questions about the news operation, story coverage, and station philosophy in covering the news. But unless asked, don't offer your own philosophy because you may come across as a "know-it-all." The questions about pay and benefits are legitimate, but they should be asked at the end of the interview if the interviewer brings them up first and should not be your emphasis.

## Minority Opportunities

Women and minorities have made tremendous strides in finding jobs in broadcast news in recent years. Minority news directors, like other minority journalists, are most often found in larger markets. Those markets also are the ones most likely to have Spanish-speaking stations.

In a national survey, most news directors who responded indicated they are interested in getting applications from minorities, particularly African Americans, who have strong writing, reporting, and anchoring skills.

Will Wright, an African-American news director at WWOR-TV in metropolitan New York and former vice president and news director of KRIV-TV in Houston, says African Americans are at a disadvantage because they do not complete enough internships that lead to many jobs in broadcast news.

Wright, one of only a few black TV news directors in the nation, recalls that he broke into broadcast news as a desk assistant for CBS News in New York some 30 years ago. Wright notes that he paid his dues at CBS, going for coffee, running copy, and stripping wires. He believes minorities must be prepared to do the same hard work through internships and entry-level jobs.

Wright adds, however, that those "who are determined to win in a business that is set up to discourage them have to be quick learners. Don't let anyone

**Figure 25.7**   WWOR-TV News Director Will Wright (right) talks to assignment editor Elaine Higgins. (Courtesy of WWOR-TV)

have to tell you twice what to do," he advises. "Do it right the first time and you will succeed."

*CBS News* correspondent Ed Bradley agrees that "menial tasks come with the territory . . . and when I got into broadcasting, I was a gofer." He says that's the way entry-level positions work "whether you are black, white, yellow, brown, or red." Bradley says he knows young African-American men and women "who are eager to take entry-level positions to get their foot in the door."

When asked if being African American has had any effect on his career, Bradley said, "I think it has helped and hurt. It helped because I came along at a time when there was an effort to find more minorities who could do a job and I always showed that I could do a job no matter what they put me into." He added that being African-American may have hurt in some instances because there were people who wondered whether they should take a chance on hiring an African-American person for a given job because they had never done it before.

Asked how he thinks African Americans are treated in broadcast journalism, Bradley said, "Better than we used to be, but not as well as I'd like to see." He adds, "I'd like to see more opportunity [for blacks] on the air and off the air."

For women—black and white—advancement to management positions isn't always about race and gender. "The demands of the job are harder for women," says Penny Parrish, news director at KMSP in Minneapolis. "It's hard to run a newsroom without that being the top priority in your life. Going into television didn't help my marriage and probably led to my divorce," she notes.

Susan Stamberg, a correspondent for National Public Radio (NPR) and the first woman to host a national news show, says that women have done well at NPR, but "it was never easy. A handful of us worked hard and had to be very, very good," says Stamberg. "We punched a hole through the wall, which allowed a lot of other talented women to walk through." Now many women hold top jobs with NPR—as vice presidents, executive producers, as well as producers, editors, and reporters; however, Stamberg also notes, "Women are paid less at NPR than they are at commercial stations. But then, so are the men!"

As for the absence of female anchors on the commercial network news programs (i.e., CBS, NBC, and ABC), Stamberg calls it "ridiculous." She thinks commercial TV is still living in "the dark ages." Top policy decisions are still being made by men. Women can be accepted as anchors in the morning, but not in the evening. But the cable channels—CNN, CNBC, MSNBC, and others—understand that women can be talented news anchors at any time of day. "That's a welcome relief," says Stamberg, "to those of us who have been doing this work for many years."

Veteran broadcast news expert Lou Prato agrees that "more women are running and staffing newsrooms than ever before, but they "still have to deal with sexism, especially when it comes to pay." Female news directors, on average, make about 30 percent less than their male counterparts, but Prato says this difference may not be the result of sexism alone. He says many women are unwilling to argue for more money because "subconsciously or not, women do not want to be perceived as overly aggressive."

Consultant Nan Siemer agrees with Prato. She says most women think that "they are lucky to have a job in broadcasting and aren't supposed to negotiate for wages." Because of this attitude, Siemer began a consulting service called Breakers, which, she says, teaches women how to break the "glass ceiling."

Siemer says that one thing she had to do in her own career was "follow the negotiating examples set by men because women were not giving me any examples to draw from." She says she is trying to teach women that "negotiation is not an evil word, that they can talk about money without being uncomfortable."

# Some Final Words

The supply of entry-level job seekers greatly exceeds the demand. Entry-level applicants outnumber hiring by 10 to 1 in TV news. As a result, the average TV news director gets about 60 applications for every entry-level hire. Most of these applications are, as might be expected, for jobs as reporters and anchors. Why such an interest in broadcast news?

As many people have stated in this book, broadcast news is exciting. It is a fascinating business—one that pays you to read newspapers and magazines; to interview politicians, celebrities, and other exciting people; and to know what's going on in every part of the world before most other people. Unfortunately, because the work appeals to many people, the pay is not very good unless you have outstanding abilities that permit you to work in a large market. For many journalists, money is not the most important consideration, but rather the challenges that await reporters every day.

Trust me—you'll tell yourself how nice it is to be in a business that excites you so much that you don't look at the clock except when a deadline is involved. Although you may be exhausted at the end of the day, you often will look for colleagues to join you for coffee or drinks so that you can recreate what transpired that day, to analyze what you and the news team accomplished, and, of course, to commiserate about some of the things that went wrong. If you have trouble sleeping, it probably will not be because you're not tired but because you have trouble relaxing your mind.

You can join this exciting field, but remember: You'll need a dedication to develop your skills and a determination to pursue a career that is going to demand responsibility, accuracy, and fairness in whatever you do.

# Glossary

**Actuality**   Voices of people involved in a news story. Also called a sound bite.

**ADDA**   A system that electronically stores graphics and other information in a computer for random recall.

**Affiliates**   Radio and TV stations that are serviced by networks.

**Ambush interview**   Forcing someone to speak with you on camera against their will.

**Anchor**   Someone who reads news on the TV set.

**AP**   Associated Press, one of the major wire services.

**Assignment editor**   Newsperson who assigns stories to reporters and camera crews.

**Attribution**   The source of a news story.

**Audio**   Sound used in a radio or TV newscast.

**Back timing**   The timing of the final part of a broadcast to assist the newscaster or producer to get off the air on time.

**Beat**   An assignment given to a reporter on a continuing basis.

**Black**   Control track on a videotape. Also, a complete fade from a picture.

**Blind lead-in**   A general lead-in to a report from the field, used when you do not know what the reporter will say at the top of the report.

**Box**   Used primarily with ADDA or ESS to indicate that picture, freeze-frame video, or graphic will appear in a box next to the anchor's head. Some newsrooms use BSS, which stands for box, still store.

**Bridge**   Words that connect one piece of narration or sound bite to another.

**B-roll**   A film term still often used to describe the use of video to cover an interview or narration.

**Bulletin**   Important late-breaking news item.

**Bump tease**   A short audio headline covered by video, used before commercials in a TV newscast, to hold the audience's attention.

**Character generator**   Electronic device used to produce supers (fonts).

**Chroma-key**   The electronic placement of pictures behind the newscaster.

**Close**   The ending of a reporter's news story. Also referred to as a sig-out.

**Copy**   Material written for broadcast. Also, wire copy distributed by wire services.

**Cover footage**   Video shot at the scene of a news story; used to replace the newsmaker and/or reporter while their voices are heard.

**Crash**   Colloquialism for serious problems in a newscast.

**CU**   Close-up camera shot.

**Cue words**   The words at the start and end of audiotape or videotape to identify how a sound bite begins and ends.

**Cutaway**   A video shot used to avoid a jump cut.

**Cutoff time**   The time when a reporter must leave the scene of a story in order to make broadcast.

**Delayed lead**   Keeping the most important information in a story until the middle or end to create suspense.

**Dissolve**   Special video effect that slowly replaces one image on the screen with another.

**Drive-time**   Indicates the time of day when people are going to or coming from work. Usually the highest rated time periods for radio stations.

**ESS**   Abbreviation for electronic still storage. See *ADDA*.

**Establishing shot**   A wide shot of a scene, usually used at the beginning of a news story.

**Evergreen**   A story, usually a feature, that can be used anytime.

**Fade**   A dissolve from a picture to black.

**Feeds**   Material distributed by networks and others to affiliates and other stations for use on local newscasts. Also known as syndication feeds.

**Freedom of Information Act**   Passed by Congress to permit anyone who wishes to have access to all but the most sensitive government documents. Similar acts, called "Sunshine laws," have been established in all 50 states.

**Fill copy**   (Also called *pad copy*.) Relatively unimportant news copy for use near the end of the newscast if needed to fill time.

**Flash**   Headline used by wire services to describe news of an extreme nature, like the death of a president.

**Font**   See *Super*.

**Freeze frame**   A still video image seen next to or behind the anchor while he or she is reading copy. Mostly used in a box next to the anchor's head.

**Future file**   Folder or computer file used by the assignment desk to keep track of stories that may be covered in the future.

**Graphics**   Graphs, photos, maps, and other visuals used in a TV news story or newscast.

**Hard lead**   A lead that places the most important information in the first sentence.

**Headlines**   A series of one-line sentences describing news events. Used at the top of a newscast.

**Hold for release**   Wire service story or press release that cannot be used until the time specified.

**Information overload**   Putting too much information in a lead sentence or paragraph.

**Investigative reporting**   Developing news reports in depth, usually about something that someone is trying to hide.

**Jump cut**   An erratic movement of a head that occurs when video is edited to eliminate some of a speaker's words.

**Kicker**   A light story used at the end of a newscast.

**Lead**   The first line or two of a news story or the first story in a newscast.

**Leading question**   Asking a question during an interview that tries to elicit information the reporter wants to hear.

**Lineup**   The arrangement of stories in a newscast. Also called the rundown.

**Live**   Reporting from the scene of a story as it is happening

**Local angle**   Details of a news story that are of special interest to the audience in your community.

**Local news**   Stories dealing with your community.

**Long shot (LS)**   Wide view of the scene. See *Establishing shot.*

**Medium shot (MS)**   Between a close-up and long shot.

**Microwave**   Beaming a TV signal between two points using microwave antennas.

**Minicam**   A lightweight video camera.

**Negative lead**   A lead sentence that contains the word "not". To be avoided.

**News director**   The person in charge of the news operation at a radio or TV station.

**News judgment**   Ability to recognize the relative importance of news

**O/C**   Abbreviation for on camera.

**Out cue**   Last words in a sound bite.

**Package**   A story put together by a reporter that includes interviews, narration, and cover footage.

**Pad copy**   See *Fill copy.*

**Peaks and valleys**   A TV production technique that spreads important stories throughout a newscast, not only at the top.

**Primetime**   The time when radio and TV have their largest audiences.

**Privacy Act**   A law that is designed to prevent unwarranted invasion of a person's privacy.

**Producer**   The newsperson who decides which material will go into a newscast and in which order. Also, in larger markets, someone who helps reporters put together packages.

**Prompter**   Electronic device that projects news scripts on monitors so they can be read by anchors. Also known as teleprompters.

**Reader**   A story without video read by an anchor on camera.

**Reuters**   British news agency.

**Reversal**   A shot of the reporter looking at the person being interviewed; an editing device.

**Reverse question**   Shot of the reporter repeating questions asked during the interview; an editing technique considered by some newspeople as somewhat unethical.

**Rip and read**   The broadcasting of radio wire copy without any rewrite.

**RTNDA**   Radio and Television News Directors' Association.

**Running story**   A news story in which there are new developments, usually for more than one day.

**Shotgun lead**   A news story lead that includes information about more than one related story.

**SIL**   Abbreviation for silent; used on the video side of split page to indicate the use of videotape that has no sound.

**Slug**   Word or two written in the upper left corner of script to identify the story.

**Soft lead**   A lead in which the most important fact is not given immediately.

**SOT**   Abbreviation for sound-on-tape; used on the video side of the split page to indicate the tape has sound.

**Sound bite**   Portion of statement or interview that is in news broadcast or package.

**Sound under**   Keeping the natural sound low when used under the voice of a reporter or newscaster.

**Source**   Someone who provides information used in a news story.

**Split page**   The standard TV news script. The left side of the page is used for video directions, and the right side is for the script and audio cues.

**Staging**   Unethical practice in which a reporter asks people to behave in a certain way—one that is not natural—when they are on camera.

**Stand-up**   A report on camera at the scene.

**Super**   (Also called a *font*.) Short for superimposing lettering, graphics, or videotape. Used mostly for the names, addresses, and titles of people being identified in a news package or newscast.

**Suspense lead**   A lead that keeps the most important part of the story until the very end.

**Syndication**   The sale and distribution of news material to stations by independent companies and the networks.

**Tag**   A sentence or two used by a reporter or anchor at the end of a story or newscast. Sometimes referred to as an on-camera tag

**Talking head**   Colloquial for person being interviewed on camera.

**Tease**   A short headline that describes a story to follow a commercial. In TV, usually accompanied by a few seconds of the upcoming video story. Commonly referred to as a bump tease

**Time coding**   The recording of the time of day on the edge of videotape as it is being shot.

**Two-shot**   Camera shot of two people.

**Upcut**   The loss of words at the beginning of audio- or videotape.

**Update**   New details in a news story that require a rewrite.

**UPI**   United Press International, one of the major wire services.

**Urgent**   A wire service term indicating an important story, but not as important as a bulletin or flash story.

**V/O**   Abbreviation for voice-over. Used on the left-hand side of the split page to indicate that the anchor is speaking over video. Also to indicate a reporter doing narration over cover footage.

**Voicer**   A story read by a radio reporter that has no sound bites.

**VTR**   Videotape recording.

**Wire**   News services provided by AP, UPI, Reuters, and other organizations.

**Word processing**   The use of computers to write and store information.

**Wrap**   To complete work on a story. Also short for "wraparound," in which a reporter's voice is heard at the beginning and end of a sound bite.

**WS**   Wide camera shot.

# Index

Page references followed by "f" denote figures